y Basics

Computer Security Basics

Deborah Russell and G.T. Gangemi Sr.

O'Reilly & Associates, Inc.
103 Morris Street, Suite A
Sebastopol, CA 95472

Computer Security Basics
by Deborah Russell and G.T. Gangemi Sr.

Editor: Deborah Russell

Printing History:

July 1991:	First Edition.
December 1991:	Minor corrections.
July 1992:	Minor corrections.

ISBN: 0-937175-71-4

Table of Contents

Figures

Tables

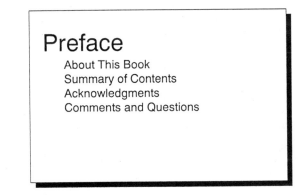

Preface

About This Book
Summary of Contents
Acknowledgments
Comments and Questions

About This Book

This book is about computer security—what it is, where it came from, where it's going, and why we should care about it. It introduces the many different areas of security in clear and simple terms: access controls, trusted systems, network security, TEMPEST, biometric devices, and more. If you're at all interested in computer security, or if computer security is a part of your job (whether you want it to be or not!), you should find this book useful. We've tried to give you the big picture and quite a few helpful details, including a lot of reference material about computer security requirements and resources.

This book is also about the many standards that exist for computer security. More and more government rules, contracts, and requisitions require that systems adhere to security standards. Chief among these is the "Orange Book," the government's *Trusted Computer System Evaluation Criteria*, which specifies the security features a system must have to be considered "trusted." If you sell or consult to the security-conscious U.S. government, you'll find this presentation particularly helpful as you make your way through the maze of government programs and procedures.

This book is not a technical reference, and it's not full of mathematical equations and flowcharts. We've tried to pull together the basics about many different areas of computer security, and put that information in understandable words. If you need particularly technical information about a specific area of computer security—for example, making your specific system secure, designing a trusted operating system, or configuring a secure network, we'll refer you to other, more specialized books.

Summary of Contents

This book is divided into five parts; it includes ten chapters and five appendices:

Part I, *Overview*, presents a brief overview of what computer security is, where it came from, and where it's going.

Chapter 1, *Introduction*, introduces computer security: what it is and why it's important. It summarizes the threats to computers and the information stored on them, and it introduces the different types of computer security.

Chapter 2, *Some Security History*, briefly describes the history of computer security: where it came from, and what government mandates, laws, and standards address it.

Part II, *Computer Security*, discusses computer security—methods of protecting information stored in a computer system, primarily by controlling access to that information.

Chapter 3, *Computer System Security and Access Controls*, introduces computer system security and describes how it controls access to systems and data.

Chapter 4, *Viruses and Other Wildlife*, gives definitions of viruses, worms, and other types of malicious code.

Chapter 5, *Secure System Planning and Administration*, describes the administrative procedures that improve security within an organization.

Chapter 6, *Inside the Orange Book*, introduces trusted systems and describes the Orange Book security requirements and evaluation classes.

Part III, *Communications Security*, discusses communications security—methods of protecting information while it's being transmitted over communications lines.

Chapter 7, *Encryption*, explains what encryption is, and how it protects data.

Chapter 8, *Communications and Network Security*, introduces network concepts and discusses some basic communications security issues.

Part IV, *Other Types of Security*, describes several additional types of security.

Chapter 9, *Physical Security and Biometrics*, introduces physical security and describes different types of biometric devices.

Chapter 10, *TEMPEST*, describes what TEMPEST is and why it's important.

Part V, *Appendices*, provides a number of quick-references to computer security requirements, programs, and other sources of information.

Appendix A, *Acronyms*, lists computer security acronyms.

Appendix B, *Computer Security Legislation*, lists laws and federal mandates that enforce computer security in areas of information protection, computer crime, and privacy.

Appendix C, *Orange Book and Other Summaries*, provides a summary of Orange Book requirements and several other tables of trusted system requirements introduced earlier in the book.

Appendix D, *Government Security Programs*, lists procedures for how the government evaluates trusted systems, cryptographic products, and TEMPEST products.

Appendix E, *A Security Source Book*, tells you where to go for security standards, government programs, security user groups, and other literature.

The *Glossary* provides a complete glossary of computer security terms.

Acknowledgments

We'd like to thank the many people who contributed to this book. Tim O'Reilly of O'Reilly & Associates and Victor Oppenheimer of Cambridge Computer Associates believed in the idea of a computer security series and encouraged us to develop this book as part of that series. Paul Mei, Nick Hammond, Len Schneider, and Perry Flinn of SecureWare reviewed a first draft of the book and supplied examples we've included in the text. James Burrows, Director of the National Institute of Standards and Technology's Computer Systems Laboratory, Stuart W. Katzke, Chief of CSL's Computer Security Division, and Dennis K. Branstad, Miles Smid, Robert Rosenthal, Gene Troy, and Irene Gilbert of CSL also reviewed the book and made many constructive suggestions; thanks as well to F. Lynn McNulty, CSL's Associate Director for Computer Security, for his help. Mitch Wright of I-NET, Inc., reviewed a draft of the book and tracked down some material for us, and Tim O'Reilly read several drafts and made many helpful suggestions. Simson Garfinkel and Gene Spafford, authors of *Practical UNIX Security*, another book in our computer security series, reviewed parts of the book and contributed valuable information. Special thanks to Andrew Odlyzko of AT&T, who reviewed the encryption chapter, to Bob Tinkelman and Bradley Ross of Cambridge Computer Associates, who commented on the communications security chapters, and to Daniel Faigin of ACM/SIGSAC, who found some typos and other errors we missed in the first printing.

Many people from O'Reilly & Associates helped to produce this book. Mike Sierra, Kismet McDonough, and Rosanne Wagger entered text, created beautiful formats (with help from Len Muellner), and overcame the icons and the killer tables. Edie Freedman designed the cover for this book and the other books in the security series. Chris Reilley prepared all of the wonderful illustrations. John Dockery tracked down hard-to-find articles, dates of obscure legislation, and more. Donna Woonteiler and Sue Willing handled all the details of production and printing scheduling. Many thanks!

Some of the chapters in this book are based on an internal document that Cambridge Computer Associates prepared for Wang Laboratories' Secure Systems group several years ago. Thanks to Wang Laboratories for use of this material.

Comments and Questions

Please write to tell us about any flaws you find in this book or how you think it could be improved. Our U.S. mail address, e-mail address, and phone number are:

O'Reilly & Associates, Inc.
103 Morris Street, Suite A
Sebastopol, CA 95472

In USA: 1-800-338-6887
International: +1 707-829-0515
UUCP: uunet!ora!bookquestions
Internet: bookquestions@ora.com

"But for the security of the future I would do everything."

James Abram Garfield, speech on assassination of Lincoln, April 15, 1865.

Part I:

OVERVIEW

Part I presents a brief overview of what computer security is, where it came from, and where it's going.

- Chapter 1, *Introduction*, introduces computer security: what it is and why it's important. It summarizes the threats to computers and the information stored on them, and it introduces the different types of computer security.

- Chapter 2, *Some Security History*, briefly describes the history of computer security: where it came from, and what government mandates, laws, and standards address it.

1

Introduction

Attack of the Giant Worm (and Other Tales)
What Is Computer Security?
Threats to Security
Why Buy Security?
What's A User To Do?

Attack of the Giant Worm (and Other Tales)

On November 2, 1988, a computer worm began to inch its way through the Internet, a government-funded network that at that time linked more than 60,000 computers across the United States. From computers in Cambridge, Massachusetts and Berkeley, California, it spread to Princeton, then to the NASA Ames Research Center in California's Silicon Valley, to the University of Pittsburgh, to Los Alamos National Laboratory, and to other universities, military bases, and research establishments.

The worm (many called it a virus) moved relentlessly across network lines from computer to computer. Once installed, it multiplied, creating processes and rapidly clogging the computer's available space, until other work virtually ground to a halt. The worm collected user and network information and exploited a number of UNIX security holes, including the *sendmail* debug facility and a bug in the *fingerd* daemon, which tells remote users who is logged into a particular machine. It also carried a dictionary of commonly used passwords and took advantage of the "trusted host" system of UNIX network communication. The worm camou-flaged itself (by changing its name to that of a standard UNIX command inter-preter) and tried to cover its tracks by vanishing after exiting.

The number of computers affected? Suns and VAXes using Berkeley Standard Distribution (BSD) 4.3 UNIX fell victim to the worm. Original estimates were that as many as 6000 computers had been affected; later research indicated the actual number to be in the 2100–2600 range. No one is really sure, and the exact num-ber isn't very significant, because even those computers not directly infected by the worm had to be tested. Little tangible damage was done. The worm entered computers, generated new processes, and paralyzed processing, but it apparently was never intended to destroy data.

An informal nationwide team of UNIX experts mobilized almost instantly to bring the worm under control. Within 12 hours of infection, the Computer Systems Research Group (CSRG) at the University of California at Berkeley developed a first attempt at stopping the spread of the worm. Later the same day, another effective method was discovered at Purdue University and was widely distri-buted. The network communications that originally allowed the worm to spread so quickly also provided the means for stopping it. Programmers scattered throughout the country used the net to communicate their findings by electronic mail, to trade recommended fixes, and to collaborate on decompiling the worm program. Although many sites reacted by disconnecting from the network, this actually hindered the swift distribution of information and remedies.

The total cost? Although no data was destroyed, a great deal of system and administrative time had to be spent shutting down machines and vital network gateways, losing electronic mail, research time, and the ability to meet deadlines. Estimates of the cost of system fixes and testing range from $1 million to as high as $100 million.

The culprit? Robert T. Morris, a Cornell University graduate student, was quickly identified as the worm-maker. He claimed that the worm was an experi-mental program containing a bug that caused it to run rampant. The FBI investi-gated. So did the National Computer Security Center, the General Accounting Office, and Cornell University. The press had a field day.

The effect on Morris? On January 23, 1990, he was convicted by a federal jury in Syracuse, New York under the 1986 Computer Fraud and Abuse Act (the first per-son to be so convicted). He faced up to five years in jail, a $250,000 fine, and res-titution for damages. On May 4, 1990, U.S. District Court Judge Howard Munson sentenced Morris to a three-year probation and ordered him to pay a $10,000 fine, perform 400 hours of community service, and pay an additional $91 per month for supervision during probation. (Morris' conviction was subsequently upheld on appeal.)

The effect on society? The Internet worm stunned the computer community and shook the outside world as well. Public awareness of computer security has increased dramatically. A new generation of security consultants—what *Business Week* has termed "hackerbusters"—have hung out their shingles, and computer security is on its way to becoming a multi-billion dollar industry. Computer security has also hit the newsstands, with more and more articles warning the public about viruses and other perils. The loss of trust in research networks and open communication among network users may prove to be the most lasting damage left by the worm.

A number of organizations now stand ready to provide expert assistance in case it happens again. Funded by the Defense Advanced Research Projects Agency (DARPA), the Computer Emergency Response Team (CERT) at the Software Engineering Institute at Carnegie Mellon University is now available to serve as a clearinghouse for information and support for any future Internet crises. The Carnegie Mellon center is supplemented by more than 100 experts, available by phone around the country. The Department of Energy has also established a Computer Incident Advisory Capability (CIAC) oriented to its own agency needs. The National Security Agency and the National Institute of Standards and Technology (formerly the National Bureau of Standards) are pooling their resources to create a a clearinghouse for government responses to computer security crises.

Several vendors have also set up organizations that are prepared to come to the aid of any of their customers who find security holes or face attacks. Sun Microsystems' Customer Warning System (CWS) is an example of such an organization. A number of other academic, research, and corporate institutions, both in the U.S. and abroad, are also establishing their own emergency organizations.

But despite the level of spending, public awareness, and preparedness in certain quarters, most organizations haven't significantly tightened security—and most users don't yet think of computer security as anything but a nuisance. At most sites, there's *still* a sense that "it can't happen here."

The Internet worm may be the most newsworthy system attack in recent years, but it's not the only one. Consider a few other examples:

KGB Connection.
In 1988, in his book, *The Cuckoo's Egg*, astronomer-turned-detective Cliff Stoll* recounted how he spent a year tracking and eventually trapping another system cracker from West Germany who tried to break into 450 computers (he succeeded with 30) over worldwide networks, including the Lawrence Berkeley Laboratory where Stoll worked. The intruder browsed through military

---

*Stoll, Cliff, *The Cuckoo's Egg: Tracing a Spy Through the Maze of Computer Espionage*, Doubleday, New York (NY), 1989.

files containing information about nuclear, biological, and chemical warfare, and nearly disrupted a medical experiment (with potentially deadly results). With the enticement of phony files bearing references to SDI, and the help of phone taps, Stoll baited the intruder and tracked him to his lair. When West German authorities found that Stoll's intruder and his compatriots had been selling information to the KGB, they charged the intruders with espionage.

NASA Shutdown.
In 1990, an Australian computer science student was charged with shutting down a computer system of the National Aeronautics and Space Administration (NASA) in Norfolk, Virginia, for 24 hours. The student, who called himself Phoenix, apparently penetrated numerous Australian and U.S. computers. In addition to the NASA shutdown, he allegedly made "alterations to data" on a computer at Lawrence Livermore National Laboratory in California.

Airline Computers.
In 1988, a major travel agency discovered that someone had penetrated its reservations and ticketing systems to print airline tickets illegally. The break-in has raised questions about the possibility that terrorist organizations could penetrate airline systems to obtain passenger information and plan attacks. There's been speculation that the 1988 terrorist attack in which members of the Kuwaiti royal family were held hostage on board an aircraft might have resulted from such advance information.

HBO Attack.
In April of 1986, a Home Box Office channel was taken over by an intruder known as Captain Midnight who worked as a part-time satellite uplink operator and retailer of home receiving dishes. He overpowered the HBO uplink transmitter signal with a stronger, unauthorized signal, and sent out his own messages to eight million viewers. The attack also sent a strong message of warning that this kind of airwaves penetration could potentially be used for terrorist purposes.

Constitution Loss
In 1991, just before the final vote on Colombia's new Constitution, a computer technician who was making final updates to the online text of the Constitution on a borrowed computer made an error that caused the text to be erased. There were no current backups. Members of the Constitutional drafting committee found themselves rooting through trash cans for earlier drafts and notes on final changes to the text of the Constitution.

Friday the 13th Virus.
In January of 1988, a student at Hebrew University in Jerusalem discovered that thousands of university computers were infected with a virus. The virus slowed down processing on certain Fridays the 13th and was scheduled to erase the hard disks of financial, research, and administrative computers on

May 13, 1988. Since this resilient virus first reared its ugly head, it appears to have popped up at many different times in different spots around the world. A recent attack on computers at the Royal National Institution for the Blind in England wiped out months of work. In the U.S. it reappeared as the Columbus Day, or Datacrime, virus.

Satellite Positioning System.
In 1989, a 14-year-old Kansas boy used an Apple home computer to crack an Air Force satellite positioning system. An adept computer user since the age of eight, the boy dialed unauthorized long-distance access codes and also browsed through the confidential files of more than 200 businesses. When apprehended, he said he hoped to persuade the businesses to hire him as a computer security consultant.

Virus Flambé.
In 1988, a virus infecting a firm of computer consultants in San Jose, California did more than damage data—it damaged equipment as well. The virus altered the scan rate of an IBM PC monitor's electronic beam, and the monitor burst into flames!

White House Computers.
In 1988, a researcher working for the Tower Commission investigating the Iran contra affair explored the computer systems used by Oliver North. He discovered that sensitive National Security Council notes that North had deleted from a "secure" White House computer system had actually been dumped into a mainframe computer and were now accessible to users of that system. While many people applauded this particular result, the potential for penetrating White House computers is alarming.

Bank Theft.
In 1984, a bank funds transfer netted $25 million for a branch manager who manipulated a computer system by entering offsetting entries that evaded auditing.

Cases of viruses, computer theft, and online vandalism—ranging from large-scale network break-ins to localized voice mail terrorism—have increased dramatically in recent years. The Computer Virus Industry Association reports that the Brain virus alone has affected 250,000 PC users.

Computer crime has also become a major threat to business. According to the Federal Bureau of Investigation, computer crime is the most expensive form of commercial crime—with an average cost of $450,000 per theft. It also represents a far greater risk to corporations than fire or any other type of hazard. Estimates of the total dollar figure for computer theft are as high as $5 billion per year.

Even though there has been substantial publicity in recent years about computer system risks and attacks, it turns out that most system penetrations go unreported. Some reports estimate that as many of 90 percent of computer crimes and intrusions are never revealed outside the victimized organizations, and only a fraction of the cases reported are actually prosecuted. Corporations and government agencies are often hesitant to report and prosecute computer break-ins because of the risk of adverse publicity, the loss of public confidence, and the possible charge of managerial incompetence. Many organizations fear lawsuits based on the emerging "standard of due care."

In fact, there are reports that some businesses are paying hush money to intruders. In London, a number of firms have reportedly signed agreements with computer criminals offering them amnesty for returning part of the money stolen and, more importantly, by keeping quiet about their thefts. In one case, an assistant programmer at a merchant bank diverted eight million pounds to a Swiss account. In an agreement that protected him from prosecution, the programmer promised not to disclose the system penetration—and he got to keep one million pounds! The reports on the British front have prompted a London insurer to offer a new policy covering viruses and other computer catastrophes. (A number of U.S. insurers have specifically excluded computer virus damage from their coverage.)

What Is Computer Security?

With computer systems increasingly under attack, it's no wonder that people are starting to take computer security more seriously. But despite this increased interest, many computer users still don't really understand what computer security is—and why it should be important to them. The headlines about the Internet worm, KGB agents, and million-dollar funds transfer frauds tell only part of the story, and it's a part most of us can't identify with as a day-to-day concern.

Computer security protects your computer and everything associated with it—your building, your terminals and printers, your cabling, and your disks and tapes. Most importantly, computer security protects the information you've stored in your system. That's why computer security is often called *information security*.

There's a longstanding view of computer security that its purpose is to protect against one particular danger—outside intruders who break into systems to steal money or secrets, or simply to prove they can do it. And although such intruders do exist, they aren't the only, or even the primary, danger to computer systems. There are many more immediate dangers, ranging from sharing your password with a friend, to failing to back up a disk, to spilling a soda on a terminal keyboard. These dangers aren't as newsworthy as flamboyantly named viruses, but they're more likely to cause you problems on a daily basis. The following sections define computer security and outline the wide range of dangers to computer systems.

A Broader Definition of Security

The popular conception of computer security is that its only goal is secrecy—keeping the names of secret agents from falling into the hands of the enemy, and keeping a nationwide fast food chain's new advertising strategy from being revealed to a competitor. Secrecy is a very important aspect of computer security, but it's not the whole story.

There are three distinct aspects of computer security: secrecy (sometimes called confidentiality), accuracy (sometimes called integrity), and availability. In some systems or application environments, one aspect of security may be more important than others. Your own assessment of what type of security your organization requires will influence your choice of the particular security techniques and products needed to meet those requirements.

Secrecy and Confidentiality

A secure computer system must not allow information to be disclosed to anyone who is not authorized to access it. In highly secure government systems, *secrecy* ensures that users access only information they're allowed, by the nature of their security clearances, to access. In business environments, *confidentiality* ensures the protection of private information, such as payroll data, as well as sensitive corporate data, such as internal memos and competitive strategy documents.

Secrecy is of paramount importance in protecting national defense information and highly proprietary business information. In such environments, other aspects of security (e.g., integrity and availability), while important, may be less critical. Chapter 3, *Computer System Security and Access Controls*, discusses several major methods of enforcing secrecy or confidentiality in your system: controlling who gets access to your system, and controlling what individual users are able to do in your system. Chapter 7, *Encryption*, discusses encryption, another excellent way to keep information a secret.

Accuracy, Integrity, and Authenticity

A secure computer system must maintain the continuing integrity of the information stored in it. *Accuracy* or *integrity* means that the system must not corrupt the information or allow any unauthorized malicious or accidental changes to it. It wasn't deliberate, but when a simple software error changed entries in Bank of New York transactions several years ago, the bank had to borrow $24 billion to cover its accounts until things got straightened out—and the mistake cost $5 million in extra interest.

In network communications, a related variant of accuracy known as *authenticity* provides a way to verify the origin of data by determining who entered or sent it, and by recording when it was sent and received.

In financial environments, accuracy is usually the most important aspect of security. In banking, for example, the confidentiality of funds transfers and other financial transactions is usually less important than the verifiable accuracy of these transactions. Chapter 7, *Encryption*, discusses message authentication, a method that ensures the accuracy of a transmission. With this method, a code is calculated and appended to a message when that message is sent across a network. At the receiving end, the code is calculated again. If the two codes are identical, the message sent is the same as the message received—proof that it wasn't forged or modified during transmission.

Availability

A secure computer system must keep information available to its users. *Availability* means that the computer system's hardware and software keeps working efficiently and that the system is able to recover quickly and completely if a disaster occurs.

The opposite of availability is *denial of service*. Denial of service means system users are unable to get the resources they need. The computer may have crashed. There may not be enough memory or processes to run a program. Needed disks, tapes, or printers may not be available. Denial of service can be every bit as disruptive as actual information theft. When the Internet worm attacked systems, it didn't actually destroy or modify any data. Instead, it attacked system availability by spreading through networks, creating new processes, and effectively blocking all other work on the infected computers.

In some ways, availability is a baseline security need for everyone. If you can't use your computer, you won't be able to tell whether your secrecy and accuracy goals are being met. Even users who abhor "security" agree that their computer systems have to keep working. Many of them don't realize that keeping systems running is also a type of security.

Chapter 5, *Secure System Planning and Administration*, and Chapter 6, *Inside the Orange Book*, discuss two important ways to ensure the availability of a system: careful system administration and sound system design.

Threats to Security

There are three key words that come up in discussions of computer security: vulnerabilities, threats, and countermeasures. A *vulnerability* is a point where a system is susceptible to attack. A *threat* is a possible danger to the system; the danger might be a person (a system cracker or a spy), a thing (a faulty piece of equipment), or an event (a fire or a flood) that might exploit a vulnerability of the system. The more vulnerabilities you see in your system, and the more threats you believe are out there, the more carefully you'll need to consider how to protect your system and its information. Techniques for protecting your system are called *countermeasures*.

Computer security is concerned with identifying vulnerabilities in systems and in protecting against threats to those systems.

Vulnerabilities

Every computer system is vulnerable to attack. Security policies and products may reduce the likelihood that an attack will actually be able to penetrate your system's defenses, or they may require an intruder to invest so much time and so many resources that it's just not worth it—but there's no such thing as a completely secure system.

Typical points of vulnerability in a computer system include those mentioned in the sections that follow.

Physical Vulnerabilities

 Your buildings and computer rooms are vulnerable. Intruders can break into your computer facilities just as they can break into your home. Once in, they can sabotage and vandalize your computer, and they can steal diskettes, disk packs, tape reels, and printout.

Locks, guards, and biometric devices (devices that test a physical or behavioral trait—for example, a fingerprint, a voiceprint, or a signature—and compare it with the traits on file to determine whether you are who you claim to be) provide an important first defense against break-ins. Burglar alarms and other ordinary types of protection are also effective deterrents.

Natural Vulnerabilities

 Computers are very vulnerable to natural disasters and to environmental threats. Disasters such as fire, flood, earthquakes, lightning, and power loss can wreck your computer and destroy your data. Dust, humidity, and uneven temperature conditions can also do damage.

Hardware and Software Vulnerabilities

Certain kinds of hardware failures can compromise the security of an entire computer system. For example, many systems provide hardware protection by structuring memory into privileged and nonprivileged areas. If memory protection features fail, they wreak havoc with your system, and they open security holes.

Software failures of any kind may cause your system to fail, may open your system to penetration, or may simply make the system so unreliable that it can't be trusted to work properly and efficiently. In particular, bugs in security features may open the floodgates to accidents or intrusion.

Even if individual hardware and software components are secure, an entire system can be compromised if the hardware components are connected improperly or if the software isn't installed correctly.

Media Vulnerabilities

Disk packs, tape reels, and printouts can be stolen, or can be damaged by such mundane perils as dust and ballpoint pens. Most disk and tape operations involve rewriting header files, not actually erasing the entire disk or tape, so sensitive data may be left on magnetic media, or magnetic flux (remanence) may remain after the magnetic force has been removed.

Emanation Vulnerabilities

 All electronic equipment emits electrical and electromagnetic radiation. Electronic eavesdroppers can intercept the signals emanating from computer systems and networks, and can then decipher them. The information stored and transmitted by the systems and networks then becomes vulnerable.

Communications Vulnerabilities

 If your computer is attached to a network, or even if it can be accessed by telephone, you greatly increase the risk that someone will be able to penetrate your system. Messages can be intercepted, misrouted, and forged. Communications lines connecting computers to each other, or connecting terminals to a central computer, can be tapped or physically damaged.

Human Vulnerabilities

The people who administer and use your computer system represent the greatest vulnerability of all. The security of your entire system is often in the hands of a system administrator. If that administrator isn't trained, or decides to take to a life of crime, your system is in grave peril. Ordinary computer users, operators, and other people on your staff can also be bribed or coerced into giving away passwords, opening doors, or otherwise jeopardizing security in your system.

Exploiting Vulnerabilities

There's a lot of variation in how easy it is to exploit different types of vulnerabilities. For example, tapping a cordless telephone or a cellular mobile phone requires only a $199 scanner from your local electronics store. Logging into a system that has no password protection, or very minimal controls, is almost as easy. Tapping an encrypted fiber optic communications link, on the other hand, or intercepting emanations from specially-shielded equipment is very difficult, even for a dedicated intelligence operation.

Threats

Threats fall into three main categories: natural, unintentional, and intentional.

Natural and Physical Threats

These are the threats that imperil every physical plant and piece of equipment: fires, floods, power failures, and other disasters. You can't always prevent such disasters, but you can find out quickly if one occurs (with fire alarms, temperature gauges, and surge protectors). You can minimize the chance that the damage will be severe (e.g., with certain types of sprinkler systems). You can institute policies that guard against hazards posing special dangers to computers (like smoking or soda spills). You can also plan for a disaster (by backing up critical data off-site and by arranging for the use of a backup system that can be used if an emergency does occur).

Unintentional Threats

These are the dangers that ignorance brings—for example, a user or a system administrator who hasn't been trained properly, who hasn't read the documentation, and who doesn't understand the importance of following proper security procedures. A user might drop a disk, or might try to use a database package to perform a simple update, and inadvertently wipe out a file. A system administrator might become the superuser and change the protection on the password file or on critical system software. Much more information is corrupted and lost through ignorance than through malice.

Intentional Threats

These are the interesting threats, the newsworthy ones, and the ones that security products do the best job of protecting against. The villains come in two varieties: outsiders and insiders. Some types of attacks are feasible only for certain types of attackers. For example, a casual "browser" isn't likely to intercept and decipher electromagnetic emanations, or perform a determined cryptographic analysis. Attacks of those kinds can typically be mounted only by so-called "high-grade attackers" who have substantial resources (in computing power, money, time, and personnel) behind them.

Outsiders include a number of different categories:

Foreign Intelligence Agents.
They're not lurking behind every bush, but they really do exist! Products using TEMPEST technology or sophisticated encryption devices are most

appropriate at installations where attacks on classified information are a realistic threat.

Terrorists.

Luckily, we haven't seen too much computer terrorism yet, though there have been a few attacks on university computer centers, armed service recruiting centers, court buildings, and the like. The government worries about computer terrorism. So do airlines, oil companies, and other businesses that protect information that's vital to the national interest.

Criminals.

Computer crime is lucrative, and, unlike many other types of crimes, can be carried out in a tidy, anonymous electronic fashion. The goal may be outright theft or embezzlement, or it may be extortion of some kind; for example, "If you don't pay me—or hire me—I'll set my virus loose and tell the press about it."

Corporate Raiders.

More and more corporations rely on computers, network connections, and electronic mail. Corporate records, memos, and informal messages have become more vulnerable than ever to attacks by competitors.

Crackers.

Kenneth Thompson calls this category of intruders "computer joy riders." When people talk about crackers, or hackers,* they usually mean intruders who are more interested in the challenge of breaking in than in the spoils of victory. These intruders may browse through systems, peeking at interesting data and programs, but they usually don't do it for monetary or political gain. More typically, they break into systems for the challenge of defeating each new security feature they encounter. They often break in via network connections they've accessed using stolen telephone credit cards. They may share their knowledge with other crackers via electronic bulletin boards. They may also document their successes in hardcopy or electronic publications (some now defunct) such as *2600 Magazine*, *Phrack*, W.O.R.M., and the *Computer Underground Digest* (the USENET newsgroup **alt.cu-digest**).

---

*The word "hacker" has a long and honorable history. It originally meant anyone with a strong interest in computers and an eagerness to experiment with them and test their limits. More recently, the word has been used to refer to those who break into systems in an unlawful way. Because many law-abiding "hackers" object to this pejorative meaning of the word, we've chosen in this book to call those who deliberately break into system "crackers" or "intruders," rather than "hackers."

Insiders and Outsiders

Outsiders may penetrate systems in a variety of ways: simple break-ins of buildings and computer rooms; disguised entry as maintenance personnel; anonymous, electronic entry through modems and network connections; and bribery or coercion of inside personnel.

Although most security mechanisms protect best against outside intruders, survey after survey indicates that most attacks are by insiders. Estimates are that as many as 80 percent of system penetrations are by fully authorized users who abuse their access privileges to perform unauthorized functions. As Robert H. Courtney, Jr. put it, "The enemy is already in—we hired them."

There are a number of different types of insiders. The fired or disgruntled employee might be trying to steal; more likely, he's just trying to wreak revenge by disrupting office operations. The coerced employee might have been blackmailed or bribed by foreign or corporate enemy agents. The greedy employee might use her inside knowledge to divert corporate or customer funds for personal benefit. The insider might be an operator, a systems programmer, or even a casual user who's willing to share a password.

Don't forget, one of the most dangerous insiders may simply be lazy or untrained. He or she doesn't bother changing passwords, doesn't learn how to encrypt files, doesn't get around to erasing scratch tapes, and leaves sensitive printout in piles on the floor. More energetic types may take advantage of this laziness and do serious damage.

Often, the most effective system attacks are those that combine a strong outside strategy (for example, breaking into competitors' files to steal their marketing plans) with access by an insider (for example, a marketing assistant who's been bribed to give away a password or steal reports).

Countermeasures

There are many different types of countermeasures—methods of protecting computers and information. In this book, we try to provide a survey of these methods in several basic categories.

Computer Security

Earlier in this chapter, we've used the term "computer security" in a broad sense to cover the protection of computers and everything associated with them. It's more precise to say that computer security is the protection of the information stored in a computer system (as opposed to protecting information that's being transmitted, or protecting the physical equipment itself). Computer security focuses on operating system features that control who can access a system and the data stored in it.

Part II of this book discusses computer security controls—including passwords, auditing of security actions, and administrative procedures like backups that protect stored data. That part also draws a distinction between the two basic types of security policies available in multi-user computer systems: discretionary access control (DAC) and mandatory access control (MAC). Part II also briefly discusses how the government sets standards for computer security, and certifies products that meet those standards, through its COMPUSEC (Computer Security) program.

Communications Security

Communications security is the protection of information while it's being transmitted by telephone, cabling, microwave, satellite, or any other means. This branch of security focuses on network access to computer systems, and the technologies that increase the security of systems allowing such connections to the outside world.

Part III of this book describes encryption, a highly effective method of protecting data either in storage or during transmission. It also discusses a number of other methods of increasing network security, along with the government COMSEC (Communications Security) program that certifies cryptographic and other communications security products.

Physical Security

Physical security is the protection of physical computer equipment from damage by natural disasters and intruders. Physical security methods include old-fashioned locks and keys, as well as more advanced technologies like smart cards and biometric devices.

Part IV of this book discusses physical security and TEMPEST, a technology that shields computer equipment to keep electromagnetic emissions from being intercepted and deciphered by eavesdroppers. It also describes the government's TEMPEST program, which tests and certifies TEMPEST equipment.

Why Buy Security?

Computer security has historically been viewed as being an unnecessary impediment to getting work done. With pressure from the government, the courts, and the press, security now seems to have graduated to a necessary evil. It may be on its way to being viewed as a full-fledged system feature.

Who's buying security and why?

Estimates of the size of the computer security market vary. International Data Corporation estimates that computer security now represents a $3 billion a year market opportunity—and this number is expected to increase dramatically over the next decade. Other studies predict that the market may rise to as much as $8 billion during this period.

As you'd expect, the U.S. government drives much of the security market. Because of its special concern for classified information relating to national defense and intelligence, the U.S. government has historically been the major force behind security research and technology. The government has a great many secrets (6.8 million new pieces of information are classified each year!) and computer security products thrive on secrecy.

It's difficult to get hard numbers on government security spending because military and other classified programs account for a large piece of the security market, and dollar figures for those classified programs aren't publicly available. Best estimates are that as much as half the total computer security purchases are government-related (although the commercial area is expected to increase dramatically during the 1990s and to outstrip government purchases by a wide margin by the end of the decade).

The Department of Defense, the intelligence agencies, and government contractors are particularly heavy users of security products—especially cryptographic products, highly secure computer systems, and systems that use TEMPEST technology (the TEMPEST market is almost exclusively a government one). But virtually every government department and agency buys security products. Most of them have little choice. They're required by government regulations to protect the information they process with appropriate security.

Businesses and government agencies have different goals and different cost/risk tradeoffs. Because financial considerations are the focus of business, security has to be cost-effective, or business won't buy or build it. A big market question is what people will be willing to pay for security over time—both in dollars and in potential loss of convenience and user friendliness.

Why buy security? There are two especially good reasons, described below.

Government Requirements

If you sell to the government, you almost certainly need to use many of the security technologies described in this book. If you're a computer vendor who's trying to sell a lot of computer workstations, for example, you may be forced to build security into your products, or to buy the technology from others.

More and more government requisitions specify security requirements along with operational requirements. The operating system you use may have to adhere to a particular security level specified in the "Orange Book" standard for trusted systems. You may need to use a particular form of encryption to protect stored and transmitted data. For high-security applications, your hardware may need to use TEMPEST shielding.

In addition to being the major purchaser of computer security, the government has historically been the driving force behind the development of security products and the standardization of what makes a system "secure." Chapter 2, *Some Security History*, describes what these security standards are and how they developed.

Information Protection

Government agencies are required by law to protect both classified information and also what's called "sensitive unclassified" information. Examples include such information as productivity statistics (Department of Commerce), currency production and transfer information (Department of the Treasury), and embassy personnel information (Department of State). What makes this information sensitive is the fact that its theft or modification could potentially disrupt the nation's economy or compromise its employees. Similarly, the breach of individual health and financial records maintained by such agencies as the Social Security Administration, the FBI, the IRS, and the Census Bureau could have severe legal and personal repercussions.

If your business involves the use of sensitive corporate information, you need security too. In some cases, you'll be concerned about keeping information secret. Obvious examples of such information include banking funds transfers, oil resource data, stock futures strategies, medical research data, and airline reservation information. In other cases, you'll need to ensure the integrity of the information. A primary example is electronic funds transfer (EFT). The Society for

Worldwide Interbank Financial Telecommunications (SWIFT), for example, provides EFT services to banks and financial institutions, processing about 700,000 transactions per day for more than 1800 banks in 46 countries. SWIFT and other financial institutions require absolute accuracy in their transactions. As described earlier, message authentication and related techniques play an important part in ensuring the accuracy of such financial information.

Even if your business doesn't involve national defense secrets and international funds transfers, the information you process is critical to your own business. Information may well be your most important business asset. Any theft or compromise of information is as much an attack on your business as is the theft of any other company asset. And the loss of information is more likely to damage your business than would a more tangible loss. Even if you're not convinced that you need security, your insurance company and your shareholders may be. The concept of "reasonable safeguards" is having an impact on users of computer systems now; you may find that if you do not provide adequate security for your information, your insurance may not cover a loss, and you may lose a court battle over "computer malpractice," "preventable loss," or the "standard of due care."

What's A User To Do?

Even if you work alone at home on a PC, computer security affects you. You'll need to worry about power failures and other natural disasters, and you'll need to back up your data in case you erroneously wipe out a disk. If you work on a multi-user system, you're going to have to contend more with security. You'll find that new system releases are adding security features—and most organizations are starting to insist that their users *use* these features.

More and more "standard" operating systems, not just those intended for use in classified military or intelligence environments, are offering strong security. Virtually every multi-user system provides at least password controls and some type of file protection scheme. Increasingly, systems are providing a number of different levels of security so an organization can choose whether to exercise certain options or not. For example, the Open Software Foundation's OSF/1 operating system allows an organization to select the desired level of "Orange Book" security from several options, and many other popular systems allow the degree of security to be fine-tuned to suit a customer's needs.

If your organization has installed a highly secure system, you may have to accept substantial restrictions on the administrative tasks you might have performed in the past—for example, freely switching directories, copying files, and viewing print queues. If your system supports mandatory access controls, you'll find that even if another user wants to let you read or print one of his or her files, the system may not let you. If you're using a window manager, you may find that you can't cut and paste between windows containing different types of information.

Some organizations or systems may not impose strict security controls. In this case, you're on your own. We hope we can convince you that security is good for you and your data—that it's worth it for you to spend a small amount of extra time worrying about viruses, protecting your login account, and otherwise practicing safe computing to the best of your (and your system's) ability.

Remember that security means more than keeping the bad guys out. It also means backing up and protecting your files in case your system or disk fails, or in case you delete data by mistake. And it means keeping your system running smoothly by not letting certain users, or systems in a network, slow down processing for everyone else. Throughout this book, interspersed with the text we'll include boxed summaries containing helpful hints suggesting what you personally can do to enforce security in your system.

2

Some Security History

Information and its Controls
Computer Security: Then and Now
Early Computer Security Efforts
Building Toward Standardization
Computer Security Mandates
    and Legislation
Privacy Considerations
International Security Activity
The Growth of Modern Standards

Computer security is a hot issue today, but it's an issue that's been simmering for many years. The development of government security regulations and standards, research into security mechanisms, and debates over the threats to information and the costs of protecting against these threats—all of these activities are well into their third decade. Computer security itself isn't new. What's new is security's broader focus (now, security means more than just keeping outsiders out) and its wider appeal (now, security is important to business as well as government).

This chapter describes how we got to where we are today. It summarizes key events in the history of computer security, focusing particularly on the government standards and programs detailed later in this book.

Information and its Controls

Information security is almost as old as information itself. Whenever people develop new methods of recording, storing, or transmitting information, these innovations are almost inevitably followed by methods of harnessing the new technologies and protecting the information they process. And they're also followed by government investigations and controls. For example:

- With Samuel F.B. Morse's introduction of the telegraph came concerns for protecting the confidentiality of transmitted messages. In 1845, just a year after the invention, a commercial encryption code was developed to keep the transmitted messages secret.

- Within five years of the introduction of the telephone in 1881, a patent application was filed for a voice scrambler.

- In the 1920s, the use of telephone wiretaps by both government and criminal forces resulted in a public outcry, Congressional hearings, and, ultimately, legislation prohibiting most wiretapping.

- In the 1940s, concerns about controlling the proliferation of information about atomic energy led to the Atomic Energy Act of 1946. This act created a Restricted Data category of information requiring special protection and penalties for dissemination. Similar controls have been imposed on new advances in other scientific fields.

- In the 1980s, the Defense Authorization Act specified controls on technical information about emerging military and space technologies.

Like any other new technology, computers have raised substantial questions about the degree to which the technology should be controlled—and by whom. Even newer technologies—for example, imaging systems that may impact the integrity of legal and financial documents—will no doubt raise the same types of complex issues.

One ongoing debate in the computer security world is over the government's restriction of technological information.

The government needs to protect certain kinds of information, such as national defense data. Particular security technologies—for example, cryptographic products—are very effective at safeguarding such information. Should the government be able to control who can and cannot buy such technologies? Should there be any limits on such sales? For example, should enemy governments be able to buy cryptographic products that may make it more difficult for U.S. intelligence

operations to monitor these nations' communications? What a[
about the technologies themselves; for example, technical pap(
graphic algorithms? Should these have to be submitted for gove
tion and possible censorship? Can technology and the free exc
tual data flourish in an environment that tries to control certain kinds of intellec-
tual exchanges?

Another debate concerns the involvement of the government in mandating the
protection of nongovernment information.

Should the government have any control over the protection of such information?
Who gets to decide whether information such as productivity statistics, geological
surveys, and health information must be protected from public scrutiny? From
whom is it being protected? Should the government impose the same security
standards on systems used to process government and commercial information?

As you'd expect, different people have a variety of opinions about these questions. We'll try to touch on questions and representative opinions throughout this
book.

Computer Security: Then and Now

In the early days of computing, computer systems were large, rare, and very
expensive. Naturally enough, those organizations lucky enough to have a computer tried their best to protect it. Computer security was simply one aspect of
general plant security. Computer buildings, floors, and rooms were guarded and
alarmed to prevent outsiders from intruding and disrupting computer operations.
Security concerns focused on physical break-ins, the theft of computer equipment, and the physical theft or destruction of disk packs, tape reels, punched
cards, and other media.

Insiders were also kept at bay. Few people knew how to use computers, and only
those who knew the secrets of the machine were privileged to stand in its presence. Most users never saw the computers that crunched their numbers. Batch
processing meant that users submitted carefully screened jobs—often through
protected slots in the doors of computer rooms—to operators who actually put the
machine through its paces.

Times changed. During the late 1960s and 1970s, computer technology was
transformed, and with it the ways in which users related to computers and data.
Multi-programming, time-sharing, and networking dramatically changed the rules

of the game. Users could now interact directly with a computer system, via a terminal, giving them more power and flexibility but also opening up new possibilities for abuse.

Telecommunications—the ability to access computers from remote locations and to share programs and data—radically changed computer usage. Large businesses began to automate and store online information about their customers, vendors, and commercial transactions. Networks linked minicomputers together and allowed them to communicate with each other and with mainframes containing large online databases. It became much easier to make wholesale changes to data—and much easier for errors to wreak widespread damage. Banking and the transfer of assets became an electronic business.

The increased ease and flexibility of computer access also had a dramatic impact on education. Universities and other schools that could not afford their own computer installations now found it possible to tie into computer networks and centralized computers and databases. More and more students had an opportunity to experiment with computers, and computers increasingly became a part of the curriculum. The result was a huge increase in the number of people who knew how to use computers.

Inevitably, the increased availability of online systems and information led to abuses. Computer security concerns broadened. Instead of worrying only about intrusions by outsiders into computer facilities and equipment (and an occasional computer operator going berserk), organizations now had to worry about computers that were vulnerable to sneak attacks over telephone lines, and information that could be stolen or changed by intruders who didn't leave a trace. Incidents of computer crime began to be reported. Individuals and government agencies expressed concerns about the invasion of privacy posed by the availability of individual financial, legal, and medical records on shared online databases. As computer terminals and modems became more affordable, these perils intensified.

The 1980s saw the dawn of a new age of computing. With the introduction of the personal computer, individuals of all ages and occupations became computer users. Computers appeared on desks at home and at the office. Some small children learned to use computers before they could read. As the price of systems dropped, and as inexpensive accounting packages became available, more and more small businesses automated their operations. PC technology introduced new risks. Precious and irreplaceable corporate data was now stored on diskettes, which could too easily be lost or stolen.

As PCs proliferated, so did the use of PC networks, electronic mail, and bulletin boards, dramatically increasing the ability of users to communicate with other users and computers, and vastly raising the security stakes. In the past, even a skilled cracker might have breached security only in a single computer, installation, or local area network; now he had the potential to disrupt nationwide or even worldwide computer operations.

The 1980s also saw systems under attack. Theoretical possibilities came to life as *War Games*-like break-ins played themselves out on the front pages of local newspapers: the Internet worm, the Friday the 13th virus, the West German hackers, and players at espionage. Government, business, and individual users suddenly saw the consequences of ignoring security risks.

As we enter the 1990s, we face the challenges of open systems. Along with our increasing dependence on networks and the need to share data, applications, and hardware/software resources across vendor boundaries come increasing security risks. In this decade the security business is coming of age, with more and more vendors developing trusted systems, bundling security functions, and developing biometric devices and network security products. Still, security systems are lagging behind the technologies they seek to control. And both businesses and individuals are lagging still further behind in their willingness to make security an integral part of their products and their jobs.

The challenge of the next decade will be to consolidate what we've learned—to build computer security into our products and our daily routines, to protect data without unnecessarily impeding our ability to access it, and to make sure that both security products and government and industry standards grow to meet the ever-increasing scope and challenges of technology.

Early Computer Security Efforts

The earliest computer-related security activities began in the 1950s, with the development of the first TEMPEST security standard, the consideration of security issues in some of the earliest computer system designs, and the establishment of the first government security organization, the U.S. Communications Security (COMSEC) Board. The board, which consisted of representatives from many different branches of the government, oversaw the protection of classified information.

Although these events set the scene for later computer security advances, the 1960s marked the true beginning of the age of computer security, with initiatives by the Department of Defense, the National Security Agency, the National Bureau of Standards, coupled with the first public awareness of security.

Public interest in computer security emerged toward the end of the decade. The Spring Joint Computer Conference of 1967 is generally recognized as being the locale for the first comprehensive computer security presentation for a technical audience. Willis H. Ware of the RAND Corporation chaired a session that addressed the wide variety of vulnerabilities present in resource-sharing, remote-access computer systems. The session addressed threats ranging from electro-magnetic radiation to bugs on communications lines to unauthorized programmer and user access to systems and data.

The Department of Defense, because of its strong interest in protecting military computers and classified information, was an early partisan of computer security efforts. In 1967, DoD began to study the potential threats to DoD computer systems and information. In October of that year, DoD assembled a task force under the auspices of the Defense Science Board within the Advanced Research Projects Agency (ARPA) (now known as the Defense Advanced Research Projects Agency or DARPA). The task force worked for the next two years examining systems and networks, identifying vulnerabilities and threats, and introducing methods of safeguarding and controlling access to defense computers, systems, networks, and information. Published as a classified document in 1970, the task force report, *Security Controls for Computer Systems*,* was a landmark publication in the history of computer security. Its recommendations, and the research that followed its publication, led to a number of programs dedicated to protecting classified information and setting standards for protection.

The Department of Defense took to heart the recommendations of the task force and began to develop regulations for enforcing the security of the computer systems, networks, and classified data used by DoD and its contractors. In 1972, DoD issued a directive† and an accompanying manual‡ that established a consistent DoD policy for computer controls and techniques. The directive stated overall policy as follows:

> Classified material contained in an ADP system shall be safeguarded by the continuous employment of protective features in the system's hardware and software design and configuration.

The directive also stipulated that systems specifically protect both the computer equipment and the data that it processes by preventing deliberate and inadvertent

---

*W.H. Ware, *Security Controls for Computer Systems: Report of Defense Science Board Task Force on Computer Security*, Rand Corporation, AD-A076-617/0, R-609-1, 1970, declassified 1976, reissued 1979.

†*Security Requirements for Automatic Data Processing (ADP) Systems* (DoD 5200.28), 1972, revised 1978.

‡*ADP Security Manual—Techniques & Procedures for Implementing, Deactivating, Testing, and Evaluating Secure Resource-Sharing ADP Systems* (DoD 5200.28-M), 1973, revised 1979.

access to classified material by unauthorized persons, as well as unauthorized manipulation of the computer and associated equipment.

During the 1970's, under the sponsorship of DoD and industry, a number of major initiatives were undertaken to better understand the system vulnerabilities and threats that early studies had exposed and to begin to develop technical measures for countering these threats. These initiatives fell into three general categories: tiger teams, security research studies, and development of the first secure operating systems.

Tiger Teams

During the 1970s, "tiger teams" first emerged on the computer scene. Tiger teams were government- and industry-sponsored teams of crackers who attempted to break down the defenses of computer systems in an effort to uncover, and eventually patch, security holes. Most tiger teams were sponsored by DoD, but IBM aroused a great deal of public awareness of computer security by committing to spend $40 million to address computer security issues—and tiger teams were an important part of finding security flaws in the company's own products.*

Tiger teams were an effective way to find and fix security problems, but their efforts were necessarily piecemeal. U.S. Air Force Lieutenant General Lincoln D. Faurer, former Director of the National Security Agency, wrote that the efforts of the tiger teams resulted in two significant conclusions.†

> Attempts to correct (patch) identified security vulnerabilities were not sufficient to prevent subsequent repenetrations. New tiger teams often found security flaws not found by earlier tiger teams, and one could not rely on the failure of a penetration effort to indicate that there were no exploitable security flaws.

> The only apparent means of guaranteeing the protection of system resources would be to design verifiable protection mechanisms into computer systems.

---

*Reports describing the efforts of tiger teams included:

  C.R. Attanasio, P.W. Markstein, and R.J. Phillips, "Penetrating an Operating System: A Study of VM/370 Integrity," *IBM Systems Journal*, Volume 15, Number 1, 1974.

  R. Bisbey, G. Popek, and J. Carlstedt, *Protection Errors in Operating Systems*, USC Information Sciences Institute, 1978.

  P.A. Karger and Schell, R.R., *Multics Security Evaluation: Vulnerability Analysis*, (ESD-TR-74-193), Electronic Systems Division, U.S. Air Force, Hanscom Air Force Base, Bedford (MA), 1974. (Available from NTIS: AD A001120.)

†Lincoln D. Faurer, "Computer Security Goals of the Department of Defense," *Computer Security Journal*, Summer 1984.

Tiger teams served a useful function by identifying security flaws and demonstrating how easily these flaws could be exploited. But by the end of the 1970s it was apparent that a more rigorous method of building, testing, and evaluating computer systems was needed.

Research and Modeling

During the 1970s, DoD and other agencies sponsored a number of groundbreaking research projects aimed at identifying security requirements, formulating security policy models, and defining recommended guidelines and controls.

In the research report of the Computer Security Technology Planning Study,* James P. Anderson introduced the concept of a *reference monitor*, an entity that "enforces the authorized access relationships between subjects and objects of a system." The idea of a reference monitor became very important to the development of standards and technologies for secure systems. Chapter 6, *Inside the Orange Book*, describes this concept and the function of subjects and objects in secure systems.

DoD went on to sponsor additional research and development in the 1970s focusing on the development of security policy models, also discussed in Chapter 6. A *security policy* defines system security by stating the set of laws, rules, and practices that regulate how an organization manages, protects, and distributes sensitive information. The mechanisms necessary to enforce a security policy usually conform to a specific *security model*.

A number of additional technical research reports published during the 1970s defined secure systems and security requirements.† During the 1970s, David Bell and Leonard LaPadula developed the first mathematical model of a multi-level security policy. The Bell and LaPadula model‡ was central to the development of basic computer security standards and laid the groundwork for a number of later security models, and their application in government security standards.

---

*J.P. Anderson, *Computer Security Technology Planning Study*, (ESD-TR-73-51), Electronic Systems Division, U.S. Air Force, Hanscom Air Force Base, Bedford (MA), 1972. (Available from NTIS: AD 758206.)

†These reports included:

   Secure Minicomputer Operating System (KSOS) Department of Defense Kernelized Secure Operating System, (WDL-7932), Ford Aerospace and Communications Corporation, 1978.

   P.G. Neumann et al, *A Provably Secure Operating System: The System, Its Application, and Proofs*, Final Report, Project 4332, SRI International, Menlo Park (CA), 1977.

‡D.E. Bell and L.J. LaPadula, *Secure Computer Systems: Mathematical Foundations and Model*, (M74-244), Mitre Corporation, Bedford (MA), 1973. (Available from NTIS: AD 771543.)

Secure Systems Development

A number of government-sponsored development projects undertook to develop the first "secure" systems during the 1970s. Most of these efforts were devoted to developing prototypes for security kernels. A *security kernel* (described briefly in Chapter 6) is the part of the operating system that controls access to system resources. The most significant was the Air Force-funded project that led to the development of a security kernel for the Multics (Multiplexed Information and Computing Service) system.*

Multics allows users with different security clearances to simultaneously access information that has been classified at different levels. Because it embodied so many well designed security features, the Multics system was particularly important to the development of later secure systems. Multics was a large-scale, highly interactive computer system that offered both hardware- and software-enforced security. Specific features of Multics included extensive password and login controls; data security through access control lists (ACLs), an access isolation mechanism (AIM), and a ring mechanism; auditing of all system access operations; decentralized system administration; and architectural features such as paged and segmented virtual memory and stack-controlled process architecture.

Other security kernels under development during the 1970s included Mitre Corporation's Digital Equipment Corporation PDP-11/45† and UCLA's Data Secure UNIX PDP-11/70.‡

Building Toward Standardization

Late in the 1970s, two important government initiatives significantly affected the development of computer security standards and methods. In 1977, the Department of Defense announced the DoD Computer Security Initiative under the auspices of the Under Secretary of Defense for Research and Engineering. The goal was to focus national attention and resources on computer security issues. The

---

*For information about Multics, see J.C. Whitmore et al, *Design for Multics Security Enhancements*, (ESD-TR74-176), Honeywell Information Systems, Cambridge (MA), 1973. (Available from NTIS: AD A030801.) See also Elliot Organick, *The Multics System: An Examination of Its Structure*, MIT Press, Cambridge (MA), 1975.

†W.L. Schiller, *The Design and Specification of a Security Kernel for the PDP-11/45*, ESD-TR-75-69, Mitre Corporation, Bedford (MA), 1975. (Available from NTIS: AD A011712.)

‡G.G. Popek et al, "UCLA Secure UNIX," *Proceedings, National Computer Conference*, New York (NY), 1979.

Initiative was launched in 1978 when DoD called together government and industry participants in a series of seminars. The goal of the seminars was to answer these questions:

- Are secure computer systems useful and feasible?

- What mechanisms should be developed to evaluate and approve secure computer systems?

- How can computer vendors be encouraged to develop secure computer systems?

The second important initiative came from the National Bureau of Standards. NBS (now NIST) has historically been responsible for the development of standards of all kinds. As a consequence of the Brooks Act of 1965 (described in "Computer Security Legislation" later in this chapter), NBS became the agency responsible for researching and developing standards for federal computer purchase and use and for assisting other agencies in implementing these standards. The bureau has published many federal standards known as Federal Information Processing Standards publications (FIPS PUBs) in all areas of computer technology, including computer security. Over the course of the next decade or so, NBS focused on two distinct security standardization efforts: development of standards for building and evaluating secure computer systems, and development of a national standard for cryptography.

Standards for Secure Systems

NBS's first charge was to evaluate the federal government's overall computer security needs and to begin to find ways to meet them. Early efforts, based on NBS's Brooks Act mandate, included the following:

1968   NBS performed an initial study to evaluate the government's computer security needs.

1972   NBS sponsored a conference on computer security in collaboration with the ACM.

1973   NBS initiated a program aimed at researching development standards for computer security.

1977   NBS began a series of Invitational Workshops dedicated to the Audit and Evaluation of Computer Systems. These had far-reaching consequences for the development of standards for secure systems.

At the first Invitational Workshop in 1977, 58 experts in computer technology and security assembled to define problems and develop solutions for building and evaluating secure systems. Invitees represented NBS, the General Accounting Organization (GAO), other government agencies, and industry. Their goal? To determine:

> What authoritative ways exist, or should exist, to decide whether a particular computer system is "secure enough" for a particular intended environment or operation, and if a given system is not "secure enough," what measures could or should be taken to make it so.

Workshop participants considered many different aspects of computer security, including accuracy, reliability, timeliness, and confidentiality. The NBS workshops resulted in the publication of several reports.* These concluded that achieving security required attention to all three of the following:

Policy   What security rules should be enforced for sensitive information?

Mechanisms   What hardware and software mechanisms are needed to enforce the policy?

Assurance   What needs to be done to make a convincing case that the mechanisms do support the policy even when the system is subject to threats?

The NBS report stated:

> By any reasonable definition of "secure" no current operating system today can be considered "secure". . . We hope the reader does not interpret this to mean that highly sensitive information cannot be dealt with securely in a computer, for of course that is done all the time. The point is that the internal control mechanisms of current operating systems have too low integrity for them to . . . effectively isolate a user on the system from data that is at a "higher" security level than he is trusted . . . to deal with.

This conclusion was an important one in terms of the multi-level security concepts discussed in Part II of this book.

---

*Z. Ruthberg and R. McKenzie, ed., *Audit and Evaluation of Computer Security*, Special Publication 500-19, National Bureau of Standards, Gaithersburg (MD), 1980. (Available from GPO: SN 003-003-01848-1.)

Z. Ruthberg, ed., *Audit and Evaluation of Computer Security II: System Vulnerabilities and Controls*, Special Publication 500-57, (MD78733), National Bureau of Standards, Gaithersburg (MD), 1980. (Available from GPO: SN 003-003-02178-4.)

The NBS workshops recommended that a number of actions be taken. One action was to formulate a detailed computer security policy for sensitive information not covered by national security policies and guidelines. Another was to establish a formal security and evaluation and accreditation process, including the publication of a list of approved products to guide specification and procurement of systems intended to handle sensitive information. A third was to establish a standard, formalized, institutionalized technical means of measuring or evaluating the overall security of a system.

As an outgrowth of the NBS workshops, the Mitre Corporation was assigned the task of developing an initial set of computer security evaluation criteria that could be used to assess the degree of trust that could be placed in a computer system that protected classified data. Beginning in 1979, in response to the NBS workshop and report on the standardization of computer security requirements, the Office of the Secretary of Defense conducted a series of public seminars on the DoD Computer Security Initiative. One result of these seminars was that the Deputy Secretary of Defense assigned to the Director of the National Security Agency (NSA) responsibility for increasing the use of trusted information security products within the Department of Defense.

National Computer Security Center

As a result of NSA's new responsibility for information security, on January 2, 1981, the DoD Computer Security Center (CSC) was established within NSA to expand upon the work begun by the DoD Computer Security Initiative. The official charter of the CSC is contained in the DoD Directive entitled "Computer Security Evaluation Center" (5215.1).

Several years later, the computer security responsibilities held by CSC were expanded to include all federal agencies and the Center became known as the National Computer Security Center (NCSC) in August, 1985. The Center was founded with the following goals:

- Encourage the widespread availability of trusted computer systems.

- Evaluate the technical protection capabilities of industry- and government-developed systems.

- Provide technical support of government and industry groups engaged in computer security research and development.

- Develop technical criteria for the evaluation of computer systems.

- Evaluate commercial systems.

- Conduct and sponsor research in computer and network security technology.

- Develop and provide access to verification and analysis tools used to develop and test secure computer systems.

- Conduct training in areas of computer security.

- Disseminate computer security information to other branches of the federal government and to industry.

In 1985, NSA also merged its communications and computer security responsibilities together under the Deputy Directorate for Information Security Systems (INFOSEC).

Birth of the Orange Book

The Center met an important goal by publishing the *Department of Defense Trusted Computer System Evaluation Criteria (TCSEC)*, commonly known as the Orange Book because of the color of its cover. Based on the computer security evaluation criteria developed by Mitre* and on such developments as the security model developed by Bell and LaPadula, this publication was distributed to government and industry experts, revised, and finally released in August of 1983.

The Orange Book is the bible of secure system development. It describes the evaluation criteria used to assess the level of trust that can be placed in a particular computer system. It effectively makes security a measurable commodity so a buyer can identify the exact level of security required for a particular system, application, or environment. The Orange Book presents a graded classification of secure systems. It defines four broad hierarchical divisions, or levels, of protection—D, C, B, and A, in order of increasing security. Within each division, the Orange Book defines one or more classes, each defined by a specific set of criteria that a system must meet to achieve a rating in that class. Some divisions have only a single class, others have two or three. The original Orange Book was revised slightly and was reissued in December of 1985.

Using the Orange Book criteria, NCSC performs evaluations of products submitted by vendors for certification at a particular level of trust. Products that are successfully evaluated through NCSC's Trusted Products Evaluation Program (TPEP) are placed on the Evaluated Products List (EPL). Chapter 6, *Inside the Orange Book*, describes the Orange Book evaluation criteria (and also mentions some of the complaints about these criteria). Appendix D, *Government Security Programs*, describes the evaluation process.

---

*G.H. Nibaldi, *Proposed Technical Evaluation Criteria for Trusted Computer Systems*, (M79-225), Mitre Corporation, Bedford (MA), 1979. (Available from NTIS: AD A108832.)

G.H. Nibaldi, *Specification of a Trusted Computing Base*, (M79-228), Mitre Corporation, Bedford (MA), 1979. (Available from NTIS: AD 108831.)

Although evaluations performed in accordance with the Orange Book focus on multi-purpose trusted computer systems, evaluations are also performed for network communications products and for security subsystems and specialty products. In the years since the publication of the Orange Book, NCSC has published a number of additional books describing how the Orange Book may be interpreted for such security products. Chapter 6 introduces these documents, and Appendix E, *A Security Source Book*, tells how you can obtain them.

Standards for Cryptography

During the 1970s, interest in a national cryptographic standard began to build within the government. The idea was to find an algorithm that could be used to protect sensitive unclassified government information (classified algorithms were already being used to protect classified information) and sensitive commercial data such as banking electronic funds transfers. In 1973, the National Bureau of Standards, part of the Department of Commerce, invited vendors to submit data encryption techniques that might be used as the basis of an encryptions algorithm.

Under the auspices of the Institute of Computer Science and Technology (ICST) (now known as the National Computer Systems Laboratory), NBS organized a series of workshops for government and industry representatives. The method eventually selected by NBS became known as the Data Encryption Standard (DES).

The DES was adopted as a Federal Information Processing Standard (FIPS PUB 46) in 1977 as the official method of protecting unclassified data in the computers of U.S. government agencies, and was subsequently adopted as an American National Standards Institute (ANSI) standard.

The DES consists of two components: an algorithm and a key. The DES algorithm is a complex, iterative process that is public information. This algorithm uses a secret value—the key—to encode and decode messages.

DES technology has been embedded in the products of many commercial products. Until 1986, the National Security Agency endorsed products containing DES-based algorithms. In 1986, NSA announced that it would no longer endorse such products. There has been a substantial reaction to this decision by vendors, users, and other government agencies. Chapter 7, *Encryption*, describes the DES in greater detail and outlines some of the issues surrounding the use of the algorithm.

While the DES algorithm is likely to remain the standard for commercial data encryption for many years to come, cryptographic researchers have continued to work on the development of more advanced algorithms, and NSA is now encouraging vendors to develop products based on these algorithms. Through the

Commercial Communications Security Endorsement Program (CCEP), government and industry representatives develop, test, and endorse new cryptographic products. (CCEP is described in Appendix D, *Government Security Programs*.) Products that meet the requirements of the program are placed on Endorsed Cryptographic Products List (ECPL).

Standards for Emanations

As early as the 1950s, concerns began to develop about the possibility that the electrical and electromagnetic radiation that emanates from computer equipment (as it does from all electronic equipment) could be intercepted and deciphered. In an effort to counter this threat, the U.S. government established the first standard for the level of emanations that were acceptable for equipment used to process classified information in the late 1950s. During the 1960s and 1970s, as standardization efforts proceeded in areas of secure systems and cryptography, they also resulted in the refinement of the initial TEMPEST standard and the establishment of a program to endorse products that met the requirements of this standard.

The Industrial TEMPEST Program was established in 1974 with three main goals:

1. Specify a TEMPEST standard that sets allowable limits on the levels of emission from electronic equipment.

2. Outline criteria for testing equipment that, according to its vendors, meets the TEMPEST standard.

3. Certify vendor equipment that successfully meets the TEMPEST standard.

The National TEMPEST Standard (National Communications Security Emanations Memorandum 5100), known as NACSEM 5100, was published in 1970. This standard has been revised several times. The current standard, announced in 1981 as National Communications Security Information Memorandum 5100A (NACSIM 5100A), is entitled "Compromising Emanations Laboratory Test Standard, Electromagnetics (U)." NACSIM 5100A sets the standards for equipment used to handle classified data.

Through ITP, government and industry representatives have worked together to set standards and to develop, test, and certify TEMPEST equipment. The U.S. government evaluates TEMPEST products submitted by vendors through the Endorsed TEMPEST Products Program (ETPP) described in Appendix D. For information about TEMPEST, see Chapter 10.

Computer Security Mandates and Legislation

Throughout history, new advances in the availability, processing, and transmission of information have inevitably been followed by new security methods, federal laws, and procedural controls. These are typically aimed at protecting information that's considered to be essential to national security or other national interests.

In the 1970s and into the 1980s, national concerns about the Soviet interception of domestic communications intensified, leading to a large number of security-related pieces of legislation, Presidential directives, and national policy statements. These fall into several categories:

Protection of Classified or Sensitive Information.
Legislation mandating computer security practices by federal agencies and contractors. The idea of this legislation is that organizations that process classified or sensitive unclassified government information must be careful to protect that information from unauthorized access. Table B-1 in Appendix B, *Computer Security Legislation*, summarizes the legislation in this category, and the following sections describe the main laws.

Computer Crime.
Legislation defining computer crime as an offense and extending other regulations to cover thefts and other abuses carried out by computers and other new techniques. Table B-2 in Appendix B summarizes the pieces of legislation that have been extended to include computer fraud and abuse, as well as additional existing statutes that have been used to prosecute computer criminals. In addition to the federal policies listed in Table B-2, virtually all of the states have enacted their own legislation prohibiting computer crime and abuse.

Privacy.
Legislation protecting the privacy of information maintained about individuals (e.g., health and financial records). The section entitled "Privacy Considerations" discusses privacy issues relevant to computer security. Table B-3 in Appendix B summarizes the legislation in this category.

The following sections outline some of the most important federal computer security laws and guidelines.

NSDD 145

The National Security Decision Directive 145 (NSDD 145), entitled the National Policy on Telecommunications and Automated Information Systems Security, and signed by President Reagan on September 17, 1984, has had far-reaching significance in the world of computer security. NSDD 145 mandated the protection of both classified and unclassified sensitive information. It also gave NSA the obligation to "encourage, advise, and if appropriate assist" the private sector. Because it gave NSA jurisdiction in the private sector, NSDD 145 has been a controversial directive. Eventually, NSDD 145 was revised and reissued as NSD 42, as described in a later section.

NSDD 145 requires systems that handle classified information to be secured as necessary to prevent access by unauthorized individuals. It also requires that systems protect sensitive information, whether it has originated in the government or outside it, in proportion to the potential damage that disclosure, alteration, or loss poses to national security. Examples of sensitive information include productivity statistics; information that might relate to the disruption of public services (e.g., air traffic control information); and virtually all information collected by such organizations as the Social Security Administration, the Federal Bureau of Investigation, the Internal Revenue Service, and the Census Bureau (e.g., individual health and financial records).

NSDD 145 had another important administrative effect. It effectively created a federal interagency structure for the management of computer security within the government. Under the provisions of NSDD 145, the government's System Security Steering Group oversees NSDD 145's implementation. This organization is composed of a power team: the Secretaries of Defense, State, and the Treasury, the Attorney General, the director of the Office of Management and the Budget, and the director of the CIA. Under the direction of the Steering Group, the National Telecommunications and Information Systems Security Committee (NTISSC) develops operations policies and provides guidance to government agencies. This committee has representatives from a variety of government agencies and departments, including the Departments of Defense, State, Treasury, Commerce, Transportation, and Energy, and the Joint Chiefs of Staff, GSA, FBI, Army, Navy, Air Force, Marine Corps, DIA, CIA, and NSA.

NTISSP 2

In an effort to clarify the meaning of sensitive information and better interpret the requirements for its protection, the National Telecommunications and Information Systems Security Publication 2 (NTISSP 2), "National Policy on Protection of Sensitive but Unclassified Information in Federal Government

Telecommunications and Automated Systems," was published on October 29, 1986.

NTISSP 2 defined sensitive information as follows:

> Sensitive, but unclassified information is information the disclosure, loss, misuse, alteration, or destruction of which could adversely affect national security or other federal government interests. National security interests are those unclassified matters that relate to the national defense or the foreign relations of the U.S. government. Other government interests are those related, but not limited to the wide range of government or government-derived economic, human, financial, industrial, agricultural, technology, and law enforcement information, as well as the privacy or confidentiality of personal or commercial proprietary information provided to the U.S. government by its citizens.

NTISSP 2 applies to all government agencies and contractors. It describes the general categories of information that might relate to national security, foreign relations, or other government interests. It instructs the heads of Departments and agencies to determine what information is sensitive but unclassified and to provide system protection for that information when it is electronically communicated, transferred, processed, or stored.

Computer Fraud and Abuse Act

Issued in 1986, the Computer Fraud and Abuse Act (18 U.S. Code 1030, now called Public Law 99-474) prohibits unauthorized or fraudulent access to government computers and establishes penalties for such access. Anyone convicted under this act faces a fine of $5000 or twice the value of anything obtained via unauthorized access, plus up to five years in jail (one year for first offenders). The act prohibits access with the intent to defraud, as well as intentional trespassing. For example, posting passwords to federal computers on pirate electronic bulletin boards is a misdemeanor under this act. Robert T. Morris, author of the infamous Internet worm, was the first person convicted under the Computer Fraud and Abuse Act (Section 1030 (a)(5)), setting a precedent for future cases.

There are complaints about the wording of the Computer Fraud and Abuse Act on both sides of the issue.

The frustration of the Justice Department in prosecuting espionage cases in which classified information has been obtained by computer has led the Department to try to change the wording of the Computer Fraud and Abuse Act. The current law says it's a felony for anyone knowingly to gain unauthorized access to a computer and obtain classified information "with the intent or reason to believe that such information so obtained is to be used to the injury of the United States or to the advantage of any foreign nation." The Justice Department wants to drop that clause. The revised law would simply require proof that the intruder obtained certain information, not that the information was delivered or transmitted to anyone else.

Amendments to the Computer Fraud and Abuse Act has been proposed in Congress to expand the act's current government and banking focus to any systems used in interstate commerce or communications. The amendments would also change the orientation of the act from simple unauthorized access to the use of a computer system in performing other crimes.

On the other side of the issue, there have been complaints that the language of the Computer Fraud and Abuse Act is too general and could apply to anyone who writes or teaches about computer security. There have also been suggestions that the act should explicitly treat different types of offenses in different ways. At present, there is no clear distinction between people who use computers for hacking, for computer crime, and for terrorism.

As yet, no changes have been made to the language of the Computer Fraud and Abuse Act.

Computer Security Act

An important outgrowth of NSDD 145 was the development of the Computer Security Act of 1987 (H.R. 145), which later became Public Law 100-235. This act has expanded the definition of computer security protection and has increased awareness of computer security as an issue. It's the closest thing the U.S. has to a federal data protection policy. The Computer Security Act, which went into effect in September of 1988, requires every U.S. government computer system that processes sensitive information to have a customized computer security plan for the system's management and use. It also requires that all U.S. government employees, contractors, and others who directly affect federal programs undergo ongoing periodic training in computer security. All users of systems containing sensitive data must also receive computer security training corresponding to the sensitivity of the data to which they have access.

The Computer Security Act further defined sensitive information as information whose "loss, misuse, unauthorized access to, or modification of could adversely affect the national interest, or the conduct of federal programs, or the privacy to which individuals are entitled under . . . the Privacy Act" (described under "Privacy Considerations" later in this chapter).

This act gave NIST new responsibility for federal computer security management. It assigned to the Institute for Computer Sciences and Technology within NIST responsibility for assessing the vulnerability of federal computer systems, for developing standards, and for providing technical assistance, as well as for developing guidelines for the training of federal personnel in computer security-related areas. NSA was assigned a role as advisor to NIST regarding technical safeguards.

The Computer Security Act does not affect the protection of classified information. It also allows requirements to be waived if they'll disrupt or slow down the implementation of what's considered to be an important federal agency mission.

Searching for a Balance

Following the adoption of the Computer Security Act, concerns were voiced by Congress, industry, professional groups, and the general public about the potential for abuse. These concerns focused on NSA's role in the private sector—in particular, relating to the control of unclassified information. Banks and other data-intensive industries feared that the act would impose disruptive restrictions on their operations. Civil libertarians were concerned about infringements on personal privacy. These concerns culminated in a series of Congressional hearings during 1987. During these hearings, NTISSP 2 was rescinded in March of 1987, and a review of NSDD 145 was ordered. Debate continues about the appropriate role of government in protecting and mandating the protection of information (see inset).

In 1990, NSDD 145 was revised and reissued as National Security Directive 42 (NSD 42). The new directive narrowed the original scope of NSDD 145 to primarily defense-related information.

Recent Government Security Initiatives

NSA, NIST, and DoD have all played an important part in developing computer security standards and in carrying out security programs. The exact balance of responsibility has not always been clear, and the boundaries continue to shift. Typically, NSA has had responsibility for the protection of classified military and intelligence information via computer security techniques, while NIST has been responsible for developing standards and for developing computer security training programs. At times, both NSA and NIST have claimed responsibility for safeguarding unclassified, sensitive information, though most recently this type of information has been in NIST's bailiwick. Although standards for the evaluation of secure systems came about under NIST's auspices, actual evaluations are performed by the National Computer Security Center, a part of NSA. Different pieces of legislation seem to shift the balance one way or the other.

Hackers' Rights

Through most of the computer industry, there's a push to take security more seriously. But some big guns say we've gone too far. In the wake of law enforcement sweeps such as Operation Sun Devil, which seized 42 computers and 23,000 floppy disks in 14 cities, shut down several bulletin board systems, and made four arrests in spring of 1990 (some resulting from publication of information about the BellSouth 911 emergency telephone service and other "hacker tutorials"), a new group has been formed to provide legal aid to those it says have been victimized.

Federal and state law enforcers have been searching the homes of computer crackers, many of them members of the Legion of Doom organization—and some who say they're not crackers at all. Mitch Kapor (of Lotus and ON Technology fame) and John Barlow (author and Grateful Dead songwriter) have banded together, in conjunction with some well-known New York and Boston law firms, to form a defense team known as the Electronic Frontier Foundation, which seeks to protect the civil liberties of legitimate computer users.

Members of the team charge that in trying to protect the government, industry, and individuals from cracker attacks, government agents have violated constitutional rights. They also warn that the intimidation of today may thwart the technology of tomorrow. Senator Patrick Leahy, Democrat from Vermont, insists that we need to punish lawbreakers, but comments, "We cannot unduly inhibit the inquisitive 13-year-old who, if left to experiment today, may tomorrow develop telecommunications or computer technology to lead the United States into the 21st century. He represents our future and our best hope to remain a technologically competitive nation."

As a consequence of NSDD 145, the balance of responsibility seemed to shift to NSA (only to shift back again to NIST with the Computer Security Act and the revision of NSDD 145). NIST's Computer Security Program now encompasses a wide range of security activities, including developing and publishing computer security standards (in conjunction with organizations such as ANSI, ISO, and IEEE, described later in this chapter); conducting research in areas of security testing and solutions; and providing computer security training and support to other government agencies.

NSA and NIST have signed a memorandum of understanding about how they will cooperate on issues affecting the protection of sensitive unclassified information, mainly focusing on the implementation of the Computer Security Act. Their agreement is still subject to interpretation, and the balance continues to be a fragile one.

In late 1990, NSA and NIST announced that they were embarking on a joint venture that might result in new computer security criteria for computer procurements by federal agencies. NIST's survey of Orange Book users may result in the publication of new interpretations and for expansions of the original book.

The joint venture is also expected to take into consideration the European Community's Information Technology Security Evaluation Criteria (ITSEC), requirements that are under consideration as an international security standard (described in "International Security Activity" later in this chapter).

Under funding by DARPA, the National Research Council published a report, entitled *Computers at Risk*, that expresses concern about the state of computer security in the United States, and makes recommendations about the need for a more coordinated security structure. Recommendations include the creation of a private-sector, not-for-profit foundation. The committee's report also suggests the publication of a comprehensive set of what are known as Generally Accepted System Security Principles (GSSP), which would clearly define necessary security features and requirements. Since publication, a number of companies have worked together to establish what is now known as the International Information Security Foundation (IISF).

Privacy Considerations

The ability to collect and manage information doesn't necessarily confer the right to save, analyze, and publicize that information. Since the dawn of the computer age, there has been tension between, on the one hand, the technologies that enable huge amounts of information to be stored and accessed with accuracy and efficiency, and, on the other hand, the right to personal privacy.

During the 1960s, the increasing availability of large-scale computers made possible for the first time the development and use of centralized, computerized databases. In 1965, recommendations were made for the establishment of a National Data Bank to serve as a central repository of all personal information gathered by federal agencies about U.S. citizens. This proposal awakened concerns about the computer's potential for invading individual privacy. Extended and heated testimony was heard before the U.S. House of Representatives Subcommittee on the Computer and Invasion of Privacy. There was considerable national discussion about the potential for abuse of centralized databases and about the need for legal actions to protect society against such abuses.

By 1968, the National Data Bank proposal had been abandoned. Over the next decade, Congressional and individual efforts led to several important studies and legislative acts aimed at harnessing the government (and, in some cases, business) by controlling its use of computer systems that handle personal information.

One very important piece of privacy legislation, the Privacy Act of 1974 (Public Law 93-579), requires the U.S. government to safeguard personal data processed by federal agency computer systems. It also requires the government to provide ways for individuals to find out what personal information is being recorded and to correct inaccurate information. It spells out physical security procedures, information management practices, and computer/network controls.

More recently, the Electronic Communications Privacy Act, passed in 1986, extended the legal protection defined in earlier laws to cover new types of communications. It prohibits the unauthorized interception of communications regardless of how transmission takes place (e.g., video and data communications, transmission via wire, radio, electromagnetic, photo-electronic, or photo-optical systems).

Table B-3 in Appendix B, *Computer Security Legislation*, lists the main privacy studies and acts, as well as several key earlier federal rulings and pieces of legislation that establish privacy guidelines:

In addition to the federal statutes listed in the appendix, virtually every state has enacted privacy legislation governing the use and collection of information about its citizens; most of the states now explicitly prohibit computer crime as well. Massachusetts recently enacted a groundbreaking piece of computer crime legislation that will attempt to balance security needs against the privacy and First Amendment rights of computer users. The bill makes it a crime to enter someone else's computer system unlawfully and to do damage either deliberately or accidentally. The compromise bill addressed the fears of those who said that an original version of the bill would have made it illegal to teach a course on computer security, for example, because the course would spread information that could be used to crack computers.

Confrontations between technology and privacy continue. Recently, Lotus's Marketplace Households product, would have provided a CD-ROM database of names, addresses, and related marketing information on 120 million U.S. consumers. After news about the product was promulgated on USENET (along with information about how and where to complain), the product was cancelled when more than 30,000 people insisted their names be removed from the database.

International Security Activity

Although the focus of this chapter has been U.S. legislation and other developments leading to security standards in this country, there is a good deal of security activity in other countries as well.

In the area of standards development, the *Information Technology Security Evaluation Criteria (ITSEC)*, published by the Federal Republic of Germany in 1990, defines a standard that's under development for international security. The ITSEC, now known as Europe's "White Book," were developed by European representatives from industry and academia in the United Kingdom, France, Germany, and the Netherlands under the auspices of the German Information Security Agency (GISA). The criteria represent a first step in establishing a single international, or at least a common European, security standard. As Europe becomes more and more a united market, such a standard is seen as being essential.

The ITSEC are based to some extent on the U.S. Orange Book, as well as on several European standards (the different shades of Green Books published in Germany and the United Kingdom). Unlike the Orange Book, which defines a hierarchical progression of systems offering low to high security, the ITSEC define multiple types of systems supporting specific types of security requirements, some of which may be more appropriate in certain environments than others. For example, some categories focus on confidentiality requirements, others on integrity requirements.

For a summary of the ITSEC requirements, see Appendix C, *Orange Book and Other Summaries*.

There is pressure in the U.S. to develop security standards that take the European White Book into consideration. Vendors who sell internationally are concerned that otherwise they'll have to comply with two distinct security standards. NIST is currently working on developing a standard that will be compatible with the White Book.

In the area of computer crime legislation, the United Kingdom has recently passed a new law, the U.K. Computer Misuse Act of 1990, that spells out a range of offenses for different levels of unauthorized access. This legislation may serve as a model for the U.S. in trying to assess how far to go in prosecuting different types of computer-related offenses. According to the law, the first level of offense, unauthorized access to a computer system, is punishable by up to six months in prison. The second level of offense, unauthorized access in an attempt to further a more serious crime, is punishable by up to five years in prison. The third level of offense, unauthorized modification of information stored in a computer system (e.g., by the introduction of a virus or other malicious code), is also punishable by up to five years in prison.

In the area of privacy and the protection of individual data, the United States has lagged behind other countries. For example, Japan adopted a National Computer Policy (NCP) as early as 1972. France enacted a law on Data Protection and Individual Liberties, and many European countries have followed suit. In most other countries, legislation has established a central organization charged with ensuring the privacy and accuracy of data. For example, Sweden's organization is known as the Data Inspection Board. Government agencies and, in many cases, corporations that want to develop record-keeping systems must apply for permission and must follow a set of rules. An individual whose privacy has been invaded can apply for remedial action through this organization. In addition to remedying privacy abuses, the organization is typically responsible for monitoring record-keeping organizations for compliance with the law.

In contrast, in the U.S., there is no central privacy advocate, and both legislation and remedial actions are piecemeal. Although the Office of Management and the Budget provides very loose supervision of privacy legislation, you're basically on your own. If you feel that your privacy has been invaded, you, perhaps with the help of various consumer protection agencies, must locate, confront, and seek redress against any of the 6000 record-keeping organizations that store information about private citizens.

The Growth of Modern Standards

As open systems proliferate, the standardization of security functions across computers and networks is becoming more and more essential. In the past, standardization efforts have been driven by the government, and many have complained that government-sanctioned standards have not kept up with technology. In recent years, standardization efforts have increasingly been initiated by computer user organizations. Both users and vendors are coming together to agree on what security functions are appropriate for the world of open systems.

Table 2-1 summarizes what's going on in the standards area that's relevant to computer security. Appendix E, *A Security Source Book*, explains how you can find out more about these standards and organizations.

Table 2-1. Security-relevant Standards Organizations

Organization	Description
ABA	The American Bankers Association develops computer standards for financial and banking areas. The ABA is the Secretariat for X9, ANSI's Accredited Standards Committee for Financial Services. Standards developed by this committee focus on encryption and message authentication for financial institutions. The ABA also develops standards for personal identification numbers (PINs) and key management. (See the discussion of encryption standards in Chapter 7, *Encryption*, for information about these concepts.)
ANSI	The American National Standards Institute is the officially designated national standards organization in the United States and is the formal U.S. representative to ISO. ANSI does not develop its own standards, but is the clearinghouse for U.S. and international standards—for example, ASCII code, languages (e.g., C and FORTRAN), and communications protocols. ANSI committees are working on such security concerns as encryption and message authentication.
CBEMA	The Computer and Business Equipment Manufacturers Association develops standards in a variety of areas, including languages, graphics, and database technologies, and submits these standards to ANSI for approval as ANSI standards. CBEMA is the Secretariat for X3, ANSI's Accredited Standards Committee for Information Processing.
CCITT	The Comité Consultatif Internationale Telegraphique et Telephonique (International Telegraph and Telephone Consultative Committee) was established under the United Nations. It is responsible for the X.25 (packet-switched networks) and X.400 (electronic mail) standards and for other international communications standards. CCITT works with ISO on international standards for security.

Table 2-1. Security-relevant Standards Organizations (continued)

Organization	Description
ECMA	The European Computer Manufacturers Association is an association of approximately 50 European computer manufacturers. Its security groups are involved in developing standards for security in such areas as distributed interactive processing, distributed office applications, and open systems.
EIA	The Electronic Industries Association is a trade organization that has developed standards such as the RS-232 standard for terminals and computer connections.
IEEE	The Institute of Electrical and Electronic Engineers is a professional organization that develops standards and submits them for ANSI approval.
	The IEEE 1003.1 standard, announced in 1988, is the official POSIX (Portable Operating System Interface for Computer Environments) standard for application portability in open systems. Along with many other POSIX standards efforts, it was developed in cooperation with the ISO (described below). Although the POSIX interface standard (also known as POSIX-1) is based on the UNIX system model, POSIX specifies how an interface must perform, not how it is implemented, so UNIX need not be the base operating system. POSIX.1 evolved in 1981 from */usr/group*, the forerunner of UniForum, the Association of UNIX System Users. The */usr/group* standard was an early attempt to specify a standard for a portable mechanism.
	The IEEE 1003.1 standard has also been published by NIST (described below) as FIPS PUB 151 and by ISO (also described below) as ISO/IEC 9945-1.

Table 2-1. Security-relevant Standards Organizations (continued)

Organization	Description
	IEEE has a number of committees, some of them security-related. The IEEE 1003.6 Security Extensions Committee grew out of UniForum's Technical Committee's Security Subcommittee. This committee is dedicated to developing standards for making a POSIX-compliant system a trusted system. Security subgroups are at work on security issues such as discretionary access control, mandatory access control, privileges, and audit trails, and standards are expected within the next few years. (See Chapter 3, *Computer System Security and Access Controls*, for a discussion of these concepts.)
IFIP	The International Federation of Information Processing is a multinational federation of professional and technical organizations involved with computer and information processing. It was originally established under the auspices of UNESCO. IFIP has a number of committees. The Technical Committee 11 (TC-11) on Security and Protection in Information Systems does extensive work in proliferating security information internationally and in developing standards.
ISO	The International Standards Organization (Organisation Internationale de Normalisation) founded in 1946, is an international organization composed of a number of national standards organizations. ISO's Open Systems Interconnection (OSI) basic reference model is a standard conceptual model for discussing data communications. (This layered model is described in Chapter 8, *Communications and Network Security*.) ISO and other organizations are working on extending the OSI model to define security-related architectural elements. Several groups within ISO are developing standards using cryptography as a mechanism for network security. Such standards will provide for data confidentiality, data integrity, peer entity authentication, access control, key distribution, and digital signatures. (See Chapter 8 for information about these concepts.)

Table 2-1. Security-relevant Standards Organizations (continued)

Organization	Description
MAP/TOP	The Manufacturing Automation Protocol/Technical Office Protocol is a consortium of factory automation users. Sponsored by General Motors (MAP) and Boeing (TOP), MAP/TOP has worked on pieces of ISO standards.
NCSC	The National Computer Security Center publishes the Rainbow Series of computer security standards for trusted systems, chief among them the Orange Book. The books in the Rainbow Series are listed in Appendix E, *A Security Source Book.*
	The NCSC sponsors the Trusted UNIX Organization, which consists of a group of vendors, including AT&T, involved in developing trusted UNIX systems. Security standards developed by TRUSIX will be POSIX-compliant.
NIST	The National Institute of Standards and Technology (formerly the National Bureau of Standards) specifies standards for many government-related products and procedures.
	FIPS PUBs (Federation of Information Processing Standards publications) are written by NIST's National Computer Systems Laboratory (NCSL). FIPS PUBs are required standards for the acquisition of equipment and the processing of information by government agencies and contractors. The many FIPS PUBs that address security issues are listed in Appendix E.
	GOSIP (the Government Open Systems Interconnect Profile program) is sponsored by NIST with participation by a number of other government agencies. GOSIP specifies a set of data communications protocols based on the OSI model. All government agencies that buy networks must now comply with the GOSIP/OSI standard. In 1988, Version 1 of the GOSIP standard for networks and services was published as FIPS PUB 146. The standard is being revised to address security concerns and other issues.

Table 2-1. Security-relevant Standards Organizations (continued)

Organization	Description
X/Open	The X/Open Organization was founded in 1984 as a consortium of five American and European computer manufacturers. It has evolved into an international group that's dedicated to developing a standard for application portability in open systems called the Common Application Environment. X/Open-compliant systems must support a stated set of security features, described in the *X/Open Security Guide*.

In addition to these organizations, a number of commercially-oriented security user groups play an active role in disseminating security information and, in some cases, attempting to develop commercial standards for security. These include the Computer Security Institute (CSI), the American Society for Industrial Security (ASIS), and the Information Systems Security Association (ISSA); see Appendix E for information about these groups and others. A number of large corporations are also working on security standards that they feel will be more appropriate to business than the defense-oriented Orange Book and other government standards (for example, Electronic Data Systems (EDS) and American Express are working together on Commercial International Security Requirements [CISR]).

"No one can build his security upon the nobleness of another person."

Willa Sibert Cather, *Alexander's Bridge*, 1912.

Part II:

COMPUTER SECURITY

Part II discusses computer security—methods of protecting information that's stored in a computer system.

- Chapter 3, *Computer System Security and Access Controls*, introduces computer system security and describes how it controls access to systems and data.

- Chapter 4, *Viruses and Other Wildlife*, gives definitions for viruses, worms, and other types of malicious code.

- Chapter 5, *Secure System Planning and Administration*, describes the administrative procedures that improve security within your organization.

- Chapter 6, *Inside the Orange Book*, introduces trusted systems and describes the Orange Book security requirements and evaluation classes.

3

Computer System Security and Access Controls

What Makes a System Secure?
System Access: Logging Into Your
System
Data Access: Protecting Your Data

Computer security covers a lot of territory: locking your computer room and your machine, protecting your login accounts with passwords, using file protection to keep your data from being destroyed, encrypting network communications lines, and using special shields to keep electromagnetic emanations from leaking out of your computer. But when people talk about computer security, they usually mean what in this chapter we call computer system security.

What Makes a System Secure?

In the most basic sense, computer system security ensures that your computer does what it's supposed to do—even if its users don't do what they're supposed to do. It protects the information stored in it from being lost, changed either malicious or accidentally, or read or modified by those not authorized to access it.

How does computer system security provide protection? There are four primary methods:

1. **System Access Controls**. Ensuring that unauthorized users don't get into the system, and by encouraging (and sometimes forcing) authorized users to be security-conscious—for example, by changing their passwords on a regular basis. The system also protects password data and keeps track of who's doing what in the system, especially if what they're doing is security-related (e.g., logging in, trying to open a file, using special privileges).

   The section "System Access: Logging Into Your System" introduces the basics of system access controls. Chapter 6, *Inside the Orange Book*, describes the Orange Book accountability requirements, which specify the system access controls defined for different levels of secure systems. In particular, see the section entitled "Accountability Requirements" in that chapter.

2. **Data Access Controls**. Monitoring who can access what data, and for what purpose. Your system might support discretionary access controls; with these, *you* determine whether other people can read or change your data. Your system might also support mandatory access controls; with these, *the system* determines access rules based on the security levels of the people, the files, and the other objects in your system.

   "Data Access: Protecting Your Data" introduces the basics of data access controls. In Chapter 6, the section entitled "Security Policy Requirements" describes the Orange Book security policy requirements, which specify the data access controls defined for different levels of secure systems.

3. **System and Security Administration**. Performing the offline procedures that make or break a secure system—by clearly delineating system administrator responsibilities, by training users appropriately, and by monitoring users to make sure that security policies are observed. This category also involves more global security management; for example, figuring out what security threats face your system and what it will cost to protect against them.

   Chapter 5, *System Security Planning and Administration*, introduces the basics of system security planning and administration. In Chapter 6, the section entitled "Assurance Requirements" describes the Orange Book system administration requirements defined for different levels of secure systems.

4. **System Design**. Taking advantage of basic hardware and software security characteristics; for example, using a system architecture that's able to segment memory, thus isolating privileged processes from nonprivileged processes.

Although a detailed discussion of secure system design is outside the province of this book, the section "System Architecture" in Chapter 6 describes briefly the major Orange Book design requirements for different levels of secure systems.

System Access: Logging Into Your System

The first way in which a system provides computer security is by controlling access to that system: Who's allowed to log in? How does the system decide whether a user is legitimate? How does the system keep track of who's doing what in the system?

What's really going on when you try to log into a system? It's a kind of challenge. You tell the system who you are, and the system proves that you are (or you aren't) who you claim to be. In security terms, this two-step process is called *identification* and *authentication*.

Identification and Authentication

Identification is the way you tell the system who you are. Authentication is the way you prove to the system that you are who you say you are. In just about any multi-user system, you must identify yourself, and the system must authenticate your identity, before you can use the system. There are three classic ways in which you can prove yourself:

1. **Something you know**. The most familiar example is a password. The theory is that if you know the secret password for an account, you must be the owner of that account. There is a problem with this theory: You might give your password away or have it stolen from you. If you write it down, someone might read it. If you tell someone, that person might tell someone else. If you have a simple, easy-to-guess password, someone might guess it or systematically crack it.

2. **Something you have**. Examples are keys, tokens, badges, and smart cards you must have to "unlock" your terminal or your account. The theory is that if you have the key or equivalent, you must be the owner of it. The problem with this theory is that you might lose the key, it might be stolen from you, or

someone might borrow it and duplicate it. Electronic keys, badges, and smart cards are gaining acceptance as authentication devices and as access devices for buildings and computer rooms. With the proliferation of automatic teller machines (ATMs), people are becoming increasingly familiar with this type of authentication.

3. **Something you are.** Examples are physiological or behavioral traits, such as your fingerprint, handprint, retina pattern, voice, signature, or keystroke pattern. Biometric systems compare your particular trait against the one stored for you and determine whether you are who you claim to be. Although biometric systems occasionally reject valid users and accept invalid ones, they are generally quite accurate. The problem with these authentication systems is that, on the whole, people aren't comfortable using them.

Passwords are still, far and away, the authentication tool of choice. Even when authentication devices like tokens and biometric devices are used, they're usually supplements to, not replacements for, conventional login IDs and passwords. Biometrics and key cards typically act only as a first line of defense against intruders, not as the only defense. (See Chapter 9, *Physical Security and Biometrics*, for a discussion of authentication devices.)

In most systems, you identify yourself to the system by entering some kind of unique login identifier, followed by a password. The identifier is typically a name, initials, a login number, or an account number assigned by the system administrator based on your own name and/or group. The password is typically a string of letters and/or numbers known only to you. Login identification sequences are much the same from system to system. For example, UNIX systems display the prompt:

```
login:
```

and expect a first or last name (or any other handle you've been given) in response. Other systems may expect an identifier of a specific length—for example, a three-character ID (usually your initials) or an account number.

The typical password interaction is usually a relatively simple and user-friendly one. After you enter your login ID, the system prompts:

```
Password:
```

You type the password (which is ordinarily never echoed, or displayed, on the terminal screen), and the system authenticates your identity by verifying that the entered password is valid for your account. You'll be able to proceed only if the password you enter matches the password stored for you in the system.

Hints for Protecting Passwords

Both system administrators and users share responsibility for enforcing password security. Remember, password security is everyone's responsibility. In addition to damaging your own files, someone who uses your password to break into a system can also compromise all of the files in your system or network.

From the USENET: "A password should be like a toothbrush. Use it every day; change it regularly; and DON'T share it with friends."

- Don't allow any logins without passwords. If you're the system administrator, make sure *every* account has a password.

- Don't keep passwords that may have come with your system. Change all test or guest passwords—for example, **root, system, test, demo,** etc., before allowing users to log in.

- Don't ever let anyone use your password.

- Don't write your password down—particularly on your terminal, computer, or anywhere around your desk. If you ever do write your password down, don't identify it as a password and don't write the phone number of the computer on the same piece of paper.

- Don't type a password while anyone is watching.

- Don't record your password online or send it anywhere via electronic mail. In *The Cuckoo's Egg*, Cliff Stoll reports how his intruder scanned electronic mail messages for references to the word "password."

- Don't make a bad situation worse. If you do share your password—deliberately or inadvertently—change it immediately (or ask your administrator to change it).

- Don't keep the same password indefinitely. Even if your password hasn't been compromised, change it on a regular basis.

Passwords are your main defense against intruders. To protect your system and your data, you must select good passwords, and you must protect them carefully.

Once you've been authenticated, the system uses your ID (and the security information associated with it) to determine what you're allowed to do in the system. The system uses this information to make access decisions. For example, if you try to modify a sensitive file, the system checks your authenticated user ID against the list of IDs representing users who are authorized to read and write the data in that file. Only if your ID appears in that list will the system allow you to access the file. (File access is discussed in "Data Access: Protecting Your Data" later in this chapter.)

Secure systems use your ID to maintain individual accountability—in other words, to keep track of what you're doing in a system, particularly if you're affecting security in any way. If Jack Hacke repeatedly tries to access files he's not authorized to view, the system will *know*! (The discussion of auditing in Chapter 6, *Inside the Orange Book*, describes how this tracking works.)

At one time, a system cracker would have to try to guess your password, one password attempt at a time (a so-called *brute force attack*). Like everything else, this process has been automated. Crackers now use computers to do the guessing. In theory, the longer the password, the longer it takes to try every combination of characters. For example, with a password containing eight random characters, there are 2,800,000,000,000 combinations; even with a computer capable of guessing one million passwords per second (a lot faster than the machine your average cracker is likely to be using!), figuring out the right combination would take an average of forty-five years.

The problem is, users don't select random, or even decently secure passwords, and a cracker doesn't need to figure out *your* password—any password will do. Unfortunately, users typically pick passwords that are laughably easy to guess— their initials, their childrens' names, their license plates, etc. Studies indicate that a very large percentage of users' passwords can easily be guessed. With the help of online dictionaries of common passwords (English words, names of people, animals, cars, fictional characters, places, and so on), crackers are quite likely to be able to guess a good many of the passwords most people are likely to choose. But if you select a good password (see the hints in the inset), an intruder shouldn't be able to guess it—with or without a dictionary.

Hints for Picking Passwords

If you're allowed to choose your own password, pick passwords that are hard to guess. Here are some suggestions:

- Pick passwords that aren't words (English or otherwise) or names (especially your own, that of a fictional character such as Hamlet or Gandolf, or that of a family member, a pet, or a car).
- Pick a mix of alphabetic and numeric characters. Never use an all-numeric password (especially your phone number or social security number).
- Pick long passwords. If your password is only a few letters long, an attacker will find it easy to try all combinations. Most systems insist that your password be at least 6-8 characters. Some systems support passwords of up to 40 or more characters.
- Pick different passwords for the different machines or network nodes you access.
- Be careful about including special characters in passwords. Some special characters (e.g., # and @) have special meaning to terminal emulation software. Other control characters, like CONTROL-S, CONTROL-H, CONTROL-/, and CONTROL-\, can also cause confusion. Check with your system administrator.

The best passwords contain mixed uppercase and lowercase letters, as well as at least one number and/or special character. The password you pick doesn't need to be gibberish. In fact, if it is, you'll be tempted to write it down, defeating the purpose of your careful selection. Some suggestions are:

- Combine several short words with numbers or special characters; for example, `I;did3it`.
- Use an acronym you've built from a phrase you'll remember. For example, the acronym for "When in the course of human events" is `Witcohe`, but that one could be guessed. It's better to pick a phrase that's not recognizable. For example, the acronym for "Oh no, I forgot to do it" is `Oniftdi`.
- Add a number or a special character for more security. For example: `Onif;tdi` or `On5iftdi`.
- Pick a nonsense word that's still pronounceable; for example `8Bektag` or `shmoaz12`.

Your ID is associated with all of the processes you create. In many systems, you can effectively change your identity to that of another user; in traditional, untrusted UNIX systems, for example, you do this with the **su** command. When you change identity, the system may lose its ability to keep track of who's doing what. In secure systems, the system may still allow you to change identity, but it typically keeps track of your original identity as well, so processes you create are still stamped with your "real" ID.

Systems typically maintain a file containing information about your privileges and characteristics; in some systems, this is called a security profile, an authentication profile, or a user list. Your profile might tell the system what your clearance is (e.g., SECRET), whether you're allowed to change your own password, whether you can log in on weekends, whether you can run backup programs and other privileged programs, and a myriad of other information. In some cases, your profile is in the same file as the password list; in other cases, the information might be kept in separate files. In any case, it's vital that your system protect this information; any compromise can jeopardize the security of the entire system.

One of the important pieces of information that appears in your authentication profile or user list is an indication of what kind of user you are. Most systems support several categories of users, or roles; a typical set includes regular users, a system administrator, and an operator. Highly secure systems may define a security officer as a separate category. Each category of user has specific privileges and responsibilities—for example, specific programs the user can run. The system administrator, for example, may effectively be able to do *anything* in the system, including overriding or circumventing security requirements. The power of the system administrator is a major issue in secure systems; see the discussion of administrative controls and least privilege in Chapter 5, *Secure System Planning and Administration*.

Protecting Passwords

Access decisions are the heart of system security, and access decisions are based on passwords, so it's vital that your system protect its passwords and other login information.

Most systems protect passwords in two important ways: they make passwords hard to guess and login controls hard to crack, and they protect the file in which passwords are stored.

Protecting Your Login and Password on Entry

Most vendors offer a whole smorgasbord of login controls and password management features that the system administrator can mix and match to provide optimal protection of a particular system. Because these security features are commercially attractive and relatively easy to implement, most systems tend to have a lot of them. Examples of such features are shown in Table 3-1.

Table 3-1. Sample Login/Password Controls

Feature	Meaning
System messages	Most systems display welcome and announcement messages before and/or after you successfully log in. Some systems allow the system administrator to suppress these messages, because they may provide a clue to an observer as to the type of system being accessed. If an intruder dials in and finds out he's talking to a VMS system, for example, that's a valuable clue.
Limited attempts	After a certain number of unsuccessful tries at logging into the system (the number can be specified by the system administrator), the system locks you out and prevents you from attempting to log in from that terminal. Some systems lock you out without informing you that this has happened. This allows for the possibility of taking evasive action—identifying the account as a suspicious one without letting you know you're under investigation.
Limited time periods	Certain users or terminals may be limited to logging in during business hours or other specified times.
Last login message	When you log in, the system may display the date and time of your last login. Many systems also display the number of unsuccessful login attempts since the time of your last successful login. This may give you a chance to discover that your account was accessed by someone else—for example, by noticing a login in the middle of the night or by noticing a pattern of repeated attempts to log in. If you weren't responsible for these attempts, notify your system administrator right away.

Table 3-1. Sample Login/Password Controls (continued)

Feature	Meaning
User-changeable passwords	In many systems, you're allowed to change your own password at any time after its initial assignment by the system administrator.
System-generated passwords	Some systems require you to use passwords generated randomly by the system, rather than relying on your own selection of a difficult-to-guess password. The VAX/VMS Version 4.3 system, and many other systems, ensure that these passwords are pronounceable. Some systems let you view several random choices from which you can pick one you think you'll be able to remember. A danger of system-generated passwords is that they're often so hard to remember that users may tend to write them down. Another danger is that if the algorithm for generating these passwords becomes known, your entire system is in jeopardy.
Password aging and expiration	When a specified time is reached—for example, the end of the month—all passwords in the system may expire. The new passwords usually must not be identical to the old passwords. The system should give reasonable notice before requiring you to change your password; if you have to pick a password quickly, you're likely to pick a poor one.

In some systems, the system administrator can respond to a security breach by forcing a particular password, or all passwords, to expire immediately. This controls further access to the system until the damage can be assessed.

The system may keep track of your passwords for an extended period to make sure you don't reuse one that might have been guessed. |
| Minimum length | Because short passwords are easier to guess than long ones, some systems require that passwords be a certain length, usually six to eight characters. |

Table 3-1. Sample Login/Password Controls (continued)

Feature	Meaning
Password locks	Locks allow the system administrator to restrict certain users from logging in or to lock login accounts that haven't been used for an extended period of time.
System passwords	System passwords control access to particular terminals that might be targets for unauthorized use. Usually a system password must be entered before you enter your individual password.
Primary and secondary passwords	Some systems require that two users, each with a valid password, be present to log in successfully to certain extremely sensitive accounts.
Dial-in password	Some systems require that special passwords be used to access dial-in lines.

Protecting Your Password in Storage

Every system needs to maintain its authentication data. Typically, valid passwords are stored in a password file. This file typically is accessed only under certain limited circumstances—when a new user is registered, when you change your password, or when you log in and need to be authenticated.

Protection of passwords is extremely critical to system security. Systems commonly use both encryption and access controls to protect password data.

Encryption. Most systems encrypt the data stored in the system's password file. Encryption (described in Chapter 7) transforms original information into altered information that usually has the appearance of random text. Encryption ensures that even if file security is somehow breached, the intruder won't be able to read the passwords in the file; they'll look like gibberish.

Most systems perform one-way encryption of passwords. One-way encryption means that the password is never decrypted—that is, deciphered into its original form. When the system administrator supplies you with your initial password, it's encrypted before it's stored in the password file. The original password is not preserved, not even in memory. Each time you log in and enter your password, the system encrypts the password you enter and compares the encrypted version with the encrypted password stored in the password file to be sure you've entered a valid password. Remember too that the password is never displayed on the terminal screen.

Access Controls. Even encrypted passwords might be able to be cracked by a determined foe. Many systems store encrypted password data in files known as shadow password files, which have the most restrictive protection available in the system. In most systems, access is limited to the system administrator, usually by specifying only the administrator's ID in an access control list (ACL) on the file. (See the discussion of access control lists in the next section.)

Data Access: Protecting Your Data

The second important way in which a system provides computer security is by controlling access to the data stored in a system: Who can read your files? Who can change your files? Can you decide to share your data with other users? How does the system make decisions about access control?

If you work alone on a PC, you don't need to worry about access controls. You own all of your files, and you can read and write them as you wish. If you want to share a file with someone, you can copy it onto a diskette and hand it over.

With shared computers, it isn't as easy. As soon as you begin to work on a system that supports multiple users, you'll have to start worrying about data protection and access controls. You may not want every user in the system to be able to read your files. You certainly won't want them to change your files.

Even if you trust everyone on the system to keep away from your data, you need to protect against accidents. Suppose you and Joe Slow are working in separate areas of a shared directory. Both of you are working on the same projects, and you've both picked identical names for some of your files. With a few unfortunate keystrokes, Joe can change directories and delete one of your files, thinking it's his own. If your files aren't protected in any way, the system doesn't put any obstacles in his path. Access controls on files (they usually apply to other system objects, such as directories and devices as well) provide protection against such disasters.

There are two basic types of access controls that provide different levels of protection to the files in your system: discretionary access control and mandatory access control.

With *discretionary access control* (DAC) you decide how you want to protect your files, and whether to share your data. With the more complex *mandatory access control* (MAC) the system protects your files. In a MAC system, everything has a label. Using the security policy relationships established for your organization, the system decides whether a user can access a file by comparing the label of the user with the label of the file. The following sections introduce these types of access controls.

Discretionary Access Control

Discretionary access control (DAC) is an access policy that restricts access to files (and other system objects such as directories and devices) based on the identity of users and/or the groups to which they belong.

What's discretionary about discretionary access control? In contrast to mandatory access control, in which the system controls access, DAC is applied at your own discretion. With DAC, you can choose to give away your data; with MAC, you can't.

Not only does DAC let you tell the system who can access your data, it lets you specify the type of access allowed. For example, you might want everyone in the system to be able to read a particular file, but you might want only yourself and your manager to be able to change it. Most systems support three basic types of access:

Read   If you have read access for a file, you can read the file.

Write   If you have write access for a file, you can write (change or replace) the file.

Execute   The execute permission is relevant only if the file is a program. If you have execute permission for a file, you can run the program.

Ownership

There are many types of discretionary access control. One simple method involves ownership of files, directories, and devices.

If you create a file, you're the owner of the file. Your login ID, or some other identifier, is entered in the file header. A system might base all of its access decisions on file ownership. If you're the owner of the file, the system lets you read and change the file. If you're not the owner, you have no rights to the file. This is a simple scheme, but not a very practical one. For one thing, it doesn't let you share the file with anyone.

Virtually every system keeps track of file ownership and bases many access decisions upon it (for example, regardless of other mechanisms, the system might let you delete a file only if you're the file owner).

File Types and File Protection Classes

File types and file protection classes provide more powerful access mechanisms. Some systems let you assign a file type or a file protection class when you create a file. You can pick from a limited set of options for file access. Many systems let you define a file as a public, semipublic, or private file. The Wang SVS/OS CAP 1.0 system provides the following choices for a file protection class:

Blank   Public. Anyone can read or write the file.

@   Execute-only. Anyone can execute the file (run the program). Only the file owner and the system administrator can read or write it.

$ Read-only. Anyone can read or execute the file. Only the file owner and the system administrator can write it.

\#   Private. Only the file owner and the system administrator can read, write, or execute the file.

A-Z   System-dependent. For example, the system administrator might set up the system so only users with access rights to class P files (defined in user profiles) may be allowed to access PAYROLL files (protected with a file protection class of P).

Self/Group/Public Controls

In many systems, you control access to your files by dividing the world of users into three categories, and telling the system what the users in each category can do to your file. Some systems call these *self/group/public* controls. In UNIX, they're called *user/group/other* (UGO) controls:

Self   You—the creator or owner of the file.

Group   A set of users. For example, all the users in a particular department may be in the R&D group.

Public   Everyone else—users other than you and the other members of your group.

Each file has a set of bits called *file permissions* associated with it. File permissions often have the meanings shown in Figure 3-1.

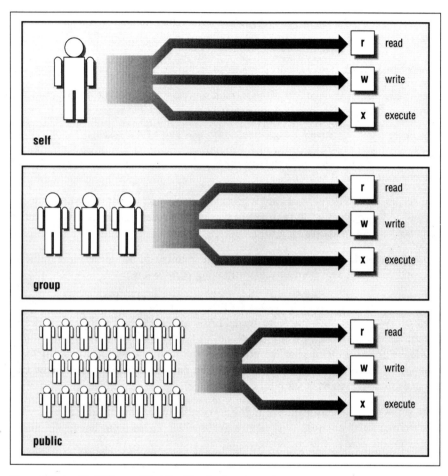

Figure 3-1. Self/Group/Public Controls

If you list your files (with the correct option) in a UNIX system, you'll see such file permissions as the following:

```
-rw-rw-r--   1 frank   r&d   81904   Nov 7 13:25   UPDATES
```

If a dash (–) appears in place of a permission, the user does *not* have the corresponding permission to read, write, or execute the file. For example, in the above example, the file owner (**frank**) can read and write the UPDATES file (**rw–**), members of the file group (**r&d**) can read and write the file (**rw–**), and the rest of the world can only read the file (**r––**). (Ignore the first – above; it has a special meaning to UNIX.)

Consider a few more examples:

The CHESS file contains a game; its permissions look like this:

```
-rwxrwxrwx   1 libr   games   61799   May 19  10:11  CHESS
```

Everyone can read, write, and execute this file.

The SRC95 file is a segment of code that several people in the **r&d** group are working on; its permissions look like this:

```
-rw-rw----   1 sarah   r&d   55660   Dec 19  11:42  SRC95
```

The owner and the other members of the group can read and change the file. No one else can access it at all.

The self/group/public controls are a good way to protect files. But what happens if you need to protect a file in different ways for different users, or if you want to keep one user from accessing a file?

If Sarah owns the FLAG file and wants Joe (a member of her group) to be able to read and change it, she'll specify the following permissions:

```
-rw-rw----   1 sarah   r&d   22975   Jan 19  10:14  FLAG
```

If Sarah wants Joe to be able to read FLAG, and Mary to be able to read and change it, she could make Mary the owner of the file (with **r** and **w** permissions) and leave Joe as a member of the group that can read (**r**) only. But what if Joe's group contains other users who aren't trusted enough to read FLAG? How can Sarah exclude the sinister Sam, for example?

With some complicated maneuvering, it's possible to accomplish these goals with self/group/public controls, but the more special cases you have, the more unwieldy this kind of file access becomes.

Access Control Lists

Access control lists (ACLs) are lists of users and groups, with their specific permissions. They offer a more flexible way of providing discretionary access control. ACLs are implemented differently on different systems. For example, in a UNIX-based trusted system that uses the UNIX security kernel developed by Atlanta-based SecureWare, you'd protect PAYROLL with ACLs in the form:

```
<john.acct, r>

<jane.pay, rw>
```

where:

- **john** and **jane** are login IDs of users who are allowed access to the PAYROLL file.

- **acct** and **pay** are group IDs of the users.

- **r** and **w** indicate the type of access allowed; **r** means that the user can only read PAYROLL, **w** that he or she can also change it.

If **john** is in the **acct** group, he can only read the file. If he belongs to any other group, by default he has no access. Similarly, if **jane** is in the **pay** group, she can read and write the file. Figure 3-2 illustrates how ACLs control file access.

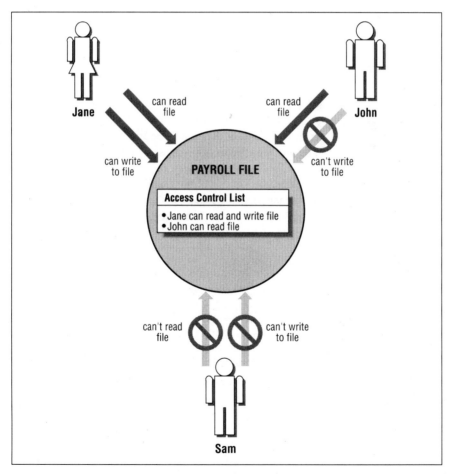

Figure 3-2. Discretionary Access Control With an Access Control List

ACLs usually support wildcard characters that let you specify more general access to files. For example, you might specify:

```
<*.*, r>
```

to indicate that any user (*) in any group (*) can read (**r**) the file. You might specify:

```
<@.*, rw>
```

to indicate that only the owner (@) of the file can read (**r**) and modify (**w**) it.

In some systems, you can indicate that a particular user is specifically *not* allowed to access a file—for example, by specifying a null character or the word **none** or **null**) in place of an access character such as **r** or **w**.

```
<sam.*,none >
```

Mandatory Access Control

Mandatory access control (MAC) is an access policy supported for systems that process especially sensitive data (e.g., government classified information or sensitive corporate data). Systems providing mandatory access controls must assign sensitivity labels to *all* subjects (e.g., users, programs) and *all* objects (e.g., files, directories, devices, windows, sockets) in the system. A user's sensitivity label specifies the sensitivity level, or level of trust, associated with that user; it's often called a clearance. A file's sensitivity label specifies the level of trust that a user must have to be able to access that file. Mandatory access controls use sensitivity labels to determine who can access what information in your system.

Together, labeling and mandatory access control implement a *multi-level security policy*—a policy for handling multiple information classifications at a number of different security levels within a single computer system.

In the past, military systems were set up to handle one, and only one, level of security. The policy for such systems, known as a *system high policy*, required everyone who used the system to have the highest clearance required by any data in the system. A system that handled SECRET data, for example, could not be used by anyone who did not have a SECRET clearance (regardless of how well protected the SECRET data was). Although many government sites still operate in system high mode, others support multiple security levels. This is done by dividing, or compartmentalizing, the data. Such systems support simultaneous use by users with the highest and the lowest clearances (or, potentially, with no clearances at all), and with access to many different types of sensitive compartmented intelligence (SCI). (Compartments are introduced in the next section.)

Although this section tries to touch on the major issues involved with labeling, security levels, and mandatory access control, these are complicated topics, with a lot of security history behind them. Chapter 6, *Inside the Orange Book*, discusses briefly how the Orange Book specifies requirements in these areas. If you need to know more, consult some of the more technical books referenced in Appendix E, *A Security Source Book.*

Sensitivity Labels

Every subject and object in a system supporting mandatory access controls has a sensitivity label associated with it. A sensitivity label consists of two parts: A classification and a set of categories (sometimes called compartments). For example:

```
SECRET    [VENUS,  TANK,  ALPHA]
```
/   \
classification   *categories*

The *classification* is a single, hierarchical level. In the so-called military security model (based on the Department of Defense multi-level security policy), there are four distinct levels:

```
TOP SECRET
SECRET
CONFIDENTIAL
UNCLASSIFIED
```

Each classification is more trusted than the classification beneath it.

The actual definition of classifications is up to a site's system administrator or security officer. If your site is processing government classified information, your labeling setup will have to support the military model. But in general, labels represent whatever set of classifications and categories make sense in your own environment. For example, at a commercial site, you might define the following corporate hierarchy:

```
CORPORATE
BRANCH
DEPARTMENTS
```

Or you might define gradations in levels of trust:

```
EYES ONLY
OFFICERS ONLY
COMPANY PROPRIETARY
PUBLIC
```

The *categories* or *compartments* are nonhierarchical, and represent distinct areas of information in your system. Together, the categories make up a category set or a compartment set. A set may contain an arbitrary number of items.

In a military environment, you might have categories such as:

```
SDI
TANK
SUB
VENUS
STEALTH
```

In a commercial environment, your categories might correspond to company departments, product names, ad campaigns, or any other setup you wish to implement:

```
ACCOUNTING
PR
MARKETING
SALES
R&D
```

The idea is that even someone who has the highest classification isn't automatically cleared to see all information at that level. To see information in the SDI category, for example, you must "need to know" that information. The section entitled "Access Decisions" in this chapter describes how a system determines whether you can access a particular piece of information.

Data Import and Export

In a mandatory access control system, it's very important to control the import of information from other systems, and the export of information to other systems. MAC systems have a lot of rules about data import and export. They also control which system devices you can use to copy and print information; for example, you might not be allowed to print sensitive information on a printer located in a public area of your building. There are also rules for labeling devices and printed output (with banner pages and page headers and trailers). The discussion of specific labeling requirements in Chapter 6, *Inside the Orange Book*, touches on some of these rules.

Access Decisions

In a mandatory access control system, all access decisions are made by the system. Unlike discretionary access control, which allows you to specify, at your own discretion, who can and cannot share your files, mandatory access control puts all such access decisions under the control of the system. The decision to allow or deny access to an object (e.g., a file) involves an interaction between all three of the following:

- The label of the subject—for example, your clearance:

  TOP SECRET [VENUS TANK ALPHA]

- The label of the object—for example, a file named LOGISTIC with a sensitivity label:

  SECRET [VENUS ALPHA]

- An access request—for example, your attempt to read the LOGISTIC file.

When you try to read the LOGISTIC file, the system compares your clearance to the file's label to determine whether you'll be allowed to read it. Figure 3-3 shows how mandatory access control works.

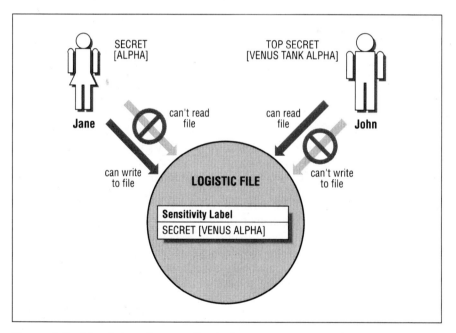

Figure 3-3. Mandatory Access Control

Although multi-level security systems provide many benefits, they're the source of many frustrations as well. If you're beginning to use a system that supports labeling and mandatory access controls, you may find yourself frustrated by trying to read and write files. For example, under some circumstances, you may write a file and then find that you can't read it! Basically, mandatory access control comes down to the read and write rules described below.

Read. To read an object, the subject's sensitivity level must dominate the object's sensitivity level. Dominate? What that means is that to read the LOGISTIC file (whose label is SECRET [VENUS ALPHA]), your classification must *equal or exceed* SECRET (it must be SECRET or TOP SECRET). In addition, the categories you're allowed to read must include the categories specified in the file label. In this case, suppose your clearance includes three categories: VENUS, TANK, and ALPHA. You'll be able to read LOGISTIC because its label contains only VENUS and ALPHA.

But suppose your clearance is CONFIDENTIAL [VENUS ALPHA]. No good! Your classification isn't high enough. It must be SECRET or TOP SECRET.

Now suppose your clearance is TOP SECRET [VENUS]. Still no good! Your classification is high enough, but to read LOGISTIC you need clearance to the ALPHA compartment as well.

Write. To write an object, the object's sensitivity level must dominate the subject's sensitivity level. To change any information in the LOGISTIC file, your sensitivity level must *equal or be less than* the sensitivity level of the file, *and* your categories must all be included in the file's category set. Because your label is TOP SECRET and the file's is SECRET, you can't change the file.

This write rule may seem odd. Does this, in fact, mean that you're *too* trusted to change the LOGISTIC file? Shouldn't it work the other way? That is, shouldn't TOP SECRET users be able to change SECRET files? Well, no. The reason has to do with something called a *downgrade of information*, or a *write-down of information*. Sometimes security people talk about information *flowing* to a lower or a higher level.

Consider the case where a user with a TOP SECRET clearance reads a number of TOP SECRET documents and tries to copy sections of them into an UNCLASSIFIED memo. That would be a downgrade of information (TOP SECRET information becoming UNCLASSIFIED), and it's not allowed because it would provide a way to share highly sensitive information with people not authorized to access it.

The other side of the write rule is known as *upgrade of information*. Suppose you have a CONFIDENTIAL clearance. The system will let you write a SECRET memo, but then it won't let you read the memo. Why? By writing CONFIDENTIAL information into a SECRET memo, you've essentially made that information SECRET. The system does allow an upgrade of information, but it doesn't suspend the normal access rules.

Note that these rules become substantially more complicated when your system supports information labels as well as sensitivity labels. Information labels are required for compartmented mode workstations, a technology described in Chapter 6, *Inside the Orange Book.*

Comparability. In the previous example, the label:

TOP SECRET [VENUS ALPHA]

is "higher" than either of the labels:

SECRET [VENUS ALPHA]

TOP SECRET [VENUS]

But you can't really say that the label:

TOP SECRET [VENUS]

is higher than the label:

SECRET [ALPHA]

Because neither label contains all the categories of the other, the labels can't be compared. They're said to be *incomparable*. In a mandatory access control system, you won't be allowed access to a file whose label is incomparable to your clearance.

Bell-LaPadula Model. It's important to note the origin of the policies outlined above. In 1973, David Bell and Leonard LaPadula first described the DoD multi-level military security policy in abstract, formal terms, as mentioned in Chapter 2, *Some Security History.* In the Bell and LaPadula model, they used mathematical notation and set theory to define the concept of a secure state, the modes of access, and the rules for granting access. They called their model the Basic Security Theorem. In their model, Bell and LaPadula defined the read and write rules we've simplified above. The *simple security condition* stated that the subject's sensitivity label must dominate the object's sensitivity label (the read rule we previously described). The **-property*, or *star property* stated that the object's sensitivity label must dominate the subject's sensitivity label (the write rule we previously described). Several of the more technical books referenced in Appendix E, *A Security Source Book,* describe these rules more rigorously. Refer to them for additional details.

4

Viruses and Other Wildlife

Viruses
Worms
Trojan Horses
Bombs
Trap Doors
Spoofs
Other Wildlife
Remedies

The word "virus" has become a rather trendy term for describing a number of different types of attacks on computers. Just about everybody has heard of computer viruses, but most people aren't clear about what they are and how they differ from worms and other threats to software. The computer security threats described in this chapter have been given many names (some of them unprintable). The most popular are *malicious code*, *programmed threats*, *rogue programs*, and *vandalware*. This chapter provides some definitions of these threats.

Viruses

A *virus* is a code fragment that copies itself into a larger program, modifying that program. Unlike a worm, described in the next section, a virus is not an independent program. A virus executes only when its host program begins to run. The virus then replicates itself, infecting other programs as it reproduces. A virus might start reproducing right away, or it might lie dormant for some time, until it's triggered by a particular event. For example, a particular triggering date may arrive (as with the infamous Friday the 13th virus), or a particular event may occur (for example, deleting a particular person's name from a payroll file, perhaps indicating that he's been fired). See the section on "Bombs" later in this chapter for more information about triggers.

A virus may infect memory, a floppy disk, a tape, or any other type of storage. Like a biological virus, a computer virus invades other organisms, causing those organisms to proliferate and spread the virus. It degrades system performance in addition to whatever other damage (e.g., data deletion) it does. A virus may spread via a network, through the use of infected software on diskettes, or by electronic bulletin boards linked by telephone lines. Although viruses have become a significant problem on personal computers, they are less common on larger shared computers, which are more likely to protect the operating system from modification by users and programs without special privileges.

Viruses and worms are often confused. During the 1988 outbreak on the Internet, there was much debate about whether the invader was a virus or a worm. Security people sometimes distinguish between the two by categorizing a virus as destructive (it might destroy or compromise data) and a worm as non-destructive (it might browse through the system or simply slow down service). Because system and network slowdowns can themselves be very destructive, this distinction may not be a very meaningful one.

Both viruses and worms typically protect themselves by hiding in their host programs, by operating in delayed fashion, and sometimes by destroying evidence of their wrongdoing. All this may hinder attempts to control and eradicate the offending code.

Gene Spafford of Purdue* credits David Gerrold with being the first to use the word "virus" as a computer attacker in Gerrold's science fiction stories about the G.O.D. machine.† Spafford describes the origins of the virus:

> A subplot in that book described a program named VIRUS created by an unethical scientist. A computer infected with VIRUS would randomly dial the phone until it found another computer. It would then break into that system and infect it with a copy of VIRUS. This program would infiltrate the system software and slow the system down so much that it became unusable (except to infect other machines). The inventor had plans to sell a program named

---

*Eugene H. Spafford, "The Internet Worm Program: An Analysis," Purdue Technical Report CSD-TR-823, West Lafayette (IN), November 29, 1988.

†These stories were later combined and expanded into the book *When Harlie Was One*, Ballantine Books, First Edition, New York (NY), 1972). In later editions of the book, the virus plot was removed.

VACCINE that could cure VIRUS and prevent infection, but disaster occurred when noise on a phone line caused VIRUS to mutate so VACCINE ceased to be effective.

In 1984, Ken Thompson* described the development of what can be considered the first computer virus (though he didn't give it that name). Thompson wrote a self-reproducing program in the C programming language. He modified the program to "learn" new syntax and then planted a Trojan horse (described later) that deliberately miscompiled the UNIX **login** command, enabling him to log into the system as any user. Next, he added a second Trojan horse aimed at the C compiler. After compiling the modified source with the normal C compiler to produce a bugged binary, he installed this binary as the official C, and removed the bugs from the source of the compiler. Then, whenever the new source of the compiler was compiled, the new binary reinserted the bugs. The **login** command remained bugged, with no trace in the source.

A number of people developed computer viruses on IBM PC and Apple II computers (though they were not called viruses) during the early 1980s. (According to Spafford, "Festering Hate" and "Cyberaids" were among the infections.)

Fred Cohen from the University of Southern California was the first to define formally the term "computer virus." (The term was suggested by Cohen's advisor, Len Adleman, after Cohen developed an experimental program for a security seminar.) According to Cohen, a computer virus is:

> ...a program that can "infect" other programs by modifying them to include a possibly evolved copy of itself. With the infection property, a virus can spread throughout a computer system or network using the authorizations of every user using it to infect their programs. Every program that gets infected may also act as a virus and thus the infection grows.†

In his experiments, Cohen showed how quickly a virus could propagate throughout an entire operating system.

A large number of viruses now inhabit computer systems—particular in uncontrolled PC environments. According to Dr. Harold Joseph Highland, more than 350 distinct viruses have been identified to date.‡ Viruses are often named for

---

*Kenneth Thompson, "Reflections on Trusting Trust," *Communications of the ACM*, Volume 27, Number 8, August 1984.

†Fred Cohen, "Computer Viruses: Theory and Experiments, *Computers and Security*, Volume 6, Number 1, 1987 (first presented at 1984 meeting of IFIP Technical Committee 11 on Security and Protection in Information Systems).

‡Harold Joseph Highland, "Random Bits and Bytes," *Computers and Security*, Elsevier Advanced Technology, Volume 10, Number 1, February 1991.

the place where they are first discovered (e.g., the Bulgarian Factory of viruses), or for some message displayed by the virus (e.g., the AIDS virus). Examples of PC viruses include the Brain virus, the Fu Manchu virus, the Icelandic virus, and the Bouncing Ball virus. Examples of Apple Macintosh viruses include the Dukakis virus and the Peace virus.*

Worms

A *worm* is an independent program. It reproduces by copying itself in full-blown fashion from one computer to another, usually over a network. Like a virus, a worm compounds the damage it does by spreading rapidly from one site to another. Unlike a virus, which attaches itself to a program, a worm keeps its independence; it usually doesn't modify other programs. And, unlike a virus, which ordinarily causes some kind of destruction, a worm doesn't destroy data. But a worm is certainly not benign; it typically does a lot of damage by harnessing the resources in a network (as it maintains and reproduces itself), by tying up these resources, and, eventually, by shutting down the network.

The notion of a worm as a computer intruder apparently dates from John Brunner's 1975 science fiction novel, *The Shockwave Rider*. In Brunner's book, programs called "tapeworms" lived inside computers, spread from machine to machine, and were "indefinitely self-perpetuating so long as the net exists."†

Around 1980, John Schoch and Jon Hupp, researchers at Xerox Palo Alto Research Center, developed the first experimental worm programs as a research tool.‡ The worms were designed to spread from one computer to another. Shoch and Hupp described their worms as follows:

> A *worm* is simply a computation which lives on one or more machines . . . The programs on individual computers are described as the *segments* of a worm . . . The segments in a worm remain in communication with each other; should one segment fail, the remaining pieces must find another free

---

*For a full taxonomy, see Eugene H. Spafford, Kathleen A. Heaphy, and David Ferbrache, *Computer Viruses: Dealing with Electronic Vandalism and Programmed Threats*, ADAPSO, Arlington (VA), 1989. (Order from ADAPSO: (703) 522-5055.)

†John Brunner, *Shockwave Rider*, Ballantine, New York (NY), 1975.

‡John F. Shoch and Jon A. Hupp, "The Worm Programs—Early Experience with a Distributed Computation," *Communications of the ACM*, Volume 25, Number 3, pp. 172-180, March 1982. (An earlier version was presented at the Workshop for Fundamental Issues in Distributed Computing, ACM/SIGOPS and ACM/SIGPLAN, December 1980.)

machine, initialize it, and add it to the worm. As segments (machines) join and then leave the computation, the worm itself seems to move through the network.

The Xerox PARC worms were, on the whole, useful creatures; they handled mail, ran distributed diagnostics, and performed other distributed functions. A few errant, experimental worms did get out of control, however, before a "worm watcher" was added to the network.

Trojan Horses

 A *Trojan horse* is a code fragment that hides inside a program and performs a disguised function. It's a popular mechanism for disguising a virus or a worm.

In classical mythology, a Trojan horse was a large hollow horse made of wood by Odysseus during the Trojan War. The Greeks hid soldiers inside the horse and left it at the gates of Troy. After the Trojans were persuaded to bring the horse inside the gates, the hidden soldiers opened the doors for the rest of the army, which attacked the city and won the war.

In the modern computer world, a Trojan horse hides in an independent program that performs a useful or appealing function—or appears to perform that function. Along with the apparent function, however, the program performs some other unauthorized operation. A typical Trojan horse tricks a user into running a program, often an attractive or helpful one. When the unsuspecting user runs the program, it does indeed perform the expected function. But its real purpose is often to penetrate the defenses of the system by usurping the user's legitimate privileges and thus obtaining information that the penetrator isn't authorized to access. Trojan horses are often hidden in programs that entice users by displaying information about new system features or by playing new games.

Dan Edwards of NSA is credited as being the first to use the term "Trojan horse."*

A classic Trojan horse attack is described by Dennis M. Ritchie.† An attacker writes a "password grabber" program that simulates the normal login process and runs it on an unattended terminal. When an unsuspecting user sees the `login:`

---

*Morrie Gasser, *Building a Secure Computer System*, New York (NY), Van Nostrand Reinhold, 1988. Also, Donn B. Parker, "The Trojan Horse Virus and Other Crimoids," in Denning, Peter J., ed., *Computers Under Attack: Intruders, Worms, and Viruses*, ACM Press, Addison Wesley, Reading (MA), 1990.
†Dennis M. Ritchie, "On the Security of UNIX", *UNIX System Manager's Manual (SMM)*, 4.3 Berkeley Software Distribution, University of California, Berkeley (CA), 1986.

prompt and attempts to log in, the program runs through the normal login sequence so the user thinks that he or she is logging in the ordinary way.

However, once the program containing the Trojan horse has received the login and password, it copies (or mails) this information to a file owned by the program implementor and prints out a `login incorrect` message. The user assumes that the password has been mistyped and re-enters it. In the meantime, the program containing the Trojan horse has exited and the real login program is now in control. The next time the user successfully logs in, not suspecting that login and password information has been revealed.

Some people call this particular type of Trojan horse a "Trojan mule" because, unlike a program that displays helpful system information or plays a game, the password grabber is simply a trap. It doesn't even try to perform a useful function. Another distinction that's sometimes made between Trojan horses and Trojan mules is that, while Trojan mules disappear from the system once they've done done their dirty work, Trojan horses often remain in the system until they're eradicated.

A clever Trojan horse leaves no trace of its presence, does no detectable damage, may reside indefinitely in unsuspecting software, and may even be programmed to self-destruct before it can be detected.

Bombs

A *bomb* is a type of Trojan horse, used to release a virus, a worm, or some other system attack. It's either an independent program or a piece of code that's been planted by a system developer or a programmer. A bomb works by triggering some kind of unauthorized action when a particular date, time, or condition occurs.

Technically there are two types of bombs: time and logic. A bomb that's set to go off on a particular date or after some period of time has elapsed is called a *time bomb*. The Friday the 13th Virus, which started doing damage on the first Friday the 13th in 1988, is an example of a time bomb. A bomb that's set to go off when a particular event occurs is called a *logic bomb*. Software developers have been known to explode logic bombs at key moments after installation—for example, if the customer fails to pay a bill or tries to perform an illicit copy.

A.K. Dewdney describes a logic bomb in the French spy novel by Thierry Breton and Denis Beneich, *Softwar: La Guerre Douce*:*

> ...they spin a chilling yarn about the purchase by the Soviet Union of an American supercomputer. Instead of blocking the sale, American authorities, displaying studied reluctance, agree to the transaction. The computer has been secretly programmed with a "software bomb." Ostensibly bought to help with weather forecasting over the vast territory of the Soviet Union, the machine, or rather its software, contains a hidden trigger; as soon as the U.S. National Weather Service reports a certain temperature at St. Thomas in the Virgin Islands, the program proceeds to subvert and destroy every piece of software it can find in the Soviet network.

Trap Doors

 A *trap door*, or a *back door*, is a mechanism that's built into a system by its designer. The function of a trap door is to give the designer a way to sneak back into the system, circumventing normal system protection. Unlike a logic bomb, which usually explodes in someone else's system, a trap door gives the original designer a secret route into the software.

Sometimes, programmers leave trap doors (entry points) in a program to allow them to test the program, or monitor its operation, without having to follow what may be cumbersome access rules or security measures. These trap doors also provide a way to get into the program in case there's a problem with the access routines. Although such trap doors are ordinarily removed before the program is shipped to the customer, sometimes they're left in the code by accident or by design.

A trap door is typically activated by the person who planted it. Usually, the means of access is not apparent—for example, an unlikely set of keystrokes or sequence of events, or a particular login. Once the developer gets in through the trap door, he or she may get special program privileges. In the 1983 movie, *War Games*, the hero gained access to a NORAD computer system by inadvertently entering a trap door planted by its creator (allowing him to log in without an authorized account), setting off a Global Thermonuclear War game that became all too real.

---

*A.K. Dewdney, "A Core War Bestiary of Viruses, Worms, and Other Threats to Computer Memories," *Scientific American*, Volume 252, Number 3, pp. 14-23, March 1985.

Spoofs

A *spoof* is simply a generic name for a program that tricks an unsuspecting user into giving away privileges. Often, the spoof is perpetrated by a Trojan horse mechanism in which an unauthorized user is tricked into inadvertently running an unauthorized program. (The Trojan horse login described above is an example of a spoof.) The program then takes on the privileges of the user and may run amuck!

Sometimes, a spoof in which someone pretends to be another user is called a *masquerade*.

Other Wildlife

There are several variants on the malicious code described in this chapter:

- *Bacteria* are programs that do nothing but make copies of themselves, but by doing this they eventually use all the resources (e.g., memory, disk space) of your system.

- *Rabbits* are another name for rapidly reproducing programs.

- *Crabs* are programs that attack the display of data on computer terminal screens.

- *Creepers* are the worm-like creatures that crawled through the ARPANET in a demonstration program developed by Bob Thomas, and enhanced by Ray Tomlinson, both of Bolt Beranek and Newman in the early 1970s.* The message, "I'm the creeper, catch me if you can!" spread from terminal to terminal until the creepers were eradicated by "the reaper."

- *Salamis* slice away (rather than hack away) tiny pieces of data. For example, a salami attack alters one or two numbers or a decimal point in a file, or it shaves a penny off a customer's bank interest calculations and deposits the pennies in the intruder's account. No one is likely to notice such tiny discrepancies, which can often be attributed to computer truncation and rounding errors. It does not act precipitously, and it can do a lot of damage without calling attention to itself.

---

*Cited in Anne W. Branscomb, "Rogue Programs and Computer Rogues: Tailoring the Punishment to Fit the Crime," in *Rogue Programs: Viruses, Worms, and Trojan Horses*, Lance J. Hoffman, ed., Van Nostrand Reinhold, New York (NY), 1990.

Hints for Protecting Against Malicious Code

Whether you're a system administrator or a user, be careful not to infect your system with viruses and other wildlife that may creep in from other systems.

- Boot your computer from a known, good, write-protected operating system floppy disk (not from the hard disk).

- Install only licensed software bought from reputable sources (but be aware that even such sources have experienced infection). Save the original copies in a secure off-site location in case you need them later.

- Don't use software that arrives with its packaging open.

- Don't install software brought to the office from your home computer.

- Install only the software needed on your system.

- Be wary about new public-domain or shareware programs. Don't be the first to try such programs. Check your local electronic bulletin boards to see if other users have reported any problems with the programs. In an office environment, don't allow users to install software obtained from such sources. All software should be checked out by a system administrator. Don't share any software without system administrator approval.

- Whenever you're using a program for the first time, especially if it's public domain software, "vaccinate" it first with one of the many available virus-checking programs on the market. Most of these programs work by checking all of your executable files for signs of viruses. Some even check every new disk automatically when you insert it in your computer. Other types of virus checkers are resident programs that monitor any attempt to create or change a file.

- Be sure to back up all your data (see "Performing Backups" in Chapter 5, *Secure System Planning and Administration*). Remember to inspect your backups before you restore a system that's been invaded by a virus. If the virus has infected any of the backed up files, you'll be in trouble again.

Remedies

There are now many programs that can help you keep viruses and other wildlife away from your system—and can wipe out the critters if they gain access. Known as vaccinators, immunizers, inoculators, or antibodies (Flu Shot and Antidote are a few examples), these programs are available from both commercial and public domain sources. These products, and the system administration procedures that go along with them, have two overlapping goals: They don't let you run a program that's infected, and they keep infected programs from damaging your system.

Personal computer magazines periodically run articles and reviews of anti-viral software. You can also get help from such organizations as the Computer Virus Industry Association (see Appendix E, *A Security Source Book*). Remember, if you use an anti-virus program, get it from a reliable source, or you may make things worse!

5

Secure System Planning and Administration

Administrative Security
Overall Planning and Administration
Day-to-day Administration
Separation of Duties

Secure system planning and administration is the human side of computer security. Even in a highly trusted system, security isn't automatic. It's still the system administrator who carries out your organization's security policy, and it's the system administrator who makes or breaks system security. For example, your organization's security policy may require regular backups, but it's the administrator who must actually run the backups. Training users, setting up and protecting the password file and other system-critical files, and examining audit logs: these are some of the many other ways that a system's abstract security policy gets translated into human terms.

Administrative Security

Administrative security falls into three general categories:

1. **Overall security planning and administration.** This category includes working with management to set a security policy for your organization, publicizing it and gaining management support for it, performing risk analysis

and disaster planning, monitoring employees, training users, answering their questions, and so on.

2. **Day-to-day security administration.** This category includes creating accounts and assigning security profiles for users—for example, their initial passwords, their password controls (e.g., how often they must change their passwords), their login controls (e.g., what hours they can log in), making sure there aren't security holes in your system, and so on.

3. **Day-to-day system administration.** This category includes keeping the system running, doing daily backups, creating user accounts, and so on. This type of system administration is vital to *any* system—whether it processes highly secure information or not. Although these mundane tasks may not seem especially security-relevant, they're actually vital to security. Remember that "availability" is a key goal of overall computer security. Day-to-day system administration keeps the system available.

Because system administration is so system-specific, the details of how to administer particular systems aren't in the province of this book. This chapter provides some general hints for sound administration. In addition, most vendors provide reasonably good system administrator documentation describing the security features of their own systems. There are also several excellent, commercially available references that describe how to keep your system secure.*

If your organization has government contracts, you may need to observe more stringent security policies established by the government for high-security sites. When your organization gets a security clearance, you'll find out the details of what you need to do.

Because of size, staffing, or budget, some organizations may not have a system administrator who takes responsibility for security administration. If your organization can't afford full-time system administration, or doesn't have the appropriate staff to administer a security policy that adequately protects your equipment and information, we recommend that you consider hiring a security consultant on a short-term or periodic basis. Such a person can analyze your security risks and needs, help you set up a workable security policy, and conduct periodic security audits. (See the discussion in "Performing a Security Audit" later in this chapter.)

---

*If you're running a UNIX system, we particularly recommend *Practical UNIX Security* by Simson Garfinkel and Gene Spafford, O'Reilly & Associates, Sebastopol (CA), 1991).

Overall Planning and Administration

System administrators sometimes find themselves in the position of being the security advocates within their organizations—having to sell security both to users (who may question why they need to use features they may find cumbersome) and to upper management (who may question why it all costs so much money).

This section describes a number of overall security decisions someone needs to make about security at your site. Depending on the staffing and security consciousness of your organization, these decisions may be made by a system administrator or by senior management.

Analyzing Costs and Risks

Computer security is a tradeoff. When you're considering building, buying, or even using a security product, you'll have to balance the cost of the product against the risk of doing without it. Some organizations formalize this process and call it a risk analysis. *Risk analysis* is a procedure used to estimate potential losses that may result from system vulnerabilities and to quantify the damage that may result if certain threats occur. The ultimate goal of risk analysis is to help select cost-effective safeguards that will reduce risks to an acceptable level. Basically, risk analysis is a way of figuring out how important your system is, and how far you're willing to go—in terms of equipment, people, and budget—to protect it.

Standard risk analysis involves looking at your tangible assets—for example, your buildings, your computers, and your other equipment—and figuring how to protect them. Because your organization's most valuable asset may be the information processed by your computers, not the computers themselves, you need to take a good look at how best to protect that information as well.

When you're evaluating your organization's information asset and considering whether and how to protect it, you'll have a number of important questions to ask:

What information do you have and how important is it?

There are many different types of information: national defense information describing military resources and deployment; corporate records showing projected profits, losses, and strategies; personnel records describing health, financial, academic, and employment history.

You'll need to assess how important that information is to your own organization. Information of inestimable value to one organization may have little or no value to another organization.

How vulnerable is the information?

Some information may be very important to you, but may be of little interest to anyone else. (The novel you're writing on your PC may fall into this category.) Other information may be of great interest, but may be so inaccessible that additional security controls aren't really justified. (Classified military information that's encrypted and stored on a heavily guarded computer with one authorized user and no network connections may fall into this category.)

Everyone needs to worry about physical threats (e.g., fire and power loss) and accidents caused by careless or untrained employees. Beyond these obvious perils, you'll need to evaluate whether realistic attempts are being made, or could be made, to break into your system, and to assess how likely it is that a break-in will occur in the future. If you're responsible for national defense information, you'll have to worry about foreign intelligence. If you're protecting your business's data, you'll be a lot more concerned about your competitors, about crackers, and about insider threats. Remember too that threats to information tend to grow as people learn about your system's vulnerabilities, and as methods of exploiting those vulnerabilities get cheaper and easier.

What is the cost of losing or compromising the information?

Just as there are many different types of costs of security information, there are many different types of consequences. If we're talking about the loss of vital national defense information, the cost might be cataclysmic. If a medical experiment is disrupted or patient records are lost or compromised, people might die. If the security of an ATM is breached, a bank might lose a lot of money—and, when the news hits the press, the bank might also suffer a loss of confidence by customers and possibly lawsuits by shareholders.

What about corporate strategy information? Personal health or financial information? Each has its own risks, costs, and consequences, both tangible and intangible, ranging from the loss of competitive advantage to the risk of losing government benefits to personal embarrassment.

What is the cost of protecting the information?

There are certain basic costs that you must incur. You *must* back up your data. No matter what security violation occurs—a natural disaster, a user mistake, or a break-in—having a recent backup of your data will allow you to go on.

There are many different types of additional costs. Will you need to buy new equipment? Will the use of a security product slow down response time and performance in a system that must provide quick customer service? Will security controls detract from the user-friendliness of a system that you're marketing as easy to use?

Here too, you'll have to consider the different types of costs within your own organization and to assess the impact of security costs in relation to expected security benefits. One rule of thumb is that the cost of securing information shouldn't exceed the financial and administrative cost of recovering that information—although certain types of information, like national defense information, can't necessarily be quantified in this way. It's also hard to quantify the damage done by publicity and the loss of public confidence. Dennis Steinauer of the National Institute of Standards and Technology put it this way, "Controls that are more expensive than the value of the information they protect are not cost-effective. Absolute security is achieved only at unlimited cost."

Based on the answers to these questions, you'll need to make a determination, balancing your assessment of the value of your information asset against the risks of losing it and the financial and human costs of protecting that information. Then you'll need to decide what your priorities are, and what types of security— physical, operating system, communications lines, encryption, biometric devices, and so on—best fit your information, your risks, and your budget. And then you'll need to make an educated guess about what to protect and how.

Planning for Disaster

One of the most important things you can do to protect your organization from disaster is to plan for that disaster. A disaster recovery plan is a plan for keeping your computer equipment and information available in case of an emergency. Disaster planning may spell the difference between a problem and a (possibly business-threatening) catastrophe.

Your organization's disaster recovery plan will involve such activities as backing up data for storage at remote secure facilities and arranging for the use of other computer facilities or equipment in case of an emergency. Such arrangements may be informal (for example, you might make a reciprocal agreement with another department or organization to use each others' equipment if a disaster occurs), or they may be formal (for example, you might prepare a separate emergency site or contract with an organization that handles disaster preparedness).

Emergency sites are usually characterized as cold or hot. *Cold sites* are emergency facilities containing air conditioning and cabling, but no computers. You can move replacement equipment into this site and continue processing. *Hot sites* are emergency facilities containing computers, backup data—the works!

In addition to protecting your organization's equipment and information, a disaster recovery plan may greatly increase public confidence—as well as the confidence of your employees and managers—in your ability to safeguard data and continue to provide service.

Computers and their ongoing availability are absolutely vital to the continued survival of most businesses. Yet few organizations actually perform risk analysis and disaster planning. In a study performed by the General Accounting Office, the GAO found that only about a third of the companies it surveyed had any kind of disaster plan in place.

Remember that backups are the key to disaster planning. If a disaster occurs and you've backed up your system, you'll be able to recover eventually. See the discussion of backups in "Backing Up Your Data" later in this chapter.

Chapter 9, *Physical Security and Biometrics*, discusses some of the natural disasters that face your organization and describes what you can do to reduce your risks.

Setting Security Rules for Employees

Some aspects of security are simply good management. Be sensible about who you hire, what computer resources you let them use, and what you do when they leave your organization. See the inset entitled "Hints for Employee Security Management" for the most basic rules.

Training Users

No matter how diligent and careful a system administrator you are, you can't enforce security alone. The users in your organization have to take some responsibility for security. Teach your users how to use the hardware and software, be sure they understand your organization's security policy, and impress upon them the importance of observing good security practices. (See the inset entitled "Hints for Safe Computing" for some very basic guidelines for individual user security.) Most importantly, be sure they know how to recognize security problems and what to do if they occur. Remember, improperly-trained users are more of a peril to system security than crackers.

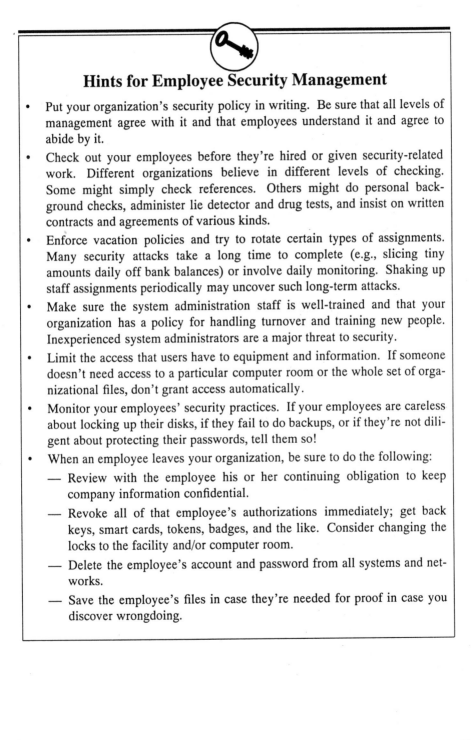

Hints for Employee Security Management

- Put your organization's security policy in writing. Be sure that all levels of management agree with it and that employees understand it and agree to abide by it.

- Check out your employees before they're hired or given security-related work. Different organizations believe in different levels of checking. Some might simply check references. Others might do personal background checks, administer lie detector and drug tests, and insist on written contracts and agreements of various kinds.

- Enforce vacation policies and try to rotate certain types of assignments. Many security attacks take a long time to complete (e.g., slicing tiny amounts daily off bank balances) or involve daily monitoring. Shaking up staff assignments periodically may uncover such long-term attacks.

- Make sure the system administration staff is well-trained and that your organization has a policy for handling turnover and training new people. Inexperienced system administrators are a major threat to security.

- Limit the access that users have to equipment and information. If someone doesn't need access to a particular computer room or the whole set of organizational files, don't grant access automatically.

- Monitor your employees' security practices. If your employees are careless about locking up their disks, if they fail to do backups, or if they're not diligent about protecting their passwords, tell them so!

- When an employee leaves your organization, be sure to do the following:

  — Review with the employee his or her continuing obligation to keep company information confidential.

  — Revoke all of that employee's authorizations immediately; get back keys, smart cards, tokens, badges, and the like. Consider changing the locks to the facility and/or computer room.

  — Delete the employee's account and password from all systems and networks.

  — Save the employee's files in case they're needed for proof in case you discover wrongdoing.

Day-to-day Administration

Day-to-day system administration encompasses many activities, but most of them focus on keeping your computer system running smoothly by maintaining equipment, making sure there's sufficient space on the system disks, and protecting the system and its software from damage. Examples include making sure users can't modify system software; checking each new release of a vendor's software, especially fixes to security problems, to be sure such problems have really been fixed; and insisting that vendors promptly patch any security holes or other bugs you find.

Most daily administrative activities are very system-specific. However, a few activities, described in this section, are essentials for any system.

Performing Backups

Backups of your system and all the data stored on your system are absolutely essential if you expect to be able to recover from a disaster. What kind of disaster? It might be a natural disaster, such as a fire or a flood. It might be a crime, such as a system intruder's meddling, vandalism of your computer room, or theft of a computer or a disk. It might be a hardware or software failure or a user error (e.g., deleting the latest version of a document or the latest release of some development software). Whatever the cause, and whatever the extent of the damage, you *will* be able to recover eventually if you have recent backups of all your system data.

Your own system documentation tells you how to perform backups. Our purpose is to persuade you to read it, do it, and do it again and again. Many organizations have well-defined rules about performing backups; if you don't follow the rules, you'll lose your job. But many other organizations have much looser policies. The scheduling and the extent of backups is far more discretionary. In these cases, it's really up to you. In the inset entitled "Hints for Backups," we've provided some general guidelines.

What does it mean to perform regular backups? That's an organizational decision; it depends on the number of users in your system, the volume of work, and many other variables. Many organizations perform a full backup (of every file in the system) every night. Others may do a full backup only once a month, but they do an incremental backup (of everything that's changed since the last full backup) every day.

Hints for Safe Computing

Security features and trusted systems do a lot to make your computer environment a secure one. But in most systems, the final word on security is your own. Here's a collection of general hints for protecting your computer and your data. Other chapters contain additional hints in specific areas.

- Obey your site's security policy. Follow the rules, make sure your work habits are secure, and don't try to bypass security. Taking a few extra minutes to protect your login, your password, and your data is a pretty good bargain compared with trying to reconstruct your work and deal with the consequences if files are stolen, lost, or damaged.

- Use any security controls and products available to you. These may include locks, security boards, and software packages and features.

- Never leave your computer, workstation, or terminal unattended. If you're going out to lunch, log out first. The easiest way for someone to crack a system is simply to use your account.

- Be careful not to leave sensitive information around in paper or magnetic form. Shred sensitive printout or place it in secure recycle bins. When you scratch a disk or a tape, erase it; don't just reinitialize it (leaving the data still on the medium). Consider using degaussing products if they're available at your site.

- Don't eat or drink near your computer or any computer media. A soda spilled into the ventilation holes of your PC can cause a tremendous amount of damage.

- Be careful not to damage your disks and other media. For example, don't write directly on their labels with a ballpoint pen.

Hints for Backups

Remember that your backups are the key to recovering your system in case of a disaster. Back up all of your files, and follow these rules:

- Encrypt your backups if they contain sensitive data.

- Keep extra backups off-site in a locked, fireproof location. You don't want a fire, lightning, or some other disaster to wipe out your system and your backups at the same time.

- Protect your backup tapes or disks. Keep them locked up. Don't let them hang unattended for someone to steal or mistakenly use.

- Verify your backups. Check periodically to make sure they've been produced correctly and haven't been damaged in any way.

- Sanitize your backups before your discard them. Be sure to delete all data by overwriting what's there. Don't just reinitialize your tapes or disks. (That typically rewrites only the header.)

- If you're throwing backups away, destroy the media first (by burning, crushing, or shredding.)

- Consider buying an automatic backup program that runs full or incremental backups (without your intervention) every night. There are also services available to encrypt and back up your data over a phone line to an "electronic vault."

Performing a Security Audit

It's a good idea to check on the security of your system by performing periodic security audits. A *security audit* is a search through your system for security problems and vulnerabilities.

Check your system files and any system logs or audit reports your system produces for dangerous situations or clues to suspicious activity. These might include:

- **Accounts without passwords.** They might have come with the system, or they might have been set up for guests or demos. Anyone can log in using such accounts.

- **Accounts with easily guessed passwords.** These might include passwords selected by users or passwords associated with administrator or guest accounts.

- **Group accounts.** Accounts that let multiple people (for example, all of the members of a particular department or a course) log in are risky; if someone breaks into a system using such an account, there's no way of knowing who was responsible.

- **Dormant accounts.** These include accounts of users who have left your organization, gone on vacation, or moved to a different group or a different system.

- **New accounts.** Be sure they're accounts you assigned and not accounts that an intruder has created.

- **Files with no owners.** An intruder might have wiped out the ownership field of a file to protect his or her identity.

- **Recent changes in file protection.** An intruder may have given special privileges to certain programs or may have made system files accessible to ordinary users. Individual users may have carelessly made their files accessible to everyone in the system.

- **Suspicious user activity.** Basically, this means that a user (or someone using that user's account) is acting in an unexpected way—for example, someone logs in from a number of different terminals, logs in at odd times of the day or the week, runs protected system programs, dials out an unusual amount, uses new networks, etc.

Separation of Duties

Separation of duties is the principle that it's better to assign pieces of security-related tasks to several specific individuals. If no one user has total control of the system's security mechanisms, no one user can completely compromise the system. This principle is related to another important security principle, that of *least privilege*, the idea that the users and the processes in a system should have the least number of privileges—and for the shortest amount of time—needed to do their work. The Orange Book least privilege requirement is described in Chapter 6, *Inside the Orange Book*.

In many systems, the system administrator has total control of the system's daily operations and security functions. In secure systems, this concentration of power in a single individual isn't allowed. It's obvious that in such systems ordinary users shouldn't be allowed to perform security-related functions (except those that are discretionary to them, such as protecting files they own). It may not be so obvious that security-related functions should not automatically be in the baili-wick of the system administrator, who takes responsibility for other important system operations.

In highly secure systems, as many as three distinct, complementary administrative functions, or roles, may be required: a system administrator, a security administrator (sometimes called an Information System Security Officer, or ISSO), and an operator.

Typical system administrator/operator functions include:

• Installing system software.

• Starting up and shutting down the system.

• Adding and removing system users.

• Performing backup and recovery.

• Mounting disks and tapes.

• Handling printers.

Typical security administrator functions include:

- Setting user clearances, initial passwords, and other security characteristics for new users, and changing security profiles for existing users.

- Setting or changing file sensitivity labels.

- Setting security characteristics of devices and communications channels.

- Reviewing audit data.

If an operator role is defined, the operator may perform some of the more mundane system administrator duties, such as doing backups.

The system administrator, the security administrator, and the operator may not always be different people, but in a secure system their roles must be clearly divided. Whenever the system administrator assumes the role of security administrator, for example, the person must switch hats thoroughly enough so the system is aware that the person is changing roles.

For example, suppose the person serving as system administrator needs to perform a security function—for example, starting up an auditing program. He or she will typically have to exit from the system administrator interface, and switch, in some system-defined way, to the security administrator interface before being able to run the program. Although cumbersome, this process clearly reinforces the system administrator/security administrator's understanding that the two roles are very different, with clearly delineated responsibilities that are monitored by the system. The system administrator and the security administrator play complementary roles that provide checks and balances on each other.

In some ways, these roles meet the objective of the so-called *two-man control* discussed in government security guidelines—the idea that it's much less likely that two people will conspire to breach security. For example, the system administrator's job is to add new users to the system; the security administrator's is to assign a password, a clearance, and other security information to that user's account. The security administrator usually must create system administrator accounts; the system administrator cannot create his own.

6

Inside the Orange Book

How secure is secure? Because different organizations—and different types of information—require different types of security, it's helpful to be able to quantify. The need to quantify security, or to measure trust, was the primary motive behind development of the government's *Trusted Computer System Evaluation Criteria* (the "Orange Book").*

If you're at all interested in computer security, you'll need to know something about the Orange Book. As more organizations become security-conscious, as more vendors develop secure systems and products, and as more government requisitions stipulate that equipment purchases be tied to Orange Book certification, there's more of a need to understand what the Orange Book is all about. Despite

---

*Department of Defense Trusted Computer System Evaluation Criteria, Department of Defense Standard (DOD 5200.28-STD), Library Number S225,711, December 1985.

challenges (see "Complaints about the Orange Book" later in this chapter), the Orange Book remains the current standard for secure systems.

In this chapter, we've tried to touch upon each of the Orange Book requirements without going into a great deal of detail. If you don't need to know about specific Orange Book requirements, you may want to read only the introductory sections of this chapter, and skip the discussion of specifics. If you want to find out the precise language of the Orange Book in a particular area, you'll want to refer to the detailed tables of security requirements in Appendix C, *Orange Book and Other Summaries*.

Introduction to the Orange Book

The Orange Book came about as a consequence of increasing security consciousness on the part of the government and industry, coupled with a growing need for standards for the purchase and use of computers by the federal government. Chapter 2, *Some Security History*, traces the history of computer security and the work that led to the publication of the Orange Book in August of 1983.

The Orange Book defines four broad hierarchical divisions of security protection. In increasing order of trust, they are:

D   Minimal security

C   Discretionary protection

B   Mandatory protection

A   Verified protection

Each division consists of one or more numbered classes, with higher numbers indicating a greater degree of security. For example, division C contains two distinct classes (C2 offers more security than C1); division B contains three classes (B3 offers more security than B2, which offers more security than B1); division A currently contains only one class. Each class is defined by a specific set of criteria that a system must meet to be awarded a rating in that class. The criteria fall into four general categories: security policy, accountability, assurance, and documentation. Table 6-1, included in "Orange Book Evaluation Classes" later in this chapter, lists each of the classes, along with representative systems that have been successfully evaluated in each of these classes.

What's the purpose of the Orange Book? According to the book itself, the evaluation criteria were developed with three basic objectives:

1. **Measurement.** To provide users with a metric with which to assess the degree of trust that can be placed in computer systems for the secure processing of classified or other sensitive information. For example, a user can rely on a B2 system to be "more secure" than a C2 system.

2. **Guidance.** To provide guidance to manufacturers as to what to build into their trusted commercial products to satisfy trust requirements for sensitive applications.

3. **Acquisition.** To provide a basis for specifying security requirements in acquisition specifications. Rather than specifying a hodge-podge of security requirements, and having vendors respond in piecemeal fashion, the Orange Book provides a clear way of specifying a coordinated set of security functions. A customer can be confident that the system he or she acquires has already been checked out for the needed degree of security.

As the Orange Book puts it, the criteria "constitute a uniform set of basic requirements and evaluation classes for assessing the effectiveness of security controls built into . . . systems."

A Summary of Security Concepts

The Orange Book discusses such concepts as trust, the Trusted Computing Base, a security policy, a security model, and a security kernel. You'll see references to these concepts later in this chapter, in the discussion of specific Orange Book requirements, and in other security literature. What do these concepts mean? The following sections give some very basic definitions.

What's a Trusted System?

The Orange Book talks about "trusted" systems rather than "secure" systems. The words aren't really synonymous. No system is completely secure. Any system can be penetrated—given enough tools and enough time. But systems can be trusted, some more than others, to do what we want them to do, and what we expect them to continue to do over time.

The central concept of the Orange Book is that it's possible to measure this trust—to build, evaluate, and certify a system that conforms to a specific set of security criteria, and that therefore merits a certain overall security rating. Appendix D, *Government Security Programs*, describes how trusted systems are evaluated and rated by the government.

What is a trusted system? The Orange Book defines it as:

> ...a system that employs sufficient hardware and software integrity measures to allow its use to simultaneously process a range of sensitive unclassified or classified (e.g., confidential through top secret) information for a diverse set of users without violating access privileges.

Measuring Trust

How does the Orange Book measure trust? The book approaches security from two perspectives:

Security Policy   A security policy states the rules enforced by a system's security features; for example, the rules governing whether a particular user is allowed to access a particular piece of information. Obviously, there are more security features in a highly secure system (e.g., a system rated as being B1 or higher) than in a less secure system (e.g., a C1 or C2 system), although at the highest levels there are actually few differences in security features. Instead, there is more "assurance."

Assurance   Assurance is the trust that can be placed in a system, and the trusted ways the system can be proven to have been developed, tested, documented, maintained, and delivered to a customer. At the higher levels of security, there are few changes in security features, but a definite increase in the degree of assurance a user can place in the system's architecture and security policies. As the Orange Book puts it, assurance "begins [at the lowest class] with an operable access control mechanism and ends [at the highest class] with a mechanism that a clever and determined user cannot circumvent."

In the lower classes (C1, C2, and B1), assurance of correct and complete design and implementation is gained mostly through testing of the security-relevant portions of the system. In the higher classes (B2, B3, and A1), assurance is derived more from system design and implementation and, at the highest level (A1 only), from formal verification tools. Assurance is described in detail in "Assurance Requirements" later in this chapter.

Trusted Computing Base

The concept of the *Trusted Computing Base* (TCB) is central to the notion of a trusted system. The Orange Book uses the term TCB to refer to the mechanisms that enforce security in a system. The book defines the TCB as follows:

> The totality of protection mechanisms within a computer system—including hardware, firmware, and software—the combination of which is responsible for enforcing a security policy. It creates a basic protection environment and provides additional user services required for a trusted computer system. The ability of a trusted computing base to correctly enforce a security policy depends solely on the mechanisms within the TCB and on the correct input by system administrative personnel of parameters (e.g., a user's clearance) related to the security policy.

Not every part of an operating system needs to be trusted. An important part of an evaluation of a computer system is to identify the architecture, assurance mechanisms, and security features that comprise the TCB, and to show how the TCB is protected from interference and tampering—either accidentally or deliberately.

Systems rated at the higher levels of trust require well-defined TCBs that are implemented in accordance with the reference monitor concept. First introduced by James Anderson in a 1972 Hanscom Air Force Base study, a *reference monitor* is a concept that "enforces the authorized access relationships between subjects and objects of a system." The mechanism that enforces this concept "validates each reference to data or programs by any user (program) against a list of authorized types of reference for that user."

The code that implements the reference monitor concept carries out the rules of the system—for example, whether a particular user can read a particular file.

The Anderson report lists the three design requirements that must be met by a reference monitor mechanism:

1. **Isolation**. The reference monitor must be tamperproof.

2. **Completeness**. The reference monitor must be invoked for every access decision, and must be impossible to bypass.

3. **Verifiability**. The reference monitor must be small enough to be able to be analyzed and tested, and it must be possible to ensure that the testing is complete.

Security Policy

A *security policy* is the set of rules and practices that regulate how an organization manages, protects, and distributes sensitive information. It's the framework in which a system provides trust. A security policy is typically stated in terms of subject and objects. A *subject* is something active in the system; examples of subjects are users, processes, and programs. An *object* is something that a subject acts upon; examples of objects are files, directories, devices, sockets, and windows.

The Orange Book defines a security policy as follows:

> Given identified subjects and objects, there must be a set of rules that are used by the system to determine whether a given subject can be permitted to gain access to a specific object.

For example, the security policy for a system determines whether a particular subject (e.g., a user) will be permitted access to a particular object (e.g., a file).

The Orange Book requires that a system express its security policy in either formal or informal terms. At the lower levels of trust (C1, C2, B1), an informally stated policy is acceptable. At the higher levels of trust (B2, B3, A1), a formally stated, mathematically precise policy is required.

Security Model

The mechanisms necessary to enforce a security policy usually conform to a specific security model. A *security model* expresses a system's security requirements precisely and without confusion.

A number of different security models have been developed. Models developed for highly secure systems are typically expressed mathematically and often use set theory to describe rules for system access.

The Orange Book criteria are based on the state-machine model developed by David Bell and Leonard LaPadula in 1973 under the sponsorship of the U.S. Air Force Electronic Systems Division (ESD). The Bell and LaPadula model is the first mathematical model of a multi-level secure computer system. The Orange Book describes the Bell and LaPadula model as follows:

> A formal state transition model of computer security policy that describes a set of system access rules. In this formal model, the entities in a computer system are divided into abstract sets of subjects and objects. The notion of a secure state is defined and it is proven that each state transition preserves security by moving from secure state to secure state; thus inductively proving that the system is secure. A system state is deemed to be "secure" if the only

permitted access modes of subjects to objects are in accordance with a specific security policy.

To determine whether or not a specific access mode is allowed, the clearance of a subject is compared to the classification of the object and a determination is made as to whether the subject is authorized for the specific access mode (for example, read or write). The clearance/classification scheme is expressed in terms of a lattice. The discussion of discretionary access control and mandatory access control in this chapter and in Chapter 3, *Computer System Security and Access Controls*, spells out more tangibly how specific security models are translated into real system behavior.

Anther security model that has gained popularity in security circles is the Biba integrity model,* which addresses the distinction between secrecy (protecting against unauthorized access) and integrity (protecting against unauthorized modification).

More recently, David Clark and David Wilson have proposed an integrity model that is especially appropriate for security in commercial activities.†

The access matrix model, the noninterference model, and the information flow model are other examples of security models. For a good analysis of different types of security models, refer to Morrie Gasser's book, *Building a Secure Computer System*.

Security Kernel

A *security kernel*, a concept developed by Roger Schell in 1972, is the operating system mechanism that actually implements the reference monitor concept. The security kernel is the heart of the TCB—the resource in the computing system that supervises all system activity in accordance with the system's security policy. The Orange Book defines a security kernel as:

> The hardware, firmware, and software elements of a Trusted Computing Base that implement the reference monitor concept. It must mediate all access, be protected from modification, and be verifiable as correct.

---

*K.J. Biba, *Integrity Considerations for Secure Computer Systems* (ESD-TR-76-372), Electronic Systems Division, U.S. Air Force, Hanscom Field, Bedford (MA), 1977. (Available from NTIS: AD-771543.)

†D.D. Clark, and D.R. Wilson, "A Comparison of Commercial and Military Computer Security Policies," *Proceedings of the 1987 Symposium on Security and Privacy*, pp. 184-195, IEEE Computer Society, Washington (DC), 1987.

The security kernel approach is the most commonly accepted approach to building highly trusted computing systems. Typically, the kernel is the bottom layer in a multiple-layer design, and additional functions are built on top of the kernel in an orderly way.

Simplicity is a very important characteristic of the TCB. As the Orange Book puts it, "The TCB should be as simple as possible, consistent with the functions it has to perform." For highly trusted systems, it's especially important that the TCB be designed and implemented so security features are clearly centralized within a security kernel. The kernel can then be rigorously tested to prove that the TCB is complete and tamperproof.

Security Perimeter

The security kernel, as well as other security-related system functions, lies within the imaginary boundary of the TCB known as the *security perimeter*. In highly trusted systems, the TCB must be designed and implemented in such a way that system elements included in it (those inside the security perimeter) are designed to perform security functions, while those elements excluded from the TCB (those outside the security perimeter) need not be trusted. It's very important that the interfaces across the security perimeter (for example, ways in which users invoke security functions) be precisely defined and enforced by the security components of the system.

With distributed systems and systems supporting networking, the term "security perimeter" may have a somewhat different meaning. An entire computer system, or even a local area network, may be inside a perimeter, connected to the outside world via a trusted system that's often called a gateway. The point is to control communication between trusted and untrusted systems and networks, and potentially to contain the damage done by a security breach.

Orange Book Evaluation Classes

Table 6-1 lists the Orange Book evaluation classes, along with representative operating systems that have been successfully evaluated, or that are currently undergoing evaluation, in each of these classes. Evaluations must be performed for systems with particular configurations on particular platforms. A system such as UNIX cannot be evaluated apart from its implementation on a particular piece of hardware, and a number of different vendors' implementations of UNIX have undergone individual evaluations.

There still haven't been too many systems evaluated according to Orange Book requirements. As of the end of 1991, fewer than 30 systems, among them the systems listed in Table 6-1, had received Orange Book ratings of any kind (most at the lower ratings); many more systems are currently being evaluated.

Table 6-1. Evaluation Classes and Sample Systems

Class	Name	Examples
D	Minimal security	None. Reserved for systems that are submitted for evaluation but fail. Basic operating systems for personal computers, such as the IBM PC running MS-DOS and the Apple Macintosh would probably fall into this category if they were evaluated.
C1	Discretionary security protection	IBM: MVS/RACF (a later version was given a C2 rating). Although ordinary UNIX systems have not been submitted for formal evaluation, many people feel that such systems (without enhanced security features) would be given a C1 rating.
C2	Controlled access protection	Computer Associates International: ACF/2/MVS Digital Equipment Corporation: VAX/VMS 4.3 Gould: UTX/32S Hewlett-Packard: MPE V/E Wang Laboratories: SVS/OS CAP 1.0
B1	Labeled security protection	AT&T: System V/MLS IBM: MVS/ESA SecureWare: CMW+ UNISYS: OS 1100
B2	Structured protection	Honeywell Information Systems: Multics Trusted Information Systems: Trusted XENIX
B3	Security domains	Honeywell Federal Systems: XTS-200 (in evaluation)
A1	Verified design	Honeywell Information Systems: SCOMP Boeing Aerospace: SNS

Comparison of Evaluation Classes

Figure 6-1 compares the Orange Book evaluation classes, showing the specific features required for each class and, in general terms, how requirements increase from class to class. Later sections, and the detailed tables included in Appendix C, *Orange Book and Other Summaries*, describe more rigorously how requirements change as you move from one class to another.

Complaints About the Orange Book

Some respected security practitioners disagree with Orange Book specifics and with the government's reliance on this book alone as a way of measuring trust. Here are some of the main claims about the inadequacies of the Orange Book.

- The Orange Book model works only in a government classified environment, and the higher levels of security aren't appropriate for the protection of commercial data, where data integrity is the chief concern.

- The Orange Book focuses on only one aspect of security—secrecy—while paying little attention to the principles of accuracy, availability, and authenticity.

- The Orange Book emphasizes protection from unauthorized access, while most security attacks actually involve insiders. (Orange Book defenders point out that the book's principle of *least privilege* addresses this issue to some degree.)

- The Orange Book doesn't address networking issues. (However, the Red Book, described in Chapter 8, *Communications and Network Security*, does address these issues.)

- The Orange book contains a relatively small number of security ratings. A system that offers a subset of Orange Book security features—plus some very strong features in other areas not addressed by the Orange Book (for example, integrity) wouldn't fit into any of the current ratings.

There's a lot of ongoing debate about these issues, and it's likely that the Orange Book will undergo a revision in the future to respond both to complaints about inadequacies and to changing technologies. For now, however, the Orange Book is the clear standard for secure systems.

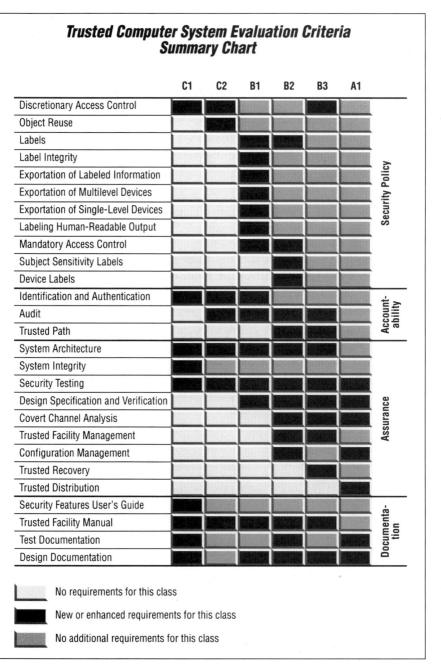

Trusted Computer System Evaluation Criteria Summary Chart

	C1	C2	B1	B2	B3	A1	
Discretionary Access Control							Security Policy
Object Reuse							
Labels							
Label Integrity							
Exportation of Labeled Information							
Exportation of Multilevel Devices							
Exportation of Single-Level Devices							
Labeling Human-Readable Output							
Mandatory Access Control							
Subject Sensitivity Labels							
Device Labels							
Identification and Authentication							Accountability
Audit							
Trusted Path							
System Architecture							Assurance
System Integrity							
Security Testing							
Design Specification and Verification							
Covert Channel Analysis							
Trusted Facility Management							
Configuration Management							
Trusted Recovery							
Trusted Distribution							
Security Features User's Guide							Documentation
Trusted Facility Manual							
Test Documentation							
Design Documentation							

No requirements for this class

New or enhanced requirements for this class

No additional requirements for this class

Figure 6-1. Comparison of Evaluation Classes

The Rainbow Series and Other Sources

The Orange Book is an abstract, very concise description of computer security requirements. (We've included a tabular summary of Orange Book requirements in Appendix C, *Orange Book and Other Summaries*.) The Orange Book provides a broad framework for building and evaluating a trusted system, but it raises as many questions as it answers about the specifics of what's really needed to satisfy particular requirements. In an attempt to help system developers, the government has published a number of additional books interpreting Orange Book requirements in particular, puzzling areas. These are known collectively as the Rainbow Series because each has a different cover color.

Chief among the documents in the Rainbow Series is the *Trusted Network Interpretation* (TNI) (the "Red Book"), which interprets the criteria described in the Orange Book for networks and network components. Published in 1987, this book identifies security features not mentioned in the Orange Book that apply to networks, and it describes how these features fit into the graded classification of systems described in the Orange Book. For example, the Red Book discusses how the concept of group identification for discretionary access control might be extended to internet addresses. (The Red Book is described briefly in Chapter 8, *Communications and Network Security*.)

Another book that's expected to be of use to developers of database management systems is the *Trusted Database Management System Interpretation* (TDI) (the "Lavender Book"), which interprets Orange Book requirements for DBMS products. For example, this book discusses how the concept of security labels might be extended to labels for stored view definitions (obtained via DBMS query commands).

There are now more than 20 books in the Rainbow Series. Some others include:

Green Book   *Password Management Guideline*

Tan Book   *A Guide to Understanding Audit in Trusted Systems*

Purple Book   *Guidelines for Formal Verification Systems*

Burgundy Book   *A Guide to Understanding Design Documentation in Trusted Systems*

A complete list of the books in the Rainbow Series is included in Appendix E along with information on how to get copies of these books.

Another set of books of use to those interested in security and government guidelines for security products and their use is the set of Federation of Information Processing Standards. Called "FIPS PUBs," these books are federal standards in many areas, some of them relevant to computer security. For example, FIPS PUB

46-1, *Data Encryption Standard*, describes the DES, the national standard for encryption of sensitive government information. FIPS PUB 112, *Password Usage*, is a standard on secure passwords. FIPS PUBs related to security are listed in Appendix E along with information about how to get copies.

There are so many government publications describing different areas of computer security that those who are interested in security or those who need to understand government regulations and procedures are often baffled. (It's our hope that this book will help you make your way through this maze by listing the publications and how to get them and telling you what's important about them.)

Evaluations of Secure Systems

The National Computer Security Center (NCSC) is responsible for evaluating secure computer systems and related security products (for example, network security products and add-on products such as fingerprint scanners and electronic access control tokens). The NCSC uses the security requirements described in the Orange Book as a guide in evaluating security products through its Trusted Product Evaluation Program (TPEP). The final section of this chapter provides a brief summary of NCSC's various evaluation programs. Appendix C, *Orange Book and Other Summaries*, describes these programs in greater detail.

Security Policy Requirements

Security policy requirements are the first set of security requirements defined in the Orange Book. As discussed earlier, a security policy states the rules enforced by the system to provide the necessary degree of security. The Orange Book defines the following specific requirements in the security policy category:

- Discretionary access control.

- Object reuse.

- Labels.

- Mandatory access control.

No Guarantees

An Orange Book rating, even a very high rating, can't guarantee security. A "trusted" system is still only as secure as the enforcement of that system. As discussed in Chapter 5, *Secure System Planning and Administration*, much actual system security is in the hands of your system administrator and/or your security administrator. Your administrative staff must understand the full range of system features, must set up all necessary security structures, and must train users to do their part. The more highly trusted a system is, the less individual users can compromise the system. But system administration remains the vital link between a system's theoretical security and its actual ability to function securely in the real world.

At the lower levels of security, a security policy is informal, and the Orange Book does not even require that it be written; it's simply the underpinnings of the trusted system—the rules that govern it. For B1 systems and above, the Orange Book requires a written security policy. At the higher levels, the security policy becomes increasingly formal and must be expressed in mathematically precise notation.

Discretionary Access Control

Discretionary access control (DAC) is a method of restricting access to files (and other system objects) based on the identity of users and/or the groups to which they belong. DAC is the most common type of access control mechanism found in trusted systems.

What's discretionary about discretionary access control? The DAC requirement specifies that users should be able to protect their own files by indicating who can and cannot access them (on a "need-to-know" basis) and by specifying the type of access allowed (e.g., read-only, read and modify, etc.). In contrast to mandatory access control, in which the system controls access, DAC is applied at the discretion of the user (or a program executing on behalf of the user). With DAC, you can choose to give away your data; with MAC, you can't.

Chapter 3, *Computer System Security and Access Controls*, introduces the concept of discretionary access control, and that discussion is not repeated here. The section "Discretionary Access Control" in that chapter introduces different types of discretionary file protection (file ownership, file protection classes, self/group/public controls, and access control lists).

DAC requirements increase as you move from a C1 system to a C2 system, and again when you move to a B3 system. The main differences are summarized in Table 6-2.

Table 6-2. Discretionary Access Control (DAC) Requirements

Class	Requirement
C1	The system does not need to distinguish between individual users, only between those who are allowed to access a file and those who are not; for example, access to a file might be restricted to members of the WEROK group. At this level, the system also does not need to distinguish between types of access (e.g., read versus write). At this level, a user does not need to own a file (or have any other special privileges) in order to give the file away. The system need not protect newly created files or other objects.
C2, B1, B2	The system must be able to distinguish between individual users. The Orange Book uses the phrase, "These access controls shall be capable of including or excluding access to the granularity of a single user." At this level, a user must have some privilege or permission in order to give the file away; most implementations require that the user be the owner of the file. The system must protect newly created files and other objects.
B3, A1	The system must be able to distinguish between types of access (e.g., read versus write). Access control lists (ACLs) are specifically required. The system must also be able to indicate that a particular user is *not* allowed access. (Many evaluated systems with lower ratings support this feature as well.) In addition, groups must be defined.

For complete information about how to interpret Orange Book requirements for discretionary access control, see the government publication, *A Guide to Understanding Discretionary Access Control in Trusted Systems* (the "Salmon Book").

Object Reuse

Object reuse requirements protect files, memory, and other objects in a trusted system from being accidentally accessed by users who aren't authorized to access them. A system's ordinary access control features determine who can and cannot access files, devices, and other objects that have been assigned to specific users. Object reuse requirements address what happens when these objects are reassigned. Object reuse requirements apply to systems rated at C2 and above.

Consider a few obvious examples of what could happen if object reuse features are not part of a trusted system. Suppose that when you create a new file your system allocates a certain area of disk to that file. You store confidential data in the file, print it, and eventually delete it. But suppose the system doesn't actually delete the data from the physical disk, but simply rewrites the header of the file to indicate deletion. There are many ways to bypass ordinary system procedures and read the data on the disk without using the normal file system.

Consider another example. Suppose that Jack J. Hacke (whose login ID is JJH) has left your company (perhaps under a cloud), and that a year later June J. Hacke arrives on the scene. The administrator assigns June a login ID (Jack's old ID, JJH). The danger is that Jack's ID might still exist somewhere in the system—for example, in an Access Control List showing the users authorized to access a file, as a member of a group, or as the owner of a disk or tape. Because the same ID is now reassigned to June, she may find that she has access to certain information previously available to Jack—information that she wouldn't have been able to access if she followed normal system access rules.

Object reuse features provide security by ensuring that when an object—for example, a login ID—is assigned, allocated, or reallocated, the object doesn't contain data left over from previous usage. In the first example above, object reuse features would erase the data by overwriting it, so it wouldn't be possible for anyone to retrieve it from the disk. In the second example, object reuse features might maintain a file containing the IDs of users deleted from the system; when a new user is added to the system, the system could check this file to ensure that the ID doesn't duplicate a previously assigned one.

With the increasing availability of intelligent terminals and printers, object reuse issues have broadened. Often, information is copied into the local storage of a terminal or a printer without the user's knowledge. For example, printer spoolers buffer individual print pages, or even entire copies of documents, in local memory. Terminals store multiple screens so you can page through them. The danger of these features is that when you log out, the buffered pages and screens may not be cleared. In trusted systems, object reuse features ensure that local memory is cleared on logout or at the end of printing a job.

Common object reuse features implemented in trusted systems include:

- Clearing memory blocks or pages before they are allocated to a program or data.

- Clearing disk blocks when a file is scratched or before the blocks are allocated to a file.

- Degaussing magnetic tapes when they're no longer needed.

- Clearing X Window System objects before they are reassigned to another user.

- Erasing password buffers after encryption.

- Clearing buffered pages, documents, or screens from the local memory of a terminal or printer.

Depending on the level of security, features may be available at the administrator's or user's option. For example, a tape initialization program may offer an erase option. Because erasing, rather than reinitializing, takes extra time, the user or administrator might be required to invoke the option only when sensitive material is present on the tape.

Labels

The section "Mandatory Access Control" in Chapter 3, *Computer System Security and Access Controls*, introduces sensitivity labels, describes briefly the use of classifications and compartments, and discusses how mandatory access controls use these sensitivity labels to determine who can access what information in your system. The discussion that follows supplements the discussion in Chapter 3 by focusing on specific Orange Book labeling requirements.

Labels and mandatory access control are separate security policy requirements, but they work together. Beginning at the B1 level, the Orange Book requires that every subject (e.g., user, process) and storage object (e.g., file, directory, window, socket) have a sensitivity label associated with it. (For B2 systems and above, *all* system resources (e.g., devices, ROM) must have sensitivity labels.) A user's sensitivity label specifies the sensitivity level, or level of trust, associated with that user; a user's sensitivity label is usually called a *clearance*. A file's sensitivity label specifies the level of trust that a user must have to be able to access that file.

Label Integrity

Label integrity ensures that the sensitivity labels associated with subjects and objects are accurate representations of the security levels of these subjects and objects. Thus, a file sensitivity label, such as:

TOP SECRET [VENUS]

must actually be associated with a TOP SECRET file containing information about the planet Venus. A clearance, such as:

COMPANY CONFIDENTIAL [PAYROLL AUDIT]

must be assigned to an accountant who's responsible for the payroll and auditing activities in your company. Similarly, when information is exported (as discussed in the next few sections), the sensitivity label written on the output must match the internal labels of the information exported.

Suppose that a user edits a TOP SECRET file to remove all TOP SECRET and SECRET information (leaving only UNCLASSIFIED information), and then changes the sensitivity label to UNCLASSIFIED. If the system crashes at this point, has it ensured that the label didn't get written to disk before the changes to the file were written? If such a thing could happen, you'd end up with a file labeled UNCLASSIFIED that actually did contain TOP SECRET data—a clear violation of label integrity. Systems rated at B1 and above must prove that their label integrity features guard against such violations.

Exportation of Labeled Information

A trusted system must be sure that when information is written by the system, that information continues to have protection mechanisms associated with it. Two important ways of securing exported information are to assign security levels to output devices, and to write sensitivity labels along with data. Systems rated at B1 and above must provide secure export facilities.

The Orange Book defines two types of export devices: multi-level and single-level. Every I/O device and communications channel in a system must be designated as one type or the other. Any changes to these designations must be able to be audited. Typically, a system administrator designates devices during system installation and setup.

Exportation to Multi-level Devices. A *multi-level device* or a *multi-level communications channel* is one to which you can write information at a number of different sensitivity levels. The system must support a way of specifying the lowest (e.g., UNCLASSIFIED) and the highest (e.g., TOP SECRET) security levels allowed for data being written to such a device.

When you write information to a multi-level device, the Orange Book requires that the system have some way to associate a security level with it. Mechanisms may differ for different systems and different types of devices. Files written to such devices must have sensitivity levels attached to them (usually written in a header record preceding the data in the file). This prevents a user from bypassing system controls by simply copying a sensitive file to another, untrusted system or device. Of course, there must be system controls on what devices can actually be used in this way—and what happens to the transferred data. A sensitivity label on a file isn't much protection if a user can simply carry a diskette home, or can post the file to an electronic bulletin board. In most trusted systems, only disks are categorized as multi-level devices.

Exportation to Single-level Devices. A *single-level device* or a *single-level communications channel* is one to which you can write information at only one particular sensitivity level. Usually, terminals, printers, tape drives, and communication ports are categorized as single-level devices. The level you specify for a device is usually dependent on its physical location or the inherent security of the device type. For example, your installation might locate printers in a number of different computer rooms and offices. You'd designate these printers as having sensitivity levels corresponding to the personnel who have access to the printers.

You might designate a printer in a public area as UNCLASSIFIED, whereas a printer in a highly protected office used only by an individual with a TOP SECRET clearance might be designated TOP SECRET. Once you've designated a device in this way, the system will be able to send to that device only information at the level associated with the device.

Unlike output sent to multi-level devices, output sent to single-level devices is *not* required to be labeled with the security level of the exported information, although many trusted systems do label such output. The Orange Book does require that there be some way (system or procedural) to designate the single level of information being sent to the device.

Labeling Human-readable Output. The Orange Book has very clear requirements for how to label hard-copy output (output that people can see). This includes pages of printed output, maps, graphics, and other displays. The system administrator must have some way of specifying the labels that are to appear on the output.

Two types of labels are required: First, each distinct output must be labeled, at the beginning and the end, with labels that represent the overall sensitivity of the output. If you're printing the contents of a file, you'll typically see a banner page before and after the file contents, clearly showing the file's sensitivity label. An example of a banner page printed by the SecureWare CMW+ system (certified at the B1 level) appears in Figure 6-2.

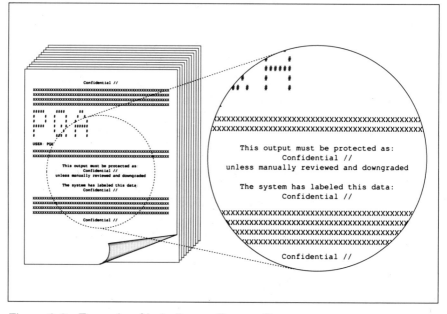

Figure 6-2. Example of Labeling on Banner Page

Second, each page of printed output must be labeled, at the top and the bottom, with labels that represent either the overall sensitivity of the output (e.g., the file sensitivity label) or the specific sensitivity of the information on that page. You'll typically see a page header and footer such as the following:

```
Confidential //
```

What do these labeling distinctions really mean? If you're printing a report containing a set of interview notes, some more sensitive than others, your system *must* label the beginning and end of the report with the highest sensitivity label of the interviews included. If one is TOP SECRET, and the rest are CONFIDENTIAL, the output must be labeled TOP SECRET. The categories (e.g., VENUS, ALPHA) included on the output must show all of the categories represented by the interviews included, but no other categories.

With the individual interviews, the Orange Book gives you a choice. You can either label (at the top and bottom of each page) all of them TOP SECRET, or you can label each appropriately (TOP SECRET for the super-sensitive one, CONFIDENTIAL for the rest), with the appropriate categories included for each interview. In the second case, the system must provide a method for you to enter and store labels for individual interviews.

Clearly, physical controls are essential to make hard-copy labeling more than an empty exercise. The operator or other individual tending the printers at your site must obviously be cleared to the level of the most sensitive information being sent to those printers. He or she must also distribute the output properly—not just leave it all in a pile somewhere for anyone to see.

Subject Sensitivity Labels

The *subject sensitivity label* requirement states that the system must notify a terminal user of any change in the security level associated with that user during an interactive session. This requirement applies to systems rated at B2 and above.

The idea of subject sensitivity labels is that you must always know what security level you're working at. Trusted systems typically display your clearance when you log in, and redisplay it if the security level changes, either automatically or at the user's request.

You may not always work at the highest level of security you're allowed to see. For example, if you have a TOP SECRET clearance, you might work at a SECRET level during a particular interactive session if, for example, you're working in a public place in the presence of a coworker who isn't cleared at the TOP SECRET level. If you do this, you'll usually be allowed to change to either a higher (TOP SECRET) or lower (CONFIDENTIAL or UNCLASSIFIED) level later in the session.

Device Labels

The *device labels* requirement states that each physical device attached to your system must have minimum and maximum security levels associated with them, and that these levels are to be used to "enforce constraints imposed by the physical environments in which the devices are located."

For a multi-level device, you'll have to specify the lowest level of information that can be sent to that device (the minimum for the device) and the highest level of information that can be sent to that device (the maximum for the device). For a single-level device, the minimum is the same as the maximum.

We've already discussed how the export of information to devices must take into account where those devices are located. Obviously, the export of sensitive information to publicly available devices would defeat the purpose of mandatory access controls. This Orange Book requirement makes that obvious conclusion an actual necessity for evaluation.

Because of its close association with exporting output to multi-level and single-level devices, the device labels requirement is usually easily met by systems supporting mandatory access controls, even though the requirement isn't required until the B2 level.

Mandatory Access Control

Mandatory access control (MAC) is the final security policy requirement. Unlike discretionary access control (DAC), which allows users to specify, at their own discretion, who can and cannot share their files, mandatory access control puts all such access decisions under the control of the system. The section "Mandatory Access Control" in Chapter 3 introduces the rules for when a user with a particular clearance may and may not be able to access a file with a particular sensitivity label.

Accountability Requirements

Accountability requirements are the second set of security requirements defined in the Orange Book. Accountability is the idea that the system knows who you are and what you're doing. The system must be able to identify all users of the system, must use information about your identity to decide whether you can legitimately access information, and must keep track of any security-related actions you take in the system (so you can't get away with doing anything you're not authorized to do).

The accountability requirements specified in the Orange Book are:

- Identification and authentication.

- Trusted path.

- Audit.

Identification and Authentication

Identification and authentication (I&A) is a requirement at all levels of system security. The Orange Book requires you to identify yourself to the system before performing any work that will require interaction with the TCB (e.g., running a program, reading a file, or invoking any function that requires the system to check your access rights). In most multi-user systems, you identify yourself to the system by entering some kind of login identifier, followed by a password, as described in "System Access: Logging Into Your System" in Chapter 3.

Most systems require you to log in regardless of who you are or what functions you intend to perform, although some systems allow certain types of users to access certain system functions without logging in. (An example is a system operator who needs to perform quick maintenance operations in a physically protected computer room. At the lower levels of security, this scenario might be allowed; at the higher levels, it would not.)

NOTE

The Orange Book states that passwords must be protected, but not how. Two additional government publications provide more concrete suggestions: The *Department of Defense Password Management Guideline* (the "Green Book"), and FIPS PUB 112—*Password Usage*. The Green Book advocates three major password features:

- Users should be able to change their own passwords.

- Passwords should be machine-generated rather than user-created.

- Certain audit reports (e.g., date and time of last login) should be provided by the system directly to the user.

It also provides a set of specific guidelines for good password development and user practices. These are incorporated into the discussion of passwords in Chapter 3, *Computer System Security and Access Controls*. Most trusted systems comply explicitly with the Green Book.

At higher levels of security, the login procedure may involve prompts for a security level or a clearance. In this case, you can enter a security level up to your clearance. The system checks the level you've entered against the clearance stored in your security profile. For example, if your clearance is SECRET, you can enter a clearance of CONFIDENTIAL to indicate that you'll be working at a CONFIDENTIAL level during this session; you can't override security by entering a level of TOP SECRET.

Specific identification and authentication requirements are summarized in Table 6-3.

Table 6-3. Identification and Authentication (I&A) Requirements

Class	Requirement
C1	The system distinguishes only between authorized users and unauthorized users; authorized users log into the system in some fashion, but do not need to have individual login IDs.
C2 and above	At all levels above C1, the Orange Book requires individual accountability. Each user has an individual ID. The login ID must be a unique identifier, not a company, department, group, or terminal ID.
	Once you've successfully logged in, the system uses your ID, and the security profile associated with it, to make access decisions. For example, if you attempt to modify a sensitive file, the system is able to check your authenticated user ID against the list of IDs representing users who are authorized to view and modify the data in that file. Only if your ID appears in that list will the system allow you to access the file.
	The system also uses your ID to audit your actions—that is, to keep track of what you're doing in the system. If Jack Hacke repeatedly tries to access files he's not authorized to view, the system will *know!* The section "Audit" describes how this tracking takes place.

Trusted Path

A *trusted path* provides an unmistakable means by which a user (typically at a terminal or a workstation) can communicate directly with the TCB without having to interact with the system through untrusted (and possibly untrustworthy) applications and layers of the operating system. A trusted path is a requirement for systems rated at B2 and above.

The simplest approach to implementing a trusted path is also the most expensive and the most unwieldy. Supply each user with two terminals—one is hardwired to the TCB and is used for communication with the TCB (for certain security-critical functions such as logging in, changing sensitivity labels and security levels, etc.); the other is used for ordinary work. Because this isn't a very practical approach, most trusted paths involve setting up a particular key sequence on a terminal that signals the TCB to halt any (possibly untrustworthy) process that is running on the terminal and to establish the direct link to the TCB. The key sequence must be one that's used *only* to invoke secure software, and one that untrusted software can't intercept or spoof.

For example, on the VAX/VMS Version 4.3 system, the secure terminal server feature provides an optional trusted path. Before logging in, you press the BREAK key, followed by the RETURN key. This sequence invokes the VAX/VMS secure terminal server feature (if it has been enabled by the security manager). The system halts any currently executing process for the terminal (including any spoof programs) and invokes the trusted login process on your behalf. It thereby ensures that the TCB login program, not any other mimicking process, is in control.

Why is a trusted path important? A trusted path is the flip side of the identification and authentication requirement. Identification and authentication mechanisms authenticate the user; they guarantee to the TCB that the user is entitled to gain access to the system. Trusted path mechanisms, on the other hand, authenticate the TCB; they guarantee to the user that he or she is communicating with trusted software, not with some other intermediary program or process that might mimic the trusted software—for example, to spoof you into giving away your password. Because a trusted path is a direct communication link between the user and the TCB, it avoids the need to interact with untrusted system or application software in which a Trojan horse or some other peril might lurk. (See the discussion of Trojan horses, viruses, worms, and other dangerous wildlife in Chapter 4, *Viruses and Other Wildlife*.)

The type of terminal hardware has a significant impact on the implementation of a trusted path. If an intelligent terminal or a personal computer is being used as a terminal, it becomes more difficult to ensure that a path is trusted. For example, some intelligent terminals have escape sequences that tell the terminal to send the current line to the system as if it had just been entered by the user. A personal computer, even if it is used solely as a terminal, nevertheless has the capability of running applications that can result in inadvertent or deliberate access or damage to secure information. Some vendors have met the trusted path requirement by stipulating that dumb terminals must be used in the system configuration. Systems utilizing PCs as terminals may involve evaluation of the PC software as well as the host software and, often, the development of a TCB on the PC itself.

Compartmented mode workstations (CMWs) typically implement the trusted path feature through functions based on the X Window System. CMW windowing capabilities prohibit user processes from reading or writing the screen during initial login and authentication; no windows are displayed on the screen during this phase. CMWs typically reserve a portion of the screen and a portion of each window only for trusted path communication. For example, the SecureWare CMW+ system allows you to invoke a trusted path menu in several ways; the most common is to click on a trusted path button that appears on each top-level window's label bar. When you do this, a menu such as the one shown in Figure 6-3 allows you to select such security-critical functions as changing a password, changing file or window labels, or shutting down the system.

For information about these workstations, see "Compartmented Mode Workstations" later in this chapter.

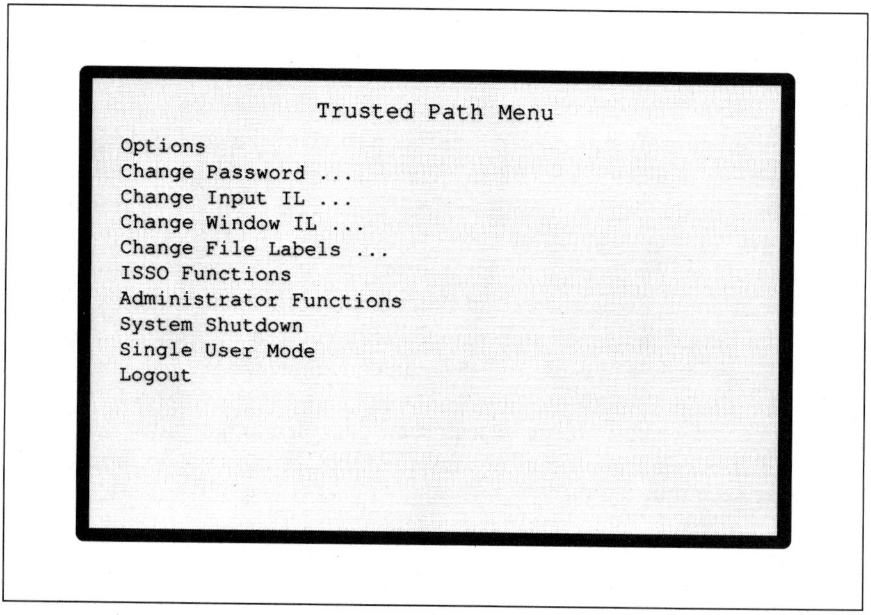

```
                    Trusted Path Menu
      Options
      Change Password ...
      Change Input IL ...
      Change Window IL ...
      Change File Labels ...
      ISSO Functions
      Administrator Functions
      System Shutdown
      Single User Mode
      Logout
```

Figure 6-3. Sample Trusted Path Menu

Audit

Auditing is the recording, examining, and reviewing of security-related activities in a trusted system. A security-related activity is any activity that relates to a subject's access of an object. In audit terms, such activities are often called events, and auditing itself is sometimes called event logging.

Typical events include:

*   Logons (successful or unsuccessful).

*   Logouts.

*   Remote system accesses.

- File opens, closes, renames, and deletions.

- Changes in privileges or security attributes (e.g., a change in a file's sensitivity label or a user's clearance).

Why audit these events? The primary reason is that even the most secure system is vulnerable to attack, and auditing provides an excellent way of determining whether and how such attacks may take place.

Beginning at the C2 level, the Orange Book requires auditing. Your authenticated ID must be able to be associated with all auditable actions that you perform. Audit trails produced by the system show the ID of the user who initiated each action. This means that if you try to log in (whether you succeed or fail), if you try to access a file you're not entitled to see, or if you try to assume the privileges of the system administrator, the system knows!

Auditing lets you perform two very useful security functions: surveillance and reconstruction. *Surveillance* is the monitoring of user activity. This type of auditing might prevent security violations from occurring, if only because users know they're being observed. *Reconstruction* is the ability to put together, in the event of a security violation, a record of what happened, what needs to be fixed, and who's responsible.

Each time an auditable event occurs, the system writes at least the following information (mandated by the Orange Book) to the audit trail:

- Date and time of the event.

- Unique ID of the user who initiated the event.

- Type of event.

- Success or failure.

- Origin of the request (e.g., terminal ID).

- Name of object involved (e.g., file being deleted).

- Description of modifications to security databases.

- Subject and object security levels (B1 and above).

An example of an audit log displayed by the Wang SVS/OS CAP 1.0 system (rated C2) is shown in Figure 6-4.

Wang VS Security Log
Events Logged on May 10, 1991

Page 9

Time	Subject Jobname	UID	@WS	Event (* = Violation)	Data	Recorder Jobname	UID	@WS
16:02:08.2		SRH	84	CHANGE ACCESS LISTS CHANGE ACL	File: @1602079 Lib: WPPSRH Vol: SYS400 Owner: SRH Fileclass: New: ( ) PART 1 OF 1		SRH	84
16:02:08.9		SRH	84	CHANGE FILE ATTRIBUTES	File: @1602079 Lib: WPPSRH Vol: SYS400 Owner: SRH Fileclass: Attribute: EXPIRATIONDATE Old: 91130 New: 91129		SRH	84
16:02:09.0		SRH	84	OPEN FOR POSSIBLE MOD	File: @1602079 Lib: WPPSRH Vol: SYS400 Owner: SRH Fileclass: Device: DISK Open Mode: OPEN FOR IO MODE		SRH	84
16:02:20.6		SRH	84	RENAME	OFile: @1602079 OLib: WPPSRH OVol: SYS400 NFile: AF010838 NLib: WPPSRH Owner: SRH Fileclass: Type: RENAME OF A FILE		SRH	84
16:02:20.7		SRH	84	CLOSE	File: AF010838 Lib: WPPSRH Vol: SYS400 Device: DISK 257 I/O cnt: 2 Open Mode: OPEN FOR IO MODE		SRH	84
16:02:39.5		SRH	84	SCRATCH	File: @160237 Lib: #027000W Vol: SYSCAP Owner: SRH Fileclass:		SRH	84
16:02:42.4		SRH	84	PROGRAM INVOCATION	File: WPEMUSSL Lib: @SYSTEM@ Vol: SYSCAP Owner: WJT Fileclass:		SRH	84
16:02:42.8		SRH	84	OPEN FOR POSSIBLE MOD	File: @1602414 Lib: WPPSRH Vol: SYS400 Owner: SRH Fileclass: Device: DISK Open Mode: OPEN FOR IO MODE		SRH	84
16:02:43.4		SRH	84	SCRATCH	File: @AF010838 Lib: #WPPSRH Vol: SYS400 Owner: SRH Fileclass:		SRH	84

Figure 6-4. Sample Audit Output

Although the Orange Book specifies examples of events that must be audited, to a large extent an individual site determines the precise set of events. As you move from a lower to a higher evaluation class, the number and type of auditable events increases, as shown in Table 6-4 later in this section.

Auditing is a vital system administration tool. By observing patterns of suspicious activity (e.g., a large number of login failures from a particular terminal, or a user's repeated attempts to read files he's not allowed to access), you can effectively monitor the security of your system. You can see who's trying to bypass protection mechanisms—either deliberately or inadvertently—and you can use this information to deter such attempts in the future.

What do you do with the information you collect? That's up to you and your management. You might confront deliberate offenders. You might decide to provide additional training in security-related areas. You might take immediate action, such as shutting down vulnerable ports or locking certain office doors.

Auditing interacts with many of the other Orange Book requirements—in particular, with identification and authentication. Once the system has authenticated your identity (that is, confirmed that you are who you say you are), your ID is an unchangeable stamp that's associated with every process you create and every program you run.

Audit data tends to be voluminous (imagine several hundred users and fifty or more auditable events)—in fact, so voluminous that it can cease to be useful because no one is willing to wade through it all. Therefore, a trusted system must provide tools allowing the system administrator to audit selectively. The Orange Book requires that you offer selective collection and reduction tools for auditing. *Selective collection* allows you to produce a report showing just one user's (perhaps suspicious) activities. *Selective reduction* allows you to boil down, or extract from, audit data that's already been collected.

Most vendors provide utilities allowing audit trails to be printed for particular users, particular types of events, or particular files. Typical event types include system events (e.g., operator messages), file events (e.g., file opens and closes), and user events (e.g., user logins and logouts). Other techniques for audit implementation include data compression; special handling for storage media (for example, to ensure that audit data is not lost when the disk fills up); and the use of write-once devices (to ensure that audit data can't be modified).

Specific Orange Book audit requirements are summarized in Table 6-4.

Table 6-4. Audit Requirements

Class	Requirements
C2	The system must audit security-related events and must protect audit data. A related identification and authentication requirement states that the system must associate a user's identity with all auditable actions taken by that user. The system must be able to audit selectively by user.
B1	The system must be able to audit any changes in security levels. Any security overrides must be audited. The system must be able to audit selectively by security level (e.g., all users with TOP SECRET clearances).
B2	The system must audit events that might be used to exploit covert storage channels. (See the section "Covert Channel Analysis" later in this chapter.)
B3, A1	The system must be able to monitor the accumulation of security events that may indicate an "imminent violation of security policy." The mechanism must notify the system administrator in some fashion—for example, by sounding an alarm or sending a particular type of message—when certain predefined thresholds are exceeded, and must take what the Orange Book calls "the least disruptive action to terminate the event." This might involve logging an offending user off the system.

You'll want to consider how your own site ought to proceed in case evidence of a system intruder is found. Instead of immediately logging a caught-in-the-act intruder off the system (clearly sending the message that he's been discovered), it might make a lot more sense to observe the activity for awhile (while ensuring that vital data is not compromised), and try to find out more about the intruder's identity. In *The Cuckoo's Egg*, Cliff Stoll describes how he did just this. Stoll's book is highly recommended for both entertainment and instruction.

For complete information about how to interpret Orange Book requirements for auditing, see the government publication, *A Guide to Understanding Audit in Trusted Systems* (the "Tan Book").

Assurance Requirements

Assurance requirements are the third set of security requirements defined in the Orange Book. Assurance is a guarantee (or at least a reasonable confidence) that the security policy of a trusted system has been implemented correctly and that the system's security features accurately carry out that security policy.

The Orange Book identifies two types of assurance: operational assurance and life-cycle assurance. *Operational assurance* focuses on the basic architecture and features of the system. *Life-cycle assurance* focuses on controls and standards for building and maintaining the system.

As you move up the ladder from less trusted to more trusted systems, you'll encounter more and more assurance requirements. In fact, at the highest levels (B3 and A1), there are very few additional security features beyond those available in lower-level systems; highly secure systems are distinguished primarily by the far greater assurance, or trust, that can be placed in the security features.

The operational assurance requirements specified in the Orange Book are:

- System architecture.

- System integrity.

- Covert channel analysis.

- Trusted facility management.

- Trusted recovery.

The life-cycle assurance requirements specified in the Orange Book are:

- Security testing.

- Design specification and verification.

- Configuration management.

- Trusted distribution.

Operational Assurance

Operational assurance features ensure that the architecture of a trusted system and its specific implementation enforce the system's security policy. An example of a key operational assurance is a feature that clearly separates security-relevant code from user code in the system's memory.

System Architecture

The *system architecture* requirement has to do with the way a system is designed to make security possible—if not inevitable.

Although systems at the lower levels (C1 through B1 or even B2) need not be designed specifically for security, they must support sound principles of hardware and operating system design, as well as the ability to support specific security features that might be added to these systems. Most well-designed modern multi-processing, multi-user systems follow the key design principles necessary to satisfy Orange Book system architecture requirements through at least C2 or B1, although these principles aren't necessarily oriented to security. For example, the protection features that keep users from destroying each others' programs and data, and provide users with timely, reliable service, are clearly needed in any operating system, but they're security features too.

Those familiar with the Orange Book say that almost any system can evolve into a B1 or even a B2 system, but B3 and higher systems must be born that way. It's almost impossible simply to pile on security features to achieve a high system rating. Retrofitting a system to satisfy the higher-level requirements can't readily be done, because these requirements demand less, not more—less complexity, simpler semantics, and a clearer separation between protection-critical and non-critical modules.

System design is a large and complicated topic, and it's not one to which we can do justice in a few paragraphs. This section only touches on a few key principles of good design that are emphasized in the Orange Book. The details of how these principles are translated into specific system architectures are not in the province of this book. If you're a system user, the details of system design are probably not of concern to you (as long as your system continues to work properly).

The Orange Book requires architectural features such as those summarized in Table 6-5.

Table 6-5. System Architecture Requirements

Class	Requirement
All classes	A protected execution domain for security-relevant functions (protected from both deliberate tampering and inadvertent modification). For example, this means that privileged programs (such as those that audit security events) can't be interfered with by user programs. The Orange Book dictates that the TCB must maintain its own domain, free from external interference or tampering.
	Some systems have a clear distinction between user and system areas. Other systems have more complex, ring-based architectures in which there may be as many as ten distinct, increasingly more privileged domains. In a typical ring-based architecture, the TCB, or security kernel, occupies the innermost ring; user programs occupy the outermost ring; in between are such intermediate processes as operating system services and administrative programs.
All classes	Protection of resources so they're subject to access control and auditing. This includes the protection of obvious security-critical resources—for example, such techniques as putting an access control list on the password file—as well as the protection of user files so they won't be erroneously or deliberately accessed by other users.
B1 and above	Process isolation through distinct address spaces. This ensures that when multiple processes run concurrently, they won't interfere with each other—by accident or design—by writing each other's memory, changing each other's instructions, and so on. It also ensures that the system can keep track of everything it needs (e.g., registers, status information) to switch from one process to another, an essential element of a multi-processing system. Virtual memory techniques are often used to keep multiple processes each in their own virtual address spaces without interfering with, or even being aware of, each other.

Table 6-5. System Architecture Requirements (continued)

Class	Requirement
B2 and above	TCB modularity and the enforcement of *least privilege* in the design of these modules. Least privilege has a number of meanings in a trusted system. In terms of system architecture, it means that processes have no more privilege than they need to perform their functions. Only those modules that really need complete system privileges are to be located in the security kernel (e.g., in the innermost ring). Other, less critical, modules should call on more privileged routines only as needed and only for the duration of the needed operation.
B2 and above	Hardware features such as segmentation. Segmentation is a hardware protection feature. Systems supporting segmentation divide their virtual memory into segments. A process occupies as many of these segments as it needs when it executes. Typically, segments are of several types. System processes can access all types; user processes cannot access segments that are restricted to system use. Certain instructions are restricted and can be issued only by privileged system processes. The result is that unprivileged user processes cannot access or modify the memory used by the operating system.
B3 and above	A precise and simple protection mechanism that enforces such features as layering, abstraction, and data hiding. Systems of this kind have a very structured, hierarchical design in which system functions are layered. The lower layers of the hierarchy perform certain basic functions; the higher layers may perform more complex functions. Layers communicate with each other through calls via clearly defined interfaces. Data hiding means that a layer in the hierarchy has no access to data outside itself; data handled by other layers is hidden.

System Integrity

System integrity means that the hardware and firmware must work and must be tested to ensure that they keep working. For all levels, the Orange Book states that "Hardware and software features shall be provided that can be used to periodically validate the correct operation of the on-site hardware and firmware elements of the TCB."

Clearly, system integrity is a vitally important goal for all system developers, not only developers of trusted systems. As we've mentioned before, a very important element of system security is the ability of that system to function as expected and to remain available for operation.

Many vendors meet the system integrity requirement by providing a set of integrity tests. Unlike most tests, which are run only during an initial testing phase, integrity tests are a regular exercise. A typical approach is to run through integrity tests for hardware and firmware components (e.g., CPU, memory, controllers, peripheral devices) each time the system is powered up. The system will not boot unless the tests work successfully. More substantial diagnostics are usually performed at scheduled preventive maintenance periods.

Covert Channel Analysis

A *covert channel* is an information path that's not ordinarily used for communication in a system and therefore isn't protected by the system's normal security mechanisms. Covert channels have a nice subversive sound to them. They're a secret way to convey information to another person or program—the computer equivalent of a spy carrying a newspaper as a signal: *The New York Times* means the blueprints have been smuggled out of the plant, and *The Washington Post* means there's been a problem.

In theory, virtually every piece of information stored in or processed by a secure computer system is a potential covert channel. The reason covert channels aren't more of a problem is that getting meaningful information in this way is quite cumbersome. The Orange Book wisely reserves covert channel analysis and protection mechanisms for the highest levels of security (B2 systems and above), where the information gained by exploiting covert channels is more likely to be worth the quest.

There are two types of covert channels: storage channels and timing channels. *Storage channels* convey information by changing stored system data of some kind. *Timing channels* convey information by affecting performance or otherwise modifying timing by using a system resource in some measurable way.

Specific Orange Book covert channel requirements are summarized in Table 6-6.

Table 6-6. Covert Channel Requirements

Class	Requirement
B2	The system must protect against covert storage channels. System developers must perform a "covert channel analysis" (a thorough search), often using information flow methods, for all covert storage channels.
B3, A1	The system must protect against both covert storage channels and covert timing channels. System developers must perform a covert channel analysis for both types of covert channels.

The Orange Book also recognizes that, because covert channels are so endemic in systems—however secure—and because they typically convey such a small amount of information, there needs to be some sensible way of determining how bad a particular covert channel is. "A Guideline on Covert Channels," included in the Orange Book, uses the concept of a bandwidth to quantify covert channels.

A *bandwidth* is the rate at which the covert channel can convey information; the Orange Book measures bandwidth in bits per second. It specifies both the bandwidth that is considered "too high" for evaluation (currently 100 bits per second) and also stipulates that systems must audit the use of covert channels with bandwidths exceeding 1 bit in ten seconds. Part of the covert channel analysis involves determining the bandwidth (by measurement or engineering estimation). At the A1 level, the covert channel analysis must be performed using formal methods. (See "Design Specification and Verification" for information about these methods.)

Covert channels are much more of an issue in networks than they are in operating systems. In networks, there are simply many more places for channels to hide. It's also the case that in networks there are certain techniques, like noise and traffic generation, that can limit the effectiveness of covert channels. See Chapter 8, *Communications and Network Security*, for more information.

Covert Storage Channels. Covert storage channels convey information via small changes in data—or even by the presence of the data itself.

A simple example of exploiting a covert storage channel involves changing a name of some kind to convey information. The number of characters available in a filename, a group name, or a directory name provides a reasonable amount of information, as do the field names on reports. For example, consider a somewhat implausible case where you change filename JULY_ACCOUNTS to JULY_ACCOUNTS_JJHOKI8IT (where JJH and OKI8IT are a login ID and password that can be used to penetrate the system).

A more plausible example involves changing the characteristics of objects in the system; for example, the amount of free space on the hard disk. A program with access to TOP SECRET information could convey information to a less secure program by changing the amount or the pattern of free space—perhaps even using patterns corresponding to Morse code. Using all the processes available in the system, or filling an entire disk with garbage, provides a dramatic way to convey information. Changing the characteristics of files—for example, changing the length, the modification date, or even the security protection of a file—is another example of exploiting a covert channel. Even changing the format (e.g., the spacing or alignment) of a message or a report can potentially provide information.

The examples mentioned above imply that you're using covert channels to convey information to a partner in crime—or more typically that a Trojan horse that's been planted somewhere in the system is reporting information to someone. But other types of covert channels may quite inadvertently leak valuable system information simply by revealing their existence. Consider a login message that repeatedly prompts you to enter a login ID, corrects your syntax by helpfully informing you that the "Login ID cannot exceed three characters," and then, after you've finally made a lucky guess, prompts for the associated password. Or consider what happens when you try to create a new file, group, or directory. If the system tells you that a file of that name already exists, you've learned something. Now you can figure out how to break into that particular file.

Covert Timing Channels. Obtaining information via covert timing channels may seem even more implausible, but such methods have been used to breach system security. Timing channels typically work by taking advantage of some kind of system clock or other timing device. Information is conveyed by such timing considerations as the elapsed time required to perform an operation, the percentage of CPU time expended, and the time occurring between two events.

By modulating the use of a system resource very slightly (for example, by slowing down processing by running a subroutine multiple times, by inserting a meaningless loop in a process, or by performing a repetitive user function, such as displaying directory contents), you can use the slight change in system timing and performance to convey some small amount of information.

Trusted Facility Management

Trusted facility management is the assignment of a specific individual to administer the security-related functions of a system. It's somewhat surprising that trusted facility management is an assurance requirement only for highly secure systems (B2, B3, and A1), because so many systems evaluated at lower levels of security are structured to try to meet this requirement.

Trusted facility management is closely related to the concept of *least privilege*, a concept introduced earlier in terms of system architecture. In the context of trusted facility management, least privilege means that the users in a system should have the least number of privileges—and for the shortest amount of time—needed to do their work. It's also related to the administrative concept of *separation of duties*, the idea that it's better to assign pieces of security-related tasks to several specific individuals; if no one user has total control of the system's security mechanisms, no one user can completely compromise the system.

The section "Separation of Duties" in Chapter 5, *Secure System Planning and Administration*, outlines the different roles that users may assume in trusted systems, and summarizes the major responsibilities of the system administrator, the security administrator (sometimes called the information systems security officer, or ISSO), and the operator.

Specific Orange Book requirements for trusted facility management are summarized in Table 6-7.

Table 6-7. Trusted Facility Management Requirements

Class	Requirement
B2	The system must support separate operator and administrator roles.
B3, A1	The system must clearly identify the functions of a security administrator, whose job role is limited, as much as possible, to performing security-related functions. The security administrator and the system administrator/operator need not be different people necessarily, but their roles must be clearly divided. Whenever the system administrator assumes the role of security administrator, this role change must be audited. The security administrator's job is to perform security functions; non-security functions are strictly limited.

Trusted Recovery

Trusted recovery ensures that security is not breached when a system crash or some other system failure occurs. Trusted recovery is required only for B3 and A1 systems.

Trusted recovery actually involves two activities: preparing for a system failure and recovering the system.

Your main preparation responsibility is to back up all system-critical files on a regular basis. The recovery procedure will be far more straightforward if you are restoring only a day or two of processing. (See the discussion of "Performing Backups" in Chapter 5.) If an unexpected system failure such as a crash or a power outage occurs, you will be called upon to recover the system according to certain procedures that ensure the continuing security of the system. These procedures may also be required if you detect a system problem, such as a missing resource, an inconsistent database, or any kind of system compromise, and you need to halt and reboot the system.

A system failure represents a possibly serious security risk because it is a time when the system is not functioning in the ordinary way. For example, if the system crashes while sensitive data is being written to disk (where it is protected by the system's access control mechanisms), the possibility exists that the data will be left unprotected in memory.

Trusted recovery requirements involve both software mechanisms and administrative procedures. It is the responsibility of the system administrator to halt the system when an error occurs, and to run the necessary trusted recovery programs before letting other users access the system.

Specific trusted recovery procedures depend upon your own system's requirements. Typical recovery activities include the following:

- Reboot the system to get it running in single-user mode.

- Recover all file systems that were active at the time of the system failure.

- Restore any missing or damaged files and databases from the most recent backups.

- Recover required security characteristics—for example, file security labels.

- Check security-critical files, such as the file containing system passwords.

Once you have performed all necessary trusted recovery procedures, you can be sure that system data cannot be compromised, and you can let other users access the system.

Life-cycle Assurance

Life-cycle assurance features ensure that a trusted system is designed, developed, and maintained with formal and rigidly controlled standards. These features are basically human administrative controls. Because so much trust is placed in the system's basic hardware and software capabilities, it's vital to protect that hardware and software from tampering or inadvertent modification at any stage in the system's life cycle—during design, development, testing, updating, or distribution. An example of a key life-cycle assurance is configuration management, which carefully monitors and protects all changes to the system's hardware, software, firmware, test suites, and documentation.

Security Testing

As you might expect, the Orange Book has a substantial interest in testing the security features in evaluated systems. The *security testing* assurance requirement is closely related to the test documentation requirement (see "Test Documentation"). The system developer tests all security features, ensures that the system works as described in the documentation, and documents the results of testing these features. The NCSC evaluation team then undertakes its own testing.

There are two basic types of security testing: mechanism testing and interface testing. *Mechanism testing* means testing of security mechanisms; these mechanisms include discretionary access control, labeling, mandatory access control, identification and authentication, trusted path, and auditing. *Interface testing* means testing all user routines that invoke security functions (i.e., those that are at the user interface of the TCB).

Different types of testing are considered adequate at different security levels. At the C1, C2, and B1 levels, mechanism testing is usually sufficient. At the B2, B3, and A1 levels, interface testing of every interface is required.

There are specific testing requirements at every level of evaluation, with both the quantity and the quality of the testing increasing at each successive level. The specific Orange Book requirements are outlined in Table 6-8.

Table 6-8. Security Testing Requirements

Class	Requirement
C1	Tests must show that the security mechanisms work as described in the documentation, and that there are no obvious ways for an unauthorized user to bypass or defeat these mechanisms.
C2	Additional tests must search for obvious flaws that would allow violation of resource isolation or permit unauthorized access to audit or authentication data.

Table 6-8. Security Testing Requirements (continued)

Class	Requirement
B1	Additional tests (performed by an expert team) must search thoroughly for system flaws that would allow an unauthorized user to defeat discretionary or mandatory access controls or that would cause the TCB to enter a state in which it's unable to respond to user requests. (This is a denial of service problem.) All such flaws must be corrected or neutralized (i.e., the system must be able to keep an intruder from doing damage if he does, in fact, break in as a consequence of one of these flaws).
B2	All such flaws must be corrected (neutralizing them isn't sufficient), and the system will then be retested. Additional tests must demonstrate that the TCB is consistent with the descriptive top-level specification (DTLS), described in the next section. At this level, the Orange Book states that the TCB must be found to be "relatively resistant to penetration."
B3	Testing must uncover no more than a few correctable implementation flaws (the exact number and type has to be worked out with the evaluation team), and there must be reasonable confidence that few additional flaws remain. At this level, the Orange Book states that the TCB must be found "resistant to penetration."
A1	Additional tests must demonstrate that the TCB is consistent with the formal top-level specification (FTLS), described in the next section.

The "Guideline on Security Testing" included in the Orange Book describes the approach taken by the NCSC testing team for each trusted system division (A, B, and C). It outlines very specific educational qualifications and experience of each member of the team and provides an estimated elapsed time for testing.

Design Specification and Verification

Design specification and verification requires a mathematical and automated proof that the design description for a system is consistent with the system's security policy. To some extent, this requirement blends with the design documentation requirement. But whereas the focus of the documentation requirement is on a hard-copy description of the TCB design, the focus of the design specification and verification requirement is on an automated proof that this design description is consistent with the system's security policy.

At each level of security beginning with B1, the Orange Book requires an increasingly formal (mathematically precise) model of the system's security policy, along with increasing proof that the system design is consistent with this model.

What is a formal proof? It's a complete and convincing mathematical argument that your system is secure—or at least that your system design and implementation carries out the security policy for your system. For example, it shows mathematically the conditions under which certain subjects (e.g., users) can access certain types of objects (e.g., files), and it proves that users can't circumvent these access conditions.

Whereas traditional system tests verify the correctness of a system design and implementation, formal verification effectively reduces the operating system to a theorem, and replaces piecemeal testing with a rigorous mathematical proof. Formal verification is a fundamental part of the design and implementation phases.

The specific Orange Book design specification and verification requirements are summarized in Table 6-9.

Table 6-9. Design Specification and Verification Requirements

Class	Requirement
B1	The design documentation (see the section "Design Documentation") must contain either an informal or a formal model of the security policy (including subjects, objects, modes of access, security properties, and transitions from an initial system state to a secure system state).
B2	A formal security policy model is required. The design documentation must contain a mapping of all security properties to the security policy. At this level, an accurate (confirmed by testing) descriptive top-level specification (DTLS) of the TCB is also required. The DTLS is written in informal (i.e., not mathematical) language.
B3	The design documentation must show a one-to-one, unambiguous mapping between the DTLS and the TCB. The mapping must also show that the DTLS is consistent with the formal security policy model.

Table 6-9. Design Specification and Verification Requirements (continued)

Class	Requirement
A1	A formal top-level specification (FTLS) is also required. The FTLS is written in a mathematical form that is precise and unambiguous. It is typically generated and processed via a formal specification and verification tool that's been endorsed as a testing tool by NCSC, as described later in this section. The design documentation must show a one-to-one, unambiguous mapping between the FTLS and the TCB and must show that the FTLS is consistent with the formal security policy model.

The Orange Book requires that, at the A1 level, "Verification evidence shall be consistent with that provided within the state-of-the-art of the particular National Computer Security Center-endorsed formal specification and verification system used." As more highly trusted systems become available, the number of tools for testing and verifying these systems is expected to grow as well. The NCSC has instituted the Formal Verification Systems Evaluation Program (FVSEP) to evaluate and endorse the tools required for use in designing and testing A1 systems.

The Formal Verification Systems Evaluation Program has a lot in common with the Trusted Product Evaluation Program (TPEP) that's responsible for evaluating trusted operating systems. Verification tools that successfully pass evaluation are placed on the Endorsed Tools List (ETL), published in the quarterly *Information Systems Security Products and Services Catalogue*. See Appendix D, *Government Security Programs*, for a summary of the FVSEP steps, and see the government publication, *Guidelines for Formal Verification Systems* (the "Purple Book") for complete information about building and evaluating formal verification tools.

Tools already endorsed by NCSC include the Gypsy Verification Environment (GVE) by Computational Logic, Inc., and the Formal Development Methodology (FDM) by the UNISYS Corporation.

Configuration Management

Configuration management protects a trusted system while it's being designed, developed, and maintained. Configuration management involves identifying, controlling, accounting for, and auditing all changes made to the baseline TCB, including hardware, firmware, and software—for example, any code changes—during the design, development, and maintenance phases, as well as all documentation, test plans, and other security-related system tools and facilities. Although configuration management is a requirement only for highly secure (B2, B3, and A1) systems, it's also recommended for systems evaluated at lower levels. Quite apart from any security considerations, most developers of complex systems (especially those involving many programmers) use some type of configuration management system simply because it makes good sense.

There are a number of commercially available online configuration management programs, such as UNIX's Source Code Control System (SCCS) or Revision Control System (RCS), but a manual system of careful tracking is also acceptable to NCSC.

Configuration management has several goals. First, it maintains control of a system through its life cycle, ensuring that the system being used is the correct system, implementing the correct security policy. The "correct system" is the system that has been evaluated, or that is currently being evaluated. In other words, configuration management prevents an old version of the system (or a new, untested version of the system), or any of its components, from being viewed as being the correct system.

Second, configuration management makes it possible to roll back to a previous version of the system. This might be important if, for example, a security problem is found in a version of the system other than the most current one.

The specific Orange Book configuration management requirements are summarized in Table 6-10.

Table 6-10. Configuration Management Requirements

Class	Requirement
B2, B3	Configuration management procedures must be enforced during development and maintenance. Configuration management must be enforced for changes to the descriptive top-level specification (DTLS), other design data, implementation documentation, source code, the running version of the object code, and testing resources and documentation. Tools must be available to generate a new TCB from the source code and to compare a newly generated version with the previous version.
A1	Configuration management procedures must be enforced during the entire system life cycle (i.e., during design, development, and maintenance). Configuration management must be enforced for all of the items listed for B2 and B3 systems, as well as security-relevant hardware, firmware, and software that modifies the formal model and the formal top-level specification (FTLS). Safeguards (technical, physical, and procedural) must protect the master copy of the TCB from modification.

To carry out the configuration management requirements, it's helpful to implement such policies as the following:

- **Assign a unique identifier to each configuration item**. This allows components to be tracked individually. A *configuration item* is the smallest portion of the system subject to independent configuration management. Typical examples include individual hardware components, programs, user manuals, and so on. It's helpful if the identifier consists of a number of fields that describe, in some fashion, the item it identifies. For example, one field might represent the system or software version, and another the item itself.

- **Develop a configuration management plan**. Define exactly how each configuration item is to be tracked (e.g., who proposes, evaluates, and approves or disapproves changes, how are emergency or time-sensitive changes accomplished, etc.).

- **Record all changes to configuration items (either online or offline)**. Provide a way to audit that information when verifying configuration information.

- **Establish a Configuration Control Board**. Such a body typically consists of representatives from different areas of system development (e.g., system engineering, quality assurance, technical support, technical documentation, security engineering, user groups). The board meets, or at least interacts, periodically to consider proposals for system changes and to ensure that only approved changes are implemented in the system.

For complete information about how to interpret Orange Book requirements for auditing, see the government publication, *A Guide to Understanding Configuration Management in Trusted Systems* (the "Coral Book").

Trusted Distribution

Trusted distribution protects a trusted system while the system is being shipped to a customer site. The trusted distribution requirement applies only to systems evaluated at the A1 level. The trusted distribution requirement has two goals: protection and site validation.

Protection means that at the vendor end (and during transmission from vendor to customer), trusted distribution ensures that the system that arrives at a customer site is the exact, evaluated system shipped by the vendor. This includes both original releases and updates of the hardware, software, firmware, and documentation that make up or describe the TCB. You must provide protection during packing, transfer between any intermediate sites, at warehouse facilities, and during the actual transmission to the customer.

Site validation means that at the customer end, trusted distribution detects counterfeit systems (those sent by anyone except the legitimate vendor) or modified systems (those tampered with en route to the customer's site). This goal addresses the threat of *subversion* (the deliberate, malicious modification of a system).

Although most vendors of A1 systems provide methods in both of these categories, a sufficiently strong solution in either one may meet the overall trusted distribution requirement. The NCSC recommends that a variety of overlapping techniques be adopted.

For trusted distribution to work successfully, other assurance requirements must also be met. If a system has already been tampered with at the vendor's site, all the trusted distribution features in the world won't make it trustworthy. Other assurance requirements (in particular, configuration management, described in an earlier section) address the security of the vendor's system development.

To meet the trusted distribution requirement, you must submit a plan during evaluation describing the procedures and methods that will be used to protect the system during distribution. The NCSC does not mandate the specific methods used to protect the system, but makes suggestions in the government publication, *A Guide to Understanding Trusted Distribution in Trusted Systems* (the "Dark Lavender Book"). These fall into several categories:

- **Protective packaging of hardware, software, firmware, and documentation**. Packaging provides protection against environmental damage (e.g., dust and water), as well as tampering. Double-wrapping of materials also provides additional security by keeping the sender and the package contents anonymous. Methods include shrink wrapping, cables with alarms, and tamper-resistant seals.

- **Couriers**. This includes internal employees, bonded outside personnel, or special military couriers.

- **Registered mail**. In itself, this is not a sufficient technique but can be used in conjunction with other methods.

- **Message authentication codes**. At the vendor's end, an encryption process appends a code to the contents of the transmission (e.g., the TCB). At the customer's end, the decryption process also generates a code. If the two codes are not the same, this is an indication that the contents have been tampered with.

- **Encryption of the whole transmission**. (See the discussion of encryption and message authentication codes in Chapter 7.)

- **Testing**. The customer tests that the TCB hardware, software, and firmware are exact copies of the master copy at the vendor's site. Methods include inventory checks, engineering inspections, and checksum programs. Checksum programs work by performing computations based on the contents of the transmission. The program is run at both the vendor's end and the customer's end. Any difference in the result indicates that the contents of the transmission may have been modified.

- **Communication**. Whenever a system delivery is being made, the vendor must inform the customer exactly what is being sent (including serial numbers of equipment), when to expect it, and by what method. Communication decreases the possibility that a system or some documentation sent by an intruder in any fashion (most likely by electronic means) will be installed at the customer site.

Documentation Requirements

The fourth and final set of requirements defined in the Orange Book is the set of *documentation requirements*. Developers of trusted systems sometimes complain that documenting a trusted system takes more time than building it. The documentation required for the evaluation of a trusted system is formidable. The Orange Book mandates four specific documents. These won't necessarily correspond to four specific books. In the case of the *Security Features User's Guide* for a C1 or C2 system, a single chapter of a general user manual may be sufficient; in the case of the test and design documentation, many volumes of text and diagrams may be needed. The documentation requirements are:

- *Security Features User's Guide* (SFUG).

- *Trusted Facility Manual* (TFM).

- Test documentation.

- Design documentation.

As you'd expect, the amount and depth of the documentation increases as you move up the trusted system ladder.

In addition to the sheer volume of the text required by the Orange Book, there are several important reasons why trusted system documentation is usually so voluminous.

First, in addition to the specific books mandated by the Orange Book, a number of other documents must be written—and often rewritten ad infinitum—during evaluation. These include a written system security policy, a mapping of technical and security features, and numerous memos and explanatory documents.

Second, because the evaluation process for a complete system is likely to be very lengthy, many evaluation milestones may be established. Each milestone has associated with it a sizable documentation requirement.

Third, because the evaluation of a trusted system often culminates in commercial release of the system as well, the vendor's documentation group is usually also hard at work preparing user and technical manuals targeted for the commercial release. As security features are developed, reviewed during evaluation, and changed—maybe many times—to meet evaluation guidelines, the changes must be propagated to the many books that describe those features.

Security Features User's Guide

The *Security Features User's Guide* (SFUG) is is aimed at ordinary, unprivileged system users. It tells them everything they need to know about system security features and how to enforce them. Typical topics include:

- **Logging into the trusted system**. How do I enter my login ID and password? How do I change my password, what messages will I see, and how can I use those messages to enforce security in my system?

- **Protecting files and other information**. How do I specify an Access Control List (or similar protection)?

- **Importing and exporting files**. How do I read new data into the trusted system and write data to other systems without jeopardizing security?

- **Dealing with system restrictions**. Often, a user's reaction, particularly to a system supporting mandatory access controls, will be frustration. Why can't I read this file? Why don't all the files show up in the directory listing? Why can't I copy this file? Why do I have to ask the system administrator to do it for me? It's important that the SFUG address issues of this kind.

The SFUG requirements are the same for all evaluation classes.

Trusted Facility Manual

The *Trusted Facility Manual* (TFM) is aimed at system administrators and/or security administrators. It tells them everything they need to know about setting up the system so it will be secure, enforcing system security, interacting with user requests, and making the system work to its best advantage. The Orange Book requires that the TFM contain warnings about the functions and privileges that must be controlled in a trusted system. But an administrator's job is complex, and a simple set of rules can't cover all of the situations that may need to be faced. At the lower levels of security, in particular, a system may offer many choices, not all of which have the same security significance. It's very important that the TFM tell the administrator what the tradeoffs are between security and performance so he or she can make appropriate decisions for the particular site.

Typical topics include those listed in Table 6-11.

Table 6-11. Trusted Facility Manual (TFM) Requirements

Class	Requirement
All classes	Why security? Introduction to security concepts, rationale for using the security features described in the TFM (features that may seem onerous).
All classes	How do I administer identification and authentication features? How do I add users, set up authentication profiles, change passwords and enforce their use and protection? How do I help users with login problems?
All classes	How do I administer discretionary access controls? How do I protect system files using mechanisms such as Access Control Lists, and what problems might users may have using them?
C2 and above	How do I administer the auditing capabilities? How do I set up my system for auditing, select the appropriate events to record, do selective auditing, maintain auditing files and media, and examine audit data?
B1 and above	How do I administer mandatory access controls? How do I set up the appropriate classifications and categories for my site, assign sensitivity labels, change user security levels, and deal with problems users may have accessing files and other system objects?
B2 and above	How do I generate a new TCB from source?

Table 6-11. Trusted Facility Manual (TFM) Requirements (continued)

Class	Requirement
B3 and above	How do I start the system in a secure manner? How do I resume secure system operation after a system failure? How do I perform separate system administrator and operator functions?

The TFM is a requirement at all levels of security. As security requirements become more complex at the higher levels, the TFM must address increasingly complex topics as well.

Test Documentation

As discussed in the section "Security Testing" in this chapter, a trusted system is trusted largely because it's proved itself able to carry out the system's security mechanisms and, at the higher levels of security, to withstand attacks on these mechanisms. The *test documentation* requirement is an important piece of security testing.

Good test documentation is usually simple but voluminous. It's not uncommon for the test documentation for even a C1 or C2 system to consist of many volumes of test descriptions and results.

For all Orange Book levels, the test documentation must "show how the security mechanisms were tested, and results of the security mechanisms' functional testing." Specific Orange Book test documentation requirements are listed in Table 6-12.

Table 6-12. Test Documentation Requirements

Class	Requirement
C2 and above	Test documentation must describe the test plan, test procedures, and test results.
B2	Test documentation must include the results of testing the effectiveness of methods used to reduce the incidence of covert channels.
A1	Test documentation must include the results of mapping between the formal top-level specification (FLTS) and the TCB source code.

The way the tests and results are presented is up to the system developer. Test documentation must contain a test plan, assumptions about the test environment, the test procedures, expected results, and actual results. The key question the testing and test documentation must address is whether any design or implementation flaws in the TCB would permit a user to read, change, or delete data that he or she normally wouldn't be authorized to access.

Most developers test the system in a rigorous, module-by-module sequence, and present the tests in the same way. If mechanism testing is performed (see the section "Security Testing"), the test documentation addresses testing of the following security mechanisms: discretionary access control, labeling, mandatory access control, identification and authentication, trusted path, and auditing.

Often, much of the testing is performed using automated testing programs, and most vendors adapt these programs to generate test documentation in automated fashion as well.

Design Documentation

Design documentation is a formidable requirement for most system developers. The idea of design documentation is to document the internals of the system's (or at least the TCB's) hardware, software, and firmware. The focus of the design documentation is on "the manufacturer's philosophy of protection and . . . how this philosophy is translated into the TCB." A key task is to define the boundaries of the system and to clearly distinguish between those portions of the system that are security-relevant and those that are not.

There are two major goals of design documentation: to prove to the evaluation team that the system fulfills the evaluation criteria, and to aid the design and development team by helping them define the system's security policy and how well that policy carries into the implementation. A peripheral result of good design documentation is that it provides a useful training tool for new system engineers.

At the higher levels of security, the design documentation's description of the system's security policy becomes increasingly more formal. The specific Orange Book requirements are summarized in Table 6-13; see "Design Specification and Verification" earlier in this chapter for more details.

Table 6-13. Design Documentation Requirements

Class	Requirement
B1	Allows either an informal or a formal description of the security policy model.
B2	Requires a formal description of the security policy model and proof that it is sufficient to enforce the security policy. It also requires a descriptive top-level specification (DTLS) and a description of how the TCB implements the reference monitor concept.
B3	Requires that informal techniques show the TCB to be consistent with the DTLS and requires a mapping between TCB and DTLS elements.
A1	Requires a description of components internal to the TCB, and requires that a combination of formal and informal techniques show the TCB to be consistent with the formal top-level specification (FTLS) and requires a mapping between TCB and FTLS elements.

Typical design documentation consists of several volumes describing the overall architecture of the hardware and the operating system, followed by separate documents or chapters describing each of the major modules of the system (e.g., process management, file management, auditing).

Because there are always so many questions about the scope, organization, and quantity of design documentation during system development and evaluation, the government has published *A Guide to Understanding Design Documentation in Trusted Systems* (the "Burgundy Book"). This document summarizes all of the specific design documentation requirements (36 in all!), provides rules of thumb for quantity (the design documentation for a system should be roughly comparable in bulk to the system source listings) and level of effort (as much as a person year at the C1 and C2 levels, and more for more highly trusted systems), and gives concrete examples of design documentation titles and scope in a number of specific evaluated systems at different levels of security. It also tries to lend some inspiration to what most system developers regard as the most dreary task in the development and evaluation effort:

> The design documentation is intended to guide the implementation of the product; it is not intended merely as an abstract philosophical exercise completely divorced from the "real" product . . . Design documentation also increases the developer's level of understanding of the system . . . plays an important role in providing . . . life-cycle assurance, (and) serves as a useful training tool.

Design documentation . . . should not be viewed as a burden to system development . . . Developers should recognize the importance of meeting the purpose and intent of the TCSEC design documentation requirements as opposed to meeting them in a strictly mechanical fashion.

Easier said than done!

Summary of Classes

The following sections summarize very briefly the high points of each of the Orange Book evaluation classes described in this chapter.

D Systems: Minimal Security

According to the Orange Book, division D "is reserved for systems that have been evaluated but that fail to meet the requirements for a higher evaluation class." The Orange Book lists no requirements for division D. It's simply a catch-all category for systems that don't provide the security features offered by systems more highly rated.

In fact, there are no evaluated systems in this class; a vendor wouldn't go to the trouble of getting a system evaluated if it didn't offer a reasonable set of security features. It's likely that the most basic personal computer systems (e.g., IBM PC running MS-DOS, Apple Macintosh) would fall into the division D category if they were evaluated.

C1 Systems: Discretionary Security Protection

C1 systems provide rather limited security features. The Orange Book describes C1 systems as an environment of "cooperating users processing data at the same level(s) of security." At this level, security features are intended primarily to keep users from making honest mistakes that could damage the system (e.g., by writing over system memory or critical software) or could interfere with other users' work (by deleting or modifying their programs or data). The security features of a C1 system aren't sufficient to keep a determined intruder out.

The two main user-visible features required in the C1 class are:

- **Passwords (or some other mechanism).** These identify and authenticate a user before letting him or her use the system.

- **Discretionary protection of files and other objects**. With systems of this kind, you can protect your own files by deciding who will be allowed to access them. (See "Discretionary Access Control" in Chapter 3 for a discussion of methods of protection, including file protection classes, self/group/public controls, and access control lists).

C1 systems must also provide a system architecture that's capable of protecting system code from tampering by user programs. The system must be tested to ensure that it works properly and that the security features can't be bypassed in any obvious way. There are also specific documentation requirements.

Few vendors consider having their systems evaluated at this low a level of security. The IBM MVS/RACF system is rated at C1, but a later version of the system was given a C2 rating. Many people feel that if an ordinary UNIX system (with no enhanced security features) were submitted for evaluation, it would be given a C1 rating. (Others claim that it would get a C2 rating.)

C2 Systems: Controlled Access Protection

C2 systems provide much more stringent security than C1 systems. In addition to providing all the features required at the C1 level, C2 systems offer the following additional user-visible features:

- **Accountability of individual users**. Through individual password controls and auditing (maintaining a record of every security-related action every user performs), the system is able to keep track of who's doing what in the system.

- **More detailed discretionary controls**. The Orange Book describes C2 requirements as follows: "These access controls shall be capable of including or excluding to the granularity of a single user." Through access control lists or some other mechanism, you must be able to specify, for example, that only Mary and Joe can read a file and that only Sam can change it.

- **Object reuse**. This feature makes sure that any data left in memory, on disk, or anywhere else in the system doesn't accidentally become accessible to a user. (See the section describing "Object Reuse" earlier in this chapter for an explanation.)

The C2 system architecture must allow system resources to be protected via access control features. C2 systems also require more rigorous testing and documentation.

Quite a few C2 systems have been evaluated and given ratings, although most recently submitted systems are seeking higher ratings. (Some of these offer the ability to tune the system to provide either C2 or B1 security, as appropriate for a particular site or department.) Examples of C2-rated systems include Digital Equipment Corporation's VAX/VMS 4.3, Gould's UTX/32S, Wang Laboratories' SVS/OS CAP 1.0 (Controlled Access Protection), Control Data Corporation's Network Operating System (NOS), and Prime's Primos, revision 21.0.

B1 Systems: Labeled Security Protection

B1 (and higher) systems support mandatory access controls (MAC), as described in "Mandatory Access Control" in Chapter 3, *Computer System Security and Access Controls*. In a MAC system, every file (and other major object) in the system must be labeled. The system uses these sensitivity labels, and the security levels of the system's users, to enforce the system's security policy. In MAC systems, protection of files is no longer discretionary. You can't give another user access to one of your files unless that user has the necessary clearance to the file. The Orange Book imposes many specific labeling requirements on B1 systems (described in this chapter), including labeling of all information that's exported from the system.

B1 systems must have a system architecture that more rigorously separates the security-related portions of the system from those that are not security-related. B1 systems also require more stringent testing and documentation. In the B1 class, your documentation must include a model of the security policy supported by the system. This policy need not be a mathematical one (as is required in the higher classes), but it must be a clear statement of the rules enforced by the system's security features.

Examples of systems already evaluated at the B1 level are SecureWare's CMW+, AT&T's System V/MLS, IBM's MVS/ESA, and UNISYS' OS 1100. The Open Software Foundation's OSF/1 system offers customers the option of configuring to support either C2 or B1 security.

B2 Systems: Structured Protection

B2 and higher systems don't actually add many more specific user-visible security features to the set already required of B1 systems. Instead, they extend these features, and they require additional assurance that the features were designed and work properly. (Assurance is described in detail in the "Assurance" section of this chapter.) The Orange Book says that B2 systems must be "relatively resistant to penetration."

In the B2 class, labeling features are extended to include all objects in the system, including devices. B2 systems also add a trusted path feature, allowing the user to communicate with the system in a direct and unmistakable way—for example, by pressing a certain key or interacting with a certain menu. The system design must offer proof that an intruder can't interfere with, or "spoof," this direct channel.

B2 systems support *least privilege*, the concept that users and programs should possess the least number of privileges they need, and for the shortest time necessary, to perform system functions. This concept is implemented via a combination of design, implementation, and assurance requirements. One example is the requirement that there be a separate system administrator and operator.

From a system design point of view, B2 systems require substantially more modularity and use of hardware features to isolate security-related functions from those that are not security-related. B2 systems also require a formal, mathematical statement of the system's security policy, as well as more stringent testing and documentation. They also require that a configuration management system manage all changes to the system code and documentation and that system designers conduct a search for covert channels—secret ways that a developer could use the system to reveal information (see "Covert Channel Analysis" later in this chapter).

Few systems have been successfully evaluated at B2 and higher. Honeywell Information Systems' Multics system (introduced in Chapter 2) and Trusted Information Systems' Trusted XENIX (a PC-based system) are two examples of systems with B2 ratings.

B3 Systems: Security Domains

There are no requirements for new user-visible features at the B3 level, but the system design and assurance features are substantially more rigorous. Trusted facility management (assignment of a specific individual as security administrator) is required, as is trusted recovery (procedures ensuring that security doesn't fail if the system does) and the ability to signal the administrator immediately if the system detects an "imminent violation of security policy."

The most notable difference between B3 and lower systems is the requirement that the system satisfy the reference monitor requirement (introduced in "Security Policy" earlier in this chapter) by being simple, tamperproof, and impossible to bypass. The Orange Book says that B3 systems must be "highly resistant to penetration." The TCB is very tightly structured to exclude code not required for the enforcement of system security.

B3 systems aren't very common. It's difficult enough to obtain a B3 rating that vendors may choose to go all the way for an A1 rating. The only system currently under evaluation at the B3 level is XTS-200 by Honeywell Federal Systems.

A1 Systems: Verified Design

At present, A1 systems are at the top of the security heap, although the Orange Book does discuss the possibility of defining requirements for systems that exceed current A1 requirements in areas of system architecture, testing, and formal verification.

A1 systems are pretty much functionally equivalent to B3 systems. The only actual feature provided by A1 systems beyond B3 requirements is trusted distribution, which enforces security while a trusted system is being shipped to a customer. What makes a system an A1 system is the additional assurance that's offered by the formal analysis and mathematical proof that the system design matches the system's security policy and its design specifications. (See the section "Design Specification and Verification" earlier in this chapter.)

The only systems that have received an A1 rating to date are Honeywell Information Systems' Secure Communications Processor (SCOMP) and Boeing Aerospace's SNS system.

Compartmented Mode Workstations

Compartmented Mode Workstations (CMWs) are a new type of trusted system that's recently gained a lot of attention, particularly in military and intelligence applications. A CMW is a secure workstation providing a high-resolution monitor, a window manager, and a detailed set of security functions. Unlike workstations that act simply as terminals, CMWs have enough built-in security to operate as trusted computers. Although CMWs can operate in stand-alone mode, they are more typically attached to a local area network (LAN), communicating with other workstations and often with a central computer.

The idea of a CMW was initiated by the Defense Intelligence Agency (DIA), based on research done by Mitre. From a security point of view, CMWs are very useful because they allow workstation users to process multiple compartments of data simultaneously. As described in earlier sections, each compartment contains a certain type of data. A user who is cleared to access TOP SECRET [VENUS] data, for example, may not necessarily be cleared to access TOP SECRET [ALPHA] data. The workstation keeps the compartments internally separated and typically uses windowing capabilities to control access to data.

The DIA saw CMWs as being effective tools, particularly for intelligence analysts. The idea was that an analyst could open several windows simultaneously, examine a variety of intelligence sources (possibly those at different levels of security and in different compartments), and compose reports by "cutting" from source documents and "pasting" into a final document. The system would control the cutting and pasting by ensuring that the analyst couldn't read documents at a higher security level than his own (or in a compartment he's not cleared to access). The system would also keep the analyst from creating a document at a lower security level than that of the source documents pasted into the final document.

The DIA originally sent out a Request for Proposal in November of 1987, soliciting competitive bids for prototypes of CMWs that would become commercially available. At the time of the first RFP, DIA stated the need within the DoD intelligence community for approximately 25,000 initial workstations. DIA selected five vendors to develop competitive CMW technologies: IBM, Harris, Sun Microsystems, Digital Equipment Corporation, and SecureWare. Several CMWs, developed by the original vendors or based on the technology of these vendors, have been submitted for joint evaluation by DIA and NCSC. The first fully operational systems have already been endorsed, placed on the Evaluated Products List (EPL) and the Trusted Extensions List (TEL), and are now available for government and commercial use.

Actual CMW evaluations are performed using the security requirements stated in the DIA's *Security Requirements for System High and Compartmented Mode Workstations* (called the CMWREQS). System high workstations differ from CMWs in a few important ways; for example, system high workstations process information at only one sensitivity level.

The CMWREQS are similar to the Orange Book requirements for B3 system; for example, they require mandatory access controls, access control lists, a trusted path, trusted facility management, and trusted recovery. Appendix C, *Orange Book and Other Summaries*, provides a complete list of CMWREQS for both system high workstations and compartmented mode workstations.

Information labels are an important addition to the standard Orange Book requirements imposed on CMWs. Information labels must be associated with all objects (e.g., files, windows, processes) that are accessible to the user. An information label is similar to a sensitivity label. However, in addition to the hierarchical classification (e.g., TOP SECRET) and the nonhierarchical compartments or categories (e.g., VENUS, TANK), an information label contains required markings—including codewords and handling caveats—to be used for labeling data. In the following example, information can be released only to U.S. sources and those in the United Kingdom:

TOP SECRET [VENUS, TANK REL UK]

In the next example, information cannot be released to foreign nationals:

```
SECRET [ALPHA, BETA, DELTA   NO FORN]
```

There are two other important differences between sensitivity labels and information labels:

- Sensitivity labels permit access decisions to be made between subjects and objects; information labels simply represent the sensitivity of the information contained in a subject or an object.

- Sensitivity labels typically remain static for the life of the label; information labels are automatically adjusted as the information content of a subject or object changes. For example, in an X Window System-based CMW, the information label of a window would change as new information moves into the window. This adjustment of labels is called *floating*.

There are elaborate rules for how sensitivity labels and levels interact with information labels and levels.

Government Computer Security Programs

The National Computer Security Center (NCSC) is the government's primary computer security liaison with industry. If you're building a secure computer system, you'll work closely with the NCSC during the design, development, and testing of your product. An NCSC evaluation team will review early drafts of your system's documentation. The team will test your system—both its overall functionality and its security. And eventually, if the evaluation is successful, the NCSC will place your product on the government's Evaluated Products List (EPL), will write a report describing your system's security characteristics, and will make it publicly available from the Government Printing Office (GPO) and the National Technical Information Service (NTIS).

At various stages of a system evaluation, brief descriptions of your product will appear in the EPL section of the government's *Information Systems Security Products and Services Catalogue*. A quarterly publication (which appears in full in January and July, with updates in April and October), the catalogue continuously updates its listings to give the security community an up-to-date picture of what products are being developed, certified, and, in some cases, abandoned. The catalogue is available from the GPO; see Appendix E, *A Security Source Book*, for details.

The primary NCSC computer security evaluation programs are the following:

Trusted Product Evaluation Program (TPEP).
Evaluates complete hardware/software systems. Examples of computer systems evaluated under this program are Digital Equipment Corporation's VAX/VMS 4.3 (rated at C2), AT&T's System V/MLS (rated at B1), and Honeywell's Multics (rated at B2).

Trusted Product Evaluation Program (For Networks).
Evaluates network products. Examples of network products evaluated under this program are CSC's Network Operating System (NOS) (rated at C2) and Verdix Corporation's VSLAN system (rated at B2).

Trusted Product Evaluation Program (For Database Management Systems).
Evaluates DBMS products.

Trusted Product Evaluation Program (For Subsystems).
Evaluates add-on security products. Examples of subsystems evaluated under this program are Gordian Systems' Access Key, Enigma Logic's Safeword, and Wang Laboratories' MicroControl.

Formal Verification Systems Evaluation Program (FVSEP).
Evaluates formal design and verification tools (used in the design and testing of highly trusted operating systems). Examples of tools evaluated under this program are Computational Logic's Gypsy Verification Environment (GVE) and UNISYS' Formal Development Methodology (FDM).

Appendix D, *Government Security Programs,* describes these programs, along with other NCSC computer security activities.

"Our watchword is security."

William Pitt, Earl of Chatham.

Part III:

COMMUNICATIONS SECURITY

Part III discusses communications security—methods of protecting information while it's being transmitted.

- Chapter 7, *Encryption*, explains what encryption is, and how it protects both stored data and communications.

- Chapter 8, *Communications and Network Security*, introduces network concepts and discusses basic communications security issues.

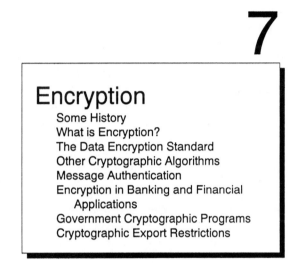

7

Encryption

Encryption is a method of information protection that dates back 4000 years, an ancient art that's taken on new significance in the modern computer age. It's a particularly effective way to protect sensitive information—for example, passwords—that's stored in a computer system, as well as information that's being transmitted over communications lines.

Through the ages, encryption has protected communications while they were being transmitted through a hostile environment—usually one involving war or diplomacy. Hundreds or even thousands of years ago, this might have meant encrypting a letter from a battlefield general to the home front; encryption protected the communication in case the soldier carrying the letter was captured. In modern times, this might mean encrypting an electronic mail message containing sensitive information (of military, corporate, or personal importance) transmitted across a network; encryption protects the information in case an intruder taps into the network.

Information that's encrypted remains secure even when it's transmitted over a network that doesn't provide strong security—in fact, even if the information is publicly available. In most versions of the UNIX operating system, for example, the file containing user passwords stores those password in encrypted form. Encryption protects these passwords so effectively that, except in quite secure systems, the password file is publicly readable. Anybody can read it, but nobody can understand the passwords in it.

Because encryption has historically been an expensive method of computer security (expensive in terms of product cost as well as computer time needed to encrypt), it has most often been used to protect only classified or particularly sensitive information—for example, military information, intelligence information, information about funds transfers, and information about the passwords in a computer system. Encryption is now becoming a more popular and inexpensive method of protecting both communications and sensitive stored data. For example, the nationwide Internet network recently began offering an encryption service to its users. As awareness of encryption benefits grows, as more penalties are introduced for failing to protect information, and as encryption technology becomes more accessible and affordable, encryption is more likely to be used as a matter of course to protect data—whether it's classified information being transmitted over a network, or ordinary user data stored on an office computer system.

This chapter describes basic encryption techniques and how they're used to protect data. Chapter 8, *Communications and Network Security*, discusses communications security (of which encryption is an important part) and networking concepts, and elaborates on how encryption fits into overall communications security.

Cryptography is a complex topic. This chapter provides an introduction to basic encryption techniques, but it doesn't try to describe the mathematical basis of encryption algorithms or explore all the complexities of the topic. For detailed information, an excellent reference is Dorothy Denning's *Cryptography and Data Security*.*

Some History

The earliest ciphers date back to early Egyptian days—around 2000 B.C., when funeral messages consisting of modified hieroglyphs were carved into stone—not to keep the messages a secret, but to increase their mystery. In *The Codebreakers*,† David Kahn's definitive work on codes and those who have broken them through the centuries, Kahn traces the history of cryptography from ancient Egypt

---

*Dorothy E.R. Denning, *Cryptography and Data Security*, Addison-Wesley, Reading (MA), 1983.
†David Kahn, *The Codebreakers*, Macmillan Company, New York (NY), 1972.

to India, Mesopotamia, Babylon, Greece, and into Western civilization and eventually the dawn of the computer age.

From the Spartans to Julius Caesar, from the Old Testament ciphers to the Papal plotters of the Fourteenth Century, from Mary, Queen of Scots to Abraham Lincoln's Civil War ciphers, cryptography has been a part of war, diplomacy, and politics. Mary, Queen of Scots, for example, lost her life in the sixteenth century because an encrypted message she sent from prison was intercepted and deciphered. During the Revolutionary War, Benedict Arnold used a codebook cipher to communicate with the British. Throughout history, governments and individuals have protected secret communications by encoding them. The development of ciphers and ciphering devices over the centuries has culminated in the complex computer-based codes, algorithms, and machines of modern times.

The protection of communications has always been particularly critical in times of war and political strife. The development of modern cryptography owes much to the research conducted under the pressures of World War II, and particularly to the breaking of the Enigma machine.*

The Enigma machine was originally developed in Germany by an electrical engineer, Arthur Scherbius, during World War I. He offered an early version of the machine to the German navy and foreign office as early as 1918. The machine was originally rejected, but after some additional security enhancements were made to the commercial model, the German navy began using Enigma machines early in 1926.

The Enigma machine (shown in Figure 7-1) worked as follows: An operator typed the original text of the first letter of the message to be encrypted on the machine's keyboard-like set of buttons. The battery-powered machine encrypted the letter and, using a flashlight-type bulb, illuminated a substitute letter on a glass screen. What was special about the Enigma machine was a set of wheels known as *rotors*. Made of rubber or some other nonconducting material, the rotors contained electrical contacts which were wired in such a way that turning the rotors would change the correspondence between letters. Before the encryption began, the operator would set these rotors to an initial position. When the operator typed the first character—"A", for example, the machine might illuminate a light corresponding to "P". The operator would then copy the letter "P" onto an encryption worksheet, would advance the rotors, and would enter the next letter. With the new rotor settings, the correspondence between letters would change. An "A" might now be translated to an "X". This process would continue until the entire message was encrypted. The encrypted message could now be transmitted by radio to its destination, usually a U-boat in the Atlantic.

---

*For a full and fascinating discussion of the Enigma machine and the breaking of its codes, see David Kahn's *Seizing the Enigma*, Houghton Mifflin, Boston (MA), 1991.

Figure 7-1. The Enigma Machine*

---

*Reproduced by permission of the Smithsonian Institution.

At the other end of the communication, the operator trying to decrypt a message coded by the Enigma machine would need another, identically built Enigma machine and would also need to know the original settings of the rotors.

The first breakthrough in solving the Enigma codes came from Poland. In the late 1920s, the Poles formed a cryptanalysis unit that began to work on breaking the German codes. Marian Rejewski and two other mathematicians cracked some of the early Enigma messages.

In the early 1930s in France, a German named Hans-Thilo Schmidt offered French intelligence some information about setting the Enigma keys. The French cryptanalysts didn't have the resources to take advantage of this information and the British also rejected the information as being insufficient. The French offered the information to Poland, where Rejewski used it to make additional brilliant advances in cracking the Enigma codes.

After the fall of Poland in 1939, the Poles passed their information on to the French and the British. As the Germans continued to change keys and to modify the design of the Enigma machine, the British built on the Polish solution. Under the direction of mathematician Alan Turing, and with the help of Enigma documents captured from U-boats sunk during the remainder of the war, the highly secret "Ultra" project began to decrypt German naval messages on a regular and timely basis. In the early 1940s, Americans—some of them from IBM—made their own contributions, based on knowledge they'd gained reconstructing Japanese diplomatic cipher machines through the "Purple" project in the U.S.

In the decades since World War II, the use of computers to break codes has transformed the codebreaking game and has contributed greatly to the use of cryptography in military and intelligence applications, as well as in systems used in everyday computer systems.

What is Encryption?

Encryption (sometimes called *enciphering*) transforms original information, called *plaintext* or *cleartext*, into transformed information, called *ciphertext*, *codetext*, or simply *cipher*, which usually has the appearance of random, unintelligible data. The transformed information, in its encrypted form, is called the *cryptogram*.

Encryption is reversible. After transmission, when the information has reached its destination, the inverse operation (*decryption*, sometimes called *deciphering*) transforms the ciphertext back to the original plaintext.

The technique or rules selected for encryption—known as the *encryption algorithm*—determines how simple or how complex the process of transformation will be. Most encryption techniques utilize rather simple mathematical formulas that are applied a number of times in different combinations. Most also use a secret value called a *key* to encrypt and decrypt the text. The key is a kind of password, usually known only to the sender and the recipient of encrypted information. The encryption algorithm mathematically applies the key, which is usually a long string of numbers, to the information being encrypted or decrypted.

Unlike a regular password, a key doesn't directly give you access to information. Instead, it's used by the algorithm to transform information in a particular way. With the key, information that's been locked (encrypted) by the key can readily be transformed; without the key, that information is inaccessible. The examples shown later in this chapter will help make encryption keys more understandable.

The study of encryption and decryption is called *cryptography*, from the Greek *kryptos* meaning "hidden," and *graphia*, meaning "writing." The process of trying to decrypt encrypted information without the key (to "break" an encrypted message) is called *cryptanalysis*.

The type of encryption algorithm, the secrecy of the key, and a number of other characteristics together form what's called the *strength* of the encryption; cryptographic strength determines how hard it is to break an encrypted message.

An important consideration in assessing the strength of any encryption algorithm is not whether it can be broken (given sufficient pairs of plaintext and ciphertext, any secret message—except one encoded with a so-called "one-time pad," described later in this chapter—can theoretically be decrypted) but how likely it is that decryption can be performed in a reasonable amount of time. A message that can be broken, but only with a network of supercomputers grinding away for decades, is very safe indeed.

Remember that a poorly chosen, or improperly protected, encryption key opens the door to an intruder, just as a shared or stolen password does. If an intruder gets access to an encryption key, even the strongest encryption algorithm won't protect your data.

Figure 7-2 shows simple encryption and decryption.

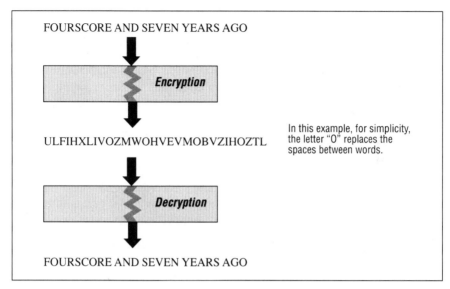

Figure 7-2. Simple Encryption and Decryption

Why Encryption?

Encryption provides security in three of the four security categories introduced in Chapter 1, *Introduction*. (Encryption is not a particularly effective way to achieve the fourth category, availability.)

Secrecy or Confidentiality. Encryption is very good at keeping information a secret. Even if someone is able to steal your computer or to access an encrypted file, that person will find it extremely difficult to figure out what's in the file.

Accuracy or Integrity. Encryption is also very good at ensuring the accuracy or the integrity of information. In addition to keeping information secret, certain types of encryption algorithms protect against forgery or tampering. This type of processing detects even the slightest change—malicious or inadvertent—in the information. While military, intelligence, and many corporate users care a lot about secrecy, financial institutions are more concerned about accuracy: making sure that a decimal point or a zero hasn't slipped, or that an electronic embezzler hasn't rounded off a few transactions here and there. Integrity checking is also a way that network users can ensure that their communications have not been affected by viruses or other penetrations.

Authenticity. Encryption is also very good at making sure that your information is authentic. Certain encryption techniques let you confirm absolutely who sent a particular piece of information. This is extremely important to financial or legal transactions. An authentication technique that's becoming a popular encryption tool is a digital signature. A digital signature is unique for every transaction and can't be forged. (Digital signatures are described later in this chapter.)

Transposition and Substitution Ciphers

There are two basic types of encryption ciphers:

Transposition   *Transposition ciphers* (sometimes called *permutation ciphers*) rearrange the order of the bits, characters, or blocks of characters that are being encrypted or decrypted.

Substitution   *Substitution ciphers* replace the actual bits, characters, or blocks of characters with substitutes (for example, one letter replaces another letter).

With a very simple transposition cipher (shown in Figure 7-3), the letters of the original text (the plaintext) are scrambled. With this type of cipher, the original letters of the plaintext are preserved; only their positions change.

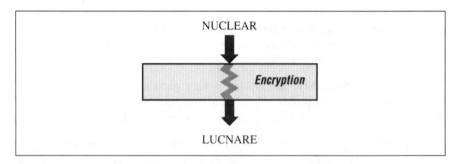

Figure 7-3. A Simple Transposition Cipher

With a very simple substitution cipher (two variations are shown in Figure 7-4), the letters of the plaintext are replaced with other letters, numbers, or symbols. With this type of cipher, the original positions of the letters of the plaintext are preserved, but the letters themselves change.

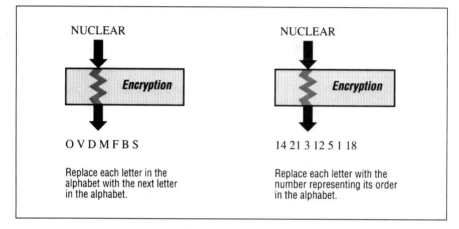

Figure 7-4. Simple Substitution Ciphers

More About Transposition

In *The Codebreakers*, David Kahn recounts the development of a number of early transposition and substitution ciphers in ancient civilizations. In the fifth century B.C., the Spartans used a particularly interesting type of transposition cipher. During the Peloponnesian War, Spartan rulers encoded official messages by writing them on a long strip of parchment wound in a spiral around a wooden staff called a skytale. A message written in this fashion could be deciphered only by an official Spartan reader who had been given a baton of identical diameter. Thucydides, Plutarch, and Xenophon all have written about the use of this early cryptographic device.

Figure 7-5 shows another example of a transposition cipher.

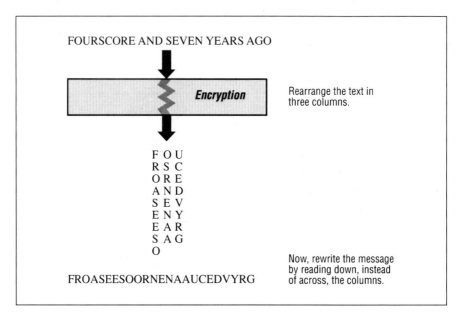

Figure 7-5. Another Transposition Cipher

More About Substitution

Although earlier substitution ciphers existed, Julius Caesar's military use of such a cipher was the first clearly documented case. Caesar's cipher, shown in Figure 7-6, was a simple form of encryption in which each letter of an original message is replaced with the letter three places beyond it in the alphabet.

The cipher used in Edward Allen Poe's short story, "The Gold Bug," is a good example of a substitution cipher. Another example from literature is the cipher used in Sir Arthur Conan Doyle's Sherlock Holmes tale, "The Adventure of the Dancing Men."

Usually, cipher alphabets are much more complex than these examples. Sometimes an alphabet will have multiple substitutes for a letter, sometimes the alphabet will include substitutes that mean nothing, and sometimes several alphabets are used in rotation or combination.

The Enigma machine described earlier in this chapter used substitution to encrypt communications.

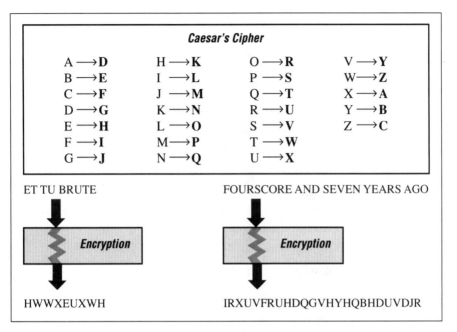

Figure 7-6. The Caesar Substitution Cipher

Cryptographic Keys: Private and Public

More complex ciphers do not use simple substitutions or transpositions. Instead, they use a secret key to control a long sequence of complicated substitutions and transpositions. The operation of the algorithm upon the original information and the key produces the cipher "alphabet" that encrypts the information.

Modern cryptographic systems fall into two general categories (identified by the types of keys they use): private key and public key systems:

Private Key Cryptography.

Private key (sometimes called symmetric key, secret key, or single key) systems use a single key. That key is used both to encrypt and to decrypt information. A separate key is needed for each pair of users who exchange messages, and both sides of the encryption transaction must keep the key secret. The security of the encryption method is completely dependent on how well the key is protected. The Data Encryption Standard (DES) algorithm, described later in this chapter, is a private key algorithm.

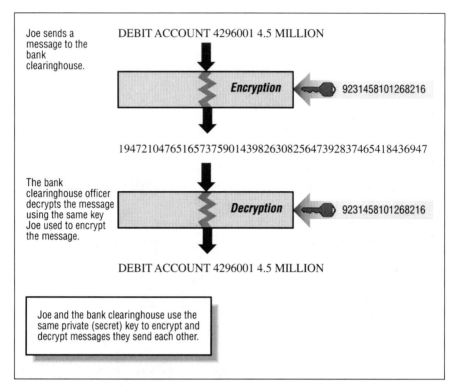

Joe sends a message to the bank clearinghouse.

DEBIT ACCOUNT 4296001 4.5 MILLION

Encryption ← 9231458101268216

194721047651657375901439826308256473928374654184369 47

The bank clearinghouse officer decrypts the message using the same key Joe used to encrypt the message.

Decryption ← 9231458101268216

DEBIT ACCOUNT 4296001 4.5 MILLION

Joe and the bank clearinghouse use the same private (secret) key to encrypt and decrypt messages they send each other.

Figure 7-7. A Simple Example of Private Key Encryption/Decryption

Public Key Cryptography.

Public key (sometimes called asymmetric key or two key) systems use two keys: a public key and a private key. Within a group of users—for example, within a computer network—each user has both a public key and a private key. A user must keep his private key a secret, but the public key is publicly known; public keys may even be listed in directories of electronic mail addresses.

Public and private keys are mathematically related. If you encrypt a message with your private key, the recipient of the message can decrypt it with your public key. Similarly, anyone can send anyone else an encrypted message, simply by encrypting the message with the recipient's public key; the sender doesn't need to know the recipient's private key. When you receive an encrypted message, you, and only you, can decrypt it with your private key. The RSA cryptographic algorithm, described later in this chapter, is an example of a public key algorithm.

In addition to providing an encryption facility, some public key systems provide an authentication feature which ensures that when the recipient decrypts your message he knows it comes from you and no one else.

In Figure 7-8, a banker named Joe uses his private key (known only to him) to encrypt a message. When the message is sent to the bank clearinghouse, the clearinghouse officer applies Joe's public key (known to everyone within the bank). Because decryption produces an intelligible message, the officer knows that only Joe could have created the message, and proceeds to follow Joe's instructions.

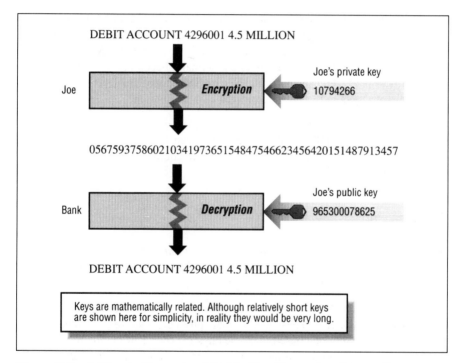

DEBIT ACCOUNT 4296001 4.5 MILLION

Joe   **Encryption**   Joe's private key
10794266

05675937586021034197365154847546623456420151487913457

Bank   **Decryption**   Joe's public key
965300078625

DEBIT ACCOUNT 4296001 4.5 MILLION

Keys are mathematically related. Although relatively short keys are shown here for simplicity, in reality they would be very long.

Figure 7-8. A Simple Example of Public Key Encryption/Decryption

Key Management and Distribution

A major problem with encryption as a security method is that the distribution, storage, and eventual disposal of keys introduces an expensive and onerous administrative burden. Historically, cryptographic keys were delivered by escorted couriers carrying keys or key books in secure boxes. In some cases, this is still the way it's done. With most modern high-security cryptographic products, government agencies do the actual key distribution, delivering the keys on magnetic media to individual sites. Another approach is to distribute a master key, which is then used to generate additional session keys. A site must follow strictly enforced procedures for protecting and monitoring the use of the key, and there must be a way to change keys. Even with all of these restrictions, there's always a chance that the key will be stolen or compromised.

Of course, if a key is lost, there's another problem. Because deciphering encrypted information depends on the availability of the key, the encrypted information will be lost forever if you can't locate the key.

The difficulty of key distribution, storage, and disposal has limited the wide-scale usability of many cryptographic products in the past. Automated key variable distribution is problematic because it's difficult to keep the keys secure while they're being distributed, but this approach is finally becoming more widely used. The Department of Defense-sponsored Secure Telephone Unit (STU-III) project is an example of a system that uses automated key distribution.

Standards for key management have been developed by the government and by such organizations as ISO, ANSI, and the American Banking Association (ABA); see "Encryption in Banking and Financial Applications" later in this chapter for some relevant publications.

One-time Pad

One approach, known as a *one-time pad* or a *one-time cipher key*, can be proven mathematically to be foolproof. As its name indicates, the pad is used only once, and the key must be destroyed after a single use.

With a one-time cipher, you create two copies of a pad containing a set of *completely* random numbers. (These are numbers produced by a secure random number generator, possibly one based on some physical source of randomness. Sometimes, one-time pads are based on the process of nuclear radioactive decay.) The set contains at least as many numbers as the number of characters in your message. The sender of the message gets one copy of the pad; the recipient gets the other. On a computer system, one way to encrypt or decrypt a one-time message is to use a mathematical function called an exclusive OR, or XOR. When the sender XORs the message with the first copy of the pad, the process creates the encrypted message. When the recipient XORs the encrypted message with the second copy of the pad, the process recreates the original message, as shown in Figure 7-9.

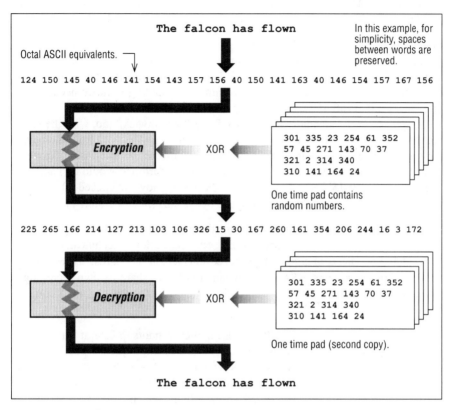

Figure 7-9. A One-time Pad

One-time pads are sometimes used to encrypt important diplomatic communications, but they're not practical for most communications because of the difficulty of distribution. (For each possible pair of users who might wish to communicate, a key has to be generated and distributed to those users; the key must be longer than all the messages they might wish to exchange.)

The Data Encryption Standard

During the 1960s, with the burgeoning of computer technology and concerns about the secrecy and privacy of communications, interest in a national encryption standard began to build. The idea of this standard was that it could be used by the many different types of government computer systems and networks, as well as in the systems used by government contractors, and potentially in commercial systems as well. The drive toward a national cryptographic standard culminated in the development of the Data Encryption Standard (DES).

Since 1965, when the Brooks Act was passed, the National Bureau of Standards (NBS, now known as the National Institute of Standards and Technology, or NIST) had held the authority to research and develop standards for the protection of computer systems. NBS's study of government computing security needs, spanning the years 1968-1971, touched upon the need for an encryption standard. Development of the standard was clearly in NBS's bailiwick, and, with the cooperation of NSA, NBS initiated a cryptography program. The goal from the beginning was to develop a single public standard for protecting unclassified government or sensitive private-sector information—a standard that would be viable for approximately 10-15 years (a goal the DES has already far exceeded) and that would be able to be used on different types of systems (interoperability).

NSA already had its own encryption algorithms used for the protection of classified military and intelligence information. NSA lent a lot of technical support to NBS, including the evaluation of proposed encryption standards. However, for national defense reasons, NSA never intended either to share its own secret algorithms with the public or to use the public standard to encrypt classified communications.

In the *Federal Register* of May, 1973, NBS invited vendors to submit data encryption techniques that might be used as the basis of a high-quality public cryptographic standard. Only a few responses were received, and these were unacceptable to the NSA evaluators. In August of 1974, NBS tried again. This time, with the prodding of NSA, IBM submitted an algorithm, which proved acceptable to NSA.

At IBM, work had been proceeding for some time on the development of several encryption algorithms. One was a 64-bit algorithm used to protect financial transactions. Another was a 128-bit algorithm known as Lucifer. IBM was particularly interested in the protection of automated funds transfers, especially those involving communication between online terminals.

There have been charges that NSA deliberately weakened the Lucifer algorithm before accepting it as the basis for a national cryptographic standard—some say to allow the agency to crack encrypted communications. These charges were fueled by the fact that NSA urged IBM to submit its algorithm, and by the modifications made in the Lucifer algorithm (the shortening of the key from 128 bits to 56 bits and changes in the algorithm's substitution functions, or S-boxes). A U.S. Senate panel has investigated these charges and has upheld the integrity of the DES.

NBS solicited comments about the DES in the *Federal Register* of March and August, 1975, and in a letter sent to Federal Information Processing Standards (FIPS) contacts in federal agencies. In an effort to be responsive to comments and to the controversy brewing around NSA's involvement in the algorithm, NBS sponsored two workshops. One examined the feasibility—both technical and financial—of cracking the DES through computational brute force. The other examined the mathematical basis of the DES. In addition, NBS discussed with the Department of Justice issues regarding competition.

The approval of the DES by the Department of Commerce in 1976, and its publication in 1977 as the *Data Encryption Standard* (FIPS PUB 46, updated and revised as FIPS PUB 46-1 in 1988) as the official method for protecting unclassified data in the computers of U.S. government agencies was a landmark in the history of cryptography. The approval included a provision that NBS review the algorithm every five years to determine whether it should be reaffirmed as a public standard. The DES was subsequently adopted as an American National Standards Institute (ANSI) standard.

The following FIPS PUBs and ANSI X3 (Information Processing) Committee publications contain standards for the DES and its use; see Appendix E, *A Security Source Book*, for information about obtaining these standards.

FIPS PUB 46-1   *Data Encryption Standard*

FIPS PUB 74   *Guidelines for Implementing and Using the NBS Data Encryption Standard*

FIPS PUB 81   *DES Modes of Operation*

FIPS PUB 113   *Computer Data Authentication*

ANSI X3.92   *Data Encryption Algorithm (DEA)*

ANSI X3.105   *Data Link Encryption*

ANS X3.106   *DEA Modes of Operation*

ANSI's X9 (Financial Services) Committee has also published standards related to the use of DES in the banking community; see the section on "Encryption in Banking and Financial Applications" later in this chapter.

In 1986, ISO also recommended the use of the DES as an international standard (to be called DEA-1). However, as a consequence of NSA's withdrawal of wholehearted DES support (described in a later section) and ISO's reconsideration of the advisability of supporting a single international encryption standard, ISO has now withdrawn this recommendation.

Government export regulations restrict the freedom of U.S. vendors of DES-based products to sell these products outside the United States. Even software implementations of the algorithm—for example, the SunOS **des** command—can't be included in international distributions. See the discussion of these restrictions in "Cryptographic Export Restrictions" later in this chapter.

What is the DES?

FIPS PUB 46 describes the DES as follows:

> The Data Encryption Standard (DES) specifies an algorithm to be implemented in electronic hardware devices and used for the cryptographic protection of computer data ... Encrypting data converts it to an unintelligible form called cipher. Decrypting cipher converts the data back to its original form. The algorithm ... specifies both enciphering and deciphering operations which are based on a binary number called a key ... Data can be recovered from cipher only by using exactly the same key used to encipher it.

FIPS PUB 46 recommends that certain kinds of data be protected by the DES:

> Data that is considered sensitive by the responsible authority, data that has a high value, or data that represents a high value should be cryptographically protected if it is vulnerable to unauthorized disclosure or undetected modification during transmission or while in storage. A risk analysis should be performed under the direction of a responsible authority to determine potential threats.

Federal Standard 1027, *Telecommunications for Use in the DES, in the Physical Layer of Data Communications*, published by the General Services Administration in 1982, is a standard for how the DES algorithm should be built into cryptographic hardware or firmware—for example, in unclassified link encryption, voice encryption, and satellite systems. Equipment bought by the government for unclassified use must meet the 1027 standard.

NOTE

> Although a number of software implementations of the DES have been developed, such implementations do not meet the official DES standard because they can be modified. There is no federal standard for software encryption.

The DES consists of two components: an algorithm and a key. The published DES algorithm involves a number of iterations of a simple transformation, which uses both transposition and substitution techniques applied alternately. This algorithm uses a single key to encode and decode messages. DES is a so-called private key cipher. With this type of cipher, data is encrypted and decrypted with the same key. Both the sender and the receiver must keep the key a secret from others. Because the DES algorithm itself is publicly known, learning the encryption key would allow an encrypted message to be read by anyone.

The DES key is a sequence of eight bytes, each containing eight bits (seven key bits and a parity bit). During encryption, the DES algorithm divides a message into blocks of 64 bits (plaintext). It operates on a single block at a time, dividing the block in half and encrypting the characters one after another. The characters are scrambled 16 times, under control of the key, resulting in 64 bits of encrypted text (ciphertext). The key has 56 meaningful bits (the eight parity bits are discarded by the first permutation). Figure 7-10 (adapted from a diagram included in FIPS PUB 46-1) shows the basic processing performed during DES encryption. If you are interested in the details, you can consult that publication for an explanation of DES processing.

The DES provides four distinct modes of operation that differ in complexity and use. The following summarizes these modes very briefly. For a description of how the modes work, and an explanation of chaining and other technical terms, see FIPS PUB 81.

ECB   Electronic Codebook. A basic block encryption method. This mode operates like a codebook; for a given block of plaintext and a given key, it always produces the same block of ciphertext. The ECB mode is sometimes used to encrypt keys.

CBC   Cipher Block Chaining. An enhanced version of the ECB that chains together blocks of ciphertext. Unlike the ECB mode, which encrypts identical input blocks to produce identical output blocks (perhaps revealing a pattern), the CBC mode encrypts each block using the plaintext, the key, and a third value, which is based on the previous block. This repetitive encryption, called *chaining*, hides repeated patterns.

CFB   Cipher Feedback. Uses previously generated ciphertext as input to the DES to generate pseudo-random output. This output is combined with plaintext to produce ciphertext, thus chaining together resulting ciphertext. The CFB mode is often used to encrypt individual characters.

OFB   Output Feedback. Very similar to the CFB. Whereas previous DES ciphertext is used as input in CFB mode, previous DES output is used as input in OFB mode. OFB does not chain the ciphertext. The OFB mode is often used to encrypt satellite communications.

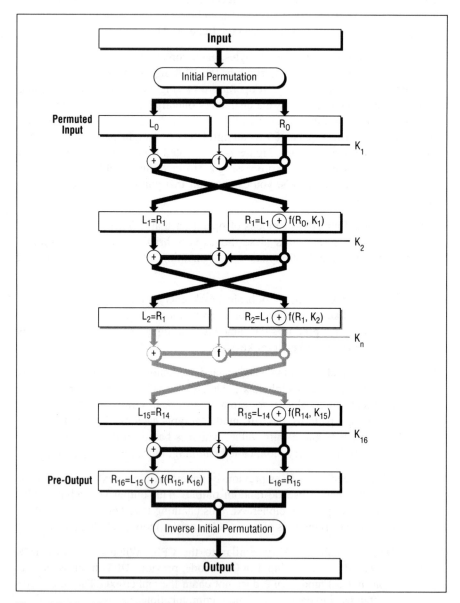

Figure 7-10. How the DES Works

The CBC and CFB modes perform message authentication as well as encryption. Message authentication ensures that the information received matches the information sent. During encryption by the DES, the blocks of text are linked; in CBC and CFB modes, the encryption of each block depends on the results of encoding the block that preceded it. Because of this link, the final encrypted block is changed if a single character is altered anywhere in the message. The final block serves as a message authentication code—a cryptographic checksum used to check the accuracy of the transmission and to detect whether there's been any tampering with the message.

See the discussion in "Message Authentication" later in this chapter.

Future of the DES

DES technology has been embedded in many commercial products and is, far and away, the encryption algorithm of choice by commercial users. A few of the companies with DES-based offerings include Computer Sciences Corporation, Digital Equipment Corporation, General Electric, IBM, Motorola, and Racal-Milgo. One example of a DES-based product is a mobile radio that uses a chip built on the DES algorithm to encrypt voice communications. Other DES products include encryption boxes for use with microwave, satellite, and other types of communications.

Although the government cannot use the DES to protect classified or extremely sensitive unclassified information, DES products have been very popular in all but the most secret government agencies. For example, in the Department of Energy, more than thirty networks use DES devices. In the Department of Justice, 20,000 DES radio units are in use. The DES is the basis of the Department of the Treasury's electronic funds transfer program; the Federal Reserve uses the DES to encrypt connections between Depository Financial Institutions and Federal Reserve banks. Outside the government, the DES is clearly the algorithm of choice. When the Internet decided recently to add an encryption facility, it chose the DES.

Historically, NSA has supported the DES through the Government Endorsed Data Encryption Standard Equipment Program. Through this program, NSA evaluates DES-based products, places successfully evaluated products on the NSA Endorsed Data Encryption Standard Products List (NEDESPL), and publishes this list in the *Information Systems Security Services and Products Catalogue*, available from the Government Printing Office. See Appendix E, *A Security Source Book*, for details. Buyers of endorsed DES products receive the keys necessary to operate the DES equipment directly from NSA.

In 1986, the agency surprised the industry by announcing that as of January, 1988, it would not endorse DES-based products as complying with Federal Standard 1027. In addition, the agency said that it would recommend that NIST not reaffirm the DES when the standard next came up for review (in 1988). NSA did say that products already endorsed would continue to be available and would continue to be listed, and that NSA would continue to provide keys as needed for these products. In addition, the agency would continue to evaluate modifications to previously endorsed products, as long as the modifications did not affect the security of the products.

NSA's rationale for dropping DES support was that DES had become so popular that it was likely to be a target for penetration. But, although cryptographic researchers have tried to break the DES,* experts have concluded that the algorithm is very well designed. In all of the DES's years of service, there has not been a single reported case of actual cracking, and security experts feel that the algorithm, which provides 72,000,000,000,000,000 (72 quadrillion) possible DES keys, is very likely to withstand all but a dedicated cracking effort by foreign intelligence.

A single machine performing one DES encryption per microsecond would take 2000 years to find a given key. (The corresponding number of years estimated for a brute force attack on the RSA algorithm, described in the next section, is two billion years.) It has been estimated that a special-purpose multi-processor built out of custom DES chips at a cost of about ten million dollars would perform such an attack in about one day, but there are few organizations with the resources or motivation to build such a machine.†

What's the alternative to the DES? NSA wants its own classified algorithms to be used by both government and industry. Through the Commercial Communications Security Endorsement Program (CCEP), described in "Government Cryptographic Programs" later in this chapter, qualified vendors may get access to these algorithms. They're able to include hardware using these algorithms, embedded in tamperproof integrated circuit modules, in their products.

There has been a sizable amount of reaction, much of it negative, to NSA's decision to drop DES endorsement. In 1987, in the wake of NSA's announcement, when NIST published a request for comments, 31 of 33 responding organizations (including federal agencies, the American Bankers Association, and the Computer and Business Equipment Manufacturers Association) supported reaffirmation of the standard. (Of the other two, one did not oppose reaffirmation, and the

---

*At the 1991 CRYPTO conference, Eli Biham and Adi Shamir of the Weizmann Institute reported that they used differential analysis to break a version of the DES with eight rounds (the actual DES uses 16 rounds) in less than two minutes on a PC.
†Private communication from Andrew Odlyzko.

other supported reaffirmation for financial encryption.)* Respondents pointed out that the DES is used extensively in existing products and applications and that there is no clear and currently available alternative. Without the DES, information might be left unprotected while organizations wait for an appropriate alternative algorithm.

Vendors have other concerns about losing the DES. They're worried about the the future market for existing DES-based products. They're also worried that they may not be allowed to acquire classified cryptographic technology, and that the need to embed this technology in their products may introduce new and complex levels of classified information handling into their product building processes. There are also some concerns that NSA itself will be in a position to be able to penetrate their encrypted communications. Finally, because the classified algorithms have more stringent export restrictions than DES-based products, companies that use these products in their U.S. and foreign offices (and in communications between these offices) could be seriously affected.

Users of DES-based products are worried about the lack of continuing support for these products, and they're also questioning whether these products are secure enough.

Industry complaints, many coordinated by the American Bankers Association on behalf of banks and financial institutions (prime users of the DES for encryption of financial transactions), led NSA to reconsider its decision. NSA has now, after substantial discussion with the industry, announced that it will continue to support the DES indefinitely for the encryption of financial data—for example, for FedWire transactions. In a memo to the Treasury Department, NSA wrote, "We agree . . . with continued Treasury certification of DES equipment until transition to a new cryptographic technology is possible." NSA is also considering what to do about export restrictions on products that use the new cryptographic algorithms, particularly for businesses with worldwide operations.

Overwhelming support for the DES, coupled with the fact that the DES remains technically adequate, caused NIST to recommend to the Secretary of Commerce that the DES be reaffirmed for five more years (it comes up again in 1992). At least for now, the DES remains the required federal standard for the protection of sensitive, unclassified data and the only publicly available cryptographic algorithm that has been endorsed by the U.S. government.

---

*Miles E. Smid, and Dennis K. Branstad, *The Data Encryption Standard: Past and Future*, National Institute of Standards and Technology, Gaithersburg (MD).

Other Cryptographic Algorithms

Even before NSA announced its decision about its new cryptographic algorithms, DES wasn't the only game in town. There are a number of enhanced or alternative cryptographic algorithms.

Variations on the DES

Cryptographic researchers have suggested that the use by the DES of a 128-bit block, rather than an 64-bit block (i.e., 16 numbers instead of 8), of encrypted data would significantly strengthen the DES algorithm. Some users of the DES have modified their own implementations of the algorithm to use this strategy. Another approach to strengthening the DES algorithm is to apply the algorithm successive times, thus getting more than the 16 cycles of encryption and decryption offered by the original algorithm. With this approach, the DES algorithm enciphers and deciphers data two or three times in sequence, using different keys.

Public Key Algorithms

The DES is an example of a private key algorithm. A completely different type of cryptographic algorithm, the public key algorithm, was introduced by Whitfield Diffie and M.E. Hellman in 1976.* (See "Cryptographic Keys: Public and Private" earlier in this chapter for an introduction.) Two examples of public key cryptography (PKC) are the Merkle and Hellman trap door knapsack encryption method (which was broken in 1982)† and the RSA algorithm introduced by Ronald Rivest, Adi Shamir, and Leonard Adleman.‡

The very first public key algorithm, proposed by Diffie and Hellman, cannot be used for encrypting messages or files by itself, but can be used to exchange keys to be used with other cryptosystems, and also for identification and related purposes. The security of the Diffie-Hellman public key system is based on the mathematical difficulty of the discrete logarithm problem. For this scheme to be secure, the keys have to be long.

---

*W. Diffie, and M.E. Hellman, "New Directions in Cryptography," *IEEE Transactions on Information Theory*, Volume IT-22, Number 6, November 1976.

†R. Merkle, and M.E. Hellman, "Hidden Information and Signatures in Trapdoor Knacksacks," *IEEE Transactions in Information Theory*, September 1978.

‡R. Rivest, A. Shamir, and L. Adleman, "A Method for Obtaining Digital Signatures and Public Key Cryptosystems," *Communications of the ACM*, Volume 21, Number 2, February 1978.

One particular implementation of the Diffie-Hellman algorithm, included by Sun Microsystems as part of its Network File System (NFS), used keys of 192 bits. In 1989, at AT&T's Bell Laboratories, Andrew Odlyzko and Brian LaMacchia broke this particular discrete logarithm problem. With their solution, it's possible to calculate the secret key using only a few minutes of computer time (although the program that implements the calculation took months of time by cryptography experts). The Odlyzko-LaMacchia programs* are based on principles available in the literature. Their work shows that for secure operations one has to use public key algorithms with longer keys, which increases the computational burden on the machines that are used.

The RSA Algorithm

The RSA algorithm is a very powerful public key algorithm that has resisted efforts at penetration. Typically, private key algorithms like the DES can't protect against fraud by the sender or the receiver of a message. The RSA algorithm, on the other hand (as well as some other public key algorithms), provides authentication (a way of ensuring that a message was sent by a certain user), as well as encryption. Named for its developers, Rivest, Shamir, and Adleman, who invented the algorithm at MIT in 1978, the algorithm uses two keys: a private key and a public key. With RSA, there is no distinction between the function of a user's public and private keys. A key can be used as either the public or the private key.

The keys for the RSA algorithm are generated mathematically—in part, by combining prime numbers. The security of the RSA algorithm, and others like it, depends on the use of very large numbers. (Most versions of the RSA use 154-digit, or 512-bit keys.) Until now, it has been impossible to factor extremely large numbers (those that are hundreds of digits long) with currently available technology. Some research efforts have succeeded in cracking very large numbers (see the inset "Playing the Numbers"), but it's still highly unlikely that an intruder will choose number-cracking as a cost-effective way to break into a system.

Rivest, Shamir, and Adleman licensed the patent on the algorithm from MIT, and in 1982 began offering the algorithm as a commercial product. A number of government and corporate users now use the RSA algorithm; these include Lotus Development (in its Notes groupware product), the U.S. Navy, the Department of Labor, and a number of other federal agencies and universities. Although the RSA algorithm is patented inside the U.S., it cannot be patented abroad (because

---

*Andrew Odlyzko and Brian LaMacchia, "Computation of Discrete Logarithms in Prime Fields," *Designs, Codes, and Cryptography*, Volume 1, Number 1, Kluwer, 1991.

the algorithm was published before it was patented), so it is in fairly wide use outside this country.

Digital Signatures and Notaries

In addition to providing encryption and message authentication, some encryption systems also use an authentication tool called a *digital signature* to verify the origin of the message and the identity of the sender and to resolve any authentication issues between sender and receiver. A digital signature is distinct for each specific transaction. It is unforgeable and can potentially be used as a valid signature in legal contracts. Public key encryption systems such as the RSA can produce digital signatures quite readily. When a message is encrypted at the sender's end, the sender's key digitally signs the message. When the message is decrypted at the recipient's end, the key validates the digital signature. If any alteration in either signature or message occurs, the signature won't verify any more.

An algorithm that provides both encryption and a digital signature might work like this. Suppose Joe is sending a message to Claudia:

- Joe encrypts the message with his private key (to sign it).

- Joe now applies Claudia's public key to the message (to keep it a secret from anyone but Claudia).

Now, suppose Claudia has received a message, supposedly from Joe:

- Claudia decrypts the message with her private key (to validate the signature).

- Claudia now applies Joe's public key to the message (to verify that he sent the message).

There has been discussion about expanding the use of digital signatures so they can be used as digital pseudonyms. This would be a way of preventing authorities from figuring out a sender's identity via cross-matching or other techniques.

Some encryption products use the concept of arbitrated authentication. The idea is that a centralized, outside authority, sometimes called a *notary*, is responsible for determining the authenticity of a message and the identity of its sender and receiver.

Playing the Numbers

Large, hard-to-factor numbers play an important part in encrypting sensitive data. But these numbers are in increasing danger. In 1988, Arjen K. Lenstra, from the University of Chicago and Mark Manasse from Digital Equipment Corporation used a worldwide network of 400 computers to factor a 100-digit number, coming up with the two prime numbers (one 41 digits, the other 60 digits) that produce the number when multipled.

In 1990, an even larger number fell victim to factoring. This time, Lenstra (now at Bellcore) and Manasse used more than 1000 computers to crack a 155-digit number known as the ninth Fermat. This time, three factors provided the solution.* Note, however, that this number is of a special form. When written in binary, it has only two 1's, one at the beginning and one at the end, and this form helped in obtaining the factorization. It is not currently possible to factor general integers of this kind with comparable computing power.

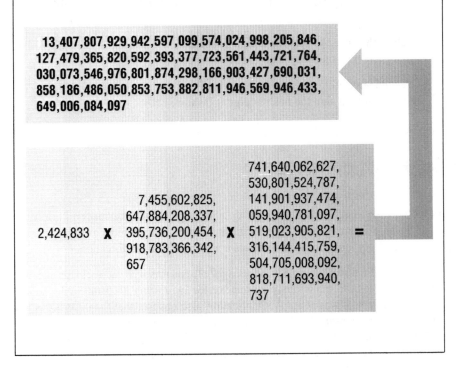

13,407,807,929,942,597,099,574,024,998,205,846,
127,479,365,820,592,393,377,723,561,443,721,764,
030,073,546,976,801,874,298,166,903,427,690,031,
858,186,486,050,853,753,882,811,946,569,946,433,
649,006,084,097

2,424,833 X 7,455,602,825,
647,884,208,337,
395,736,200,454,
918,783,366,342,
657
X 741,640,062,627,
530,801,524,787,
141,901,937,474,
059,940,781,097,
519,023,905,821,
316,144,415,759,
504,705,008,092,
818,711,693,940,
737
=

---

*Source: Mark Manasse in *Boston Globe*, June 23, 1990.

Government Algorithms

NSA has always had secret algorithms that it guards very closely. Some of these are now available to members of the Commercial Communications Security Encryption Program (CCEP) for inclusion in so-called "high-grade" cryptographic products. Founded in 1984, CCEP is a business relationship designed to combine government cryptographic knowledge with corporate product development expertise. Through CCEP, several dozen companies, including AT&T, Gemini Computers, Harris, Honeywell, Hughes Aircraft, Motorola, Rockwell International, UNISYS, Wang Laboratories, and Xerox, have developed cryptographic products. This program is described briefly in "Government Cryptographic Programs" later in this chapter, and in more detail in Appendix D, *Government Security Programs.*

NSA and NIST have recently formed a joint committee that's developing a set of new algorithms for use with sensitive, unclassified information. Several algorithms are known to be under consideration, although no definitive action has been taken to publicize these algorithms:

*   A DES-like algorithm used to protect confidentiality.

*   A public key algorithm used to distribute keys for the confidentiality algorithm.

*   An algorithm used to provide a digital signature for messages. This algorithm would perform a one-way hash of the message.

*   A second algorithm used to provide a digital signature for messages. This algorithm would sign the hash in digital fashion.

Message Authentication

As we've mentioned before, encrypting a message makes the message a secret, but it doesn't automatically authenticate it. Encryption protects a message from disclosure. Only authentication protects a message from modification.

What does authentication do for a message? It ensures that the message has not been altered, either maliciously or inadvertently, during transmission. It has arrived exactly as it was sent. Authentication also ensures that the message is not a repeat (called a *replay*) of a message previously sent, that the message came from the origin stated in the message (was not forged by an imposter), and that the message went to the intended recipient (was not falsified—for example, to alter the date of receipt).

Authentication can be used alone—just to ensure against modification and forgery—or it can be used in conjunction with encryption. In the first case, the plaintext is authenticated. In the second case, the ciphertext is authenticated.

Historically, computer and communications systems have used such techniques as checksums, parity checks, and test words to check that the information received matched the information sent, and that nothing had been modified—either intentionally or unintentionally. The message authentication capabilities included in modern encryption technologies provide an extremely reliable replacement for the old checking techniques. Both private-key and public-key encryption algorithms allow for message authentication, though public key systems are better equipped to perform this function.

With the DES algorithm, certain modes (CBC or CFB) perform message or data authentication. Encrypting data produces a message authentication code, which is appended to the encrypted message. At the receiving end, the DES independently calculates the code and compares it to the message authentication code sent with the message. If the two codes are identical, it's extremely likely that the message was sent without alteration.

There are a number of elaborations on this theme. To provide privacy as well as authentication, the DES can be used with two different secret keys, one for authentication and one for encryption. To safeguard against the sender or the receiver of a message forging or denying that he sent the message, you can use a digital signature (described above). Although it's possible to create a digital signature via the DES (using a message authentication code), public-key systems such as the RSA algorithm often do it more efficiently.

The need to ensure message authentication led to a new federal standard based on the DES. The Data Authentication Algorithm (DAA) standardizes the message authentication process described above, using a code called the Data Authentication Code.*

Encryption in Banking and Financial Applications

Encryption plays a vital role in ensuring the authenticity, as well as the secrecy, of the huge number of financial transactions transmitted over communications networks each day. In financial transactions, it's essential not only to protect the confidentiality of electronic funds transfers, but, even more importantly, to ensure the authenticity of the transactions.

---

*The DAA standard is described in detail in *Computer Data Authentication* (FIPS PUB 113).

Financial institutions are completely dependent on computers and communications networks to meet their business needs. The numbers are staggering. Transactions totaling a trillion dollars per day are transferred over banking networks such as the Clearing House Interbank Payment System (CHIPS) and FedWire.

The DES has been the backbone of financial encryption; much of the industry uses the DES, although SWIFT (the Society for Worldwide Interbank Financial Telecommunications) uses its own proprietary algorithms for authentication. Cryptography is used widely in both retail banking (transactions between private individuals and financial institutions—for example, using ATMs and point-of-sale terminals) and wholesale banking (transactions between financial institutions and corporate customers).

Within the government, NSA, NIST, and the Department of the Treasury are all involved in ensuring the security of financial applications. These agencies have signed a memorandum of understanding describing their roles in security testing (NSA), standards compliance (NIST), and financial compliance (Treasury). The Treasury Department is responsible for certifying the equipment used for electronic funds transfers, though the EFT Certification Program for Authentication Devices, described in Appendix D, *Government Security Programs*. Most of this equipment performs DES-based encryption.*

A number of standards set by NSA, NIST, and the Treasury mandate the policies to which financial institutions must adhere. Treasury Directives (TDs) and Treasury Orders (TOs) dealing with encryption include:

TD 81, Section 80   *Electronic Funds and Securities Transfer Policy*, 1984. States that federal EFT transactions must be authenticated using DES methods.

TD 81, Section 02   *Electronic Funds and Securities Transfer Policy—Message Authentication and Endorsed Security*, 1986. Extends TD 81-80 to security transfers; states that securities transfers must be authenticated using DES methods and must adhere to Federal Standard 1027.

TD 85, Section 01   Defines different categories of information to be processed by Treasury computer systems.

TD 85, Section 02   Defines C2-level security and encryption as requirements for Treasury computers. 1987.

---

*For details, refer to the Treasury publication, *Criteria and Procedures for Testing, Evaluating, and Certifying Message Authentication Devices for Federal EFT Use*, published in 1986.

TO 106, Section 09   *Electronic Funds and Securities Transfer Policy—Message Authentication and Enhanced Security*. Requires authentication measures to conform to the ANSI X9.9 standard (described in this section).

Both ANSI and the ABA have adopted a a number of standards for encryption and message authentication in the financial industry. Two committees within ANSI are particularly involved with cryptographic standards for banking and finance: X3 (Information Processing) and X9 (Financial Services). Within these committees, a number of subcommittees and working groups develop standards for personal identification numbers, key distribution in financial systems, secure personal and node authentication, and other standards relevant to cryptography. The main X9 standards include the following; X3 standards for cryptography are summarized in the section entitled "The Data Encryption Standard" above.

ANSI X9.8   *Personal Identification Number (PIN) Management and Security*, 1982—Standard for encryption (via the DES) of PINs used for access control in retail banking.

ANSI X9.9   *Financial Institution Message Authentication*, 1983—Standard for authenticating electronic transactions in wholesale banking.

ANSI X9.17   *Financial Institution Key Management (Wholesale)*, 1985—Standard for the security of the cryptographic keys used in wholesale banking for encryption and message authentication.

ANSI X9.19   *Financial Institution Message Authentication*, 1986—Standard for authentication of messages (via the DES) in retail banking.

ANSI X9.23   *Financial Institution Encoding of Wholesale Financial Messages*—Standard for encryption of messages in wholesale banking.

ANSI X9.26   *Access Security for Wholesale Financial Systems: Secure Transmission of Personal Authenticating Information and Node Authentication*—Standard for personal and node authentication in wholesale banking.

The ABA also develops standards for encryption and access control in banking and serves as the Secretariat for the ANSI X9 standards. ABA standards include:

1979   *Management and Use of Personal Identification Numbers*.

1979   *Protection of Personal Identification Numbers in Interchange*.

1981   *Key Management Standard*, Document 4.3.

The ISO, through its International Wholesale Financial Standards working group (ISO/TC-68/SC-2/WG-2), has also developed standards for authentication and key management. The following ISO standards are compatible with the corresponding ANSI standards:

DIS 8730   *Banking—Requirements for Message Authentication (Wholesale).*

DIS 8732   *Banking—Key Management (Wholesale).*

Government Cryptographic Programs

The government has a keen interest in cryptographic products. NSA, NIST, and the Department of the Treasury have all developed programs for evaluating cryptographic algorithms and products.

NSA

NSA's Communications Security Cryptographic Endorsement Program (CCEP), introduced earlier in this chapter, evaluates so-called "high-grade" cryptographic products. All algorithms used in high-grade products are designed by NSA and are classified. Chip implementations of the algorithms are provided to vendors with protective coating so they can't be reverse engineered.

NSA classifies high-grade cryptographic products developed under CCEP as either Type 1 or Type 2:

Type 1   Type 1 products are designed to encrypt classified data; they can also be used to encrypt sensitive unclassified data. An example of a Type 1 product is the Secure Telephone Unit (STU), a telephone that encrypts voice and data communications and provides secure key distribution. STU-II and STU-III are NSA-sponsored projects aimed at developing secure telephones for government agencies and government contractors. The telephones operate over ordinary telephone circuits and use encryption to provide secure voice and data communication. The first versions are being developed by AT&T, General Electric, and Motorola. DoD has recently bought thousands of STU-III units for use by both government employees and contractors. Other Type 1 products include trunk encryption devices and network communications products.

Type 2   Type 2 products are designed to encrypt sensitive unclassified data; the government doesn't allow these products to be used to encrypt classified data. Examples of Type 2 products include authentication devices, transmission security devices, and secure LANs. Type 2 equipment is effectively intended as a replacement for DES-based equipment.

Until recently, NSA's Government Endorsed Data Encryption Standard (DES) Equipment Program evaluated products based on the DES algorithm. Although NSA no longer endorses new DES-based products through this program, it does continue to list and provide keys, as necessary, for already endorsed products.

NIST

NIST's cryptographic responsibilities include the development of both standards and validation systems. NIST assists the Department of the Treasury by offering a system that tests the conformance of vendors' systems to the ANSI X9.9 message authentication standard. The system also checks for conformance to FIPS 113 (*Computer Data Authentication*). The validation is automated and can be initiated remotely via telephone lines. NIST is currently developing a system that tests the conformance of systems to the ANSI X9.17 key management standard. NIST is also working on systems that use digital message authentication codes in place of written signatures in government transactions.

Treasury

Since 1988, the Department of the Treasury has required that all of the department's electronic funds transfer messages be authenticated. The Treasury certifies authentication devices developed by vendors to ensure that they conform to Federal Standard 1027 (DES implementation) as well as to ANSI standard X9.17 (key management). The Electronic Funds Transfer (EFT) Certification Program for Authentication Devices is aided by technical input and testing services provided by NSA and NIST.

Cryptographic Export Restrictions

The U.S. government closely regulates the sale and export of cryptographic products developed within the United States. Export regulations are intended to restrict the use of products that ultimately could make an enemy nation's communications more difficult for U.S. intelligence agencies to decipher.

Like the TEMPEST products described in Chapter 10, cryptographic products can be exported outside the United States (or to a "foreign person" inside the United States) only with an appropriate export license from the Office of Munitions Control (OMC) of the U.S. Department of State.* If you want to build and sell a cryptographic product, you must register with the OMC or face a fine of up to $1 million.

Different types of cryptographic products have different restrictions:

Type 1
In general, Type 1 products can be sold only to U.S. government agencies and U.S. government contractors for use in processing classified data. Under certain circumstances, NSA may approve the use of these products by NATO and certain foreign governments (e.g., Canada, Australia).

Type 2
In general, Type 2 products can be sold only to U.S. government agencies and U.S. firms for use in processing sensitive, unclassified data. As with Type 1 products, NSA may approve the use of these products by NATO and certain foreign governments under certain circumstances.

DES Products
DES products can be sold without restriction to any organization that is located in the United States and is U.S.-owned and controlled. These products can be exported only with an appropriate license. Recently, restrictions have been relaxed somewhat to allow DES-based products to be exported for data integrity, but not for encryption applications.

Other Products
Products based on a vendor's own proprietary algorithms (usually implemented in software) can also be sold without restriction to any organization that is located in the United States and is U.S.-owned and controlled. But even commercial products that use proprietary cryptographic algorithms only to encrypt passwords (for example, the SunOS **des** function) can be exported only with an appropriate license.

In general, licenses are issued only for the governments and government contractors of the NATO countries, plus certain "friendly" governments, such as Canada, Australia, and New Zealand. License applications are considered on a case-by-case basis, but most countries—in particular the Eastern European

---

*Licensing is mandated by Category XI (C), Title 22 of Federal Regulations, Section 121 and by the International Traffic in Arms Regulations (ITARs). Export policies are also heavily influenced by the Coordinating Committee for Multilateral Export Control (CoCom), which was originally set up in 1950 to control technology transfer from the U.S. and any other "friendly" nations (e.g., NATO countries, Japan, Australia) to the Soviet Union and related countries.

countries—have historically been off-limits. NSA sometimes requires a vendor to change its own encryption algorithm to qualify for an export license. Licenses are easier to get for internationally-based financial institutions with recognized needs for encryption.

Often, once overseas customers have acquired a product stripped of its cryptographic capabilities, they'll insert a different, home-grown encryption algorithm (usually one that implements the DES) in the product.

Vendors have complained that NSA's export regulations are unnecessarily restrictive, particularly when they are applied to software products that have incidental encryption features. For example, Ashton-Tate's entry into foreign markets with its dBASE III Plus product was delayed because the product included a device that encrypts files sent over local area networks. The algorithm had to be changed before the company could get an export license. Several professional organizations have tried to intervene with NSA on behalf of vendors affected by these export restrictions. Most recently, the National Research Council's report on computer security recommended a review of export controls, particularly for DES-based products.

Many vendors are concerned that if classified NSA algorithms take the place of the DES, export restrictions will be even more stringent. End-to-end encryption for international security applications may be impossible. Miles Smid and Dennis Branstad of NIST write:

> Future international networks may require cryptographic gateways between countries where the data is translated from the cryptographic protection of one country to the cryptographic protection of the other. In such networks, end users would have to be satisfied that their data remained secure within these gateways.*

---

*Miles E. Smid, and Dennis K. Branstad, *The Data Encryption Standard: Past and Future*, National Institute of Standards and Technology, Gaithersburg (MD).

8

Communications and Network Security

What Makes Communication Secure?
Modems
Networks
OSI Model
Network Security
The Red Book and Government Network
Evaluations
Some Network Security Projects

The computer and operating system safeguards described in Part II of this book protect information very effectively as long as the information remains safely in the computer, under the operating system's control. But, in the world of networks, multi-vendor configurations, and open systems, information is increasingly on the move—being shared and communicated among different users on different systems. Information that's protected securely by an operating system becomes much more vulnerable when it's being transmitted—over telephone lines or network connections, via electronic mail or a network file transfer program. Instead of being available to only a relatively small population of users within your own organization, your computer system becomes potentially open to attack by anyone who has access to a modem or a network connection.

Whether you work on a PC or a supercomputer, you probably need access to networks. Networks let you share information (such as messages and files), as well as resources (such as printers and other remote computers). This type of communication is vital to most organizations. Information that can't be shared in a timely fashion among users—in different parts of an office, a country, or the world—may rapidly lose its value.

But sharing information over communications lines carries with it increased dangers of interception. From a computer security point of view, networks are the most vulnerable component of a system configuration. The number of possible users, the ease of access from remote, and sometimes anonymous, locations, and the opportunity for error introduced by the increasing complexity of networked systems all contribute to this vulnerability. For this reason, the most secure military and intelligence systems do not use networks at all, or restrict their use to users who are cleared to access the most secret information in the system. Many commercial systems that ordinarily provide networking support may not provide network connections for the versions of their systems that are evaluated by the government as trusted systems.

What Makes Communication Secure?

Communications security protects information while it's being transmitted by telephone lines or network connections. Secure communication enforces the security principles introduced in earlier chapters.

Secrecy or Confidentiality. Secure communication keeps information from being transmitted to anyone not authorized to receive it. Secrecy means that intruders can't tap into communications lines. With a set of interconnected systems, some of them trusted, secrecy might also mean that information can't be passed—either deliberately or because of delivery errors—to systems or networks not cleared to process that level of information.

Accuracy or Integrity. Secure communication keeps information from being lost, changed, or repeated during transmission. The information is delivered exactly as sent.

Authenticity. Secure communication keeps users on either side of a transmission from being able to forge a message or deny that they sent or received it.

Availability. Secure communication keeps the network working efficiently. Availability is a particularly important concept for networks, where even a minor slowdown in service can have a reverberating effect on an entire network. "Denial of service," described later in this chapter, is a particularly virulent problem for network security.

How can you make a communication secure? There are four main approaches:

1. Keep the communication from being intercepted. Protect your communications equipment (so an intruder can't attack a network switch or any other equipment), and choose the most secure communications medium (so an intruder can't tap the line).

2. Encrypt the data you're sending. If you're concerned primarily about protecting the secrecy of a communication, encryption (described in Chapter 7, *Encryption*) is an excellent solution, regardless of whether the medium and the equipment are physically secure. Certain encryption techniques can also ensure the accuracy and authenticity of a communication. If you're concerned about availability, however, encryption isn't much of a solution. Someone who gets access to your data may not be able to read it, but they might destroy it.

3. Apply trusted system principles. Just as a trusted operating system determines whether you're allowed to log into a system or to access a particular file, a trusted network can determine whether you're allowed to connect to another system or network, or to access a particular network service.

4. Configure your network for security. It's almost impossible to trust all the users on all the networks with which you may communicate. One way to protect your own trusted local area network without completely cutting off communication to the outside world is to set up a gateway computer (sometimes called a *firewall)* to isolate your local users. Within the security perimeter of the local network, users may be able to communicate freely. But all messages sent to or from users outside this network must pass through a firewall computer, or set of computers, that checks, routes, and labels all information that passes through it.

As with operating system security, you'll have to decide on the best method, or combination of methods, for your own equipment, environment, and assessment of the importance of your information. We mention some of the most important methods in this chapter, but there are other approaches as well. Consider one of the methods used to protect radio communications in the Pacific during World War II.* The Marines protected against eavesdroppers by having native Navahos on either side of the communication speak to each other in their own language. Because so few people speak Navaho, and because Navaho is an extremely difficult language to learn, particularly as an adult, there was virtually no chance that communications between "codetalkers" could be understood or counterfeited by the enemy.

---

*Reported by David Kahn in *The Codebreakers*.

Communications Vulnerabilities

There are many points of vulnerability when information is being communicated.

The media itself (e.g., the telephone line, the cabling, or the radio transmission) may be vulnerable. Different types of media vary significantly in how easy they are to tap. Systems such as cordless telephones can be intercepted very easily, and conventional telephone taps are both easy and inexpensive to implement. Coaxial cable is somewhat more difficult to tap. Fiber optic cable is probably the most secure medium. (See "Network Media" later in this chapter.)

Communications equipment (e.g., switching systems, signaling equipment, or testing equipment) is another point of vulnerability. The nodes where communications lines meet are very vulnerable to attack. It's extremely important to keep unauthorized people away from all communications equipment. Damage to a switching system, for example, can have a disastrous effect on a network. Communications equipment is also vulnerable to natural disasters (e.g., power problems) and to error (e.g., noise on the line).

Telephone and network connections are very vulnerable to attack. It's often easier to break into a system over a network than it is onsite. Physical controls obviously aren't effective against remote access. Using telephone and network connections, a cracker can spend a lot more time trying to break into a system remotely than would be possible onsite—and can usually stay anonymous as well.

Communications Threats

There are a number of special terms commonly used to describe communications threats. A *masquerade* occurs when someone (an imposter) pretends to be an authorized user. A *playback* or a *replay* occurs when someone records a legitimate message (perhaps a funds transfer), and later sends it again. A *repudiation* occurs when someone denies that he or she sent or received a message. A *denial of service* occurs when someone or something dominates system resources, stopping or slowing down system or network performance.

Networks, described in "Networks" later in this chapter, introduce especially serious communications security problems because exploiting even a small security hole can have far-reaching consequences when hundreds, or even thousands, of computers are linked together. Even the most serious attack on a stand-alone system is limited to that system. But in a network environment, the damage can spread quickly to other systems and networks. Remember how quickly the 1988 Internet worm spread—and consider how much more serious the consequences would have been if the worm had destroyed or modified data, instead of simply usurping system resources.

Denial of service is a problem for operating systems as well as networks. If someone shuts off power, fills up the disk, or creates as many processes as the system can support, no one will be able to get any work done. If resources aren't available on an equitable basis, some users will be very unhappy. In networks, denial of service can be a still greater problem because you have less control over the requests that come in over the network. One example of a network denial of service attack is *message flooding*, in which someone sends so many requests (perhaps meaningless messages) to a system that the system's resources are overloaded, and the system may crash as a result.

Communications interceptions, or taps, are another special network concern. There are two basic types of taps: passive and active.

Passive taps threaten the secrecy of the information that's being transmitted. Taps of this kind usually involve wiretapping or radio interception of transmitted data. Through electronic eavesdropping or monitoring, the intruder intercepts the information but doesn't attempt to modify it. It's very easy to tap telephone lines and lines connecting terminals. A single splice, or an induction loop around a terminal wire, can successfully intercept many different types of communications.

Active taps threaten the authenticity of the information that's being transmitted. Active taps usually involve breaking into a communications line and deliberately modifying information. In addition to tampering directly with the contents of the information, the intruder might threaten the transmission by tampering with its routing or authenticity—by changing the apparent origin of a message, by rerouting it to another destination, by replaying a previous message (to create a false message), or by falsifying an acknowledgment of a genuine message.

Modems

The simplest type of communication involves a single user communicating with a computer via a modem. A *modem* (short for modulator/demodulator) is a device that lets you connect to a computer from a terminal using an ordinary telephone line. Your computer can also use a modem to communicate with another computer. The modem works by converting bits to tones that can be transmitted over the telephone line. To call a computer, you must have a modem and a terminal or a personal computer at your end. The computer must also have a modem at its end.

Modems introduce security risks because they allow anyone to call your computer. In *War Games*, for example, the hero programmed his home computer to dial telephone numbers in sequence until it found one connected to a modem.

Once connected, the intruder still needs to crack your login defenses, but connecting to the computer is the first step.

There are several types of security modems that help protect your computer from unauthorized access. If you do allow modem connections, consider investing in one or more of the devices listed below, and follow the guidelines shown in the inset:

Callback or dial-back modems

If a callback modem is attached to your computer, you call the computer and enter your login ID. The modem at the computer's end then hangs up, figures out the telephone number of the office or home where the authorized owner of the login ID should be, and calls that number. Only now can you log into the system.

Unfortunately, many telephone systems won't disconnect a call until the party that initiated the call hangs up. This makes it possible for an intruder to keep the line open after the modem at the computer's end hangs up. Then, when the modem calls the authorized telephone number, the intruder can "spoof" the modem into thinking it's been properly connected. A way around this problem is to install two sets of modems, one for dial-in and one for dial-out, and two telephone lines. The incoming lines can't be used to dial out, and the outgoing lines have no telephone numbers for dial-in.

Password modems

If a password modem is attached to your computer, you must enter a password before the modem will connect you to the computer.

Encryption modems

If an encryption modem is attached to your computer, all information is encrypted as it's sent. These modems protect against wiretapping as well as access by unauthorized users. They must be used in pairs—one at your end and one at the computer's end.

Silent modems

If a silent modem is attached to your computer, the modem won't signal that the connection has been made until you've begun the login process. Silent modems are intended to keep crackers doing random dialing from knowing that they've found a computer.

Hints for Modem Security

- Be sure unauthorized users can't easily get access to your telephone and modem.

- Don't publicize your computer's telephone number.

- If you have a callback modem on your computer, don't put call forwarding on your telephone line. Call forwarding can let someone who's learned a password forward the call from the authorized terminal to his or her own (unauthorized) terminal.

- Be sure your modem works properly with the systems you're accessing. For example, make sure the modem hangs up the telephone when you log out. Make sure the modem hangs up the telephone and the system logs you out if you get disconnected. Otherwise, someone else might get access to your account—either accidentally or deliberately.

Networks

This section defines the most important terms you'll encounter when reading about networks, and it provides a brief history of where networks came from. Because the goal of this chapter is to summarize a number of network issues relevant to security, not to provide a comprehensive description of networking as such, we've only touched on the major networking topics, without trying to be too rigorous or complete. There are a number of good books describing network concepts in much greater detail.

Network Terms

A *network* is a data communications system that allows a number of systems and devices to communicate with each other. A system on a network is often called a *node*. The purpose of a network is to provide a mechanism for the users of the network's services to send information to each other and to receive information from each other. Network users communicate with each other by sending messages over a communications link. A *message* is a generic name for a single unit of communication that's transmitted over a network. A message might actually be an electronic mail message, a file, a document, an image, or any other integral piece of information.

At a very low level of message communication and routing, we can discuss network communications in two categories: connection-oriented and connectionless.

Connection-oriented communications are often compared to telephone communications. With a telephone call you pick up the telephone, dial the number, establish that the person you want to talk to is there, carry on your conversation, say goodbye, and hang up. For the duration of your conversation, a dedicated connection called a *circuit* is established between you and the person you're talking to. No other conversations take place on the circuit until your conversation is complete and you give up the circuit. In network terms, you establish a *session*—an environment in which you can send and receive messages. The two sides of the communication typically agree upon, or *negotiate*, the characteristics of the communication. With connection-oriented communications, the order of your messages is clear and predictable. The first sentence of your telephone conversation is immediately followed by the second. Connection-oriented communications are said to be reliable. *Reliable* means the network guarantees that it will deliver your data. It detects and reports any data that's missing, duplicated, or out of order.

In contrast, *connectionless communications* are often compared to U.S. mail communications. You compose a letter, write an address on the envelope, and put the letter in a mailbox. You don't need to establish that the person you're writing is available at the other end. Eventually, the letter will be left at its destination and the recipient will open, read, and maybe respond to it. With this type of communication, the order of delivery can't be predicted. Two letters, placed in the same mailbox on the same day may be delivered on two different days. Even if they arrive together, there's no way to control which the recipient will open first. Connectionless communications are said to be unreliable. *Unreliable* means the network does not guarantee that it will deliver your data. There's no sure way of telling whether a message has been delivered, or whether data is missing, duplicated, or out of order. Typically, network software deals with the problem of unreliable communications by simply retransmitting a communication if it doesn't receive an acknowledgment after a certain amount of time.

Many networks use packet-switching technologies. With *packet-switching networks*, all communications traffic is broken into small blocks called *packets*. Each message may consist of many packets. Each packet has identifying information associated with it. At the sending end, a message is broken into individual packets, each of which is transmitted through the network as an individual entity. At the receiving end, the message is reassembled from its component packets. Using the identifying information associated with the packets, the message is then routed to its proper destination. With packet-switching technology, a computer connected to a network via a single telephone line could simultaneously hold many conversations over that channel.

Multiple networks can connect to form interconnected networks known as *internets*. A common method of connecting networks is via a *gateway*—a system, or node, that's part of two networks. Communications from one network to another pass through the gateway that's attached to both of them. From a user's point of view, networks connected by gateways appear to be a single network.

There are many types of network configurations, called topologies. A *topology* is the way the nodes of a network are connected together. Examples of topologies are bus, ring, and star configurations.

Protocols and Layers

Two systems or users who want to exchange messages must agree on a common protocol. A *protocol* is a set of rules for how information is exchanged over a communications network. The protocol dictates the formats and the sequences of the messages passed between the sender and the receiver. It establishes the rules for sending and receiving messages and for handling errors. The protocol doesn't need to know the details of the hardware being used or the particular communications method.

The purpose of a *protocol model* is to provide a conceptual basis for describing how to communicate within a network in a way that's independent of the specific rules of the protocol that's being used.

The concept of layering is central to the development of a *protocol suite* or a *protocol family*. Layering divides the communications process into several, relatively independent component processes called *layers*. Each layer provides specific functions and communication with the layers above and beneath it. A protocol model specifies the general characteristics of each layer of services in a network protocol suite. The purpose of a protocol layer is to provide network services (i.e., to transmit and receive data) to the systems or users who are communicating in the layer above it. Within each layer, the two sides of the communication implement the protocols appropriate to the layer.

Examples of protocol suites are OSI (Open Systems Interconnection), TCP/IP (Transmission Control Protocol/Internet Protocol), IBM's SNA (Systems Network Architecture), Xerox's XNS (Xerox Network System), Digital Equipment Corporation's DECnet and DNA (Digital Network Architecture), and Apple's AppleTalk.

WANs, MANs, and LANs

Computer networks fall into three general categories:

WANs   *Wide area networks* are large-scale (sometimes called long-haul) networks that span a large geographic area, usually larger than a single city or metropolitan area. Worldwide military networks, public utilities, large funds transfer networks, and major corporate time-sharing systems are examples of WANs. WAN systems are usually connected by leased, high-speed, long distance data circuits, typically using a packet-switched technology.

MANs   *Metropolitan area networks* are middle-sized networks that may serve an intermediate area such as a small city or a metropolitan area. MAN systems are usually connected by technologies such as coaxial cable or microwave.

LANs   *Local area networks* are networks that are optimized for a small- to moderate-sized geographic area. Although LANs are typically intended for use with a smaller population of users than WANs and MANs, some LANs can support 1000 or more users. Office and department networks are examples of LANs. LANs often connect PC systems via technologies such as Ethernet cable or fiber optics. Usually LANs are *broadcast networks*. Instead of routing a message directly from one system to another, LANs typically broadcast messages to every system in the network. Although inherently any system can hear every transmission, by convention each system listens only for messages intended for it.

Some Network History

During the early days of computing, communications links connected central processors to remote terminals and other devices such as printers and remote job entry stations. This technology provided the basis for the first computer networks.

In the 1960s there was a great expansion in the development of computers and the use of remote multiplexers and concentrators. These devices made network communication more economical by collecting all traffic from a set of peripheral devices in the same area and sending it on a single link to a central processor. Concurrently, special processors called front ends were developed to free the CPU from having to handle all communications functions. The challenge during these early days of communications was to figure out how to transmit information efficiently and reliably.

The late 1960s and early 1970s saw the establishment of the first large-scale, general-purpose data networks. The ARPANET network, funded by the Department of Defense Advanced Research Projects Agency (ARPA, now known as DARPA), connected geographically distributed military, university, and research computer systems. The ARPANET was the first wide-area network and the first to use packet-switching technology, which revolutionized computer communication. The original ARPANET allowed different host systems to communicate on the same network via a standard network control program.

In the 1970s, IBM and Xerox also introduced their first networks—IBM's SNA and Xerox's XNS. Xerox PARC also introduced Ethernet packet-switching technology, which was standardized by Xerox, Digital Equipment Corporation, and Intel in 1978 as a network technology that allowed systems to communicate directly, without requiring the use of a central network authority. Ethernet was the first true local area network.

The present-day Internet (which now links hundreds of thousands of computers) began to take shape in the 1970s, when DARPA started converting machines to use the TCP/IP protocol suite. By 1983, TCP/IP had become the network standard for the ARPANET. TCP/IP allows systems on different networks to communicate. It's named for its two major protocols—TCP (Transmission Control Protocol) and IP (Internet Protocol). TCP/IP has become tremendously popular because it provides a way to connect systems based on different computers and communications equipment without being concerned about the details of their physical connections.

In 1984, the ARPANET split into two large networks. One branch of the ARPANET connected primarily university and research computers, and has become the backbone of the present-day Internet, which supports such networks as BITNET (for IBM computers), NFSNET (for research computers), and USENET (for UNIX sites). The other branch of the ARPANET connected classified networks, such as the MILNET (military network). These classified networks are now known collectively as the Defense Data Network (DDN).

In the 1980s, IBM introduced the first PC local area network, and interest in the use of networks in small areas such as offices grew dramatically. The 1980s also saw the introduction of the Open Systems Interconnection (OSI) Basic Reference Model, which is described in the next section.

Over the years, new communications technologies have developed, new network media have been introduced, and tremendous growth has occurred in the use of both wide area networks and local area networks. Today's network challenges include building workable network products based on standards such as OSI, developing standards for network security, and incorporating trusted system concepts and requirements into network implementations.

Hints for Network Security

- Protect your physical cables. At many sites, cabling is simply suspended from the ceiling. A vandal can disable a local area network or a part of a larger network by cutting a single wire.

- For high-security sites, run your cables through shielded electrical pipes; don't hang them from the ceiling. For the most security, seal the cables in plastic and fill the conduits with pressurized gas. If an intruder breaks through a pipe of this kind, a pressure sensor detects the drop in pressure and shuts off traffic or sounds a warning.

- Protect network connectors. Removing a terminator at the end of a network cable, or plugging a cable into wall outlets, can bring a whole network down.

- Provide extra physical security for any special systems on your network (e.g., an authentication server, a key distribution system, a network service center that collects network audit data).

- Use trusted network authentication and encryption products.

Network Media

In communications systems, electronic signals may be carried on any of the following types of network media: twisted pair cable, coaxial cable, fiber optic cable, microwave, and satellite. Each has functional advantages and disadvantages, and each has security consequences. A network may combine several of these media—for example, each building on a campus might be cabled with local Ethernet cable, but fiber may be used between buildings or floors of buildings. The guidelines in the previous inset provide some general network security hints. Supplement these with specific rules for your own cabling and environment.

Twisted Pair Cable

Twisted pair cable is the cheapest type of conventional cabling, but it's limited in distance and bandwidth (and thus in the number of communications it can carry on a single line). It's called twisted pair because it consists of two insulated wires twisted together. Twisted pair is the type of cable used for telephone systems and often for LANs.

Twisted pair cable is used most often within buildings or in small geographic areas. There are security problems with twisted pair cable, because it's very easy to tap into a twisted pair communication, and twisted pair cable is very vulnerable to electromagnetic interference. Often, twisted pair cable is shielded to control electromagnetic emissions.

Coaxial Cable

Coaxial cable is the type of communications cable that's often used to connect terminals to computers. It's frequently made of copper and it's more expensive than twisted pair cable, more resistant to electromagnetic interference, and has a much greater bandwidth (it can carry as much as a thousand times more traffic than twisted pair). Like twisted pair, coaxial cable may be shielded to control emissions.

There are two techniques for transmitting a signal over a coaxial cable: baseband and broadband. With *baseband*, only a single channel is transmitted. With *broadband*, many channels, including video, voice, and data, can be carried simultaneously over greater distances.

Coaxial cable is either thick wire Ethernet cable (often called *yellow cable*) or thin wire Ethernet cable (often called *Cheapernet* because it's less expensive than thick wire Ethernet cable).

Coaxial cable has some of the same security problems as twisted pair; it's very easy to tap into a coaxial communication.

Fiber Optic Cable

Fiber optic cable carries signals as light waves rather than as electrical impulses. Fiber optic cable offers many functional advantages (e.g., speed, longer distances, cost), and it provides far better security than other types of cable. For example:

- **Fiber is difficult to tap**. Fiber optic cable is a very difficult medium for intruders to tap because it's not electrical and it doesn't radiate. It can't be tapped by induction devices or located by metal detectors. Any tampering with a fiber optic network is readily detected, so it's difficult to insert a listening device in the cable.

- **Fiber is resistant to interference**. Because fiber optic cable is immune to electromagnetic interference (EMI) and radio frequency interference (RFI) and doesn't create its own electromagnetic interference, it's particularly appropriate in environments where such interference might be a problem (e.g., radar corridors, areas with heavy electrical equipment, or areas with equipment used to monitor critical data).

- **Fiber is resistant to hazards**. Fiber optic cable is the right choice in hazardous environments such as wet or corrosive areas, areas near high-voltage lines, and areas of frequent lightning or power surges.

Microwave

Microwave usually isn't an exclusive medium for a network. Instead, it's used in conjunction with other networks—for example, as a gateway between two LANs separated by some geographical distance (e.g., across a campus, a body of water, or a city). Microwave is less secure than fiber and coaxial and twisted pair cable, because communications can be intercepted through the air via an antenna.

One good way of increasing the security of microwave communications is to encrypt them. Common carriers such as AT&T, MCI, and U.S. Sprint provide government-endorsed protected services that provide such encryption. (See Appendix D, *Government Security Programs*, for information.)

Satellite

Like microwave, satellite is often used in conjunction with other networks to connect two distant points. Because of the delays implicit in satellite communication, satellite may be appropriate for certain types of computer communications (e.g., file transfers), but not for other types (e.g., terminal interactions). From a security point of view, satellite is not very secure. Like microwave communications, satellite communications can be intercepted through the air via an antenna.

As with microwave communications, protected services are available for encryption of satellite communications.

The Organisation Internationale de Normalisation (International Standards Organization, or ISO), which has been developing international standards since 1946, introduced the Open Systems Interconnection (OSI) model in an effort to define a conceptual model for accomplishing communication and interoperability between systems, regardless of the specific hardware or networking characteristics of the systems.

Adopted in 1984, the OSI Basic Reference Model defines a network architecture consisting of seven layers in the communications process, as shown in Figure 8-1. In very rough terms, the top layer of the OSI model (layer 7) deals with the end user interface. The next three layers (layers 6, 5, and 4) define the characteristics of the systems at the two ends of the communication. The bottom three layers (layers 3, 2, and 1) define the network facilities necessary to transfer a message.

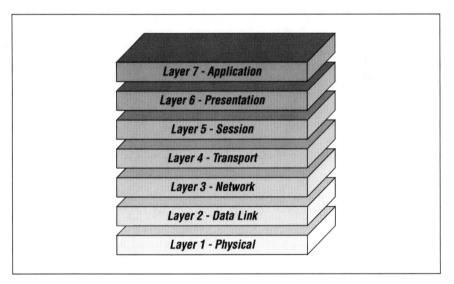

Figure 8-1. Open Systems Interconnection (OSI) Model

At the highest layer (the application layer), an application program in one computer communicates with an application in another computer. For example, you might send an electronic mail message to a user or to another computer. The mail program on the sending and receiving computers each resides in its own application layer.

Within the transmitting computer, the information to be transferred is passed down from one layer to the next layer, with each layer performing the work needed to prepare the data for physical transmission. Each side of the transmission performs an equivalent function. For example, a layer on one side would add routing information; the other side would remove it.

Each step in the process is a type of transformation, because eventually the information is transferred from one computer to the next in a very different form—for example, as radio waves, telephone line signals, or pulses of light in an optical fiber. At the other end of the communications link, the transformations have to be reversed so the other side of the communication can understand the information.

Table 8-1 shows the functions, particularly those that are security-related, performed by each layer of the OSI model.

Table 8-1. OSI Model Layers and Functions

Layer	Function
7 (Application)	Defines how a user accesses the network. Provides the end-user interface and services—for example, the specifics of electronic mail and file transfer.
6 (Presentation)	Prepares information for applications, often by data formatting—for example, blocking, data compression, and code conversion. Ensures that information is delivered in a form that the recipient can understand. May perform end-to-end encryption, as described later in this chapter.
5 (Session)	Establishes a communications session between the two sides of the communication, and synchronizes the communication. Selects the necessary network services. The session layer typically deals with starting up new tasks, if necessary, and with security (for example, authentication of nodes).
4 (Transport)	Provides transparent, reliable data transmission and end-to-end transmission control, including correcting errors and reestablishing communication after a network failure. This layer is responsible for general network management functions and resource optimization.

Table 8-1. OSI Model Layers and Functions (continued)

Layer	Function
3 (Network)	Adds routing information, and selects the appropriate facilities for transmitting the message. Controls the destination addressing and physical routing and flow of data. In packet switching networks, breaks messages into packets at the sending end and reassembles the packets into messages at the receiving end. In internets, this layer handles the routing through gateways to other networks. The network layer is often X.25, CCITT's protocol for packet-switching networks.
2 (Data Link)	Formats the messages for transmission. Handles point-to-point synchronization and error control for information transmitted over the physical link. May perform link encryption, as described later in this chapter.
1 (Physical)	Establishes the physical, mechanical, and electrical connection (e.g., the actual cable connection) and transmits the actual bits.

ISO, ANSI, and other standards organizations are working on extending the OSI model to define security-related architectural elements. NIST has also been conducting workshops for OSI implementors who are working on selecting which security options in the OSI architecture will be implemented in initial versions.* These efforts overlap with attempts to define better the security features described in the *Trusted Network Interpretation* (the "Red Book"), described later in this chapter, as well as the other network security standards summarized in the next inset.

Vendors are also developing network products that comply with the OSI model. It's expected that some OSI standards will be layered onto TCP/IP, and that eventually OSI-specific products will challenge TCP/IP as the network protocol suite of choice (particularly in Europe, where interest in OSI is already very strong). Starting in 1990, government agencies that need networking must buy networks that comply with the OSI model defined by the Government Open Systems Interconnect Profile (GOSIP) standard, introduced in Chapter 2, *Some Security History*.

---

*For complete information about the OSI model and its relationship to network security, see *ISO 7498/Part 2—Security Architecture*, Organisation Internationale de Normalisation (ISO/DP/7498).

Network Security

In the early days of networks, a network administrator usually had tight control over whether a system could connect to another remote system. These days, with the proliferation of interconnected networks and easy remote access and resource sharing, it's often impossible in open systems to identify, never mind to trust, all of the points of access to a system.

There are a number of different strategies for accomplishing security in a network environment. The choice of which and how many strategies to use depends largely on the type and scope of the network, the level of trust that can be placed in the users, and the value of the data that's being transmitted.

Trusted Networks

Many of the strategies used to make a system secure can also help to make a network secure. For example, just as a trusted operating system requires you to log in and authenticate yourself before you're allowed access to the system, a trusted network requires you to authenticate yourself before you're allowed access to any network services (for example, to log in remotely, to use a shared network resource, or to send a message across the network). Authentication and access decisions are usually much more complex in a network environment. Often, decisions about access must be made at each layer of a network protocol.

The following sections show some examples of extending to a network environment some of the trusted system concepts introduced in Part II of this book.

Identification and Authentication

Before one system can connect to another system, the user (and the system itself) must be identified and authenticated. Networks differ in how strong their identification and authentication (I&A) requirements are. In most untrusted networks, once a host system has proved its identity, it will be trusted to use network services. In more highly trusted networks, a system must prove its identity each time it requests a network service. It's risky to use a network authentication scheme that involves transmitting user passwords (particularly if they're not encrypted) from system to system for authentication—for example, to a central authentication system. A network authentication system such as Kerberos (described later in this chapter) solves this problem by using a set of encrypted keys called tickets for authentication.

More Network Security Standards

In addition to the OSI model and the government's Red Book, several other standards are important to network security:

802 Standards

The IEEE (Institute of Electrical and Electronic Engineers) has developed a set of standards, called 802 standards, primarily for local area networks; some of these standards are still in the proposal stage, and have not yet been published as final standards. The 802 standards, which include 802.1 through 802.10, basically address the lowest two layers of the OSI model. 802.10 is a standard for interoperable LAN security, known as SILS, which is oriented to the exchange of data in multivendor networks.

X.400 Standards

The X.400 standards developed by ISO (International Standards Organization) and CCITT (Comité Consultatif Internationale Telegraphique et Telephonique) are OSI-oriented protocols for message handling (for example, in electronic mail systems). They include standards for secure messaging.

X.500 Standards

The X.500 standards developed by ISO and CCITT are standards for naming. They allow users and programmers to identify an object (e.g., a file, a disk, etc.) without knowing the location of the object in a network or the path required to reach it. X.500 includes standards for authentication and secure naming.

Discretionary Access Control

In an operating system, discretionary access control (DAC) may be used to restrict file access to certain users or groups. In a network environment, discretionary access control may restrict access to certain remote users and/or systems. A particular network service might be available only to a certain group, which might be defined in a network environment as a particular Internet address (e.g., all the users of a particular system in the network).

Object Reuse

In a network environment, object reuse concerns are broadened to include such network objects as message buffers in network switches.

Labels and Mandatory Access Control

Every system in a trusted network must label its data with security attributes (e.g., sensitivity labels, information labels, login IDs, etc.). This way, the sensitivity of the data will be recognized if the data is sent to another system. Because different networks support different security policies, these labels are not necessarily in the same format.

In certain types of secure networks, each system may effectively have a label. Mandatory access control (MAC) keeps TOP SECRET data, for example, from being sent over the network to a system labeled as SECRET.

Audit

In a network environment, additional networking events must be audited on both sides of the network connection. Examples include establishing or dropping a network connection, security violations such as lost or misrouted data, and failure of a network component.

Covert Channels

Covert channels are more of an issue for networks than they are for stand-alone systems, mainly because there are so many more potential channels on which data can be transmitted.

Other Network Extensions

There are many additional network implications for system administration, system design, documentation, and other requirements introduced for operating systems in the Orange Book. For example, in a network environment, there is typically a network security officer (NSO) who's responsible for carrying out network security policy, configuring the network and all network security features, establishing the network databases used for access control, and monitoring network traffic and performance.

Perimeters and Gateways

The simplest way to protect a network from access by unauthorized users is to keep that network physically secure—for example, to provide physical protection of all internal network switches and connections, no telephone connections, and no network cabling to the outside world. But with trends toward wider communication, most organizations will at least occasionally have to communicate with outside systems and networks. Communication between trusted and untrusted networks must have very clear rules associated with it.

A trusted local area network can be thought of as being inside a security perimeter. Inside the perimeter, access controls and other security features determine who can access what information. For example, in a trusted system supporting multi-level military security, some users are cleared to access TOP SECRET data, others only SECRET, CONFIDENTIAL, or UNCLASSIFIED data. In a fairly simple network environment, all information originating outside the trusted network might be treated at a single sensitivity level. In such an environment, a gateway system, sometimes known as a *firewall computer*, a *router*, or a *trusted interface unit* (TIU), might separate the trusted system or network from the untrusted systems or networks outside it. Untrusted systems can communicate with trusted systems only through a single communications channel controlled by a trusted gateway. The gateway controls traffic from both inside and outside the network and effectively isolates the trusted network from the outside world. Because the firewall protects the other machines within the perimeter, security can be concentrated on the firewall.

In the simplest case, where everything inside the perimeter is trusted and everything outside it is untrusted, the gateway system labels and filters data. When information is imported into a trusted system from an untrusted system, the gateway system puts a sensitivity label (usually "UNCLASSIFIED") on this data. When information is exported from a trusted system to an untrusted system, the gateway system filters that information by exporting only data that the untrusted system is allowed to process (usually UNCLASSIFIED data). If multi-level security is supported, more complex network solutions are required to regulate access to the different security levels, as described in the next section.

Security in Heterogeneous Environments

More and more modern networks are attempting to serve heterogeneous computing environments. Trusted networks must have facilities for supporting a whole range of security environments, corresponding to the host systems they serve.

Using a trusted gateway to partition trusted networks from untrusted networks, as described in the previous section, works only if communications from outside the trusted network can be treated at a single level of security. In more complex environments supporting multi-level communications, more complex solutions are needed.

On the trusted network side, a system must make decisions about requests originating outside the trusted network. It must regulate which information remote users are cleared to access, and it must control which system services remote users are granted. In standard networks, in which the security attributes of the remote user aren't transmitted, the local system doesn't have sufficient information to make access decisions. This can lead to major security problems. For example, if a trusted network server on the trusted network side processes requests on behalf of an untrusted remote user, the security of the whole system is at risk.

There must be some way to propagate to the local process (the process on the trusted network side) the security attributes of the remote user (the process on the untrusted network side). This isn't as simple as sending a "TOP SECRET" label, for example, from one side to the other. Even if a user is cleared for TOP SECRET information on one system, he's not necessarily given the same courtesy when he accesses another system. Each system in the network must be able to compare the attributes of the process performing an operation with those of the file or other object on which the operation is performed, and make access decisions that are appropriate to the local system's security policy.

Trusted networks capable of handling such security decisions are still in the building stage. (See the discussion of "Project MAX" later in this chapter for an example of such a network.)

Encrypted Communications

Encryption, a process that transforms original information into enciphered information, is a very important part of network security. Because information is so vulnerable to attack when it's being transmitted over a network, encryption offers a strong assurance that even if the information is intercepted, it won't be comprehensible. (See Chapter 7 for a detailed description of encryption.)

In addition to protecting the secrecy of messages transmitted over a network by transforming them into data that appears to be unintelligible, encryption can also be used to ensure the integrity and authenticity of those messages. *Message authentication* provides a critical network security tool. Message authentication ensures that a message was received in exactly the form sent. At the sending end, the encryption process appends a message authentication code to the encrypted message. At the receiving end, the decryption process independently calculates a message authentication code and compares it with the code sent with the message. If the two are identical, the message was sent and received accurately.

A *digital signature* is another network security tool which provides electronic evidence that you, and only you, sent a signed message. Because the message incorporates a secret key that only you possess, it can't be forged. It's an immutable proof that you sent a message.

A message that's proved to be authentic by an outside authority, sometimes called a *notary*, is said to be *arbitrated*. As with a traditional notary, who provides independent evidence that someone is who he claims to be, a digital notary attests that a message is genuine. The notary may also provide proof that the message was sent and received at a particular, recorded point in time. This keeps the message from being repudiated by the sender and/or the receiver later on.

There are two communications levels at which encryption can be performed, each with different implications for network security: end-to-end encryption and link encryption.

End-to-end Encryption

With *end-to-end encryption* (sometimes called *off-line encryption*), a message is encrypted when it's transmitted and is decrypted when it's received. The network may not even need to be aware that the message is encrypted. This type of encryption may sometimes may be selected as an option by the user. The message remains encrypted through the entire communications process, from start to finish, as shown in Figure 8-2.

Link Encryption

With *link encryption* (sometimes called *online encryption*), a message is encrypted when it is transmitted, but is decrypted and then encrypted again each time it passes through a network communications node. The message may therefore be encrypted, decrypted, and re-encrypted a number of times during the communications process, and the message is exposed within each node, as shown in Figure 8-3. With link encryption, the encryption is performed just before the message is physically transmitted. Encryption is typically invisible to the user; it is simply part of the transmission process.

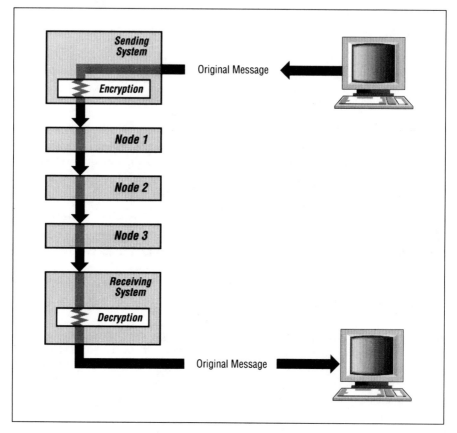

Figure 8-2. End-to-end Encryption

Comparing the Encryption Methods

There are advantages and disadvantages to each method of encryption. Advantages of end-to-end encryption are:

- It is more flexible; the user may be able to encrypt only certain information, and each user can have a distinct key.

- It makes key management and distribution easier.

- It protects data from start to finish through the entire network.

- It is more efficient; the network doesn't need to have any special encryption facilities.

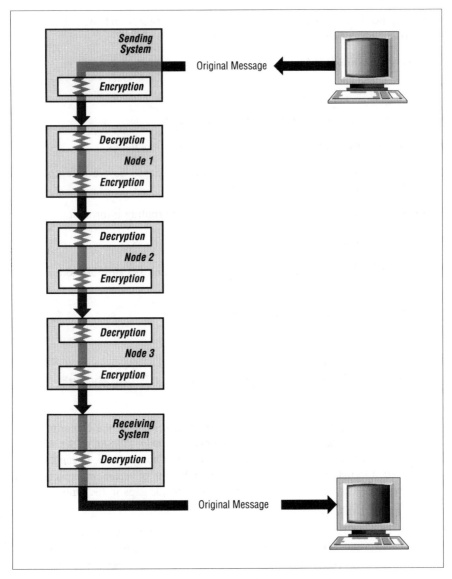

Figure 8-3. Link Encryption

Disadvantages of end-to-end encryption are:

- It may need to process some information (e.g., headers and routing information) in unencrypted form.

- Each system needs to be able to perform the same kind of encryption.

Advantages of link encryption are:

- It is easier; the user doesn't need to take any action.

- It is more convenient in a network that provides many nodes.

- It doesn't compromise the entire network if a single key is compromised. Each pair of network nodes can use a distinct key.

- It encrypts all information, including headers and routing information.

Disadvantages of link encryption are:

- Key distribution and management are more difficult because all nodes in the network must receive a key.

- There are more points of vulnerability.

The Red Book and Government Network Evaluations

Although many of the concepts and mechanisms described in the Department of Defense *Trusted Computer System Evaluation Criteria* (TCSEC) (the Orange Book) are applicable to network environments, the Orange Book doesn't define what's needed to make a network secure—and what the government expects from the network products it evaluates. There are two major gaps in the Orange Book relating to networks.

First, the Orange Book addresses single-system security. A network involves many systems, often with different architectures and different security vulnerabilities. It must be possible to have a secure network without requiring that every system connected to that network be fully trusted.

Second, the Orange Book primarily addresses the issue of access to a computer system. It focuses on two of the security principles we've introduced—secrecy (keeping unauthorized users out of a system) and integrity (keeping information from being lost or changed). It doesn't fully address two other very important principles—availability (keeping the system or network working efficiently) and authenticity (confirming that particular information was sent by a particular user) that are of great importance in networks.

Government concerns about the security of data transmitted over communications networks led to the development of standard criteria for evaluating the level of trust that can be placed in a computer network. In an effort to extend the TCSEC evaluation classes to trusted network systems and components, NCSC published the *Trusted Network Interpretation of the Trusted Computer System Evaluation Criteria* (TNI) (the Red Book) in 1987.* According to the Red Book, this publication describes the way in which:

> ...the specific security features, the assurance requirements, and the rating structure of the TCSEC are extended to networks of computers ranging from isolated local area networks to wide-area internetwork systems.

Like the Orange Book, the Red Book describes broad security principles. It doesn't explain in any detail how to put these principles into action. The Red Book distinguishes between two types of trusted networks. With one type, a set of separately evaluated and accredited systems interconnect; each is able to handle sensitive information at a particular security level or range of levels. With the other type, a single trusted network with a distinct Network Trusted Computing Base (NTCB) is evaluated. Like a trusted system, this type of trusted network has a coherent network security policy, architecture, and system design. Like a trusted operating system, a trusted network can determine which subjects (e.g., systems) can access which objects (e.g., messages, network services such as mail, or particular systems or devices).

Because network evaluation is still so ill-defined when viewed from the perspective of actual systems in complex networked environments, the Red Book requirements are likely to be revised in the near future.

The National Computer Security Center (NCSC) conducts evaluations of network products, as it does for trusted, stand-alone operating systems, through the Trusted Product Evaluation Program (TPEP), described in detail in Appendix D, *Government Security Programs*.

Trusted Network Interpretation of the Trusted Computer System Evaluation Criteria (NCSC-TG-005), Library Number S228,526, Version 1, National Computer Security Center, Gaithersburg (MD), 1987.

The Red Book divides its discussion of security features and assurance requirements into two general categories: TCSEC requirements and other security services.

TCSEC Requirements

In Part I, the Red Book describes the requirements for each evaluation class introduced in the Orange Book, and shows how the NTCB of a particular network product satisfies the requirements for that class. For example, the NTCB might satisfy the discretionary access control requirements of the C2 evaluation class by providing network identifiers (e.g., Internet addresses) for various components (e.g., hosts, gateways). The NCSC uses these interpretations of security requirements to determine what rating to assign to a network product. These ratings are the same as those described in the Orange Book (C1, C2, B1, B2, B3, A1).

Other Security Services

In Part II, the Red Book describes additional network security services that may be available in specific network products. While the NCSC doesn't evaluate such services as rigorously as it evaluates the network security features based on the Orange Book, it does assign qualitative ratings to these services. The ratings are none, minimum, fair, and good.

The network services described in this part of the Red Book fall into three general categories: communications integrity, denial of service, and compromise protection. These services are described briefly in the following sections. See the Red Book for detailed information about these services.

Communications Integrity

Communications integrity services ensure that network communications are transmitted accurately. This means that messages aren't forged, modified during transmission, or repudiated by either the sender or the receiver of the messages. The services defined in the Red Book in this category are summarized in Table 8-2.

Table 8-2. Communications Integrity Requirements

Service	Meaning
Authentication	Proves the identity of the user and system sending a message. Ensures that unauthorized users can't pretend to be another (called a *masquerade*). Also ensures that an authorized user can't record and then resend a previously sent message (called a *playback* or a *replay*).
	Network security techniques: Encryption, passwords, digital signature, time stamp on message.
Communications field integrity	Protects the accuracy and integrity of the message. Ensures that the message, including specific message fields (such as the protocol header used for routing) are not changed (via message stream modification)—either deliberately or accidentally.
	Network security techniques: Encryption, message authentication.
Nonrepudiation	Proves that a message has been sent and received. Ensures that the sender can't deny that he sent the message, and that the recipient can't deny that he received it.
	Network security techniques: Encryption, digital signature, notary (arbitrated signature).

Denial of Service

Denial of service services are designed to ensure that the network keeps working and that all services needed by users are fully available. This means that the network supports good system administration and that there are methods for keeping threats like message flooding and worms out of the network. The services defined in the Red Book in this category are summarized in Table 8-3.

Table 8-3. Denial of Service Requirements

Service	Meaning
Continuity of operations	Keeps the network working efficiently, even if components fail or if the network is attacked.
	Network security techniques: Redundant or fault-tolerant systems and devices, ability to reconfigure network in an emergency.
Protocol-based protection	Detects network problems (e.g., slowdown in transmission) using existing protocol services.
	Network security techniques: Measurement of transmission rates between systems (compare with minimum) and waiting time for responses (compare with threshold).
Network management	Monitors overall network performance to detect network attacks (e.g., message flooding, replays), failures, (e.g., message overload, noise), or inequities (some users or processes having a processing advantage over others).
	Network security techniques: Restriction of resources via network administration (e.g., limit CPU time, number of jobs, number of disks and tapes, number of files, file size).

Compromise Protection

Compromise protection services are designed to keep the information transmitted over the network a secret from those not authorized to access it. This means that the network provides methods for keeping intruders out of the network—both physically and remotely. The services defined in the Red Book in this category are summarized in Table 8-4.

Table 8-4. Compromise Protection Requirements

Service	Meaning
Data confidentiality	Protects data from being intercepted by unauthorized users during transmission.
	Network security techniques: Physical protection of cabling, access controls.
Traffic flow confidentiality	Protects data characteristics (e.g., message length, frequency, destination) from being analyzed by an intruder (*called traffic analysis*). Such an analysis might allow an observer to infer information; a classic example is that a pattern of messages between a general and troops in the field could predict that the troops are about to launch an attack.
	Network security techniques: Covert channel analysis, padding messages (to disguise their actual characteristics), sending noise or spurious messages.
Selective routing	Avoids particular threats to data by routing messages to avoid certain networks or systems (e.g., systems in certain countries or certain suspicious network nodes).
	Network security techniques: Network configuration, periodic deletion or modification of messages.

Some Network Security Projects

There are a number of innovative projects underway in the network security area. This section briefly describes some of these projects.

DISNet and BLACKER

A major network security project now underway within DoD is attempting to consolidate the department's various Defense Secure Networks into a single Defense Integrated Secure Network. Known as DISNet, the different component networks include:

- DSNet 1, which processes SECRET information.

- DSNet 2, which processes TOP SECRET information.

- DSNet 3, which processes sensitive compartmented intelligence (SCI).

The network is expected to be available within the next five years.

By using the BLACKER system under development by UNISYS Corporation, the consolidated network will use different encryption algorithms to keep separate the different security levels of information stored and transmitted over the networks. The system will employ key distribution centers for the centralized distribution of electronic cryptographic keys.

SDNS

A major effort under development by NSA is the Secure Data Network System (SDNS) Program. This program was established in 1986 as a partnership between NSA and ten major computer and telecommunications companies, including AT&T, Digital Equipment Corporation, and IBM. The goal of SDNS is to develop a security architecture based on the OSI model, as well as standard security protocols for the Government Open System Interconnect Profile (GOSIP). Through NIST, the program has published documents describing proposed standards for controlling access to a network, protecting data in networks, and managing encryption keys.* These documents are available from the National Technical Information Service; see Appendix E, *A Security Source Book*, for information about contacting NTIS.

SDNS is expected to use a distributed key generation system in which computers will be able to establish cryptographic keys as needed to communicate with other computers. (Chapter 7, *Encryption*, describes cryptographic keys and key distribution.)

Kerberos

Kerberos is an authentication system for open systems and networks. Developed by Project Athena at the Massachusetts Institute of Technology, Kerberos can be added onto any existing network protocol. Historically used with UNIX-oriented protocols like Sun's Network File System (NFS), Kerberos is expected to be used by the Open Software Foundation's OSF/1 operating system, and by other vendors. Kerberos uses an encryption system based on the Data Encryption Standard (described in Chapter 7). Each user has a private authentication key.

How does Kerberos work? Like its namesake, the many-headed dog who guards the entrance to the underworld, Kerberos guards the data transmitted between machines that communicate over the network. Kerberos uses cryptographic keys known as *tickets* to protect the security of the messages you send to the system— and the messages the system sends back to you. Kerberos never transmits passwords, even in encrypted form, on the network. Passwords reside only in a highly secure machine called a *key server*. Kerberos performs authentication both when you log into the system and when you request any type of network service (e.g., a printer or a mail system).

Project MAX

Project MAX is a network security research effort established by a number of commercial vendors, including SecureWare, Sun, and Hewlett-Packard. The goal of the project is to develop a trusted network technology that's independent of vendor platform, specific operating system, and network protocol. This will

---

*See the following:

> *Secure Data Network System (SDNS) Transport, Network, and Message Security Protocols.* (Order from NTIS: NISTIR 90-4250.)
> *Secure Data Network System (SDNS) Access Control Documents* (Order from NTIS: NISTIR 90-4259.)
> *Secure Data Network System (SDNS) Key Management Documents* (Order from NTIS: NISTIR 90-4262.)

allow information to be exchanged securely between disparate systems and networks.

The group has developed a trusted network product called MaxSix (Multilevel Architecture for X for Security Information Exchange). MaxSix consists of a set of enhancements to UNIX and networking interprocess communication. An important goal of the project is to standardize the labeling of the data that's imported into or exported from a system. In MaxSix trusted networks, the networking software transmits security attributes along with data, and inserts appropriate checks in the network subsystem that enable a local system to make access decisions (based on its own security policies) about the data imported into the system from the outside world.

MaxSix was designed to support network security standards, including DNSIX and TSIG.

DNSix is the Department of Defense Intelligence Information System (DoDIIS) Network for Security Information Exchange, a specification developed by the Defense Intelligence Agency (DIA) and Mitre for network level access control and session management. The DNSix standard is specified as a requirement for many DoD and DIA System High Workstation and Compartmented Mode Workstation procurements.

TSIG is the Trusted Systems Interoperability Group, which has developed a specification for message headers that includes attributes, such as sensitivity labels, used for trusted routing of messages in a network. TSIG has proposed a Commercial Internet Protocol Security Option (CIPSO) header that is currently being assessed.

Secure NFS

Sun Microsystems' Network File System (NFS)* is a set of file transfer protocols that has become virtually an industry standard for UNIX systems. NFS allows a client system to mount devices on a file server just as if the server were physically connected to the system. File transfers are supported over heterogeneous networks. Sun has recently introduced Secure NFS, which uses two types of encryption—the Data Encryption Standard (a private key system) and a public key encryption system.

---

*For information about NFS, see *Managing NFS and NIS* by Hal Stern, O'Reilly & Associates, Sebastopol (CA), 1991. For detailed information about Secure NFS and other aspects of UNIX network security, see *Practical UNIX Security* by Simson Garfinkel and Gene Spafford, O'Reilly & Associates, Sebastopol (CA), 1991.

"Secure from worldly chances and mishaps."

William Shakespeare, *Titus Andronicus*, Act I, Scene 1.

Part IV:

OTHER TYPES OF SECURITY

Part IV describes several additional types of security.

- Chapter 9, *Physical Security and Biometrics*, introduces physical security and describes different types of physical access devices and biometric devices.

- Chapter 10, *TEMPEST*, describes TEMPEST emanation security.

9

Physical Security and Biometrics

Physical Security
Locks and Keys: Old and New
Biometrics

Physical security protects your physical computer facilities—your building, your computer room, your computer, and your disks and other media. Biometric devices (devices that sample a physical or behavioral trait—for example, a fingerprint, a voiceprint, or a signature—and compare it with the traits on file to determine whether you are who you claim to be) provide an important first defense against break-ins. Biometric devices are beginning to be used for physical security to control access to buildings, computer rooms, and equipment.

The devices described in this chapter may also be used for system access control. For example, you might use a token, a smart card, or a fingerprint scanner to log into a computer system.

If a physical security device is an integral part of a trusted system, the National Computer Security Center can assign it a security rating, either as part of an overall system evaluation or through a separate subsystem evaluation. See Appendix D, *Government Security Programs*, for information about computer system evaluation programs.

Physical Security

In the early days of computing, computers—and the information they processed—were protected in the most fundamental way; they were locked up, with entry limited to a few authorized operators and users. Today, computers are cheaper, smaller, and more accessible to almost everyone. With computers on every desk, connected via networks to other local and remote systems, it has become less and less feasible to protect information with the old types of physical security devices. As a consequence, other types of security have increased in importance.

But despite advances in computer security and communications security, physical security remains a vitally important component of your total security plan. Physical security measures are tangible defenses that you can take to protect your facility, equipment, and information from theft, tampering, careless misuse, and natural disasters. In some ways, physical security is the easiest and the most rewarding type of security. It's very visible and reassuring. It's a tangible signal to employees and clients that you take security seriously. Building, computer room, computer, and media locks provide an important outer, physical perimeter of security. Within this perimeter, access controls and other types of security provide finer-grained protection of information.

Natural Disasters

The discussion of information security risks throughout this book has focused on man-made disasters such as sabotage, hacking, and human error. But don't forget that the same kinds of dangers that imperil all of your organization's equipment are a danger to your computer facility—fire, flood, lightning, earthquakes, and other natural disasters.

In fact, many natural threats are actually more of an issue for computers than for other types of equipment because computers and associated equipment are particularly sensitive to temperature changes, power loss, and surges in electricity. The risks are also greater for computers because, unlike buildings and office equipment, computer loss or damage involves the loss of information as well as equipment. Unlike equipment, information is not interchangeable; it may be irreplaceable—or its replacement may be so costly and disruptive as to put your organization out of business.

The suggestions provided in the following sections are very brief and basic ones. If you're in a high risk area for any of these hazards, consider acquiring fault-tolerant computers that can better tolerate adverse conditions, and get professional advice from someone whose job is disaster planning.

Fire and Smoke

• Install smoke detectors near your equipment—and check them periodically.

• Keep fire extinguishers in and near your computer rooms, and be sure everyone knows they're there.

• Enforce no-smoking policies; these are also important to controlling smoke, another hazard to computers.

• Consider using specially formulated gases such as Halon, which smothers fires and avoids the danger of water damage. Because Halon and other such gases (especially straight carbon dioxide) are potentially lethal, be sure you have an appropriate warning system.

Climate

• Some computers tolerate high and low temperatures better than others. Be sure you know your computer's limitations—and don't push the limits.

• Keep all rooms containing computers at reasonable temperatures (approximately 50-80 degrees Farenheit or 10-26 degrees Celsius).

• Keep the humidity level at 20-80 percent.

• Install gauges and alarms that warn you if you're getting out of range.

• Equip your heating and cooling systems with air filters to protect against dust (another peril to computers and especially to disks) as well.

Earthquakes and Vibration

• Keep computers away from glass windows and high surfaces, particularly if you're in a high risk area.

• Be sure that if strong vibration occurs (because of earthquakes, construction, or other sources), other objects won't easily fall on your computers.

Water

- There are various types of water damage. Flooding can result from rain or ice buildup outside, toilet or sink overflow inside, or the water from sprinklers used to fight a fire. Be sure you've protected against all types.

- If your computer does get wet, let it dry thoroughly before you attempt to turn it on again.

- Install a water sensor on the floor near your computer. If you have a raised floor, install one on the floor and one beneath it.

Electricity

- Your computer will suffer if it gets too much or too little electricity.

- For best results, install an uninterruptible power supply (UPS). It will absorb surges, will provide extra voltage during brownouts, and if power fails completely, will provide power until you're able to shut down the system. An unprotected power loss can result in serious damage. Note that surge protection won't work unless your electrical system is well-grounded.

- Install a line filter on your computer's power supply; a voltage spike can destroy your computer's power supply.

- If you can, install a special electrical circuit with an isolated ground for each of your systems.

- Install anti-static carpeting in your facility. This carpeting contains special filaments that dissipate static electricity.

Lightning

- If a lightning storm hits, try to turn off your computer and unplug it. Lightning generates an enormous power surge; it's a danger—particularly to your disks—even if you have a surge protector on your computer.

- To protect your backup tapes from the magnetic field created if lightning strikes your building, store the tapes as far away as possible from the building's steel supports. Even metal shelving may pose a hazard.

Risk Analysis and Disaster Planning

One of the most important things you can do to protect your organization from disaster is to plan for that disaster. Risk assessment and disaster planning are vital security activities, and they're rarely performed, except by the most informed organizations. For a description of what these activities are all about, see "Planning for Disaster" in Chapter 5, *Secure System Planning and Administration*.

Locks and Keys: Old and New

The first line of defense against intruders is to keep them out of your building or computer room. The locked or guarded computer room has historically been the primary means of protecting an organization's computer equipment and information from physical intrusion and unrestricted access. In most organizations these days, everyone has a terminal or a workstation, and printers are distributed around the office. It's hard in this kind of environment to lock up. But it's still a good idea to centralize the most expensive and vulnerable computer equipment— for example, to keep large shared systems, central disk or tape drives, and precious disks and tapes in a locked computer room.

To gain access to a locked facility, a user should have to pass an authentication test. Remember from Chapter 3, *Computer System Security and Access Controls*, that there are three classic ways in which you authenticate yourself (i.e., prove that you are who you say you are):

- Something you know—for example, a password.

- Something you have—for example, a key, a token, a badge, or a smart card.

- Something you are—for example, the fingerprint on your finger (which matches the one on file).

All of these authentication techniques can be used for physical security (e.g., building or computer room access) as well as for system access control. When a smart card or a fingerprint is used for computer access, it's usually only a first step. Passwords are typically required as well. When two distinct techniques are used for authentication in this way, it's called *two-factor authentication*. One factor is something you have; for example, you present your smart card or have your fingerprint or voiceprint scanned. The other factor is something you know; for example, you type a personal identification number (PIN) or a password into the system.

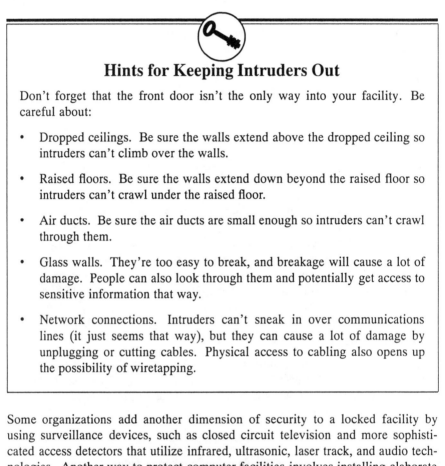

Hints for Keeping Intruders Out

Don't forget that the front door isn't the only way into your facility. Be careful about:

- Dropped ceilings. Be sure the walls extend above the dropped ceiling so intruders can't climb over the walls.

- Raised floors. Be sure the walls extend down beyond the raised floor so intruders can't crawl under the raised floor.

- Air ducts. Be sure the air ducts are small enough so intruders can't crawl through them.

- Glass walls. They're too easy to break, and breakage will cause a lot of damage. People can also look through them and potentially get access to sensitive information that way.

- Network connections. Intruders can't sneak in over communications lines (it just seems that way), but they can cause a lot of damage by unplugging or cutting cables. Physical access to cabling also opens up the possibility of wiretapping.

Some organizations add another dimension of security to a locked facility by using surveillance devices, such as closed circuit television and more sophisticated access detectors that utilize infrared, ultrasonic, laser track, and audio technologies. Another way to protect computer facilities involves installing elaborate turnstiles called *mantraps*. Systems of this kind route personnel through a double-doored facility in which you show a badge to a guard or are subjected to verification techniques, such as weight checks (to ensure against your entering the facility with an unauthorized buddy), key checks, and biometric checks, such as those described later. If you fail to pass the tests, you are trapped between the double doors, unable to enter or exit the facility until a security officer investigates the incident!

Types of Locks

In addition to locking up buildings and computer rooms, you can also secure up your computer, your network, your disk drives, and your disks. Examples of locks include:

Equipment locks   The simplest way to keep someone from walking out with your PC is simply to bolt it down. Computers, workstations, and cables may also be equipped with locks that can be unlocked only by special keys, electronic tokens, or smart cards.

Disk locks   "Secure" disks (those with encoded labels hidden inside the disk and not visible to the user) can be read only on drives equipped with special security locks and can be copied only to other secure disks, whose distribution is strictly limited. If you try to carry such a disk out of a secure area, a protection device of some kind will be activated; a buzzer may sound, a camera may take your picture, and security personnel may be notified.

Cryptographic locks   Some ultra-secure products are equipped with electronic devices known as smart keys. These keys are used to load initial cryptographic key information (usually supplied by a government agency) into the product. They typically have tamper-detection circuits, which erase the secure key storage if the circuit is broken.

Tokens

A token is an object that you carry to authenticate your identity.

In ancient times, a trusted courier might have carried the king's ring to a foreign kingdom to prove that he could speak for the king. Modern tokens are electronic devices, usually containing encoded information about the user who's authorized to carry it. Typically, a token is used in conjunction with another type of authentication, in a two-factor authentication system. For example, with certain types of PC security packages, you must insert an electronic, key-shaped token during login and authentication. After the system recognizes the token, it prompts you to type identifying information (e.g., ID and password) and compares your entry with the information encoded on the token. If the two match, you'll be allowed access. If they don't, you'll usually be given a few more chances. After multiple failures, you'll be locked out and an alarm will sound.

Challenge-response Systems

Systems like AT&T's CR1 public key authentication product are more sophisticated versions of electronic tokens. Challenge-response systems typically use a hand-held device containing an encryption program and a key. When you try to log in, the system challenges you with a random number. You type this number into the hand-held device, which encrypts it and displays the result. Now, you type that number into the system. The system compares the typed response with the result of its own encryption of the random number. If the two numbers match, you're allowed access.

Cards: Smart and Dumb

For many years, photo ID badges, often with photos, have served as credentials. You must present your license to the bank teller or supermarket clerk before you're allowed to cash a check. You must flash your employee badge before the building guard allows you to enter the building. Authentication works by having someone visually match your face to your picture.

Automatic teller machine (ATM) cards and certain types of credit cards use a more reliable type of matching by magnetically encoding identifying information on the card. For example, an automatic teller machine works by comparing the information on the card to the information you enter at the ATM—usually some combination of account number, personal identification number (PIN), and/or password—and allowing you to withdraw money only if the match is successful. Increasingly, more advanced types of cards are being used to control access to buildings, computer rooms, and computers themselves.

The typical access card is the size of a credit card. It usually contains an encoded identifying number, password, or other type of prerecorded information, often in encrypted form. Depending upon the sophistication of the system, the card may contain a large amount of additional information.

The newest types of access cards are called *smart cards*. These cards contain microchips that consist of a processor, memory used to store programs and data, and some kind of user interface. Sensitive information, which typically include the user's PIN and/or password, is kept in a secret zone of the read-only memory. This zone is encoded during manufacturing, using cryptographic techniques, and is inaccessible even to the card's owner.

Types of Access Cards

Many types of access cards have been developed; they're distinguished by the technologies used to encode information on them. The government publication, *Guideline on User Authentication Techniques for Computer Network Access Control* (FIPS PUB 83), described the following types of cards in 1980; although some of these methods have been supplanted by newer technologies, they're all included here for historical interest:

- Photo ID card. Contains a facial photograph that is checked visually by a person.

- Optical-coded card. Contains a geometric array of tiny, photographically etched or laser-burned dots representing binary zeros and ones that typically encode the user's identification number. The card is laminated with a protective layer that can't be removed without destroying the data and invalidating the card.

- Electric circuit card. Contains a printed circuit pattern. When inserted in a reader, the card selectively closes certain electrical circuits.

- Magnetic card. Contains magnetic particles that encode the card's permanent identification number. Data can be encoded on the card, but the identifying structure of the tape itself can't be altered or copied.

- Magnetic stripe card. Contains only a stripe of magnetic material, typically on one edge of the card. This is the technique used by most commercial credit cards.

- Metallic strip card. Contains rows of copper strips. The presence or absence of strips determines the code pattern.

- Capacitance card. Contains an array of small conducting plates. The capacitance of the plates determines which are isolated and which are connected.

- Passive electronic card. Contains electrically tuned circuits. The card is read using a radio frequency field, which decodes the tuned circuits to encode the unique card number.

- Active electronic card. Contains electrical coding. The card is read by an interrogation unit that examines the encoded information transmitted by the badge.

Unlike most of the other types of access card that are typically used (like badges) simply to gain entry to a facility, smart cards are often used for authentication. When a user attempts to log in or enter a secure facility, the computer system may transmit information to the smart card, which performs a series of complex calculations on it and transmits the result back to the computer. If the transmitted result matches the expected result (which is possible only if you have an authentic smart card), you're allowed to enter.

Many smart cards are built to work with card readers. You insert the card in the reader. The system displays a message, and you enter your personal identifier in response. If the identifier matches the one expected, you're allowed access.

Some smart cards use a different approach. For example, Security Dynamics of Cambridge makes a smart card that displays a code that changes every 60 seconds. To log into a system or enter a secure facility, you identify yourself (by typing your PIN or password) and you also type the code that's currently displayed on your smart card. The card is synchronized with a module attached to your main computer. This system offers a number of other special features. For example, the card is designed to stop and erase its memory at the end of its programmed lifetime. To guard against modification, batteries cannot be replaced. If you attempt to open the card to replace batteries or change it in any way, the card is permanently disabled.

Biometrics

Every person has a set of unique physiological, behavioral, and morphological characteristics that can be examined and quantified. Biometrics is the use of these characteristics to provide positive personal identification. Fingerprints and signatures have been used for many years to prove a individual's identity, but individuals can be identified in many other ways as well. Computerized biometric identification systems examine a particular trait and use that information to decide whether you have the right to enter a building, unlock a computer room, or access a system.

Biometric systems are available today that examine fingerprints, handprints, retina patterns, voice patterns, signatures, and keystroke patterns. Devices have also been proposed for such traits as footprints, lipprints, wrist vein patterns, brainwaves, skin oil characteristics, facial geometry, and weight/gait patterns.

Although the human body is intrinsically difficult to measure and quantify accurately, the biometric devices now on the market are quite reliable (especially when sensible thresholds are established for determining, for example, how closely a signature needs to match to be called "identical"). For optimal security, use biometric devices in a two-factor authentication system, in conjunction with another authentication measure such as a password.

Of the devices currently on the market, only fingerprint, handprint, and retina pattern systems are properly classified as biometric systems, because they test actual physical characteristics. Voice, signature, and keystroke systems are more properly classified as behavioral systems, because they test patterns of physiology or behavior.

The typical biometric identification system obtains data from you—for example, a handprint, a retina pattern, or a voice pattern. It then converts that analog signal into a digital representation and compares that representation to the many "templates" stored in the system. These templates are obtained when you are originally enrolled in the system. For example, in a signature verification system, you're required to sign your name several times to allow the system to sample traits and construct a template for later comparisons.

Biometric devices show great promise, but they're not yet very popular. Sales of most biometric devices number only a few thousand. Potential buyers seem to be mainly deterred by cost and by fears that unauthorized users will either impersonate authorized users or somehow bypass the devices altogether. They're also concerned that users will find the devices difficult to use or will worry that they're dangerous.

As biometric devices gain more of a foothold in the market, it's expected that software will follow. Some interesting features are already being developed. One example is a program that keeps track of unsuccessful attempts to gain access and then stores the characteristics (e.g., fingerprints) of the unsuccessful intruder so that person can be tracked down at a later time.

Another feature sends a distress signal if the system determines that you (an authorized user) are being coerced into helping an unauthorized individual to gain access. To make this work, you need an agreed-upon signal. For example, with a fingerprint system, you could signal that you needed help by pressing the left index finger, not the expected right index finger, on the glass plate of the scanner. The intruder would be unlikely to notice this subtlety. The software could be programmed to allow entry, but to alert your organization's security forces that you'd been forced to help an intruder gain entry.

There are a lot of tradeoffs associated with biometric systems. Because such systems are new and because many people just don't like being measured, there's quite a bit of personal resistance to using them. Although most of these methods are quite effective from a technical point of view, they may prove completely ineffective if people reject them and if they're seen as being intrusive, time-consuming, or even dangerous.

Some biometric methods are viewed as being quite threatening. Retina identification systems tend to be the most frightening; despite reassurances, people fear that the system will run amuck and blind them. That's quite an obstacle to acceptance! Other systems, because they're more familiar and less threatening, don't meet with the same degree of resistance. Signature systems, for example, are well-accepted because people are accustomed to having their signatures verified during banking and credit card transactions.

Surveys indicate that in order of effectiveness, biometric devices rank as follows (most secure to least secure):

- Retina pattern devices.
- Fingerprint devices.
- Handprint devices.
- Voice pattern devices.
- Keystroke pattern devices.
- Signature devices.

In order of personal acceptance, the order is just the opposite:

- Keystroke pattern devices.
- Signature devices.
- Voice pattern devices.
- Handprint devices.
- Fingerprint devices.
- Retina pattern devices.

Trade organizations for developers of biometric products are addressing technical issues associated with biometric devices and are also working on increasing public acceptance of these devices.

Fingerprints

Everybody has a unique set of fingerprints. Fingerprint verification systems examine the unique characteristics of your fingerprints and use that information to determine whether you should be allowed access.

The use of fingerprints to identify people dates from the 1800s. In the past, manual methods were used to classify and cross-check fingerprints according to certain patterns of ridges and whorls—in particular, detailed features of the print called *minutiae*. A fingerprint may have up to 150 of these minutiae. In the late 1960s, the FBI automated its system for cross-checking fingerprints, and all fingerprint checking was converted to automated systems by 1983.

A fingerprint system works like this: You place one finger on a glass plate. Light flashes inside the machine, reflects off the fingerprint, and is captured by a scanner, which transmits the fingerprint information to the computer for analysis. The fingerprint system digitizes the ridges and other characteristics of the fingerprint and compares these characteristics against the fingerprint templates stored in the system (or, in more primitive systems, against a print on a card that you carry). The system allows access only if your fingerprint sufficiently matches the template.

The more sophisticated fingerprint verification systems also perform a three-dimensional analysis of the fingerprint including infrared mechanisms for ensuring that a pulse is present. This means that an intruder can't gain entry by presenting a mold of an authorized user's finger or, worse still, an authorized finger that's no longer attached to its owner (a particularly grisly type of hacking!).

Because fingerprinting has historically been used as a law enforcement tool, fingerprint systems are pretty well-accepted by potential users of such systems—particularly in criminal justice organizations, in the military, in high-security organizations such as defense plants, and, increasingly, in banks. They have several disadvantages. They are slower than certain other types of biometric systems. In addition, their ability to work properly depends on the condition of the fingers being presented. Burns or other physical problems can affect the system's ability to match fingerprints, as can any substance (e.g., dust, perspiration, grease, glue) on fingers.

Handprints

 Everybody has unique handprints. Handprint or hand geometry verification systems examine the unique measurements of your hand and use that information to determine whether you should be allowed access.

With a handprint verification system, you place your hand on a reader, aligning all of your fingers along narrow grooves with glass between. A sensor beneath the plate scans the fingers, recording light intensity from an overhead light, and measuring fingers from tip to palm to within 1/10,000 of an inch. The information is digitized and compared against a handprint template stored for you in the system. The system will allow access only if your handprint sufficiently matches that of the stored template.

The older handprint systems examined finger length and the thickness and curve of the webbing between fingers. The newer hand geometry systems examine a whole set of topographical characteristics, such as the depth of the skin creases in the palm.

Very few handprint systems are in use today, though the technology is pretty well-accepted because it's not considered to be as intrusive as other types of biometric systems. Handprint systems are are said to be less reliable than fingerprint systems. Like fingerprint systems, their ability to work properly depends on the physical condition of the hand. Injuries, swelling, or the presence of rings, or even nail polish, on your fingers may affect the system's ability to match a handprint.

Retina Patterns

Everybody has a unique retinal vascular pattern. Unlike a fingerprint, the pattern of blood vessels in the retinal tissue can't be recorded or even photographed with ordinary equipment. Retina pattern verification systems examine the unique characteristics of an individual's retina and use that information to determine whether the individual should be allowed access.

A retina pattern verification system uses an infrared beam to scan your retina, measuring the intensity of light as it is reflected from different points and producing a digital profile of the blood vessel patterns in the retina. The system will allow access only if your retina pattern sufficiently matches those of the retina pattern stored for you in the system. The newer systems also perform iris and pupil measurements. Hand-held devices are being developed for workstation access.

Retina systems are very reliable. Their ability to work properly is affected only by very serious injuries and a few rare diseases. They have been used success-fully in national laboratories, office buildings, and prisons, but they are not well-accepted as access devices. Of all of the biometric systems, retina systems are the most threatening to people because of the fear that scanners will blind or other-wise injure them.

Voice Patterns

 Everybody has a unique vocal and acoustic pattern. Voice verification systems examine the unique characteristics of your voice. Some sys-tems also examine your own phonetic and linguistic patterns and use that information to determine whether you should be allowed access.

With a voice verification system, you speak a particular phrase. The system con-verts the acoustic strength of a speaker's voice into component frequencies and analyzes how they're distributed. The system compares your voice to a stored voiceprint. The voiceprint is a "voice signature" constructed by sampling, digi-tizing, and storing several repetitions of a particular phrase. The system will allow access only if your voice signature sufficiently matches those of the stored voiceprint.

Voice systems are fairly well-accepted (they are viewed as being non-threaten-ing) in financial organizations such as banks (particularly vaults), credit card authorization centers, and certain types of ATMs. Their ability to work properly depends to some extent on the physical condition of the larynx. Respiratory diseases, injuries, stress, and background noises may affect the system's ability to match a voiceprint.

Signature and Writing Patterns

Everybody has a unique signature and signature-writing pattern. Signa-ture verification systems examine the unique characteristics of your sig-nature, and the way in which you write your signature, and use that information to determine whether you should be allowed access.

With a signature verification system, you sign your name, using a biometric pen, typically attached by a cable to a workstation. The pen, or the pad on which you write, converts your signature into a set of electrical signals that store the dynam-ics of the signing process (e.g., changes in pressure as you press down lightly on one stroke and more forcefully on another). The system compares the signature to a signature template stored for you. It may also analyze various timing charac-teristics, such as pen-in-air movements, that are unique to you and that are much more difficult to forge than the actual static signature on a page. The system will allow access only if your signature and related characteristics sufficiently match those of the stored template.

Signature systems are a very well-accepted type of biometric system because people are accustomed to having their signatures scrutinized. Such systems are also much cheaper than many of the other biometric systems described in this section.

Keystrokes

Everybody has a unique pattern or rhythm of typing. Keystroke verification systems examine the unique characteristics of your keystrokes (your own electronic signature) and use that information to determine whether you should be allowed access.

With a keystroke system, you must type until the system can construct a reliable template of your keyboard rhythm. Once a template is available, the system will be able to examine the speed and timing of your typing during the login process, and compare it to the keystroke template stored for you. The system will allow access only if your keystroke patterns sufficiently match those of the stored template.

Because keystroke verification may be built into the ordinary login process, and doesn't require a separate verification cycle, it may eventually win wide acceptance.

Certain types of keystroke systems, which have met with some suspicion, are passive systems that continuously sample your keystrokes. The goal is to determine whether you are, in fact, the person working at your workstation and under your account, or whether an intruder has gained access. Because such systems can be used to perform surveillance of your work habits (What are you typing? At what rate?), they raise privacy issues.

10

TEMPEST

The Problem of Emanations
The TEMPEST Program
How To Build TEMPEST Products
TEMPEST Standards and Restrictions
Who Cares About TEMPEST?
Government TEMPEST Programs

Many of the security products and issues described in this book owe their origins and continuing growth to government programs and markets. Although corporate America is discovering computer security and beginning to take it to heart, government purchasing power and contracting requirements still drive much of the development and acquisition of security products. Nowhere is this fact more in evidence than in TEMPEST technology, where sales to customers other than government agencies and government contractors are almost nonexistent. TEMPEST is used mainly to protect classified information, although it's sometimes used to protect particularly sensitive unclassified information as well.

What is TEMPEST and what does it mean to the users and developers of security products? Although few people know much about TEMPEST, the technology and the government programs that promote the technology are not new. But despite its longevity, the TEMPEST program has historically been so cloaked in secrecy that even the origin of the TEMPEST name has been classified for decades. (Although meanings have been suggested, the government denies that "TEMPEST" is an acronym or has any particular meaning.) As one observer of the security scene put it, "This is the real spook stuff!"

The Problem of Emanations

All electronic equipment—hair dryers, typewriters, microchips, and supercomputers—emits electrical and electromagnetic radiation through the air or through conductors. It has long been recognized that such emanations can cause interference to radio and television reception. And recently, concerns have surfaced about possible health hazards associated with emanations (see inset).

As early as the 1950s, government and industry observers began to become concerned about another electromagnetic risk—the possibility that electronic eavesdroppers could intercept emanations, decipher them, obtain information about the signals used inside the emanating electronic equipment, and use this information to reconstruct the data being processed by the equipment. They speculated that eavesdroppers could breach security even some distance from the equipment.

Studies of signal interception and decoding have borne out these speculations. It turns out that with virtually no risk of detection, eavesdroppers using relatively unsophisticated equipment can intercept and decipher signals from an electronic source. Modern listening devices allow an eavesdropper to detect emissions and reproduce data streams or video screen images—for example, to read the computer display screens on the desktops in a remote building. Estimates are that the components needed to perform such a penetration would cost as little as $300 and would be available at a local electronics store.

Electronic eavesdropping is sometimes laughably easy. Early versions of a Heathkit terminal transmitted such strong signals that an ordinary television set, placed beside the terminal, would display everything displayed on the terminal's screen. Both technical journals and the popular press have reported examples of experiments showing how easy it is to intercept and decipher electromagnetic emanations. For example, several years ago, Wim van Eck and his colleagues at the dr. Neher Laboratories of the Netherlands PTT performed a series of experiments showing that with a relatively small investment in time and resources, they could intercept and decipher signals from video display terminals within a targeted building.* Van Eck performed a second experiment, shown on British television, which intercepted and deciphered signals emanating from the British Broadcasting Company (BBC). Vendors at computer security shows sometimes demonstrate their own products—and debunk those of others—by showing how easy it is to intercept signals emanating from their competitors' equipment.

---

*Wim van Eck, "Electromagnetic Radiation from Video Display Units: An Eavesdropping Risk?," *Computers and Security*, Volume 4, Number 4, North Holland Publisher, 1985.

The TEMPEST Program

In the late 1950s, the U.S. government established a program called TEMPEST aimed at attacking the emanations problem. TEMPEST has become an umbrella name for the technology that contains or suppresses signal emanations from electronic equipment, and for the investigations and studies of these emanations. An unclassified government publication describes TEMPEST emanations as "unintentional, intelligence-bearing ... signals which might disclose sensitive information transmitted, received, handled, or otherwise processed by an information processing system."

For some years, industry involvement in the TEMPEST program came about as the result of specific U.S. government contracts. When the government saw a need for TEMPEST protection of computer equipment, the contracting agency issued a Request for Proposal, and manufacturers proposed to build the equipment to meet the specific, and usually rather limited, needs of the project.

In 1974, government and industry began to work more closely together through the Industrial TEMPEST Program (ITP). ITP was founded with the following objectives:

- Specify a TEMPEST standard that sets allowable limits on the levels of emission from electronic equipment. The idea was to state clearly how much the equipment could leak and still be acceptable.

- Outline criteria for testing equipment that, according to its vendors, meets the TEMPEST standard.

- Certify vendor equipment that successfully meets the TEMPEST standard. (See the discussion of this standard in "TEMPEST Standards and Restrictions.") Certified equipment is listed in the government's *Information Systems Security Products and Services Catalogue*. The catalogue is available from the Government Printing Office; see Appendix E, *A Security Source Book*, for details.

The idea of ITP was to standardize TEMPEST requirements and technologies, and to encourage vendors to develop and test off-the-shelf TEMPEST equipment that the government could buy. The early TEMPEST products were typically standalone computer systems. Over the past decade, TEMPEST versions of most types of computer products have become available: complete computer systems (mainframes, minicomputers, workstations, and personal computers), peripheral devices of all kinds (printers, plotters, disk drives, tape drives, scanners, OCR

Hazardous to Your Health?

In the security world, fears about uncontrolled electromagnetic emissions focus on the interception and deciphering of these emissions by intruders. Of more immediate concern to most of us may be the growing evidence that emissions are physically dangerous as well. Since 1977, studies have looked at the health consequences of exposure to three types of fields: VLF (very low frequency, such as those given off by a computer's horizontal-scan frequency), ELF (extremely low frequency, such as those given off by a computer's vertical-scan frequency), and 60-hertz AC (alternating current, such as those given off by power lines and computer monitors' power transformers):

- In 1979, epidemiologists Nancy Wertheimer and Ed Leeper reported on an investigation showing that children living in Denver homes located near high-current electric wires died of cancer at twice the expected rate.

- In 1988, Kaiser Permanente researchers reported that of 1583 case-controlled women who attended their clinics, women who worked with VDTs for more than 20 hours a week suffered miscarriages at a rate 80 percent higher than women performing similar work without VDTs.

- In 1989, Johns Hopkins epidemiologists reported that the risk of leukemia for New York Telephone Company cable splicers, who work close to power lines, was seven times greater than that of other company workers.*

In December of 1990, the Environmental Protection Agency reported that environmental studies have shown "a causal link [between power lines and] EM fields and certain forms of site-specific cancer." Large-scale studies are now underway, and power companies and computer manufacturers and users are beginning to take these findings seriously. Chances are that the safety of VDTs and related equipment may be a major public health battlefield in the future.

In the past, TEMPEST has focused almost exclusively on the protection of classified information. But if it turns out that TEMPEST-type shielding can protect people as well as data, the TEMPEST technology described in this chapter may get a new lease on life, providing human security as well as data security.

---

*For more information about these studies and others, see Paul Brodeur's *Currents of Death*, Simon & Schuster, New York (NY), 1989, as well as the July 1990 issue of *MacWorld*.

equipment, mice, and tablets), communications equipment (modems, multi-plexers, and network equipment), cabling, and related equipment.

There are approximately 50 manufacturers of TEMPEST equipment today. They include large computer manufacturers, such as Apollo, Data General, Digital Equipment Corporation, Hewlett-Packard, IBM, UNISYS, Xerox, and Wang Laboratories, as well as numerous smaller manufacturers.

How To Build TEMPEST Products

Because they're built to control electromagnetic emanations, TEMPEST products are larger, heavier, and more expensive than comparable commercial products. TEMPEST products control emanations either by shielding the signals—building a container around them so they can't emanate beyond the container—or by sup-pressing the signals—engineering the equipment so signals don't emanate at all. (Sometimes, a product combines both methods.)

A *shield* attenuates electromagnetic signals, conducting them to ground before they can escape. A shield, which can be as small as a cable casing or as large as an entire building, is constructed in such a way that signals can't emanate outside it.

The simplest but most expensive shield approach is to install regular computer equipment in a shielded room that provides special protection against electromag-netic leaks. Smaller shields or containment devices serve the same purpose as a shielded room; shields can be constructed for computers, workstations, peripheral devices, circuit boards, and inside wiring.

Containers are made of materials that are especially capable of shielding elec-trical and electromagnetic signals. Copper, because it is a good conductor, is a popular choice. Different types and thicknesses of materials are appropriate for different frequencies of signals. Systems that rely on shielding must provide a specialized design for all component doors, air vents, filters, and communications lines that enter or exit from the equipment.

The containment approach to TEMPEST security can be a very effective one. On the negative side, shields are often expensive and time-consuming to build, and by using the equipment improperly, people can jeopardize TEMPEST security. For example, a contained central processor may need to be opened to reset it if a system crash occurs. A contained printer may need to be opened to change paper or fix a jam. If operators don't realize the importance of closing the computer or printer properly, they may inadvertently destroy the TEMPEST integrity of the product.

Another TEMPEST problem relates to the design of the product. During testing, a TEMPEST product that relies on the containment approach is fine-tuned. Although components are shielded, there are likely to be some exposed pieces that need special engineering. For example, a shielded workstation may have a speaker that requires outside access. A common approach to containing the speaker vent is to insert a mesh covering over the vent. This approach attenuates the signal and effectively shields the speaker. But, with the shielding approach, it's essential that the design of the product, as it exists at the time of product development (and government endorsement) be frozen. If substitutions in components are made at a later time, even within the containment, the TEMPEST integrity of the product may be lost. For example, if the impedance of the speaker changes, the mesh may not be as effective a shield as it was on the original product. If a contained system or component is repaired in the field, a customer engineer might erroneously replace a board with another board that hasn't been TEMPEST-certified. The result is that the container is no longer fully effective, and TEMPEST security is breached.

Some TEMPEST products use a different engineering approach. With *source suppression*, products are engineered in such a way that compromising signals are suppressed at the source, often by adding equipment that emanates confusing and spurious signals.

The source suppression approach tends to be more technologically difficult than the shield approach, but it's a more effective one from a human engineering point of view. Because the approach doesn't use shielding, it doesn't prevent users from being able to access switches and other controls. Its effectiveness doesn't depend on the proper use of the equipment by human beings. It tends to be a more appropriate approach for products installed in an office environment.

Building a TEMPEST product is quite different from building a commercial product. A prime commercial motivation is to build at the lowest reasonable cost. Product developers pick their components on the basis of cost and reliability. For example, although integrated circuit chips may differ in terms of speed, emanation of radio frequencies, and other characteristics, all of them might work acceptably and be cheap enough. If another manufacturer's chips drop substantially in price, a developer might even decide to replace a chip later in the product's life cycle. In the TEMPEST world, product developers don't have this flexibility. With a TEMPEST product, it's necessary to freeze the specs for a product at the point where the product tests acceptably.

Once a TEMPEST product has been built, it's submitted to the government for evaluation and endorsement. In theory, only successfully endorsed products can be advertised as meeting TEMPEST standards. Sometimes, a vendor will describe its product as "Designed to meet NACSIM 5100A" (the TEMPEST standard), as opposed to "Meeting the NACSIM 5100A standard" or "TEMPEST-endorsed." This is a hint that although the product may contain TEMPEST control measures, the measures either haven't been TEMPEST-tested or haven't completed testing.

TEMPEST Standards and Restrictions

TEMPEST products are developed, tested, and sold under the close scrutiny of the U.S. government.

TEMPEST Standards

The National TEMPEST Standard specifies the level of emanation permitted for TEMPEST equipment. Since the original TEMPEST standard was published in the late 1950s, this standard has been revised a number of times. The following list summarizes this history:

1950s   Original TEMPEST standard NAG1A published.

1960s   Standard revised and reissued as FS222 and later FS222A.

1970   Major revision of the standard published as National Communications Security Information Memorandum 5100 (Directive on TEMPEST Security), known as NACSEM 5100 and entitled "Compromising Emanations Laboratory Test Standard, Electromagnetics (U)".

1974   Another revision of the NACSEM 5100 standard.

1981   Current TEMPEST standard, known as NACSIM 5100A, published in conformance with National Communications Security Committee Directive 4, entitled "National Policy on Control of Compromising Emanations."

NACSIM 5100A instructs U.S. government departments and agencies to protect classified information against compromising emanations. As a result of this directive, specific procedures have been developed for agencies to use in determining the countermeasures needed for equipment and facilities that process national security information. These are detailed in National Communications Security Instruction 5004 (NACSI 5004), published in 1984.

Getting Access to the TEMPEST Standard

Both NACSIM 5100A and NACSI 5004 are classified documents, and access to these documents is available to vendors only on a strictly enforced need-to-know basis. Who needs to know? There are two situations in which a vendor will require access to these documents.

First, if you intend to develop an off-the-shelf TEMPEST product, you must have access to classified TEMPEST information. In this case, you get access by following the product evaluation process defined by the Endorsed TEMPEST Products Program (described later).

Second, many U.S. government contracts require that systems developed under the contract adhere to the TEMPEST standard. In this case, the request for and distribution of classified TEMPEST information are handled through your contract officer. When the contracting agency sponsors a vendor to the U.S. Defense Investigative Service (DIS), the agency arranges for the vendor to obtain the proper clearances and storage facilities. DIS issues a facility clearance to the company and individual clearances for employees who will be involved with the classified contract.

Foreign Standards

The North Atlantic Treaty Organization (NATO) has a parallel TEMPEST standard for the control of electromagnetic radiation. This standard, defined in 1982, is the AMSG 720B Compromising Emanations Laboratory Test Standard. Products that meet the NATO standard are placed on the NATO Recommended Products List (NRPL). This list is available from the Government Printing Office.

Several NATO countries have administrative entities that control TEMPEST use in their countries. In West Germany, the TEMPEST program is administered by the National Telecom Board. In the United Kingdom, the Industrial TEMPEST Scheme is administered by the Government Communications Headquarters (GCHQ). The United Kingdom has also adopted a second-level TEMPEST standard, called AMSG 788A, described in "Changing TEMPEST Concepts" later in this chapter.

TEMPEST Export Restrictions

The U.S. government closely regulates the sale and export of TEMPEST products. Export regulations are intended to restrict the use of products that ultimately could make an enemy nation's communications more difficult for U.S. intelligence agencies to decipher.

Like the cryptographic products described in Chapter 7, *Encryption*, TEMPEST products can be exported outside the United States (or to a "foreign person" inside the United States) only with an appropriate export license from the Office of Munitions Control (OMC) of the U.S. Department of State.* If you want to build and sell a TEMPEST product overseas, you must register with the OMC or face a fine of up to $1 million.

In general, licenses are issued only for the governments and government contractors of the NATO countries, plus certain "friendly" governments, such as Canada, Australia, and New Zealand. License applications are considered on a case-by-case basis, but most countries—in particular the Eastern European countries—have historically been off-limits.

The paperwork burden associated with obtaining the necessary export licenses for TEMPEST sales is an onerous one. If you want to sell a TEMPEST product, you must submit an application, accompanied by appropriate purchase orders, contracts or letters of intent, government forms, and (for defense contractors), letters from the sponsoring government agency. Even a complete and uncontroversial application takes many months to process. In recent years, a number of computer manufacturers have decided that bureaucratic difficulties outweigh the benefits of entering or staying in the TEMPEST market, and have closed down their TEMPEST operations.

Who Cares About TEMPEST?

Although it's relatively easy to breach security by intercepting emanations, it's pretty cumbersome to make sense of them. Someone bent on cracking a system is far more likely to try to crack the system's password defenses or to bribe an employee to reveal secrets. TEMPEST risks and technologies are of most interest in environments where the stakes are very high—those where even a small risk of detection warrants a major investment in defense. In a word, the realm of foreign intelligence!

Despite some recent commercial interest in TEMPEST, the U.S. military services, the intelligence agencies, and government contractors still buy about 90 percent of all TEMPEST equipment. The remaining TEMPEST sales are to law enforcement agencies, civil agencies (such as NASA, the Nuclear Regulatory Commission, and the Securities and Exchange Commission), and to U.S. government installations (such as embassies and consulates) abroad. Although TEMPEST

---

*Licensing is mandated by Category XI (C), Title 22 of Federal Regulations, Section 121 and by the International Traffic in Arms Regulations (ITARs).

exports are closely controlled, there is a market in the governments of friendly foreign nations such as Canada, the United Kingdom, Australia, New Zealand, and the NATO countries, as well as among contractors who work for these governments.

Increasing concern with computer security has resulted in more and more government requirements for products and programs that adhere to the TEMPEST standard. Adherence to the TEMPEST standard means that the equipment sold to the government under a government requisition, as well as the equipment the contractor uses to develop a product or provide a service under the contract, be TEMPEST-certified equipment.

Hard TEMPEST market numbers are difficult to come by, because the need for TEMPEST equipment is in many cases classified, as are the budgets for the clandestine organizations that are major TEMPEST customers. Although it's difficult to quantify the market with any precision, it's possible to approximate roughly the size and characteristics of this market by estimating the percentage of an organization's total computer hardware budget that TEMPEST requirements represent.

Approximately one-half of the U.S. government's budget for information technology is allocated to agencies that have responsibility for national security, intelligence, and international affairs—the organizations that historically have been the primary customers for TEMPEST equipment. Roughly 20 percent of all procurements by these organizations specify TEMPEST requirements. Industry experts put recent TEMPEST sales estimates at several billion dollars per year.

The TEMPEST market is an incremental one. Security observers speak of an "iceberg effect," in which a TEMPEST contractual requirement is the tip of the iceberg. In other words, the requirement for TEMPEST technology may apply only to a small portion of a total contract requisition; without being able to satisfy the TEMPEST requirement, however, a vendor may not be able to bid on an overall total contract. Many vendors whose equipment would otherwise meet the technical requirements of a government project have found that without TEMPEST products they're effectively locked out of certain sales opportunities.

Is TEMPEST Needed?

Dramatic changes in U.S. government guidelines for TEMPEST use are now being discussed within the government, and the reverberations from these guidelines are only beginning to be felt in the industry.

In the past few years, federal agencies have become increasingly concerned about the cost of TEMPEST equipment relative to its expected security benefits. TEMPEST equipment costs substantially more than non-TEMPEST equipment—traditionally about 80 percent more, and the difference is even more dramatic with certain kinds of products. In these days of government cost consciousness, this difference is especially significant. Efforts are now underway within the government to define more carefully the situations in which TEMPEST technology is needed and to reserve its use for those situations that truly warrant the additional protection, and its corresponding cost.

Several years ago, the General Accounting Office began studying the Department of Defense's TEMPEST buying practices in response to charges that program managers were buying TEMPEST equipment regardless of need. The charges originated with defense contractors who were being required by contract terms to buy and use TEMPEST equipment in their work. In its report, the GAO noted that 18 years had passed since DoD had rewritten the rules spelling out the situations in which TEMPEST equipment must be used. As a consequence, there were inconsistencies in interpreting these rules. The report stated that:

> The [military] services sometimes acquire TEMPEST countermeasures without out evaluating whether they are needed, [thus] wasting money . . . On the other hand, the military and contractors are sometimes processing classified information without evaluating the risks of compromising emanations.

The GAO recommended that DoD promptly revise its TEMPEST policy. DoD is reportedly conducting a program-by-program survey to assess TEMPEST and other security needs.

Changing TEMPEST Concepts

When is TEMPEST really needed? Efforts to define needs in a rigorous fashion have been underway for several years. The TEMPEST zoning concept is an example of an attempt to formalize when TEMPEST is and isn't needed. The zoning concept argues that certain physical configurations are already sufficiently well protected and don't require the additional security offered by TEMPEST-certified equipment.

For example, suppose that a computer system and all of its associated workstations and peripheral devices are installed in a windowless room in the middle of a large building. Suppose further that the building is surrounded by large, controlled parking lots, the facility is protected by a guarded fence, and the entire property is located in a remote part of the country. This is not a case for TEMPEST!

The basic theory behind the zoning concept was that emanations would be unlikely to leak beyond a zoned facility's perimeter and that any emanations that did leak would be unreadable and undecipherable because of the intervening barriers, the distance, and other associated noise and non-compromising emanations.

Proponents of the zoning concept attempted to specify a series of zones. Commercial, off-the-shelf equipment might be permitted within a particular zone (i.e., one in which the computer equipment is located a certain number of feet from the outer building walls and a certain number of feet from the outer perimeter of the building, etc.). TEMPEST-certified equipment might be required for other zones.

The problem with the zoning concept is that commercial equipment can't be measured in the way that TEMPEST equipment can. Commercial electronic products may contain functionally equivalent chips that don't emanate to the same degree. Even "identical" products might contain chips manufactured by different vendors. Although the chips perform identical functions, there may be substantial differences in processing speed and radiation emanation. One copy of a product might emanate a much greater distance than another copy of the same product. In an uncontrolled manufacturing process, there's no way to determine which copy will, and which won't, emanate at an unacceptable level.

Because adherents of the zoning concept did not take this characteristic of electronic emanations into account, commercial equipment standards for different zones were essentially meaningless. The original zoning concept eventually fell into disuse.

From the zoning concept has come a modified concept. According to this new concept, an installation is quantified according to a variety of characteristics, such as geographic location (region, state, city), type of facility (public, private), type of building (wood, cinderblock, brick), distance of nearest reconnaissance point, and so on. A facility's mathematically computed penetration index is compared to a stated cutoff. In general, facilities below the cutoff are free to use commercial, off-the-shelf equipment; facilities at or above the cutoff are required to use TEMPEST-certified equipment. For a particular government contract though, a contracting agency would still have the right to require a facility that's below the cutoff to acquire TEMPEST equipment for that contract.

The United Kingdom has recently adopted a further modification of this concept, one stipulating that at an intermediate cutoff point a facility's equipment may adhere to a second-level TEMPEST standard, known as AMSG 788A, which is less stringent than NACSIM 5100A in the U.S. or AMSG 720B in the NATO countries. Adoption of such a strategy in the U.S. has been discussed, and a draft document describing a second-level standard is expected to be approved and announced by 1992.

Government TEMPEST Programs

You can't simply hang out a shingle as a TEMPEST supplier. TEMPEST-certified products must be developed, tested, and endorsed according to rigorous government-monitored guidelines.

The focal point of TEMPEST development has historically been the Industrial TEMPEST Program (ITP). Since 1974, government and industry representatives have worked together through ITP to set standards and to develop, test, and certify TEMPEST equipment. TEMPEST vendors were required to be members of ITP in order to submit products for TEMPEST certification. Only ITP members were given access to the classified NACSIM 5100A standard. Successfully evaluated products developed by TEMPEST vendors under ITP were placed on the Preferred Products List (PPL) and published in the *Information Systems Security Products and Services Catalogue*, along with other information security products.

Prompted by increasing concern over the security of the products on the PPL several years ago, the government declared a moratorium on ITP membership and began a restructuring of the entire TEMPEST product endorsement and certification process. In March of 1988, the government eliminated the notion of company membership in ITP. New products and services must now be evaluated according the following new TEMPEST programs:

Endorsed TEMPEST Products Program.
This program evaluates and endorses TEMPEST products. Accepted products are placed on the Endorsed TEMPEST Products List (ETPL). Products currently undergoing evaluation are placed on the Potential Endorsed TEMPEST Products List (PETPL). Companies that have submitted products for evaluation under the Endorsed TEMPEST Products Program include IBM, Hewlett-Packard, Mitek, FiberCom, and Versitron.

Endorsed TEMPEST Test Services Program.
This program was established to support TEMPEST product development by providing quality TEMPEST test services. The program evaluates and endorses TEMPEST test services. Accepted services are placed on the Endorsed TEMPEST Test Services List (ETTSL). Companies whose test services have been endorsed under the Endorsed TEMPEST Test Services Program include Honeywell, Digital Equipment Corporation, Wang Laboratories, Chomerics, and Ford Aerospace.

Endorsed TEMPEST Test Instrumentation Program.
This program evaluates and endorses TEMPEST test instrumentation. Test instrumentation is equipment that operates in automatic fashion to quantify

and/or analyze TEMPEST characteristics of equipment under test (EUT) against the TEMPEST standard. Accepted instruments are placed on the Endorsed TEMPEST Test Instrumentation List (ETTIL).

During a transitional period, products currently listed on the PPL will remain on that list. For detailed information about the new programs and the transitional rules, see Appendix D, *Government Security Programs*.

*"Every prudent man will sooner trust
to two securities than to one."*

Earl of Chesterfield.

Part V:
APPENDICES

Part V provides computer security reference material.

- Appendix A, *Acronyms*, lists computer security acronyms.

- Appendix B, *Computer Security Legislations*, summarizes legislation that affects information protection, computer crime, and privacy.

- Appendix C, *Orange Book and Other Summaries*, provides detailed tables of trusted system requirements introduced earlier in the book.

- Appendix D, *Government Security Programs*, lists procedures for government evaluation of computer security, communications security, and TEMPEST products.

- Appendix E, *A Security Source Book*, tells you where to go for more information: security standards, government publications and programs, security user groups, and more.

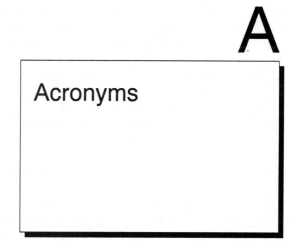

Acronyms

Most security literature is a real alphabet soup, with acronyms for just about everything. We've included acronyms for the concepts, programs, and products you're likely to read about in this book and other publications (particularly government publications).

ABA	American Bankers Association
ACF	Access Control Facility
ACL	Access Control List
ACM	Association for Computing Machinery
ACS	Access Control System
ACSE	Association Control Service Element
ADP	Automated Data Processing
AIS	Automated Information System
ANSI	American National Standards Institute
ARP	Address Resolution Protocol
ARPA	Advanced Research Projects Agency
ARPANET	Advanced Research Projects Agency Network
ATM	Automatic Teller Machine
BI	Background Investigation

C	Confidential
C3I	Command, Control, Communications, and Intelligence
CAP	Countermeasures Advisory Panel
CASE	Common Application Service Elements
CBC	Cipher Block Chaining
CBEMA	Computer and Business Equipment Manufacturers Association
CCB	Configuration Control Board
CCEP	Commercial Communications Security Endorsement Program
CCITT	Comité Consultatif Internationale Telegraphique et Telephonique (International Telephone and Telegraph Consultative Committee)
CCR	Commitment, Concurrency, and Recovery
CDRL	Contract Data Requirements List
CFB	Cipher Feedback
CFSR	Contract Funds Status Report
CHIPS	Clearing House Interbank Payments System
CI	Configuration Item
CIA	Central Intelligence Agency
CIPSO	Commercial Internet Protocol Security Options
CM	Compartmented Mode
CMW	Compartmented Mode Workstation
CMWPROT	Compartmented Mode Workstation Prototype
CMWREQS	Compartmented Mode Workstation Requirements
COMINT	Communications Intelligence
COMPUSEC	Computer Security
COMSEC	Communications Security
COTR	Contract Officers Technical Representative
COTS	Commercial Off The Shelf
CRB	Configuration Review Board
CRC	Cyclic Redundancy Check
CRC	Cyclic Redundancy Code
CSC	Computer Security Center
CSMA/CD	Carrier Sense Multiple Access with Collision Detection
CTLS	Complete Top-Level Specification
DAA	Designated Approving Authority
DAC	Discretionary Access Control
DARPA	Defense Advanced Research Projects Agency
DBMS	Data Base Management System
DCA	Defense Communications Agency
DDN	Defense Data Network
DEA	Data Encryption Algorithm
DES	Data Encryption Standard
DIA	Defense Intelligence Agency
DIA	Document Interchange Architecture

DIS	Defense Investigative Service
DISNet	Defense Integrated Secure Network
DMS	Defense Message System
DNSix	Department of Defense Intelligence Information System Network for Security Information Exchange
DoC	Department of Commerce
DoD	Department of Defense
DoDIIS	Department of Defense Intelligence Information System
DoD-STD	Department of Defense Standard
DoS	Department of State
DoS	Denial of Service
DPL	Degausser Products List
DTE	Data Terminal Equipment
DTLS	Descriptive Top-Level Specification
E3	End-to-End Encryption
EAR	Export Administration Regulations
EBDI	Electronic Business Data Interchange
EBI	Extended Background Investigation
EC	Electronic Commerce
ECB	Electronic Codebook
ECMA	European Computer Manufacturers Association
ECPL	Endorsed Cryptographic Products List
EDI	Electronic Data Interchange
EDP	Electronic Data Processing
EFT	Electronic Fund Transfer
EGP	Exterior Gateway Protocol
EIA	Electronics Industries Association
EPL	Evaluated Products List
ETCOM	European Testing for Certification for Office and Manufacturing
ETL	Endorsed Tools List
ETPL	Endorsed TEMPEST Products List
ETPP	Endorsed TEMPEST Products Program
ETTIL	Endorsed TEMPEST Test Instrumentation List
ETTIP	Endorsed TEMPEST Test Instrumentation Program
ETTSL	Endorsed TEMPEST Test Services List
ETTSP	Endorsed TEMPEST Test Services Program
EUT	Equipment Under Test
FBI	Federal Bureau of Investigation
FDDI	Fiber Distributed Data Interface
FER	Final Evaluation Report
FIPS	Federal Information Processing Standards
FOI	Freedom of Information
FOUO	For Official Use Only

FTLS	Formal Top-Level Specification
FTP	File Transfer Protocol
GAO	Government Accounting Office
GGP	Gateway-to-Gateway Protocol
GISA	German Information Security Agency
GOSIP	Government Open Systems Interconnection Protocol
GPO	General Printing Office
GSA	General Services Administration
GSSP	Generally Accepted System Security Principles
I&A	Identification and Authentication
ICMP	Internet Control Message Protocol
ICST	Institute for Computer Sciences and Technology
IGP	Interior Gateway Protocol
IP	Internet Protocol
IPAR	Initial Product Assessment Report
IEEE	Institute of Electrical and Electronic Engineers
IFIP	International Federation of Information Processing
INFOSEC	Information Security
IS/A AMPE	Inter-Service/Agency Automatic Message Processing Exchange
ISDN	Integrated Services Digital Networking
ISF	Information Security Foundation
ISO	International Standards Organization (Organisation Internationale de Normalisation)
ISSO	Information System Security Officer
IT	Information Technology
ITAR	International Traffic in Arms Regulation
ITSEC	Information Technology Security Evaluation Criteria
KDC	Key Distribution Center
LAN	Local Area Network
LRC	Longitudinal Redundancy Check
MAC	Mandatory Access Control
MAC	Message Authentication Code
MAN	Metropolitan Area Network
MAP/TOP	Manufacturing Automation Protocol/Technical Office Protocol
MC	Multiple Compartments
MDC	Manipulation Detection Code
MIC	Message Integrity Check
MILNET	Military Network
MLS	Multi-Level Security
MOA	Memorandum of Agreement
MOU	Memorandum of Understanding

MSM	Message Stream Modification
MULTICS	Multiplexed Information and Computing Service
MWT	Maximum Waiting Time
NACSI	National Communications Security Instruction
NASA	National Aeronautics and Space Administration
NATO	North Atlantic Treaty Organization
NBS	National Bureau of Standards
NCC	Network Control Center
NCSC	National Computer Security Center
NCSL	National Computer Systems Laboratory
NFIB	National Foreign Intelligence Board
NFS	Network File System
NIC	Network Information Center
NIST	National Institute of Standards and Technology
NOC	Network Operations Center
NOFORN	Not Releasable to Foreign Nationals
NOS	Network Operating System
NSA	National Security Agency
NSC	Network Security Center
NSDD	National Security Decision Directive
NSF	National Science Foundation
NSFNET	National Science Foundation Network
NTAISS	National Telecommunications and Automated Information Systems Security
NTCB	Network Trusted Computing Base
NTIS	National Technical Information Service
NTISS	National Telecommunications and Information Systems Security
NTISSC	National Telecommunications and Information Systems Security Committee
NTISSP	National Telecommunications and Information Systems Security Publication
NTP	Network Time Protocol
OFB	Output Feedback
OMB	Office of Management and the Budget
OMC	Office of Munitions Control
ORCON	Originator Controlled
OSF	Open Software Foundation
OSI	Open System Interconnection
OTA	Office of Technology Assessment
PABX	Private Automated Branch Exchange
PAC	Privilege Attribute Certificates
PDN	Public Data Network

PDU	Protocol Data Unit
PIN	Personal Identification Number
PKC	Public Key Cryptography
POSIX	Portable Operating System Interface for Computer Environments
PPD	Port Protection Device
PPL	Preferred Products List
PROPIN	Proprietary Information Involved
PSDN	Public Switched Data Network
PSN	Packet Switch Node
PTR	Preliminary Technical Report
PWDS	Protected Wireline Distribution System
RACF	Resource Access Control Facility
RAMP	Rating Maintenance Phase
RARP	Reverse Address Resolution Protocol
RDP	Reliable Datagram Protocol
RFC	Request for Comments
RFP	Request for Proposal
RFQ	Request for Quotation
RIP	Routing Information Protocol
RIPSO	Revised Internet Protocol Security Options
RSA	Rivest, Shamir, Adleman (public-key encryption algorithm)
ROM	Read Only Memory
S	Secret
SACDIN	Strategic Air Command Digital Network
SAISS	Subcommittee on Automated Information in Systems Security (of NTISSC)
SBI	Special Background Investigation
SCI	Sensitive Compartmented Information
SCI	Socket Compatibility Interface
SDI	Strategic Defense Initiative
SDNS	Secure Data Network System
SFUG	Security Features User's Guide
SIOP	Single Integrated Operational Plan
SKC	Secret Key Cryptography
SMTP	Simple Mail Transfer Protocol
SNA	Systems Network Architecture
SNMP	Simple Network Management Protocol
SNS	Secure Network Server
SQT&E	Security Qualification Test and Evaluation
SRP	Security Relevant Portion
SSDD	System Security Design Documentation
SSO	System Security Officer
STP	Security Test Plan

STPR	Security Test Procedures
STS	Subcommittee on Telecommunications Security (of NTISSC)
STU	Secure Telephone Unit
ST&E	Security Test and Evaluation
SWIFT	Society for Worldwide Interbank Financial Telecommunications
T	Top Secret
TAC	Terminal Access Controller
TAR	Technical Assessment Report
TCB	Trusted Computing Base
TCP/IP	Transmission Control Protocol/Internet Protocol
TCS	Trusted Computer System
TCSEC	Trusted Computer System Evaluation Criteria
TELNET	Teletype Network
TFE	Trusted Front-End Processor
TFM	Trusted Facility Manual
TFTP	Trivial File Transport Protocol
TLI	Transport Level Interface
TLS	Top-Level Specification
TNET	Trusted Network
TNI	Trusted Network Interpretations
TNIU	Trusted Network Interface Units
TPEP	Trusted Product Evaluation Program
TRB	Technical Review Board
TREES	Trusted Realm Environment Exchange Specification
TRUSIX	Trusted UNIX Organization
TS	Top Secret
TSIG	Trusted Systems Interoperability Group
TUI	Trusted Network Interface Unit
U	Unclassified
UDP	User Datagram Protocol
UUCP	UNIX to UNIX Copy Program
VAN	Value Added Network
VMM	Virtual Machine Monitor
VMTP	Versatile Message Transaction Protocol
VR	Vendor Report
WAN	Wide Area Network
WWMCCS	Worldwide Military Command and Control System
XNS	Xerox Network Systems

B

Computer Security Legislation

This book mentions many federal laws, executive orders, and guidelines that have shaped government computer security policy. The tables in this appendix summarize legislation in the three general areas discussed in Chapter 2, *Some Security History*, legislation that protects classified information, legislation that establishes privacy rules and guidelines, and legislation that defines and prohibits computer crime.

Table B-1. Information Protection Legislation

Legislation	Year	Effect
Brooks Act	1965	Automatic Data Processing Equipment Act (Public Law 89-306). Established the General Services Administration (GSA) and the Office of Management and the Budget (OMB) as the central procurement authorities for computer equipment, supplies, and services within the federal government. According to the Brooks Act, these controls apply to general-purpose, off-the-shelf equipment that must be commercially available. Although a system may meet the criteria for inclusion established by the Brooks Act, procurement authority in a particular case may be delegated to another agency for reasons of national security, defense, economy, or efficiency.
		Under the Brooks Act, NBS was designated as the agency responsible for federal computer standards, conducting standards research, and assisting other agencies in standards implementation.
Arms Export Control Act	1968	22 U.S. Code, 2751-2794. Specified that cryptographic and TEMPEST data to foreign nations and nationals is allowed only with an export license from the U.S. Department of State under the International Traffic in Arms Regulations (ITARs).

Table B-1. Information Protection Legislation (continued)

Legislation	Year	Effect
PD/NSC-24	1977	Presidential Directive/National Security Council-24 (unclassified in 1979). Expanded the authority of DoD to safeguard sensitive communications that "would be useful to an adversary." Created the National Communications Security Committee and gave responsibility for classified information to NSA and unclassified information to the Department of Commerce.
Foreign Intelligence Surveillance Act	1978	Public Law 95-511. Specified standards for electronic surveillance (e.g., wiretaps) of foreign intelligence.
OMB Circular A-71	1978	Security of Federal Automated Information Systems. Directed each executive agency to establish and maintain a computer security program.
Export Administration Act	1979	50 U.S. Code 2401-2420. Specified that scientific and technical data to foreign nations and nationals is allowed only with an export license from the U.S. Department of Commerce under the Export Administration Regulations (EARs).
Paperwork Reduction Act	1980	Promoted the use of efficient office systems (e.g., electronic mail, document storage, and electronic imaging systems) under the management of OMB.
OMB Circular A-123	1981	Directed agency heads and managers to set up management plans and to take responsibility for eliminating fraud, waste, and abuse in government programs. The aim of this program is to establish confidence and accountability in the protection of federal operations.

Table B-1. Information Protection Legislation (continued)

Legislation	Year	Effect
Executive Order 12333	1981	U.S. Intelligence Activities. Assigned to the Secretary of Defense responsibility for making government communications secure.
National Policy on Control of Compromising Emanations	1981	National Communications Security Committee Directive 4. Instructed government departments and agencies to protect classified information against compromising emanations via TEMPEST technology. Specific protection procedures and techniques are detailed in NACSI 5004 (see below).
Executive Order 12356	1982	National Security Information. Specified requirements for the classification, declassification, and safeguarding of "national security information."
Warner Amendment	1982	Amendment to Department of Defense Authorization Act (Public Law 97-86). Exempted certain types of DoD procurements from the Brooks Act if the function, operation, or use of a particular piece of equipment or a service involves: • Intelligence activities. • Cryptologic activities related to national security. • Command and control of military forces. • Equipment that is an integral part of a weapon or a weapon system. • An element critical to the direct fulfillment of a military or intelligence mission.
NCSC-10	1982	National Communications Security Council Policy–10. Specified a policy for the protection of U.S. national security-related information transmitted over satellite systems.

Table B-1. Information Protection Legislation (continued)

Legislation	Year	Effect
NCSC-11	1982	National Communications Security Council Policy–11. Broadened the effect of NCSC-10 to encompass all transmission systems carrying sensitive information from the government and its contractors.
OMB Circular A-127	1984	Financial Management Systems. Established a program to assure the integrity of federal financial management systems.
NSDD 145	1984	National Security Decision Directive 145. Mandated the protection of both classified and sensitive information, and created a federal interagency structure for computer security. Described in Chapter 2, *Some Security History*.
NACSI 5004	1984	National Communications Security Instruction 5004. Detailed the TEMPEST countermeasures needed for equipment and facilities that process national security information.
NACSI 6002	1984	National Communications Security Instruction 6002. Authorized the government and its contractors to purchase services for unclassified but sensitive information and to identify the communications security requirements for all contract-related telecommunications. There was debate about what "sensitive information" really entailed. NTISSP 2 tried to clarify this question.

Table B-1. Information Protection Legislation (continued)

Legislation	Year	Effect
OMB Circular A-130	1985	Management of Federal Information Resources. Established requirements for effective and efficient management of federal information resources. Requires all agency information systems to provide a level of security commensurate with the sensitivity of the information, the risk of its unauthorized access, and the harm that could result from improper access. Also requires all agencies to establish security programs to safeguard the sensitive information that they process.
NSDD 189	1985	National Security Decision Directive 189. Stated that federal policy is to *not* restrict reporting of unclassified research, regardless of whether it is federally funded.
NTISSI 4001	1985	National Telecommunications and Information System Security Instruction 4001. Established new categories of secure telecommunications and information handling equipment and associated cryptographic components: Controlled Cryptographic Items (CCIs) and Endorsed for Unclassified Cryptographic Items (EUCIs). (These categories are described in Appendix D, *Government Security Programs*.)
NTISSP 2	1986	National Telecommunications and Information Systems Security Publication 2. Defined sensitive information. As a result of Congressional and public concerns, rescinded in 1987. (See Chapter 2 for details.)
Computer Fraud and Abuse Act	1986	Public Law 99-474 (18 U.S. Code 1030). Prohibited unauthorized or fraudulent access to government computers. Described in Chapter 2.

Table B-1. Information Protection Legislation (continued)

Legislation	Year	Effect
NTISSP 200	1987	National Telecommunications and Information Systems Security Publication 200 (National Policy on Controlled Access Protection). Defined a minimum level of protection for computer systems operated by Executive branch agencies and departments of the U.S. government and their contractors, and encourages the private sector to apply this policy where needed. The policy applies to any system accessed by multiple users who do not all have the same authorization to use all of the classified or sensitive unclassified information processed or maintained by the system. NTISSP 200 stated that within five years of publication (i.e., by September of 1992), the systems affected by the policy must provide automated Controlled Access Protection (CAP) for all classified and sensitive unclassified information at the C2 level of trust defined in the Orange Book. (See Chapter 6, *Inside the Orange Book*, for a summary of C2 requirements.) NTISSP 200 has recently been rescinded.
Computer Security Act	1987	Public Law 100-235. Expanded the definition of computer security protection and clarified the role of NBS. (See Chapter 2 for details.)
NSD 42	1990	National Security Directive 42. Revised NSDD 145 to limit its role in controlling unclassified information.

Table B-2. Computer Crime Legislation

Legislation	Year*	Effect
18 U.S. Code 644	1948	Prohibits embezzlement of public money by a bank employee.
18 U.S. Code 659	1948	Prohibits theft of goods or chattel in interstate commerce.
18 U.S. Code 793	1948	Prohibits the collection or copying of information about communications or facilities (e.g., telegraph offices, research laboratories) for a foreign government or to injure the U.S., or the gathering, transmission, or loss of defense information.
18 U.S. Code 912	1948	Prohibits impersonation of a government employee to obtain something of value.
18 U.S. Code 1005	1948	Prohibits making false entries in bank records.
18 U.S. Code 1006	1948	Prohibits making false entries in credit institution records.
18 U.S. Code 1014	1948	Prohibits making false statements in loan and credit applications.
18 U.S. Code 1029	1984	Credit Card Fraud Act. Prohibits fraudulent use of credit cards, passwords, and telephone access codes.
18 U.S. Code 1030	1984	Computer Fraud and Abuse Act. Prohibits unauthorized remote access to, or modification of information in, computers containing national defense, banking, or financial information.
18 U.S. Code 1343	1952	Prohibits wire fraud using any interstate communications system (e.g., telephone, radio, television).
18 U.S. Code 1362	1948	Prohibits malicious mischief to government property.

*Year shown is the date of last revision.

Table B-2. Computer Crime Legislation (continued)

Legislation	Year*	Effect
18 U.S. Code 1905	1948	Prohibits disclosure of confidential information (e.g., trade secrets).
18 U.S. Code 2071	1948	Prohibits concealment, removal, or mutilation of public records.
18 U.S. Code 2314	1952	Prohibits interstate transportation of stolen property valued at more than $5000.
18 U.S. Code 2319	1982	Prohibits criminal infringement of a copyright.
18 U.S. Code 2512	1968	Prohibits manufacturing, selling, or use of communications interception equipment.
18 U.S. Code 2701	1986	Prohibits unauthorized access to information that's stored electronically.
18 U.S. Code 2710	1986	Prohibits unlawful access to stored communications.
18 U.S. Code 2778	1989	Prohibits the illegal export of software or data controlled by the Department of Defense.
50 U.S. Code 2510	1989	Prohibits the illegal export of software or data controlled by the Department of Commerce.

*Year shown is the date of the last revision.

Table B-3. Privacy Legislation

Legislation	Year	Effect
U.S. Constitution, Bill of Rights	1791	The Fourth Amendment guarantees protection against unreasonable search and seizure.
Communications Act	1934	Prohibits the interception of communications and the divulging of the contents of these communications unless authorized by the sender.
Omnibus Crime Control and Safe Streets Act	1968	Title III. Protects the privacy of wire and oral communications. Specifies the exact conditions under which wire and oral communications may be intercepted by authorized agencies.
Freedom of Information Act	1970	Permits individuals to access the data describing them that has been stored in federal agency files.
Fair Credit Reporting Act	1970	Public Law 91-508. Establishes individual rights in relation to the financial reporting industry.
Privacy Study	1972	Developed policy guidelines on privacy under the auspices of the U.S. Department of Health, Education, and Welfare. The Secretary's Advisory Committee on Automated Personnel Data Systems published a report in 1973 entitled *Records, Computers, and the Rights of Citizens*. This report validated "the right of individuals to participate in decisions regarding the collection, use, and disclosure of information personally identifiable to that individual."

Table B-3. Privacy Legislation (continued)

Legislation	Year	Effect
Code of Fair Information Practices	1973	As an outgrowth of the Privacy Study, government and industry representatives worked together, under the auspices of an advisory committee to the Secretary of Health, Education, and Welfare, to develop a code for organizations that gather and hold information. The code specifies that record-keeping must not be secret, that individuals must be able to access (and correct) information about themselves, that information must be used only as intended (not for any other purposes), and that the record-keeping organization must assure the reliability of the data.
Privacy Act	1974	Public Law 93-579, U.S. Code 532(a). Requires the U.S. government to safeguard personal data processed by federal agency computer systems. Also requires the government to provide ways for individuals to find out what personal information is being recorded and to correct inaccurate information. It spells out physical security procedures, information management practices, and computer/network controls. This act also mandated the creation of the Privacy Protection Study Commission.
Family Educational Rights and Privacy Act	1974	20 U.S. Code 123g. Protects student records at federally-supported institutions of learning by allowing students (or, for minors, their parents) to access their own records.
U.S. Privacy Protection Study Commission	1974	Studied infringements of individual privacy and possible protection mechanisms in the private sector. Recommendations were made in 1977.

Table B-3. Privacy Legislation (continued)

Legislation	Year	Effect
Right of Financial Privacy Act	1978	11 U.S. Code 1100. Stipulates that a depositor's bank accounts are private to that individual and can be accessed, even by the government, only with a court order and proper notice to the depositor.
Foreign Intelligence Surveillance Act	1978	Public Law 95-511. Establishes legal guidelines for the collection of foreign intelligence within the U.S. via electronic surveillance (e.g., wiretaps, radio intercepts).
Electronic Funds Transfer Act	1979	Protects the privacy of transmissions of funds over electronic funds transfer (EFT) networks and outlines the responsibilities of companies using EFTs.
Cable Communications Policy Act	1984	48 U.S. Code 551. Protects cable television subscribers by requiring service companies to restrict the use of personal information collected by them.
Electronic Communications Privacy Act	1986	18 U.S. Code 2511. Extends the legal protection provided by Title III of the Omnibus Crime Control and Safe Streets Act of 1968 to electronic communications such as electronic mail. Prohibits the unauthorized interception of communications regardless of how the communications are transmitted (e.g., video and data communications, transmissions via wire, radio, electromagnetic, photo-electronic, or photo-optical systems).
Computer Matching and Privacy Protection Act	1988	5 U.S. Code 552a. Protects against privacy violations due to information matching policies of the federal government.

C

Orange Book and Other Summaries

Orange Book (TCSEC) Requirements
Compartmented Mode Workstation
  (CMW) Requirements
System High Workstation (SHW)
  Requirements
International Security (ITSEC)
  Requirements

Orange Book (TCSEC) Requirements

The following tables show the actual text of the *Trusted Computer System Evaluation Criteria* (TCSEC) (Orange Book) security requirements. The requirements are arranged in a tabular format that shows more clearly than the Orange Book how requirements change from class to class. Note the following:

- "No requirements" in a column means the Orange Book doesn't define requirements for this feature in this class.

- "No additional requirements" means the requirements for this class are the same as those of the previous class (shown to the left in the table).

- Each column shows only new requirements for this class. In general, the requirements shown for a particular class apply in addition to any requirements for lower classes (shown to the left in a table). Occasionally, new (rather than add-on) requirements will be specified for a class.

Table C-1. Orange Book Security Policy Requirements

C1	C2	B1	B2	B3	A1
		Discretionary Access Control			
The TCB shall define and control access between named users and named objects (e.g., files and programs) in the ADP system. The enforcement mechanism (e.g., self/group/public controls, access control lists) shall allow users to specify and control sharing of those objects by named individuals or defined groups or both.	**Additional requirements:** Defined groups must specify individuals. Enforcement mechanism must provide controls to limit propagation of access rights. The discretionary access control mechanism shall, either by explicit user action or by default, provide that objects are protected from unauthorized access. These access controls shall be capable of including or excluding access to the granularity of a single user. Access permission to an object by users not already possessing access permission shall only be assigned by authorized users.	No additional requirements.	No additional requirements.	**Additional requirements:** The enforcement mechanism must be access control lists. The access controls shall be capable of specifying, for each named object, a list of named individuals with their respective modes of access to that object. Furthermore, for each such named object, it shall be possible to specify a list of named individuals and a list of groups of named individuals for which no access to the group is to be given.	No additional requirements.

Table C-1. Orange Book Security Policy Requirements (continued)

C1	C2	B1	B2	B3	A1
Object Reuse					
No requirements.	All authorizations to the information contained within a storage object shall be revoked prior to initial assignment, allocation, or reallocation to a subject from the TCB's pool of unused storage objects. No information, including encrypted representation of information, produced by a prior subject's actions is to be available to any subject that obtains access to an object that has been released back to the system.	No additional requirements.	No additional requirements.	No additional requirements.	No additional requirements.
Labels					
No requirements.	No requirements.	Sensitivity labels associated with each subject and storage object under its control (e.g., process, file, segment, device) shall be maintained by the TCB. These labels shall be used as the basis for mandatory access control decisions. In order to import non-labeled data, the TCB shall request and receive from an authorized user the security level of the data, and all such actions shall be auditable by the TCB.	**Additional requirement:** Sensitivity labels associated with each ADP system resource (e.g., subject, storage object, ROM) that is directly or indirectly accessible by subjects external to the TCB shall be maintained by the TCB.	No additional requirements.	No additional requirements.

291

Table C-1. Orange Book Security Policy Requirements (continued)

	C1	C2	B1	B2	B3	A1
			Labels (continued)			
Label Integrity:						
	No requirements.	No requirements.	Sensitivity labels shall accurately represent security levels of the specific subjects or objects with which they are associated. When exported by the TCB, sensitivity labels shall accurately and unambiguously represent the internal labels and shall be associated with the information being exported.	No additional requirements.	No additional requirements.	No additional requirements.
Exportation of Labeled Information:						
	No requirements.	No requirements.	The TCB shall designate each communication channel and I/O device as either single-level or multilevel. Any change in this designation shall be done manually and shall be auditable by the TCB. The TCB shall maintain and be able to audit any change in the security level or levels associated with a communication channel or I/O device.	No additional requirements.	No additional requirements.	No additional requirements.

Table C-1. Orange Book Security Policy Requirements (continued)

C1	C2	B1	B2	B3	A1
Exportation to Multilevel Devices:					
No requirements.	No requirements.	When the TCB exports an object to a multilevel I/O device, the sensitivity label associated with that object shall also be exported and shall reside on the same physical medium as the exported information and shall be in the same form (i.e., machine-readable or human-readable form). When the TCB exports or imports an object over a multilevel communication channel, the protocol used on that channel shall provide for the unambiguous pairing between the sensitivity labels and the associated information that is sent or received.	No additional requirements.	No additional requirements.	No additional requirements.

Labels (continued):

Table C-1. Orange Book Security Policy Requirements (continued)

C1	C2	B1	B2	B3	A1
		Labels (continued)			
Exportation to Single-Level Devices:					
No requirements.	No requirements.	Single-level I/O devices and single-level communication channels are not required to maintain the sensitivity labels of the information they process. However, the TCB shall include a mechanism by which the TCB and an authorized user reliably communicate to designate the single security level of information imported or exported via single-level communication channels or I/O devices.	No additional requirements.	No additional requirements.	No additional requirements.
Labelling Human-Readable Output:					
No requirements.	No requirements.	The ADP system administrator shall be able to specify the printable label names associated with exported sensitivity labels. The TCB shall mark the beginning and end of all human-readable sensitivity labels that properly* represent the sensitivity of the output. The TCB shall, by default, mark the top	No additional requirements.	No additional requirements.	No additional requirements.

*The hierarchical classification component in human-readable sensitivity labels shall be equal to the greatest hierarchical classification of any of the information in the output that the labels refer to; the non-hierarchical category component shall include all of the non-hierarchical categories of the information in the output the labels refer to, but no other non-hierarchical categories.

Table C-1. Orange Book Security Policy Requirements (continued)

C1	C2	B1	B2	B3	A1
		Labels (continued)			

Labelling Human-Readable Output (continued):

C1	C2	B1	B2	B3	A1
		and bottom of each page of human-readable, paged, hardcopy output (e.g., line printer output) with human-readable sensitivity labels that properly represent the overall sensitivity of the output or that properly represent the sensitivity of the information on the page. The TCB shall, by default and in an appropriate manner, mark other forms of human-readable output (e.g., maps, graphics) with human-readable sensitivity labels that properly represent the sensitivity of the output. Any override of these marking defaults shall be auditable by the TCB.			

Table C-1. Orange Book Security Policy Requirements (continued)

C1	C2	B1	B2	B3	A1
Subject Sensitivity Labels:			**Labels (continued)**		
No requirements.	No requirements.	No requirements.	The TCB shall immediately notify a terminal user of each change in the security level associated with that user during an interactive session. A terminal user shall be able to query the TCB as desired for a display of the subject's complete sensitivity label.	No additional requirements.	No additional requirements.
			Device Labels:		
No requirements.	No requirements.	No requirements.	The TCB shall support the assignment of minimum and maximum security levels to all attached physical devices. These security levels shall be used by the TCB to enforce constraints imposed by the physical environments in which the devices are located.	No additional requirements.	No additional requirements.

Table C-1. Orange Book Security Policy Requirements (continued)

C1	C2	B1	B2	B3	A1
		Mandatory Access Control			
No requirements.	No requirements.	The TCB shall enforce a mandatory access control policy over all subjects and storage objects under its control (e.g., processes, files, segments, devices). These subjects and objects shall be assigned sensitivity labels that are a combination of hierarchical classification levels and non-hierarchical categories, and the labels shall be used as the basis for mandatory access control decisions. The TCB shall be able to support two or more such security levels. The following requirements shall hold for all accesses between subjects and objects controlled by the TCB: A subject can read an object only if the hierarchical classification in the subject's security level is greater than or equal to the hierarchical classification in the object's security level and the non-hierarchical categories in the subject's security level include all the non-hierarchical categories in the	**Additional requirements:** The TCB shall enforce a mandatory access control policy over all resources (i.e., subjects, storage objects, and I/O devices) that are directly or indirectly accessible by subjects external to the TCB. The requirements shall hold for all accesses between all subjects external to the TCB and all objects directly or indirectly accessible by these subjects.	No additional requirements.	No additional requirements.

297

Table C-1. Orange Book Security Policy Requirements (continued)

C1	C2	B1	B2	B3	A1
		Mandatory Access Control (continued)			
		object's security level. A subject can write an object only if the hierarchical classification in the subject's security level is less than or equal to the hierarchical classification in the object's security level and all the non-hierarchical categories in the subject's security level are included in the non-hierarchical categories in the object's security level. Identification and authentication data shall be used by the TCB to authenticate the user's identity and to ensure that the security level and authorization of subjects external to the TCB that may be created to act on behalf of the individual user are dominated by the clearance and authorization of that user.			

Table C-2. Orange Book Accountability Requirements

C1	C2	B1	B2	B3	A1
		Identification and Authentication			
The TCB shall require users to identify themselves to it before beginning to perform any other actions that the TCB is expected to mediate. Furthermore, the TCB shall use a protected mechanism (e.g., passwords) to authenticate the user's identity. The TCB shall protect authentication data so that it cannot be accessed by any unauthorized user.	**Additional requirements**: The TCB shall be able to enforce individual accountability by providing the capability to uniquely identify each individual ADP system user. The TCB shall also provide the capability of associating this identity with all audible actions taken by that individual.	**Additional requirements**: The TCB shall maintain authentication data that includes information for verifying the identity of individual users (e.g., passwords) as well as information for detection of the clearance and authorizations of individual users. This data shall be used by the TCB to authenticate the user's identity and to ensure that the security level and authorization of all subjects external to the TCB that may be created to act on behalf of the individual user are documented by the clearance and authorization of that user.	No additional requirements.	No additional requirements.	No additional requirements.
Trusted Path:					
No requirements.	No requirements.	No requirements.	The TCB shall support a trusted communication path between itself and user for initial login and authentication. Communications via this path shall be initiated exclusively by a user.	**New requirements for B3**: The TCB shall support a trusted communication path between itself and users for use when a positive TCB-to-user connection is required (e.g., login,	No additional requirements.

Table C-2. Orange Book Accountability Requirements (continued)

C1	C2	B1	B2	B3	A1
Trusted Path (continued):					
				change subject security level). Communications via this trusted path shall be activated exclusively by a user or the TCB and shall be logically isolated and unmistakably distinguishable from other paths.	
Audit					
No requirements.	The TCB shall be able to create, maintain, and protect from modification or unauthorized access or destruction an audit trail of accesses to the objects it protects. The audit data shall be protected by the TCB so that read access to it is limited to those who are authorized for audit data. The TCB shall be able to record the following types of events: use of identification and authentication mechanisms, introduction of objects into a user's address space (e.g., file open, program initiation), deletion of objects, actions taken by computer operators and system	**Additional requirements:** The TCB shall also be able to audit any override of human-readable output markings. For events that introduce an object into a user's address space and for object deletion events the audit record shall include the name of the object and the object's security level. The ADP system administrator shall be able to selectively audit the actions of any one or more users based on individual identity and/or object security level.	**Additional requirement:** The TCB shall be able to audit the identified events that may be used in the exploitation of covert storage channels.	**Additional requirement:** The TCB shall contain a mechanism that is able to monitor the occurrence or accumulation of security auditable events that may indicate an imminent violation of security policy. This mechanism shall be able to immediately notify the security administrator when thresholds are exceeded and, if the occurrence or accumulation of the security relevant events continues, the system shall take the least disruptive action to terminate the event.	No additional requirements.

Table C-2. Orange Book Accountability Requirements (continued)

C1	C2	B1	B2	B3	A1
		Audit (continued)			
	administrators and/or system security officers, and other security relevant events. For each recorded event, the audit record shall identify: date and time of the event, user, type of event, and success or failure of the event. For identification/authentication events the origin of request (e.g., terminal ID) shall be included in the audit record. For events that introduce an object into a user's address space and for object deletion events the audit record shall include the name of the object. The ADP system administrator shall be able to selectively audit the actions of any one or more users based on individual identity.				

Table C-3. Orange Book Assurance Requirements

Operational Assurance

C1	C2	B1	B2	B3	A1
System Architecture:					
The TCB shall maintain a domain for its own execution that protects it from external interference or tampering (e.g., by modification of its code or data structures). Resources controlled by the TCB may be a defined subset of the subjects and objects in the ADP system.	**Additional requirement:** The TCB shall isolate the resources to be protected so that they are subject to the access control and auditing requirements.	**Additional requirement:** The TCB shall maintain process isolation through the provision of distinct address spaces under its control.	**New requirements for B2:** The TCB shall maintain a domain for its own execution that protects it from external interference or tampering (e.g., by modification of its code or data structures). The TCB shall maintain process isolation through the provision of distinct address spaces under its control. The TCB shall be internally structured into well-defined largely independent modules. It shall make effective use of available hardware to separate those elements that are protection-critical from those that are not. The TCB modules shall be designed such that the principle of least privilege is enforced. Features in hardware, such as segmentation, shall be used to support logically distinct	**Additional requirements:** The TCB shall be designed and structured to use a complete, conceptually simple protection mechanism with precisely defined semantics. This mechanism shall play a central role in enforcing the internal structuring of the TCB and the system. The TCB shall incorporate significant use of layering, abstraction and data hiding. Significant system engineering shall be directed toward minimizing the complexity of the TCB and excluding from the TCB modules that are not protection-critical.	No additional requirements.

302

Table C-3. Orange Book Assurance Requirements (continued)

	C1	C2	B1	B2	B3	A1
Operational Assurance (continued)						
System Architecture (continued):				storage objects with separate attributes (namely: readable, writeable). The user interface to the TCB shall be completely defined and all elements of the TCB identified.		No additional requirements.
System Integrity:	Hardware and/or software features shall be provided that can be used to periodically validate the correct operation of the on-site hardware and firmware elements of the TCB.		No additional requirements.		No additional requirements.	
Covert Channel Analysis:	No requirements.		No requirements.	The system developer shall conduct a thorough search for covert storage channels and make a determination (either by actual measurement or by engineering estimation) of the maximum bandwidth of each identified channel.	**Additional requirement**: Search for all covert channels (storage and timing).	**Additional requirement**: Formal methods shall be used in the analysis.

Table C-3. Orange Book Assurance Requirements (continued)

C1	C2	B1	B2	B3	A1
			Operational Assurance (continued)		
Trusted Facility Management:					
No requirements.	No requirements.	No requirements.	The TCB shall support separate operator and administrator functions.	**Additional requirements:** The functions performed in the role of a security administrator shall be identified. The ADP system administrative personnel shall only be able to perform security administrator functions after taking a distinct auditable action to assume the security administrator role on the ADP system. Non-security functions that can be performed in the security administration role shall be limited strictly to those essential to performing the security role effectively.	No additional requirements.
Trusted Recovery:					
No requirements.	No requirements.	No requirements.	No requirements.	Procedures and/or mechanisms shall be provided to assure that, after an ADP system failure or other discontinuity, recovery without a protection compromise is obtained.	No additional requirements.

Table C-3. Orange Book Assurance Requirements (continued)

C1	C2	B1	B2	B3	A1
Life Cycle Assurance					

Security Testing:

C1	C2	B1	B2	B3	A1
The security mechanisms of the ADP system shall be tested and found to work as claimed in the system documentation. Testing shall be done to assure that there are no obvious ways for an unauthorized user to bypass or otherwise defeat the security protection mechanisms of the TCB.	**Additional requirement:** Testing shall also include a search for obvious flaws that would allow violation of resource isolation, or that would permit unauthorized access to the audit or authentication data.	**New requirements for B1:** The security mechanisms of the ADP system shall be tested and found to work as claimed in the system documentation. A team of individuals who thoroughly understand the specific implementation of the TCB shall subject its design documentation, source code, and object code to thorough analysis and testing. Their objectives shall be: to uncover all design and implementation flaws that would permit a subject external to the TCB to read, change, or delete data normally denied under the mandatory or discretionary security policy enforced by the TCB; as well as to assure that no subject (without authorization to do so) is able to cause the TCB to enter a state such that it is unable to respond to communications initiated	**Additional requirements:** The TCB shall be found relatively resistant to penetration. Testing shall demonstrate that the TCB implementation is consistent with the descriptive top-level specification.	**Additional requirements:** The TCB shall be found resistant to penetration. No design flaws and no more than a few correctable implementation flaws may be found during testing and there shall be reasonable confidence that few remain.	**Additional requirements:** Testing shall demonstrate that the TCB implementation is consistent with the formal top-level specification. Manual or other mapping of the FTLS to the source code may form a basis for penetration testing.

Table C-3. Orange Book Assurance Requirements (continued)

C1	C2	B1	B2	B3	A1
Security Testing (continued):					
		by other users. All discovered flaws shall be removed or neutralized and the TCB retested to demonstrate that they have been eliminated and that new flaws have not been introduced.			
Design Specification and Verification:					
No requirements.	No requirements.	An informal or formal model of the security policy supported by the TCB shall be maintained over the life cycle of the ADP system and demonstrated to be consistent with its axioms.	New requirements for B2: A formal model of the security policy supported by the TCB shall be maintained over the life cycle of the ADP system that is proven consistent with its axioms. A descriptive top-level specification (DTLS) of the TCB shall be maintained that completely and accurately describes the TCB in terms of exceptions, error messages, and effects. It shall be shown to be an accurate description of the TCB interface.	Additional requirements: A convincing argument shall be given that the DTLS is consistent with the model.	Additional requirements: A formal top-level specification (FTLS) of the TCB shall be maintained that accurately describes the TCB in terms of exceptions, error messages, and effects. The DTLS and FTLS shall include those components of the TCB that are implemented as hardware and/or firmware if their properties are visible at the TCB interface. The FTLS shall be shown to be an accurate description of the TCB interface. A combination of formal and informal techniques shall be used to show that the FTLS is consistent with

Table C-3. Orange Book Assurance Requirements (continued)

C1	C2	B1	B2	B3	A1
Design Specification and Verification (continued):					
					the model. This verification evidence shall be consistent with that provided within the state-of-the-art of the particular National Computer Security Center-endorsed formal specification and verification system used. Manual or other mapping of the FTLS to the TCB source code shall be performed to provide evidence of correct implementation.
Configuration Management:					
No requirements.	No requirements.	No requirements.	During development and maintenance of the TCB, a configuration management system shall be in place that maintains control of changes to the descriptive top-level specification, other design data, implementation documentation, source code, the running version of the object code, and test fixtures and documentation. The configuration management system shall assure a consistent mapping among all documentation and code	No additional requirements.	**New requirements for A1:** During the entire life-cycle, i.e, during the design, development, and maintenance of the TCB, a configuration management system shall be in place for all security-relevant hardware, firmware, and software that maintains control of changes to the formal model, the descriptive and formal top-level specifications, other design data, implementation documentation, source code, the running version of the object

Table C-3. Orange Book Assurance Requirements (continued)

C1	C2	B1	B2	B3	A1
Configuration Management (continued)					
			associated with the current version of the TCB. Tools shall be provided for generation of a new version of the TCB from source code. Also available shall be tools for comparing a newly generated version with the previous TCB version in order to ascertain that only the intended changes have been made in the code that will actually be used as the new version of the TCB.		code, and test fixtures and documentation. The configuration management system shall assure a consistent mapping among all documentation and code associated with the current version of the TCB. Tools shall be provided for generation of a new version of the TCB from source code. Also available shall be tools, maintained under strict configuration control, for comparing a newly generated version with the previous TCB version in order to ascertain that only the intended changes have been made in the code that will actually be used as the new version of the TCB. A combination of technical, physical, and procedural safeguards shall be used to protect from unauthorized modification or destruction of the master copy or copies of all material used to generate the TCB.

Table C-3. Orange Book Assurance Requirements (continued)

C1	C2	B1	B2	B3	A1
		Trusted Distribution:			
No requirements.	No requirements.	No requirements.	No requirements.	No requirements.	A trusted ADP system control and distribution facility shall be provided for maintaining the integrity of the mapping between the master data describing the current version of the TCB and the on-site master copy of the code for the current version. Procedures (e.g., site security acceptance testing) shall exist for assuring that the TCB software, firmware, and hardware updates distributed to a customer are exactly as specified by the master copies.

Table C-4. Documentation Requirements

C1	C2	B1	B2	B3	A1
Security Features User's Guide					
A single summary, chapter, or manual in user documentation shall describe the protection mechanisms provided by the TCB, guidelines on their use, and how they interact with each other.	No additional requirements.	No additional requirements.	No additional requirements.	No additional requirements.	No additional requirements.
Trusted Facility Manual					
A manual addressed to the ADP system administrator shall present cautions about functions and privileges that should be controlled when running a secure facility.	**Additional requirement:** The procedures for examining and maintaining the audit files as well as the detailed audit record structure for each type of audit event shall be given.	**Additional requirements:** The manual shall describe the operator and administrator functions related to security, to include changing the security characteristics of a user. It shall provide guidelines on the consistent and effective use of the protective features of the system, how they interact, how to securely generate a new TCB, and facility procedures, warnings, and privileges that need to be controlled in order to operate the facility in a secure manner.	**Additional requirements:** The TCB modules that contain the reference validation mechanism shall be identified. The procedures for secure operation of a new TCB from source after modification of any modules in the TCB shall be described.	**Additional requirements:** It shall include the procedures to ensure that the system is initially started in a secure manner. Procedures shall also be included to resume secure system operation after any lapse in system operation.	No additional requirements.

Table C-4. Documentation Requirements (continued)

C1	C2	B1	B2	B3	A1
Test Documentation					
The system developer shall provide to the evaluators a document that describes the test plan, test procedures that show how the mechanisms were tested, and results of the security mechanisms' functional testing.	No additional requirements.	No additional requirements.	**Additional requirement:** It shall include results of testing the effectiveness of the methods used to reduce covert channel bandwidths.	No additional requirements.	**Additional requirement:** The results of the mapping between the formal top-level specification and the TCB source code shall be given.
Design Documentation					
Documentation shall be available that provides a description of the manufacturer's philosophy of protection and an explanation of how this philosophy is translated into the TCB. If the TCB is composed of distinct modules, the interfaces between these modules shall be described.	No additional requirements.	**Additional requirements:** An informal or formal description of the security policy model enforced by the TCB shall be available and an explanation provided to show that it is sufficient to enforce the security policy. The specific TCB protection mechanism shall be identified and an explanation given to show that they satisfy the model.	**Additional requirements:** The interfaces between the TCB modules shall be described. The security policy model must be formal and proven. The descriptive top-level specification (DTLS) shall be shown to be an accurate description of the TCB interface. Documentation shall describe how the TCB implements the reference monitor concept and give an explanation why it is tamper resistant, cannot be bypassed, and is correctly implemented. Documentation shall describe how the TCB is structured to facilitate testing and to enforce	**Additional requirements:** The TCB implementation (i.e., in hardware, firmware, and software) shall be informally shown to be consistent with the DTLS. The elements of the DTLS shall be shown, using informal techniques, to correspond to the elements of the TCB.	**Additional requirements:** The TCB implementation shall be informally shown to be consistent with the formal top-level specification (FTLS). The elements of the FTLS shall be shown, using informal techniques, to correspond to the elements of the TCB. Hardware, firmware, and software mechanisms not dealt with in the FTLS but strictly internal to the TCB (e.g., mapping registers, direct memory access I/O), shall be clearly described.

311

Table C-4. Documentation Requirements (continued)

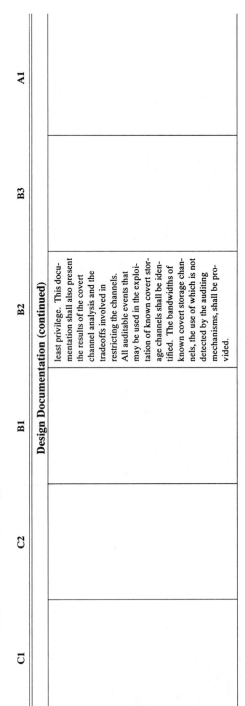

C1	C2	B1	B2	B3	A1
		Design Documentation (continued)			
			least privilege. This documentation shall also present the results of the covert channel analysis and the tradeoffs involved in restricting the channels. All auditable events that may be used in the exploitation of known covert storage channels shall be identified. The bandwidths of known covert storage channels, the use of which is not detected by the auditing mechanisms, shall be provided.		

Compartmented Mode Workstation (CMW) Requirements

This section and the next section list the requirements for compartmented mode workstations and system high workstations. Chapter 6, *Inside the Orange Book*, introduces these types of workstations and explains briefly the differences between them. The requirements are described in detail in the *Security Requirements for System High and Compartmented Mode Workstations*, available to authorized vendors from the Defense Intelligence Agency.

NOTE

"SHW" in parentheses after a security requirement indicates that this requirement is the same as the corresponding System High Workstation requirement (shown in the next section).

Table C-5. Compartmented Mode Workstation Requirements

Code	Requirement
Access Controls and Labels	
CM1	Discretionary (Need-to-know) Access Control
CM1.1a	Access Control Lists
CM1.1b	Self/Group/Public Permissions
CM2	Object Reuse
CM2.1	Object Reuse (SHW)
CM3	Information Labels
CM3.1	Information Labels (SHW)
CM3.2	Process Data Information Labels (SHW)
CM3.3	Window Information Labels (SHW)
CM3.4	Interwindow Information Labels
CM3.5	Input Information Labels (SHW)
CM3.6	File Information Labels (SHW)
CM3.7	Printed Output Labeling
CM3.8	Network Output Labeling
CM3.9	Imported Data Labeling (SHW)
CM4	Mandatory Access Control
CM4.1	Sensitivity Labels
CM4.1.1	Process Sensitivity Labels

Table C-5. Compartmented Mode Workstation Requirements (continued)

Code	Requirement
CM4.1.2	Window Sensitivity Labels
CM4.1.3	File Sensitivity Labels
CM4.2	Mandatory Access Control Policy

Accountability

Code	Requirement
CM5	User Identification and Authentication
CM5.1	Password Authentication (SHW)
CM5.2a	Local Authentication Data
CM5.2a.1a	Protected Passwords (SHW)
CM5.2a.1b	Protected Encrypted Passwords (SHW)
CM5.2b	External Authentication Data
CM5.3a	Password Generation (SHW)
CM5.3b	Password Selection (SHW)
CM6	Identification of User Terminal (SHW)
CM7	Trusted Path
CM7.1	Trusted Path
CM8	Audit (SHW)
CM8.1	Audit Data
CM8.2a	Selective Collection (SHW)
CM8.2b	Selective Reduction (SHW)
CM8.3a	Local Data Storage (SHW)
CM8.3b	External Data Storage (SHW)

Operational Assurance

Code	Requirement
CM9	System Architecture (SHW)
CM9.1	System Architecture (SHW)
CM10	System Integrity (SHW)
CM10.1	System Integrity (SHW)
CM11	Trusted Facility Management (SHW)
CM11.1	Trusted Facility Management (SHW)
CM12	Trusted Recovery

Life-Cycle Assurance

Code	Requirement
CM13	Security Testing (SHW)
CM14	Design Specification and Verification
CM15	Configuration Management (SHW)
CM16	Trusted Distribution (SHW)

Table C-5. Compartmented Mode Workstation Requirements (continued)

Code	Requirement
Documentation	
CM17	System Security Statement/Plan (SHW)
CM18	Security Features User's Guide (SHW)
CM19	Trusted Facility Manual (SHW)
CM20	Test Documentation (SHW)
CM21	Design Documentation
Environmental Protection	
CM22	Communication Security (SHW)
CM23	Physical Security (SHW)
CM24	TEMPEST (SHW)
CM25	Personnel Security (SHW)
Administrative Procedures	
CM26	Annual Accreditation (SHW)
CM27	Protection Software (SHW)
CM28	Dial-up Lines (SHW)
CM29	Access Authentication (SHW)

System High Workstation (SHW) Requirements

NOTE

An asterisk (*) in parentheses in the following table indicates that this is *not* a requirement for System High Workstations. It is shown here only for compatibility with Compartmented Mode Workstations (shown in the previous section).

Table C-6. System High Workstation (SHW) Requirements

Code	Requirement
Access Controls and Labels	
SH1	Discretionary (Need-to-know) Access Control
SH1.1a	Access Control Lists
SH1.1b	Self/Group/Public Permissions
SH2	Object Reuse
SH2.1	Object Reuse (same)
SH3	Information Labels
SH3.1a	Floating Information Labels (same)
SH3.1a.1	Information Label Contents
SH3.1a.2	Process Data Information Labels
SH3.1a.3	Window Information Labels
SH3.1a.4	Interwindow Information Labels
SH3.1a.5	Input Information Labels
SH3.1a.6	File Information Labels
SH3.1a.7	Printed Output Labeling
SH3.1a.8	Network Output Labeling
SH3.1a.9	Imported Data Labeling
SH3.1b	Stored Information Labels
SH3.1b.1	Information Label Contents
SH3.1b.2	Window Information Labels
SH3.1b.3	Interwindow Data Moves
SH3.1b.4	Input Information Labels
SH3.1b.5	File Information Labels
SH3.1b.6	Printed Output Labeling
SH3.1b.7	Network Output Labeling
SH3.1b.8	Imported Data Labeling
SH3.1c	Export Information Labels
SH3.1c.1	Information Label Contents
SH3.1c.2	Window Information Labels
SH3.1c.3	Interwindow Data Moves
SH3.1c.4	Input Information Labels
SH3.1c.5	Printed Output Labeling
SH3.1c.6	Network Output Labeling
SH3.1c.7	Imported Data Labeling
SH4	Mandatory Access Control

Table C-6. System High Workstation (SHW) Requirements (continued)

Code	Requirement
Accountability	
SH5	User Identification and Authentication
SH5.1	Password Authentication
SH5.2a	Local Authentication Data
SH5.2a.1a	Protected Passwords
SH5.2a.1b	Protected Encrypted Passwords
SH5.2b	External Authentication Data
SH5.3a	Password Generation
SH5.3b	Password Selection
SH6	Identification of User Terminal
SH7	Trusted Path
SH7.1	Trusted Path
SH8	Audit
SH8.1	Audit Data
SH8.2a	Selective Collection
SH8.2b	Selective Reduction
SH8.3a	Local Data Storage
SH8.3b	External Data Storage
Operational Assurance	
SH9	System Architecture
SH9.1	System Architecture
SH10	System Integrity
SH10.1	System Integrity
SH11	Trusted Facility Management
SH11.1	Trusted Facility Management
SH12	Trusted Recovery*
Life-Cycle Assurance	
SH13	Security Testing
SH14	Design Specification and Verification*
SH15	Configuration Management
SH16	Trusted Distribution
Documentation	
SH17	System Security Statement/Plan
SH18	Security Features User's Guide

Table C-6. System High Workstation (SHW) Requirements (continued)

Code	Requirement
SH19	Trusted Facility Manual
SH20	Test Documentation
SH21	Design Documentation*
Environmental Protection	
SH22	Communication Security
SH23	Physical Security
SH24	TEMPEST
SH25	Personnel Security
Administrative Procedures	
SH26	Annual Accreditation
SH27	Protection Software
SH28	Dial-up Lines
SH29	Access Authentication

International Security (ITSEC) Requirements

The *Information Technology Security Evaluation Criteria (ITSEC*, published by the Federal Republic of Germany in 1992), defines a standard that's under development for international security. The ITSEC, which have become known as "Europe's White Book," are described briefly in Chapter 2, *Some Security History*. The following tables show the eight distinct security functions defined in the ITSEC, along with the ITSEC "classes of functionality" and assurance levels.

Table C-7. Information Technology Security Evaluation Criteria (ITSEC)

Function	Meaning
Identification and authentication	The system's security policy specifies the subjects and objects that must be identified and authenticated. The criteria identify three authentication mechanisms: • Authentication by possession (e.g., a badge or a token). • Authentication by knowledge (e.g., a password). • Authentication by characteristic features (e.g., a fingerprint).
Administration of rights	The security policy must specify the rights that each subject and object possesses and identifies the relationships between them, any special roles in the system, and the rules for granting and changing these rights.
Verification of rights	The system must verify a subject's rights when the subject tries to access an object.
Audit	The system must audit security-related events, recording information about who did what in the system.
Object reuse	Objects must be cleared of data before they are reused so users can't accidentally access information they're not ordinarily allowed to access.
Error recovery	The security policy identifies error conditions and how the system recovers from them.
Continuity of service	The system must be able to continue to make certain key services available to maintain system security.
Data communication security	Because the ordinary system security features do not adequately protect communications, the system adds certain communication security functions and mechanisms. These are: • Peer entity authentication. • Access control. • Data confidentiality. • Data integrity. • Data origin authentication. • Non-repudiation.

Table C-8. ITSEC Classes of Functionality

Class	Meaning
F1	Derived from Orange Book class C1.
F2	Derived from Orange Book class C2.
F3	Derived from Orange Book class B1.
F4	Derived from Orange Book class B2.
F5	Derived from Orange Book class B3/A1.
F6	A distinct class for systems with high integrity (in contrast to confidentiality) requirements for data and programs. It's particularly appropriate for database systems.
F7	A distinct class for systems with high requirements for either a complete system or a special function of a system. It's particularly appropriate for process control systems.
F8	A distinct class for systems with high requirements for the safeguarding of data integrity during data communication.
F9	A distinct class for systems with high demands on the confidentiality of data during data communication. It's particularly appropriate for cryptographic systems.
F10	A distinct class for networks with high demands on the confidentiality and integrity of the information to be communicated. It's particularly appropriate when sensitive information needs to be communicated over unsecure (e.g., public) networks.

Table C-9. ITSEC Assurance Levels

Assurance Level	Meaning
E1	Testing.
E2	Configuration control and controlled distribution; roughly equivalent to Orange Book class C2 assurance.
E3	Access to detailed design and source code; roughly equivalent to Orange Book class B1 assurance.
E4	Rigorous vulnerability analysis; roughly equivalent to Orange Book class B2 assurance.
E5	Demonstrates correspondence between detailed design and source code; roughly equivalent to Orange Book class B3 assurance.
E6	Formal models and formal descriptions, linked by formal correspondences; roughly equivalent to Orange Book class A1 assurance.

D

Government Security Programs
Computer Security Programs
Communications Security Programs
TEMPEST Security Programs

This appendix is supplied for use by organizations that are involved with developing trusted systems or other high-security products.

Computer Security Programs

The U.S. government gives the umbrella name COMPUSEC (computer security) to its broad involvement in secure system policy, research, evaluation, and industry relations. According to the government's *Information Systems Security Products and Services Catalogue*, which lists products that the government has certified, the purpose of the COMPUSEC program is:

> ... to implement protective measures designed to prevent deliberate or inadvertent unauthorized access, disclosure, acquisition, manipulation, modification, or loss of information while it is being automatically processed or stored.

In contrast, the COMSEC (communications security) program, described in "Communications Security Programs," later in this appendix, is concerned with information while it is being transmitted (secure networks, encryption, etc.)

This section describes the following evaluation programs, as well as a number of additional government facilities:

Trusted Product Evaluation Program (TPEP).
Evaluates complete hardware/software systems, using the *Trusted Computer System Evaluation Criteria* (the Orange Book) requirements to determine the level of trust that can be placed in these systems.

TPEP Network Evaluation.
Evaluates network products, using the *Trusted Network Interpretation* (the Red Book) requirements to assess the products' security characteristics.

TPEP Database Management System (DBMS) Evaluation.
Evaluates DBMS products, using the *Trusted Database Management System Interpretation* (TDI) requirements to assess the products' security characteristics.

TPEP Subsystem Evaluation.
Evalutes add-on security products for specific security features, using the *Computer Security Subsystem Interpretation* (the Venice Blue Book) requirements to assess the products' security characteristics.

Formal Verification Systems Evaluation Program (FVSEP).
Evaluates formal design and verification tools (used in the design and testing of highly trusted operating systems), using the *Guidelines for Formal Verification Systems* (the Purple Book) requirements to assess the systems' security characteristics.

The Role of the NCSC

NSA's National Computer Security Center (NCSC) plays an important role in the administration of the COMPUSEC program. The NCSC is the government organization responsible for evaluating trusted systems—systems developed according to the requirements of the Orange Book. In fact, although system evaluation is a very important responsibility of the NCSC, the agency's role is a broader one.

The NCSC does the following:

• Evaluates products developed by commercial vendors. Products include trusted operating systems, compartmented mode workstations, system high workstations, network products, add-on security products, security subsystems, and formal verification tools (used to test highly trusted systems).

• Sponsors research and publicizes the results so security technology can be incorporated into trusted systems and applications. Specific areas of research interest include trusted systems, trusted networks, trusted databases, and biometrics.

- Develops and publishes technical guidelines to support Orange Book requirements.

- Provides advice, training, and tools such as DOCKMASTER, a computer system used for the dissemination and exchange of computer security information.

- Encourages organizations to report system security problems (e.g., design deficiencies in hardware, firmware, or software) to the Computer Security Technical Vulnerability Reporting Program. A vulnerability found in an evaluated product could result in a change in that product's Orange Book rating.

The NCSC also works closely with the National Institute of Standards and Technology (NIST)—mainly with NIST's National Computer Systems Laboratory (CSL), with the Defense Intelligence Agency (DIA), and with other government agencies that have an interest in computer security.

The Role of NIST

NIST's Computer Systems Laboratory (formerly the Institute for Computer Sciences and Technology) sets standards for computer security, conducts research, tests security products, and provides computer security training and support to other government agencies.

NIST's Computer Systems Laboratory does the following:

- Develops, and supports the development of, computer security standards. The CSL works closely with the accredited standards committees of organizations such as ANSI, ISO, and IEEE (described in Chapter 2, *Some Security History*). Standards that meet government needs are proposed as Federal Information Processing Standards (FIPS). A list of publications describing these standards (FIPS PUBs) is included in Appendix E, *A Security Souce Book*.

- Conducts research into security solutions. The CSL conducts research and publishes its findings in a number of current areas of computer security. For example, through the NIST Workshop for Implementors of OSI, the CSL works with vendors to identify needed security standards for the Open System Interconnection (OSI) model. The CSL also works with NSA to be sure that security standards developed for open systems meet Department of Defense requirements for protecting classified and intelligence data. The CSL's Integrated Services Digital Network (ISDN) program encourages vendors to incorporate standards into their open system products so users obtain security protection as well as interoperability from these products. The CSL is also actively pursuing research in various cryptographic areas, such as key management, message authentication, public key signatures, and electronic certification.

The CSL publishes its research results in a research journal, on its electronic bulletin board, and in special publications (known as SPEC PUBs). See Appendix E for information on these sources.

- Develops test methods. The CSL assists other agencies by offering systems that test the conformance of vendors' systems to particular federal standards (e.g., message authentication, key management). The CSL will also be contributing to developing test suites for POSIX, for OSI, and for NSA's Secure Data Network System (SDNS).

Trusted Product Evaluation Program (TPEP)

The Trusted Product Evaluation Program (TPEP) is the NCSC's primary program. Through TPEP, the agency evaluates trusted operating systems and other types of security products.

According to the NCSC, the TPEP:

> ...focuses on the security evaluation of commercially produced and supported computer systems by evaluating the technical protection capabilities against the established criteria presented in the (Orange Book).

The Trusted Product Evaluation Program supersedes the Commercial Products Evaluation Program, the NCSC's original evaluation program described in the Orange Book.

The following NCSC publications provide useful information about the evaluation of trusted systems:

- *Trusted Computer System Evaluation Criteria* (the Orange Book).

- *Trusted Product Evaluations: A Guide for Vendors* (the Aqua Book).

The following list summarizes the steps required for trusted system evaluation. This list focuses on the evaluation of trusted systems. For specific information about the evaluation of network products and other types of products, see later sections.

Proposal Review Phase (PRP)

During this phase you make initial contact with NSA's Information System Security Organization (ISSO), and sign an agreement to proceed with system design and evaluation. This phase consists of the following steps:

1. **Initial Contact.** You meet to discuss your overall plan and to learn more about the process of building and evaluating a trusted system. To make initial contact, call or write:

    > Director, National Security Agency
    > Office of Acquisition and Business Development
    > Attn: X511
    > 9800 Savage Road
    > Fort George G. Meade, MD 20755-6000
    > (301) 688-6581

2. **Certificate.** Before you begin to prepare a proposal, you must sign a Certificate Pertaining to Foreign Interests, a document stating that your company is not under foreign ownership, control, or influence (FOCI). For information, contact the same office listed above.

3. **Proposal Package Review.** You must submit four copies of a proposal containing the following items:

    - Company Profile. Information about your organization's capabilities, especially your suitability to develop a trusted product. Supply basic information such as contact names, company size, products or services offered, and recent financial reports.

    - Market Information. Information about the intended market for your proposed product. Supply information such as specific customer base, how market projections were derived, and government and commercial requirements that the product will satisfy.

    - Written Product Proposal. Technical information about the product, the security needs it will satisfy, the targeted class of trust (e.g., B1), the projected installed base, the target development schedule, and differences from similar products already in use. The NCSC publication, *Trusted*

Product Evaluations: A Guide for Vendors, summarizes many of the technical questions your proposal must answer; for example:

— Explain the security features provided by your product.

— How do users identify themselves?

— How do users authenticate themselves?

4. **Program Decision**. The Office of Acquisition Policy and Business Development considers your proposal and makes a decision about whether your product is of interest to NSA and should be accepted for evaluation.

5. **Preliminary Technical Review**. A team of three experienced evaluators meets (typically for two days) with your technical experts. This Preliminary Technical Review (PTR) assesses the product's stage of development and results in a Preliminary Technical Report (PTR).

6. **Legal Agreements**. You sign a legal agreement with NSA. NSA agrees to provide you with the necessary security information to perform an evaluation of your product, and to protect all proprietary information. You agree to provide necessary technical information, to follow all necessary procedures, to submit all product literature referencing NSA or other government programs to NSA for approval, and to prepare RAMP reports. You both agree to review the legal agreement periodically.

7. **Team Assignment**. The NCSC assigns a program manager and a technical contact from the Trusted Products and Network Security Evaluation Division. These contacts are responsible for putting you in touch with additional personnel, as necessary, to provide specific technical expertise. However, you continue to have the primary responsibility for making technical decisions and for applying the evaluation criteria and the NCSC's interpretations of these criteria.

Vendor Assistance Phase (VAP)

During this phase you develop the system, design security test procedures, and write draft documentation. The NCSC team provides support during this phase by answering questions while you complete system design and implementation. This phase consists of the following steps:

1. **Establish Product Development Milestones**. You and the evaluation team agree on a firm schedule for deliverables during this phase. The total elapsed time for this phase must not exceed one year.

2. **Deliverables**. Deliverables developed during this phase include the system design, the draft documentation, the test plan, and the RAMP plan.

Design Analysis Phase (DAP)

This phase is based primarily on design documentation, test plans, results of formal verification, and other information you supply. It involves little or no hands-on analysis. The total elapsed time for this phase must not exceed one year. This phase consists of the following steps:

1. **Evaluation Team Review.** Your NCSC evaluation team performs an in-depth examination of your product design to ensure that it is sound. Team members are drawn from a pool of evaluators within NSA (Section C71) and from three federally funded research and development centers: the Aerospace Corporation, the Institute for Defense Analysis, and the Mitre Corporation.

2. **Initial Product Assessment Report.** At the conclusion of its evaluation, the team prepares an Initial Product Assessment Report (IPAR) describing the initial evaluation of the product and including the rating that the product can expect to receive if it passes the formal evaluation phase. The IPAR summarizes each of the technical requirements for the evaluation class and describes how the product appears to meet (or does not appear to meet) that requirement.

   Note: The IPAR may also contain action items for further development by the vendor and evaluation comments.

3. **Technical Review Board.** The NCSC convenes a Technical Review Board (TRB) at which the evaluation team presents the IPAR and defends it. If the TRB recommends formal evaluation of the product, the recommendation is sent to the Chief of Section C71, who notifies the vendor of the results.

   Before a product can enter the Evaluation Phase, it must be final and marketable. The product release accepted for evaluation must not undergo any additional development.

Evaluation Phase

During this phase, the evaluation team performs a detailed analysis of the actual hardware and software and the final documentation. The phase includes hands-on testing of the system (functional testing and, if applicable, penetration testing). It also includes development of a document mapping the system's security features and assurances to the evaluation requirements for the requested rating. This phase consists of the following steps:

1. **Legal Agreement.** Upon notification of TRB approval, the vendor can decide whether to request that the product enter the Evaluation Phase. If the vendor requests formal evaluation, the vendor and the NCSC sign a legal agreement to

deliver the product, along with all necessary plans, for formal evaluation according to an agreed-upon schedule.

2. **Product Bulletin**. When the product enters formal evaluation, the process becomes public. The NCSC publishes a brief Product Bulletin (a synopsis of the system) in the next quarterly issue of the *Information Systems Security Products and Services Catalogue*. The Product Bulletin announces that the product is being formally evaluated and indicates the rating that the vendor is seeking.

3. **Evidence Review, Testing Preparation**. The evaluation team examines the system, including the mapping of security features, and prepares for testing. This activity requires access to design documentation, source code, and vendor personnel who can answer detailed questions about specific portions of the product. During this analysis, the product being evaluated must not undergo any additional development.

4. **Draft Evaluation Report**. The team prepares a draft of the Final Evaluation Report (FER) for the product. They use the IPAR as a basis for this report.

5. **Test Technical Review Board**. The NCSC convenes a Test Technical Review Board (TRB) just before the formal testing stage. This board examines the results of the initial evaluation and determines whether the product has so far satisfied all requirements.

6. **Testing**. The team observes formal testing and conducts its own security testing (and, if applicable to the desired rating, penetration testing).

7. **Final Technical Review Board**. If testing was successful, the NCSC convenes the Final TRB, which confirms the team's assessment of the product. This board reviews the draft of the Final Evaluation Report prepared by the evaluation team, as well as the Evaluated Products List (EPL) entry that will appear in the *Information Systems Security Products and Services Catalogue*.

8. **Final Evaluation Report**. The NCSC publishes the revised version of the Final Evaluation Report (FER) on behalf of the vendor. The FER describes the evaluation process, provides an overview of the product that is being evaluated, and shows how the product meets the specific requirements of the overall evaluation class rating. The FER also contains evaluator comments and a summary of evaluated components and other technical information. The report contains no proprietary information. You can obtain FERs from the National Technical Information Service or the Government Printing Office. See Appendix E, *A Security Source Book*, for details.

9. **Evaluated Products List (EPL).** The NCSC also publishes an entry for the successfully evaluated product in the Evaluated Products List section of the next quarterly issue of the *Information Systems Security Products and Services Catalogue*. The rating awarded to a system and published in the EPL is the highest class for which all of the requirements in the Orange Book have been met.

The EPL pages of the *Information Systems Security Products and Services Catalogue* are color-coded to show systems in different stages of evaluation:

White pages   Contains introductory text, indexes, lists of companies, etc.

Orange pages   Lists changes to the EPL (e.g., systems moving from one phase of evaluation to the next).

Green pages   Lists systems currently in the Vendor Assistance Phase of evaluation.

Tan pages   Lists systems currently in the Design Assistance Phase of evaluation.

Blue pages   Contains new Product Bulletins.

Rating Maintenance Phase (RAMP)

After the product has been formally evaluated and assigned a rating, the rating is published and the product can now be advertised as having that rating. Any updates to the product must be made in trusted fashion, according to additional rules.

The Rating Maintenance Phase (RAMP) keeps the EPL current. This program allows a vendor to enhance an already certified product. Under RAMP procedures, trained and certified security analysts are able to add new functions, fix bugs, and release new versions of the certified product. Participation in the RAMP program (which includes the development of RAMP plans during earlier stages of product evaluation) is required for products evaluated at C1, C2, and B1 ratings. See the section entitled "Rating Maintenance Phase (RAMP) Program" later in this chapter.

Evaluation of Network Products

The Trusted Product Evaluation Program is oriented primarily to trusted operating systems. However, the program accommodates network products as well. The following NCSC publications provide useful information about the evaluation of network products:

- *Department of Defense Trusted Network Interpretation (TNI)* (the Red Book).

- *Trusted Network Interpretation Environments Guideline of the Trusted Network Interpretation (TNI) of the Trusted Computer System Evaluation Criteria (TCSEC)* (the Dark Red Book).

- *Trusted Product Evaluations: A Guide for Vendors* (the Aqua Book).

The Red Book interprets Orange Book requirements for network products. It also addresses special concerns of a networking environment, such as communications integrity, denial of service, and data confidentiality. See Chapter 8, *Communications and Network Security*, for a discussion of Red Book requirements.

The Dark Red Book contains information that's helpful if you're integrating, operating, and maintaining trusted computer networks. It includes requirements for the minimum security required in different network environments.

The Aqua Book contains specific procedures for submitting network products for evaluation. The procedures are very similar to those described for operating systems. The Aqua Book spells out some distinct questions that must be answered for network products in the initial proposal and that must be verified during the actual evaluation. Questions include:

- What level of trust does the product meet according to Part I of the TNI?

- Which of the following functions does it provide, and at what level of trust is each functionality provided: mandatory access control, discretionary access control, identification and authentication, audit?

- What other security services mentioned in Part II of the TNI does your product provide?

- What type of carrier medium, if any, does your product use or support?

Evaluations of Database Management Systems

The Trusted Product Evaluation Program has also been extended to accommodate the special characteristics and requirements of database management systems (DBMSs). The evaluation of a database product is performed in accordance with the *Department of Defense Trusted Database Management System Interpretation* (TDI) (the Lavender book). The TDI interprets Orange Book requirements for database management products. It also addresses special concerns of database products, such as data integrity, database protection privileges, and data item security labeling. The TDI has just recently been released, and vendors and evaluators have little experience using it.

A DBMS product is a type of *trusted application*. The NCSC anticipates being able to develop guidelines for additional types of trusted applications in the future. The availability of the TDI, and projects such as Seaview, a secure database management system, are expected to spur the trusted database market.

Evaluations of Security Subsystem Products

The Trusted Product Evaluation Program has also been extended to accommodate computer security subsystem products. Subsystems are limited hardware and software products that enhance the security of computer systems. Examples of such products are access devices (e.g., smart cards and tokens), biometric devices, and security software that's layered onto existing operating systems. These products typically provide only a subset of the security functions offered by a complete operating system.

In many cases, a vendor won't bother to undergo a government evaluation for a limited security product. Even in a highly secure environment, such as a government installation, an organization's security officer (with the permission of the appropriate government contracting officer) can often give permission for a security product to be used. In some cases, however, an add-on security product will play an integral role in a trusted computer system. For example, it might control access to the workstations connected to the trusted system. In other cases, a vendor might want to make a product more marketable by being able to advertise that it's been certified.

The following NCSC publications provide useful information about the evaluation of subsystem products:

* *Trusted Product Evaluations: A Guide for Vendors* (the Aqua Book).

* *Computer Security Subsystem Interpretation (CSSI) of Trusted Computer System Evaluation Criteria (TCSEC)* (the Venice Blue Book).

The Venice Blue Book contains an interpretation of the Orange Book requirements for trusted add-on products and subsystems. The government team evaluates your product according to this interpretation.

The Aqua Book contains some information about submitting subsystems for evaluation. The procedures described are very similar to those described for operating systems. The Aqua Book also spells out some distinct questions that must be answered for subsystems in the initial proposal and that must be verified during the actual evaluation. Questions include:

- Which of the four subsystem functions does the product implement?

- What other products does the product depend upon (e.g., DOS, UNIX)?

The Aqua Book states:

> ...subsystems may not meet all of the security feature, architecture, or assurance requirements of any one security class or level of the Orange Book ... The goal ... is to provide computer installation managers with information on subsystems that would be helpful in providing immediate computer security improvements in existing installations.

The NCSC distinguishes between add-on products and subsystems.

Add-on packages are run in conjunction with a specific operating system. Evaluation of an add-on package must include a thorough evaluation of the operating system as well, because the integrity of the package depends on the integrity of the operating system. An example of an add-on package is IBM's MVS/RACF, which is layered onto a particular operating system and becomes an integral part of the systems.

Subsystems are special-purpose products that can be added onto existing operating systems to implement a subset of the security features described in the Orange Book and to increase some aspect of security—for example, identification and authentication. Examples are Gordian System's Access Key, Enigma Logic's Safeword, and Wang Laboratories' MicroControl.

To be considered for subsystem evaluation, a product must provide one or more of these capabilities:

- Discretionary access controls (DAC).

- Object reuse.

- Identification and authentication (I&A).

- Audit.

Although the NCSC basically uses Orange Book criteria to evaluate these particular functions, the agency is careful not to use the same ratings known in the Orange Book. Because subsystems, by their nature, don't meet all the requirements for a particular class, the NCSC feels that it would be misleading to assign that class's rating to a particular security product. Instead, the NCSC assigns

D-level ratings to each function offered by a subsystem, according to the following criteria:

D1   This rating is assigned for a function that, in general, satisfies the C1 Orange Book requirements (for this function only). D1 ratings are granted only for DAC, I&A, and audit functions.

D2   This rating is assigned for a function that, in general, satisfies the C2 Orange Book requirements (for this function only). D2 ratings are granted for DAC, object reuse, I&A, and audit functions.

D3   This rating is assigned for a function that, in general, satisfies the B3 Orange Book requirements (for this function only); D3 ratings are granted only for DAC and audit functions.

Government publications are careful to point out that specific ratings given individual subsystem functions do not imply an overall rating (similar to an Orange Book rating) for the subsystem, or for the system using the subsystem. For example, the Venice Blue Book states that "... incorporation of an evaluated subsystem into any system environment does not automatically confer any rating to the resulting system."

The Aqua Book contains specific procedures for submitting and evaluating computer security subsystems. The evaluation process is very similar for trusted systems and trusted subsystems. However, for subsystems, the process is simplified and consists only of two basic phases: the Proposal Review Phase and the Evaluation Phase.

Proposal Review Phase (PRP)

During this phase you make initial contact with the National Security Agency and submit a proposal for development of a trusted product. The steps you perform during this phase are very similar to those described for trusted systems in the "Trusted Product Evaluation Program (TPEP)" section. Steps include:

• Initial Contact.

• Signing of a Certificate Pertaining to Foreign Interests.

• Proposal Package Review: The Aqua Book summarizes the specific technical questions your proposal must answer for a subsystem; for example:

— Which of the four subsystem functions does the product implement?

— What other products does the product depend upon (e.g., DOS, UNIX)?

• Program Decision.

- Legal Agreements.

- Team Assignment.

(See the discussion of these steps as they're described for trusted systems above.)

Evaluation Phase

The NCSC performs an evaluation of the product. A subsystem evaluation is an analysis of the hardware and software components of the subsystem product and a mapping of the security features to the evaluation criteria for the functions offered by the product (e.g., identification and authentication, discretionary access control). The analysis includes product testing.

1. **Subsystem Evaluation Report (SER).** If the product has successfully satisfied all requirements, the NCSC publishes the Subsystem Evaluation Report on behalf of the vendor.

   The SER describes the evaluation process, provides an overview of the product that is being evaluated, and shows how the product meets the specific requirements for the functions offered by the product. It also an assessment of the product's success and usefulness in increasing computer security.

   The SER contains no proprietary information and is publicly available from the GPO or NTIS (see Appendix E, *A Security Source Book*).

2. **Evaluated Products List (EPL).** The NCSC publishes a description of the product in the Subsystem section of the Evaluated Products List contained in the next quarterly issue of the *Information Systems Security Products and Services Catalogue*.

Formal Verification Systems Evaluation Program (FVSEP)

One of the assurance requirements specified in the Orange Book for the most highly trusted systems (systems evaluated at the Orange Book A1 level of trust) is design specification and verification. This requirement is also important in the evaluation of networks. Formal verification provides assurance that the implementation of a trusted system is consistent with the system's design. The Orange Book states that, at the A1 level, security "verification evidence shall be consistent with that provided within the state-of-the-art of the particular National Computer Security Center-endorsed formal specification and verification system used."

What is formal specification and verification? Traditional system tests verify the correctness of a system design and implementation—some more systematically than others. Formal verification, on the other hand, effectively reduces the operating system to a theorem and replaces piecemeal testing with a rigorous mathematical proof. Formal verification of a system involves several steps:

* Develop a formal top-level specification of the system design.

* Verify that the specifications are consistent with the system's formal security policy model (i.e., the security requirements).

* Perform an informal mapping from the FTLS to the implementation.

Various verification tools have been developed to assist in this process.

Whereas traditional testing is performed in a testing phase, after the system has been designed and implemented, formal verification is a fundamental part of the design and implementation phases.

Formal verification tools can be very effective, but they're typically rather complicated to use. They're not canned programs, but sets of tools requiring a substantial commitment in time and energy to implement. It usually makes sense to use such tools only for the most highly trusted systems, where they're a requirement.

Because formal verification tools are required for trusted systems rated at the A1 level, the NCSC evaluates such tools via the Formal Verification Systems Evaluation Program (FVSEP), through a process very similar to the trusted operating system program described earlier in this chapter. Successfully evaluated tools are placed on the Endorsed Tools List (ETL), which is published in the *Information Systems Security Products and Services Catalogue*. Tools are described fully in Technical Assessment Reports (TARs).

Examples of formal verification tools already endorsed by the NCSC include the Gypsy Verification Environment (GVE) by Computational Logic, Inc. and the Formal Development Methodology (FDM) by the UNISYS Corporation.

The steps required for evaluation of formal verification systems are similar to those described for trusted systems and subsystems. For details, see the NCSC publication, *Guideline for Formal Verification Systems* (the Purple Book).

Degausser Products List

Vendors of degaussing products (products that erase magnetic tapes and disks) can submit their products to NSA for evaluation. Because ordinary file and device deletion procedures may not be sufficient to remove classified information from magnetic media, degaussing products contribute to the overall security of trusted systems (particularly to meeting the object reuse requirement described in Chapter 6, *Inside the Orange Book*).

NSA evaluates degaussing products according to rules stated for erasing classified material in the publication, *Techniques and Procedures for Implementing, Deactivating, Testing, and Evaluating Secure Resource-Sharing ADP Systems* (DoD 5200.28-M). Successfully evaluated systems are placed on the Degausser Products List (DPL), which is published in the *Information Systems Security Products and Services Catalogue*. Examples of endorsed degaussers include those manufactured by Ampex, Bell & Howell, Hewlett-Packard, and Data Security.

Rating Maintenance Phase (RAMP) Program

What happens when you want to change a system that's been evaluated? Because so much attention is paid during system development, documentation, and even distribution to ensure that system changes are justified and carefully monitored, it makes sense that there's a government program to handle life after evaluation.

The NCSC developed the Rating Maintenance Phase (RAMP) of the Trusted Product Evaluation Program in an effort to keep the Evaluated Products List up to date. Operating systems are dynamic entities that need to change in response to hardware advances, user requests, and other market issues. But an Orange Book evaluation is, by its very nature, static. It examines, in great detail, a particular set of system functions and assurances at a particular point in time.

RAMP is a way of maintaining the rating of an evaluated system—a way to recertify a new version of a system without requiring the vendor to have the system completely re-evaluated every time it's updated, corrected, or enhanced. It's much more efficient than a full-scale re-evaluation. Whereas a full evaluation might take 1-2 years to complete, RAMP usually results in an EPL listing for the new version of your system within a matter of months.

Through RAMP, NCSC trains a vendor's staff to do the following:

- Recognize the changes to a system that may adversely affect the implementation of the system's security policy.

- Add new functions, fix bugs, and release new versions of the evaluated system without jeopardizing system security.

- Track changes to the evaluated product via configuration management techniques.

Although not part of the original Orange Book requirements, RAMP has become a key component in evaluations of C1, C2, and B1 systems. In fact, to get a C1, C2, or B1 rating for a new system, you *must* now participate in RAMP, though systems already on the EPL do not need to be part of the program. More highly trusted systems (B2, B3, and A1) require a complete re-evaluation.

From the very beginning, RAMP plays a part in the development and evaluation of a trusted system. There are RAMP requirements at several key points in the TPEP process, described in the NCSC publication, *Rating Maintenance Phase Program Document* (the Pink Book).

System Certification and Accreditation

As we've said before, an Orange Book rating is not a guarantee of security. System administration, physical security measures, and other security features all play in part in determining whether a system can really be said to be "secure." According to the *Information Systems Security Products and Services Catalogue*, a rating ensures only that:

> The features and assurances of the product appear to provide the classes of protection characterized by the Overall Evaluation Class. The EPL entry does not constitute any general or overall endorsement by the NCSC of the product, nor does it constitute any DoD certification or accreditation of the product for use in classified or sensitive processing environments. Rather, the evaluation provides an essential part of the technical evidence required for such certification and accreditation.

If a system is being used in a government installation or at a site that's processing sensitive information (e.g., a government contractor site), the government has a vested interest in whether a secure system is actually being used securely. Certification and accreditation are the government's ways of checking on how a system is actually being used.

Certification is the process of technically assessing the appropriateness of a particular system for the processing of particular information in a particular environment. Accreditation is the government's formal approval of that system. The government defines accreditation as follows:

> The official authorization that is granted to an ADP system to process sensitive information in an operational environment based on comprehensive security evaluation of the system's hardware, firmware, and software security design, configuration, and implementation of the other system procedural, administrative, physical, TEMPEST, personnel, and communication controls.

If your organization processes classified information, accreditation is a formal process. The Designated Approval Authority (DAA) for the organization is responsible for approving the installation and use of the system. For U.S. government contractors, the DAA is the agency that administers the contract for which the system is being used. If your organization does not process classified information, your own management is responsible for approving the installation of a system and of understanding any security risks associated with its use. At government sites, it's much easier to get a system accredited if it's been successfully evaluated and assigned a rating by the NCSC.

A system's overall evaluation class rating is a very important aspect of accreditation. For example, if contract requirements call for a C2 system, for example, and if the system to be accredited has a C2 rating, accreditation is usually a simple matter. If the system is currently being evaluated but has not yet achieved its rating, the DAA has the authority to issue a security waiver under certain circumstances. This waiver indicates that there is a strong production need for the system, that the risks of the environment have been identified, and that alternative solutions have been developed to allow the system to operate in that environment. In determining whether to issue a waiver, the DAA takes into account the rating of the system, any special security characteristics of the site itself (e.g., computer room locks, shielded walls or pipes, etc.), any known threats and risks, and other alternative solutions.

DOCKMASTER

DOCKMASTER is an unclassified computer system used by the NCSC and the computer security community for online sharing of information about computer security. DOCKMASTER is a large-scale Honeywell DPS8/70M system running Multics, a B2-level operating system. The system serves federal government agencies, universities, and businesses. There are currently more than 3000 DOCKMASTER users. The system supports electronic mail connections to the ARPANET via direct mail, the MILNET, and the McDonnell Douglas Tymnet.

DOCKMASTER allows its users to retrieve listings of trusted products (the Evaluated Products List is online) and provides an electronic bulletin board for the exchange of information about computer security products, conferences, and other security issues. During a product evaluation, DOCKMASTER is a particularly useful tool. It allows the NCSC and the vendor to exchange mail, request information from each other, send document drafts back and forth, and so on. To find out who to contact for DOCKMASTER information, see Appendix E, *A Security Source Book*.

Technical Vulnerability Reporting Program

The Computer Security Technical Vulnerability Reporting Program (CSTVRP) is a clearinghouse for information about vulnerabilities and design deficiencies in computer hardware, firmware, or software. The NCSC encourages users in the government and industry to report any system weaknesses that might make a computer vulnerable to attack by either outsiders or insiders. If a vulnerability is found in a product that's under evaluation, the NCSC may respond by changing the product's rating.

Appendix E lists the office to contact for information about this program and to report vulnerabilities.

Communications Security Programs

The U.S. government gives the umbrella name COMSEC to its broad involvement in encryption and communications security. According to the *Information Systems Security Products and Services Catalogue*, which lists products that the government has certified, the purpose of the COMSEC program is:

> ...to implement protective measures designed to prevent unauthorized access, disclosure, acquisition, manipulation, modification, or loss of information while it is being communicated, regardless of the media used—e.g., by telephone, microwave, or satellite.

In contrast, the COMPUSEC (computer security) program, described in "Computer Security Programs," earlier in this appendix, is concerned with information while it is being processed or stored.

The U.S. government's COMSEC program is administered primarily by the National Security Agency. The National Institute of Standards and Technology (NIST) and the Treasury Department also play a role in setting standards for and certifying certain kinds of communications security products. The focal point of the COMSEC program is cryptographic products. Although the government has a strong interest in overall network security and in other types of communications security products, research and evaluation of those products is administered primarily by the National Computer Security Center under its COMPUSEC programs. As interest in secure networks grows, more programs may become available. For example, NIST is in the process of developing a program to test, evaluate, and endorse products based on the OSI Basic Reference Model. The goal is to determine whether these products comply with the model.

This section describes the following COMSEC programs:

Commercial Communications Security Endorsement Program.
Evaluates "high-grade" cryptographic products (described in the next section).

Government Endorsed Data Encryption Standard Equipment Program.
Evaluates cryptographic products based on the DES algorithm.

Electronic Funds Transfer Certification Program.
Evaluates products used primarily for message authentication in financial transactions.

Commercial COMSEC Endorsement Program

Until 1985, NSA served as the primary developer of high-grade cryptographic products utilizing classified cryptographic algorithms. (Chapter 7, *Encryption*, describes briefly what "high-grade" Type 1 and Type 2 products are.) NSA acquired cryptographic technology by contracting with vendors to develop specific products based on a list of basic functional requirements. In 1985, in an effort to shift the development risk to industry, and to speed up the process of getting products to market, NSA established the Commercial COMSEC Endorsement Program (CCEP). The old contract method took as long as 7-10 years to build a product; through CCEP, NSA hoped to reduce that cycle to about two years.

Through CCEP, government and industry representatives work in a business partnership to develop, test, and endorse communications security products—in particular, cryptographic products. The idea is to merge NSA's cryptographic expertise and classified algorithms with industry's business experience and financial resources. The result, NSA hopes, is to bring down the cost of the products that the government needs.

According to the government publication, *Summary of the Commercial COMSEC Endorsement Program* (CCEP), CCEP was established:

> ...to combine industry's leadership and expertise in telecommunications design, development, and high volume production with the communications security (COMSEC) experience of the National Security Agency. The primary objective of the CCEP is to provide for the widespread availability of quality, inexpensive, secure telecommunications systems for use by both the U.S. government and the private sector.

The goal is to encourage vendors to embed government classified algorithms into their communications products and to sell those products to customers who process either classified or unclassified data.

The government states its policy of endorsement under CCEP as follows:

> NSA does not make, by virtue of its endorsement, any warranty or representation regarding the efficacy or fitness for use of the products contained on the Endorsed Cryptographic Products List (ECPL).

Because high-grade COMSEC products are built according to strict rules that include the requirement that they meet the TEMPEST standard (described in Chapter 10), these products are, by definition, TEMPEST products. (This is not necessarily true of DES-based products, described later in this section.)

CCEP Eligibility

Before you can be eligible to build an NSA-endorsed cryptographic product, you must become a member of the Commercial COMSEC Endorsement Program (CCEP). To do this, you must:

- Sign a Certificate Pertaining to Foreign Interests, a document stating that your organization is not under foreign ownership, control, or influence.

- Obtain a facility clearance from the Defense Investigative Service (DIS) and appropriate individual clearances; this is necessary because the algorithms are classified, even though the final products will not be.

- Register with the Office of Munitions Control (OMC) of the U.S. Department of State.

- Establish a COMSEC Material Control System for the distribution of accountable COMSEC material.

- Appoint a COMSEC custodian to be accountable for sending and receiving official COMSEC material. The COMSEC custodian is the individual within your organization who has been approved by NSA as the authorized custodian of all COMSEC materials and information. All communications between NSA and your organization are channeled through the COMSEC custodian. The custodian receives these communications, usually through a secure mailing address, and logs and protects all communications.

- Establish an administrative channel for the distribution of other COMSEC information on a need-to-know basis.

Once you've been admitted to the CCEP, NSA assigns your organization a Program Manager. This individual is your contact for any COMSEC-related developments and the liaison to other resources within NSA.

CCEP Program Steps

The following list summarizes the major steps in the Commercial COMSEC Endorsement Program. For detailed information about these steps, see the government publication, *Commercial COMSEC Endorsement Program Procedures*.

1. **Initial Contact**. The vendor makes contact with NSA and prepares the following documents:

   - Written Product Proposal. Description of the product, its classification or sensitivity level, its security features, its integration into a larger system, its market, its competitive advantages, and its target schedule.

   - Company Profile. Description of the vendor, its expertise, and its security status.

   - Product Assurance Survey. Preliminary information about the vendor's experience, manufacturing capabilities, product integrity, configuration control, and product support.

2. **Program Decision**. NSA reviews the vendor's proposal, determines the value of and the need for the proposed product, assesses the security and suitability of the company, and considers its own priority and staffing availability. NSA must be convinced that the product will be marketable and that the company meets the minimum standards for product development. NSA also sends a survey team to the vendor's facility to assess its ability to develop and produce a COMSEC product. The team investigates the facility, using NSA's Objective Standards for Product Assurance as an evaluation guideline.

3. **Memorandum of Understanding (MOU)**. If NSA approves the vendor's proposal, NSA and the vendor sign an MOU. The MOU spells out the responsibilities of the vendor and NSA.

   The vendor agrees to supply NSA with the information necessary to evaluate the product. The vendor also agrees to adhere to all CCEP requirements. NSA agrees to provide the necessary COMSEC information and to protect the vendor's proprietary information.

4. **Product Design**. The vendor designs the product in accordance with the requirements of the MOU. The NSA Program Manager ensures that NSA provides all necessary items and actions.

5. **Memorandum of Agreement (MOA)**. After the MOU has been signed, NSA notifies the vendor of the specific security and product-related requirements that must be satisfied. NSA develops two documents: *Telecommunications Security Requirements Document* (TSRD) and the *Agreement Data Requirements List* (ADRL).

The vendor develops a number of documents. The most important are the *Theory of Equipment Operation* (TEO) and the *Theory of Compliance* (TC).

These documents are attached to the MOA, which spells out additional responsibilities of the vendor and NSA and describes the schedule for product development and evaluation.

6. **Product Development**. The vendor builds and tests the product in accordance with the requirements of the MOA. The NSA Program Manager ensures that NSA provides all necessary items and actions.

7. **Endorsement**. When all of the MOA requirements have been met, the vendor submits the product and all items specified in the ADRL that are necessary for evaluation. NSA evaluates the product and, if it complies with the TSRD, endorses it as specified in the MOA. The product is placed on the Endorsed Cryptographic Products List (ECPL), and a brief description of the product is published in the next quarterly publication of the *Information Systems Security Products and Services Catalogue*.

8. **Production**. The vendor sells the endorsed product and installs it at customer sites. All sales are subject to restrictions summarized in a later section. NSA ensures that the product is produced in accordance with the accounting procedures and that it complies with the TSRD and all terms of endorsement.

Government Endorsed DES Equipment Program

NSA instituted the Government Endorsed Data Encryption Standard (DES) Equipment Program in 1982 to provide consistent testing and endorsement of DES-based products. Under this program, vendors have historically submitted their DES products to NIST. Together, NSA and NIST have ensured that the products correctly implement the DES algorithm and that they comply with Federal Standard 1027 and other requirements for protecting national security-related telecommunications.

As described in Chapter 7, *Encryption*, NSA began in 1988 to phase out the Government Endorsed DES Program, and stopped endorsing new DES-based products (except for financial applications). DES products are still endorsed by the Treasury Department, as described in the next section.

The NSA Endorsed DES Products List (NEDESPL) continues to be published in the *Information Systems Security Products and Services Catalogue* as a convenience to users of existing DES products.

EFT Certification Program

The Department of the Treasury has its own endorsement program, the Electronic Funds Transfer (EFT) Certification Program for Authentication Devices, for products used primarily for message authentication in U.S. government financial transactions. The EFT Message Authentication Code equipment evaluated and certified under the program is tested against the following policy standards:

• Federal Standard 1027—Data Encryption Standard (DES) encryption.

• ANSI X9.17—Optional electronic key management.

See Chapter 7, *Encryption*, for a discussion of message authentication. See the Treasury publication, *Criteria and Procedures for Testing, Evaluating, and Certifying Message Authentication Devices for Federal EFT Use*, for complete information about this program.

Protected Network Services List

The government maintains a list of common carriers who provide telecommunications services approved by NSA. Services on this list are approved for the protection of sensitive unclassified information (but not classified information) that's being transferred from one point to another. The list, known as the Protected Network Services List (PNSL), is included in the *Information Systems Security Products and Services Catalogue*. It contains contact points for companies like AT&T, MCI, U.S. Sprint, and Pacific Bell.

The companies on this list provide services (not products), such as bulk trunk encryption or guaranteed routing on lines that have a degree of inherent security. Protected services are intended to safeguard voice, data, and recorded communications between government agencies and contractors via wire, cable, fiber optics, satellite, or microwave.

Protected network services fall into three categories:

PL   Private Line. Dedicated circuits leased by a customer for exclusive use. Approved private lines must use encryption or must add communications security features to unencrypted cable circuits.

FDN   Flexibly Defined Network. Network of sequential links and no permanent physical circuits.

SPRS   Switched Protected Routing Service. Under development, a system to protect sensitive information through the nationwide public switched telephone network.

Before you can claim that you provide "NSA Approved Protection," your services must be formally reviewed and approved by NSA.

Off-line Systems List (OLSL)

The government also maintains a list of cryptographic products that are offline (manual), rather than online (computerized). The list, known as the Off-Line Systems List (OLSL) is included in the *Information Systems Security Products and Services Catalogue*.

Offline products are useful in many situations because they are quickly released, easily available, portable, inexpensive, and readily tailored to the user's needs. They include such devices as:

- **Manual cryptosystems.** These include operations codes, ciphers, authentication systems, and one-time pads. Many of the systems in this category are antiquated; some systems have been in the field for more than 20 years.

- **KL-43 products.** These include automanual electronic encryption devices such as portable keyboards keyed with printed, nonperforated paper tape; these devices are often a substitute when secure voice communications are not available.

- **Signals Operation Instructions (SOI).** These are booklets containing information used to change the call signs and radio frequencies used during training and combat operations (so the enemy cannot perform traffic analysis and direction finding).

Restrictions on Cryptographic Products

Cryptographic products are developed and sold under the close scrutiny of the U.S. government. Export restrictions for cryptographic products are quite strict; these restrictions are described in Chapter 7, *Encryption*.

NSA also has stringent requirements for the design, manufacture, assembly, storage, movement, and disposal of classified and sensitive government information and the products designed to handle that information. Cryptographic products are subject to these requirements.

The handling of classified information is administered by the Defense Investigative Service (DIS). Detailed regulations are summarized in the DoD publication, *Industrial Security Manual for Safeguarding Classified Information*, and its *COMSEC Supplement*.

NSA has established two different categories for product and information handling:

CCI   Controlled Cryptographic Items. Products designed to secure classified information are known as CCIs. CCIs are unclassified (when unkeyed) but controlled. Such items must be labelled as such and are subject to continuous accounting and export restrictions. CCIs can be sold only to U.S. government agencies and contractors. Type 1 cryptographic products must be handled as CCIs. Once they've been keyed, they assume the classification level (e.g., TOP SECRET) of the key being used.

EUCI   Endorsed for Unclassified Cryptographic Items. Products designed to secure sensitive, unclassified information are known as EUCIs. EUCIs are subject to less stringent controls (e.g., point-of-sale serial number accounting and export restrictions) than CCIs. Type 2 cryptographic products must be handled as EUCIs. Type 2 products can be operated only with an unclassified key.

A vendor who wants to acquire CCI equipment must have a clearance issued by the Defense Investigative Service, as well as at least one current U.S. government contract. NSA also requires the vendor to establish a COMSEC account and to execute a legally binding agreement promising to comply with all of the requirements of a number of COMSEC documents, including the *Contractors Controlled Cryptographic Item (CCI) Manual* and the *Handling and Control of Controlled Cryptographic Items During Development and Manufacture/Assembly*.

These manuals summarize the minimum requirements for the acquisition and ownership, transportation, certified installation, key accounting, manufacturing, assembly, storage, accounting and auditing controls, and quality assurance provisions for CCI equipment. For a list of COMSEC documents, see Appendix E, *A Security Source Book*.

TEMPEST Security Programs

The U.S. government gives the umbrella name TEMPEST to its broad involvement in the study and control of signal emanations from electrical and electromagnetic equipment. This section describes the following TEMPEST programs:

Endorsed TEMPEST Products Program.
Evaluates and endorses TEMPEST products. Successfully endorsed products are placed on the Endorsed TEMPEST Products List (ETPL), which replaces the Preferred Product List. Products currently undergoing evaluation are placed on the Potential Endorsed TEMPEST Products List (PETPL).

Endorsed TEMPEST Test Services Program.
Evaluates and endorses TEMPEST test services. Successfully endorsed services are placed on the newly created Endorsed TEMPEST Test Services List (ETTSL).

Endorsed TEMPEST Test Instrumentation Program.
Evaluates and endorses TEMPEST test instrumentation. Successfully endorsed instruments are placed on the newly created Endorsed TEMPEST Test Instrumentation List (ETTIL).

These programs are administered by the Countermeasures Advisory Panel (CAP), a part of the National Telecommunications Information Systems Security Committee (NTISSC), an organization consisting of representatives of DoD, intelligence agencies, and other civil agencies.

Because these programs are new, and because many TEMPEST products now in use were endorsed according to an earlier evaluation program, the first section below describes that earlier program and its transition to the new TEMPEST endorsement programs.

Industrial TEMPEST Program and Preferred Products List

For many years, the TEMPEST program operated according to the process outlined below:

ITP Membership The focal point of TEMPEST development has historically been the Industrial TEMPEST Program (ITP). Through this program, U.S. government and industry representatives worked together to set standards and to develop, test, and certify TEMPEST equipment. TEMPEST vendors had to be members of ITP to submit products for TEMPEST certification. ITP members were given access to the classified NACSIM 5100A standard.

Product Notice An ITP member could indicate its intention to develop a new TEMPEST product by submitting a Notice of Intent to Produce a TEMPEST Product. The product itself would be submitted at a later time.

Testing Once a TEMPEST product was built, it would be certified by professional TEMPEST test personnel.

Evaluation In accordance with NACSIM 5100A standards, the U.S. government evaluated the TEMPEST test plans and TEMPEST test reports. The TEMPEST Qualification Special Committee (TQSC) of the Subcommittee on Compromising Emanations

(SOCE), comprised of representatives from the DoD and civilian agencies, had the authority to issue TEMPEST certification.

Product Listing If the product passed all tests and was accepted (approximately a 3- to 9-month process), it would be placed on the Preferred Product List (PPL). The PPL was updated on a quarterly basis, under the auspices of the Countermeasures Advisory Panel (CAP) (also staffed by representatives of DoD and civilian agencies), and published in the *Information Systems Security Products and Services Catalogue*, along with other information security products.

Recertification A certified TEMPEST product would require recertification every three years after being placed on the PPL.

In recent years, the government has been rethinking the ITP structure and its approach to product certification. Prompted by increasing concern over the security of the existing products on the PPL, the government declared a moratorium on ITP membership and began a restructuring of the entire TEMPEST product endorsement and certification process. In March of 1988, the government completed its ITP review and announced the following:

- The notion of company membership in ITP is eliminated.

- The government itself will play a more active role in evaluating and assuring the continuing quality of TEMPEST products. In contrast to the previous process, in which private industry certified TEMPEST professionals determined product compliance with the TEMPEST standard, the new process requires active involvement by the government. The government is expected both to evaluate products and to assure their continued quality by performing inspections.

- New TEMPEST products will no longer be added to the PPL.

- New products and services will be evaluated according to the new TEMPEST programs (described below). Changes to existing products will also require recertification via one of these programs.

- Products included on the PPL as of January, 1990 will continue to be recognized as certified TEMPEST products as long as the vendors satisfy the guidelines for such products.

- The government will continue to publish the PPL for five years or until the PPL no longer includes any certified products.

- Current ITP members retain their right to access classified TEMPEST information and the TEMPEST Electronic Bulletin Board for one year.

The existing Preferred Products List continues to be included in the PPL section of the *Information Systems Security Products and Services Catalogue*. Like the other TEMPEST sections of that catalogue, the PPL pages are color-coded to show TEMPEST products in different stages of endorsement.

White pages   Lists fully accredited TEMPEST products. Production units of these products have been tested and have been found to conform to the NACSIM 5100A standard.

Yellow pages   Lists products that have been removed from the White pages because the government has recently found and confirmed deficiencies in the products. Vendors have a maximum of six months to correct these deficiencies. If the deficiencies are corrected, a yellow-listed product will be restored to the White pages. Vendors in this category must warn users that deficiencies may exist in their products. Users are advised to contact the local TEMPEST authority for guidance.

Blue pages   Lists products whose accreditation has been suspended (pending accreditation termination and appeal). This is a more serious category. Vendors are not allowed to advertise the products in this category as being accredited or to take orders.

Red pages   Lists products whose accreditation has been terminated. Termination typically results from unresolved deficiencies or from failure to comply with PPL procedures or requirements. Users of these products are advised to contact the local TEMPEST authority for guidance.

Green pages   Lists products that vendors have permanently discontinued. After one year in the Green pages, these product listings will be deleted.

Endorsed TEMPEST Products Program

This section summarizes the steps you must follow to get a new TEMPEST product endorsed under the government's Endorsed TEMPEST Products Program (ETPP). The government states its policy of endorsement under this program as follows:

> NSA endorsement is a statement that the company complies with the requirements of the National TEMPEST Standard, NACSIM 5100A, Compromising Emanations Laboratory Test Standard, Electromagnetics, dated 1 July 1981, and that the company has in place and applies to the product, the manufacturing capability and product assurance controls necessary to ensure the continued TEMPEST integrity of the product subsequent to endorsement . . . The government does not make, by virtue of its endorsement, any warranty or

representation, regarding the efficacy or fitness for use of the products contained in the ETPL.

NOTE

A vendor whose product has previously been accredited and placed on the Preferred Products List (PPL) (the precursor to the Endorsed TEMPEST Products List) doesn't need to resubmit the product for endorsement under the Endorsed TEMPEST Products Program. However, the government strongly encourages vendors to resubmit its products. Once such a product is endorsed, a product listing will appear in both the existing PPL and the new ETPL. Unless a vendor's product is endorsed under the new program, the vendor won't be allowed to make any changes or additions to the product as it is listed in the PPL.

The following list summarizes the steps you must follow to get TEMPEST products endorsed. For detailed information about these steps, refer to the government publication, *Endorsed TEMPEST Products Program Procedures.*

1. **Memorandum of Understanding (MOU).** You submit a letter of intent, attaching a DD Form 441 (Department of Defense Security Agreement), stating that your organization has a SECRET facility security clearance and storage capability. (Vendors who do not yet possess a SECRET facility security clearance and storage capability should communicate with NSA's Office of Industrial Relations.)

   In conjunction with the Defense Investigative Service, U.S. government evaluators review your status and send you an MOU for signature. This document describes the terms and conditions governing the transfer of classified TEMPEST information.

   Once the MOU has been executed, you are given access to the classified National TEMPEST Standard (NACSIM 5100A) for a limited period of time. You promise to handle this classified information according to the provisions of the following documents:

   • Department of Defense, *Industrial Security Manual for Safeguarding Classified Information* (DOD 5220.22-M).

   • Department of Defense, *COMSEC Supplement to the Industrial Security Manual for Safeguarding Classified Information* (DOD 5220.22-S-1).

   • Department of Defense, *Security Classification Specification Document* (DD Form 254).

2. **Product-Specific Proposal.** Within 120 days of receiving the classified information, you must decide whether to submit a proposal. If submitted, the proposal must consist of the following:

   - Product Assurance Survey. Preliminary information about your organization's experience, manufacturing capabilities, product integrity procedures, configuration control, and product support.

   - Written Product Proposal. Description of the product, its system integration, its market, its competitive advantages, and its target schedule.

   - Company Profile. Description of your organization, its expertise, existing products, finances, security status, and key personnel, including their previous TEMPEST product development experience. The U.S. government also sends a survey team to your facility to assess your organization's ability to develop and produce a TEMPEST product. The team investigates the facility, using NSA's Objective Standards for Product Assurance as an evaluative guideline.

3. **Evaluation of Proposal.** The U.S. government reviews the Product-Specific Proposal and the findings of the survey team. In accordance with evaluation criteria, government evaluators determine the need for the proposed product and notify you of the result of the evaluation.

4. **Product Management Plan (PMP).** After the initial assessment, you negotiate with the government a Product Management Plan, which describes a mutually agreeable schedule of milestones and events, and specifies the delivery of data and reports required of each party to accomplish product development, evaluation, and endorsement. The company may withdraw its proposal at any time during this phase.

5. **Memorandum of Agreement (MOA).** You sign an MOA, a binding contract. The U.S. government agrees to deliver all required classified information and to protect the your organization's proprietary information. You agree to design, develop, produce, market, and sell a particular TEMPEST product at your own risk and expense.

   The following documents are attached to the MOA; specifications for these documents are provided by NSA:

   - *Technical and Security Requirements Document* (TSRD). Describes in detail the technical, security, and data requirements necessary for product endorsement.

- *Agreement Data Requirements List* (ADRL). Provides an itemized list of all documents that are to be submitted for TEMPEST product endorsement, with quantities and recommended media.

- *Product Management Plan* (PMP). Describes a mutually agreeable schedule of milestones, events, and deliveries.

6. **Potential Endorsed TEMPEST Products List (PETPL).** Once you have signed an MOA, the government publishes a brief description of the product in the PETPL section of the *Information Systems Security Products and Services Catalogue*. This list is an aid to potential users who may be considering what equipment to buy. NSA notes that inclusion in this list does not in any way imply that the product will actually receive endorsement.

7. **Product Development and Testing.** This activity breaks down into two major phases, the Product Evaluation Process and the Product Integrity Process.

During the Product Evaluation Process, you perform the following steps:

- Design a TEMPEST product.

- Prepare a TEMPEST control plan showing the intended construction techniques, interface techniques, security features, etc. for the product.

- Prepare a TEMPEST test plan showing the planned test methodology and test procedures.

- Perform product tests at an endorsed TEMPEST test services facility.

- Prepare a TEMPEST test report.

Under the old PPL scheme, testing was performed almost exclusively by certified TEMPEST professionals from private industry. Under the new scheme, NSA's own technical people are involved in testing and evaluating new products and in assuring their continued quality after endorsement.

During the Product Integrity Process, you prepare documents in the following categories:

- Configuration management and control (e.g., critical features list, documentation control system).

- Product assurance (e.g., product verification plan, TEMPEST deficiency resolution requirement).

- Maintenance and life cycle support (e.g., availability of maintenance services, assurance of individual qualifications).

8. **Evaluation of Product**. The U.S. government evaluates the product and all documentation. The evaluation team must be satisfied that all requirements are met and that the product complies with NACSIM 5100A, the TSRD, and the ADRL. If so, the evaluators notify you that the product has been endorsed. The entire product evaluation process takes approximately 18 months.

9. **Endorsed TEMPEST Products List (ETPL)**. If the product is endorsed, a brief description of the product is published in the next quarterly issue of the *Information Systems Security Products and Services Catalogue.*

10. **Vendor Sales and Installation**. You sell the endorsed product and install it at customer sites. Continued endorsement is contingent upon your continued adherence to all terms and conditions of the MOA and its attachments.

The ETPL pages of the *Information Systems Security Products and Services Catalogue* are color-coded to show products in different stages of certification.

White pages	Lists TEMPEST products, by equipment category, that have been successfully endorsed through the Endorsed TEMPEST Products Program. All products listed here are fully tested and endorsed in a production environment.
Yellow pages	Lists products that have been removed from the White pages because the government has recently found and confirmed deficiencies in the products. Vendors have a maximum of six months to correct these deficiencies. If the deficiencies are corrected, a yellow-listed product will be restored to the White pages. Users are advised to contact the local TEMPEST authority for guidance. In addition, NSA has initiated a TEMPEST deficiency alert program to notify TEMPEST authorities, by classified message, about product deficiencies.
Blue pages	Lists products whose accreditation has been suspended (pending accreditation termination and appeal). This is a more serious category. Vendors are not allowed to advertise the products in this category as being accredited or to take orders.
Red pages	Lists products whose accreditation has been terminated. Termination typically results from unresolved deficiencies or failure to comply with ETPP procedures or requirements Users of these products are advised to contact the local TEMPEST authority for guidance.
Green pages	Lists products that vendors have permanently discontinued.

Endorsed TEMPEST Test Services Program

The Endorsed TEMPEST Test Services Program (ETTSP) was established to support TEMPEST product development by providing quality TEMPEST test services. If you want to provide commercial TEMPEST test services, your organization must be endorsed under this program. Endorsed test services may be used for testing during your own TEMPEST product development; you may also provide these services to other TEMPEST vendors, to the U.S. government, and to government contractors.

Because TEMPEST personnel must have TEMPEST certification, the Endorsed TEMPEST Test Services Program is an adjunct to the TEMPEST Certification Program (TCP), which is responsible for the certification of TEMPEST testing professionals. The TEMPEST Certification Program is administered by the TEMPEST Countermeasures Working Group (TCMWG) of the Countermeasures Advisory Panel.

There are two types of certified test personnel: Certified TEMPEST Engineers (CTEs) and Certified TEMPEST Testers (CTTs). If you're looking for an engineering career path, consider becoming a TEMPEST engineer. Estimates are that there are only about 200 fully certified TEMPEST test engineers in the United States. Because of their scarcity, they command salaries that are considerably higher than those of uncertified TEMPEST engineers (who themselves are usually paid more than commercial engineers).

The government states its policy of endorsement under the Endorsed TEMPEST Test Services Program as follows:

> NSA endorsement of a TEMPEST test services facility is a statement that the facility complies with the technical, security, personnel, equipment, and operational requirements specified in the ETTSP Technical and Security Requirements Document (TSRD)...NSA does not make, by virtue of its endorsement, any warranty or representation regarding the quality of services provided by the endorsed facility.

The steps you follow to get test services endorsed are very similar to those described for endorsed TEMPEST products. Once endorsed, TEMPEST test services are listed on the Endorsed TEMPEST Test Services List (ETTSL), included in the *Information Systems Security Products and Services Catalogue*. Like the other TEMPEST sections of this publication, the ETTSL pages are color-coded to show services in different stages of certification.

For detailed information about test services endorsement procedures, refer to the government publication, *Endorsed TEMPEST Test Services Program*.

Endorsed TEMPEST Test Instrumentation Program

If your organization wants to be able to market endorsed TEMPEST test instrumentation, you must follow the steps described in this section for the Endorsed TEMPEST Test Instrumentation Program (ETTIP). Test instrumentation is equipment that operates in automatic fashion to quantify and/or analyze TEMPEST characteristics of equipment under test (EUT) against the TEMPEST standard.

The steps you follow to get test instrumentation endorsed are very similar to those described for endorsed TEMPEST products. Once endorsed, TEMPEST test instrumentation is listed on the Endorsed TEMPEST Test Instrumentation List (ETTIL), included in the *Information Systems Security Products and Services Catalogue*. Like the other TEMPEST sections of this publication, the ETTIL pages are color-coded to show services in different stages of certification.

For detailed information about test instrumentation endorsement procedures, refer to the government publication, *Endorsed TEMPEST Test Instrumentation Program.*

E

A Security Source Book

Government Publications
Government Program Contact Points
Emergency Organizations
Standards Organizations
Security User Groups
Electronic Groups
Computer Security Periodicals
Computer Security Books

This appendix tells you where to go for more information about computer security. It lists government publications and how to obtain them; government offices you can consult for information in specific areas; security organizations you can join; and books, magazines, and newsletters you can read for more information.

Government Publications

This section contains lists of government publications describing computer security standards, programs, and general information.

Most technical publications are available from the Government Printing Office or the National Technical Information Service. Contact:

> Superintendent of Documents
> U.S. Government Printing Office (GPO)
> Washington, DC 20402
> (202) 783-3238
>
> Hours: 8:00 a.m.–4:00 p.m. EST

You can place an order automatically anytime if you know the GPO stock number and intend to charge your order to a credit card. Contact:

> U.S. Department of Commerce
> National Technical Information Service (NTIS)
> 5285 Port Royal Road
> Springfield, VA 22161
> (703) 487-4650
>
> Sales Desk Hours: 8:30 a.m.–5:30 p.m. EST
> Identification Branch Hours: 9:00–5:00 p.m. EST

You can place an order automatically anytime if you know the NTIS number and intend to charge your order to a credit card.

The Rainbow Series

The books in the "Rainbow Series" are published by the National Computer Security Center's Technical Guidelines Program. Named for the different colors of their covers, the books in the Rainbow Series include the Orange Book, which defines trusted computer system evaluation criteria used to assess the effectiveness of security controls built into computer system products (described in Chapter 6, *Inside the Orange Book*). Other publications in this series provide detailed interpretations of certain Orange Book requirements and descriptions of evaluation program procedures.

Alas, the integrity of the Rainbow colors has been threatened by recent printings in which books have unexpectedly changed hue, and most horribly, a second book has been assigned an orange cover. If you order a particular book, be sure to specify its title and number, not just its color. To order one complimentary copy of any of these books, contact the Government Printing Office or the following office:

> Director, National Security Agency
> INFOSEC Awareness
> Attention: X71
> 9800 Savage Road
> Fort George G. Meade, MD 20755-6000
> (301) 766-8729

Table E-1. Rainbow Series

Book	Title	Number/Date
Orange Book	*Department of Defense (Dod) Trusted Computer System Evaluation Criteria (TCSEC)* Contains basic requirements in four categories for trusted operating systems: security policy, accountability, assurance, and documentation.	DoD 5200.28-STD GPO: 008-000-00461-7 12/26/85
Green Book	*Department of Defense (DoD) Password Management Guideline* Contains a set of good practices for the design, implementation, and use of password systems used for authentication. Many trusted systems comply explicitly with this guideline.	CSC-STD-002-85 GPO: 008-000-00443-9 4/12/85
Light Yellow Book	*Computer Security Requirements—Guidance for Applying the Department of Defense (DoD) Trusted Computer System Evaluation Criteria (TCSEC) in Specific Environments*	CSC-STD-003-85 GPO: 008-000-00442-1 6/25/85

Table E-1. Rainbow Series (continued)

Book	Title	Number/Date
Light Yellow Book (cont.)	Contains information on different modes of security (closed security environment, open security environment, dedicated security mode, controlled security mode, and multi-level security mode) and the "risk index" associated with each environment.	
Yellow Book	*Technical Rationale Behind CSC-STD-003-85: Computer Security Requirements—Guidance for Applying the Department of Defense (DoD) Trusted Computer System Evaluation Criteria (TCSEC) in Specific Environments* Companion to the Light Yellow Book. Contains background information on determining the class of trusted system required for different risk indexes.	CSC-STD-004-8 GPO: 008-000-00441-2 6/25/85
Tan Book	*A Guide to Understanding Audit in Trusted Systems* Contains an interpretation of the auditing requirements included in the Orange Book. Auditing keeps track of sensitive activities (e.g., login attempts) in a system and provides a way of determining who performed these activities.	NCSC-TG-001, Version 2 GPO: 008-000-00508-7 6/1/88
Aqua Book	*Trusted Product Evaluations: A Guide for Vendors*	NCSC-TG-002, Version 1 6/22/90

Table E-1. Rainbow Series (continued)

Book	Title	Number/Date
Aqua Book (cont.)	Contains procedures to follow when submitting a trusted system (or a network product, a database product, or a subsystem) to the NCSC for evaluation.	
Neon Orange Book	*A Guide to Understanding Discretionary Access Control (DAC) in Trusted Systems* Contains an interpretation of the discretionary access control requirement included in the Orange Book. DAC protects files and other objects in a system at the discretion of the owner.	NCSC-TG-003, Version 1 GPO: 008-000-00539-7 9/30/87
Teal Green Book	*Glossary of Computer Security Terms* Contains definitions for common terms used in government computer security publications.	NCSC-TG-004, Version 1 GPO: 008-000-00522-2 10/21/88
Red Book	*Trusted Network Interpretation (TNI) of the Trusted Computer System Evaluation Criteria (TCSEC)* Contains an interpretation of the Orange Book requirements for networks, and a summary of specific network services: communications integrity, denial of service, and compromise protection.	NCSC-TG-005, Version 1 GPO: 008-000-00486-2 7/31/87
(Another) Orange Book	*A Guide to Understanding Configuration Management in Trusted Systems*	NCSC-TG-006, Version 1 GPO: 008-000-00507-9 3/28/88

Table E-1. Rainbow Series (continued)

Book	Title	Number/Date
(Another) Orange Book (cont.)	Contains an interpretation of the configuration management requirements included in the Orange Book. These requirements manage changes to the Trusted Computing Base and to the system documentation.	
Burgundy Book	*A Guide to Understanding Design Documentation in Trusted Systems* Contains an interpretation of the design documentation requirements included in the Orange Book, including the suggested scope and level of effort for this documentation.	NCSC-TG-007, Version 1 GPO: 008-000-00518-4 10/2/88
Dark Lavender Book	*A Guide to Understanding Trusted Distribution in Trusted Systems* Contains an interpretation of the trusted distribution requirements included in the Orange Book. These requirements ensure that all of the elements of the TCB distributed to a customer arrive exactly as intended by the vendor. They include recommendations for packaging, security locks, courier service, etc.	NCSC-TG-008, Version 1 GPO: 008-000-00536-2 12/15/88
Venice Blue Book	*Computer Security Subsystem Interpretation (CSI) of Trusted Computer System Evaluation Criteria (TCSEC)*	NCSC-TG-009, Version 1 GPO: 008-000-00510-9 9/16/88

Table E-1. Rainbow Series (continued) (continued)

Book	Title	Number/Date
Venice Blue Book (cont.)	Contains an interpretation of the Orange Book requirements for computer security add-on products and subsystems. Subsystems typically provide features in one or more of these categories: discretionary access control, object reuse, identification and authentication, and audit.	
Dark Red Book	*Trusted Network Interpretation Environments Guideline* Companion to the Red Book (Trusted Network Interpretation [TNI] of the Trusted Computer System Evaluation Criteria [TCSEC]). Contains information helpful when integrating, operating, and maintaining trusted computer networks, including the minimum security required in different network environments.	NCSC-TG-011, Version 1 8/1/90
Pink Book	*Rating Maintenance Phase (RAMP) Program Document* Contains procedures for keeping an Orange Book rating up to date via the RAMP program. Participation in RAMP is required for C1, C2, and B1 systems.	NCSC-TG-013, Version 1 6/23/89
Purple Book	*Guidelines for Formal Verification Systems*	NCSC-TG-014, Version 1 GPO: 008-000-00546-1 4/1/89

Table E-1. Rainbow Series (continued)

Book	Title	Number/Date
Purple Book (cont.)	Contains procedures to follow when submitting a formal design and verification tool to the NCSC for evaluation.	
Brown Book	*A Guide to Understanding Trusted Facility Management*	NCSC-TG-015, Version 1 10/18/89
	Contains an interpretation of the trusted facility management requirements included in the Orange Book. These requirements mandate certain types of system and security administration—for example, the separation of operator, security administrator, and account administrator functions.	
Light Blue Book	*A Guide to Understanding Identification and Authentication in Trusted Systems*	NCSC-TG-017, Version 1 9/91
	Contains an interpretation of the identification and authentication (I&A) requirements included in the Orange Book. Identification is the way you tell the system who you are; authentication is the way you prove your identity.	
Medium Blue Book	*Trusted Product Evaluation Questionnaire*	NCSC-TG-019, Version 1 10/16/89
	Contains an extensive list of questions aimed at vendors of trusted systems. Examples are "What are the subjects in your system?" and "How can an op-	

Table E-1. Rainbow Series (continued)

Book	Title	Number/Date
Medium Blue Book (cont.)	erator distinguish the TCB-generated banner pages from user output?" The goal of this list is to help vendors understand what technical information is required for the system to be evaluated successfully.	
Grey Book	*Trusted UNIX Working Group (TRUSIX) Rationale for Selecting Access Control List Features for the UNIX System* Contains a description of access control lists (ACLs), their use in enforcing the discretionary access control (DAC) feature included in the Orange Book, and the reasons for selecting this mechanism as a standard for trusted UNIX systems.	NCSC-TG-020-A, Version 1 8/18/89
Lavender Book	*Trusted Database Management System Interpretation (TDI) of the Trusted Computer System Evaluation Criteria (TCSEC)* Contains an interpretation of the Orange Book requirements for database management systems.	NCSC-TG-021, Version 1 4/91
Neon Yellow Book	*A Guide to Understanding Trusted Recovery in Trusted Systems* Contains an interpretation of the trusted recovery requirements included in the Orange Book, including a discussion of	NCSC-TG-022, Version 1 12/30/91

Table E-1. Rainbow Series (continued)

Book	Title	Number/Date
Neon Yellow Book (cont.)	secure states and transitions, design and implementation strategies, and the relationship to other Orange Book requirements.	
Dark Green Book	*A Guide to Understanding Data Remanence in Automated Information Systems* Contains recommendations for purging magnetic media via various types of degaussing and data sanitization techniques.	NCSC-TG-025, Version 1 9/91
Salmon Book	*A Guide to Writing the Security Features User's Guide for Trusted Systems* Contains recommendations for developing the *Security Features User's Guide (SFUG)*: audience considerations, contents, possible presentation styles, etc.	NCSC-TG-026, Version 1 9/91

Other NSA Publications

The National Computer Security Center also publishes additional computer security documents that are not part of the Rainbow Series. Sample publications are listed below. Contact NCSC for complete information about available documents.

Personal Computer Security Considerations, NCSC-WA-002-85, 12/85.

Advisory Memorandum on Office Automation and Security Guidelines, NTISSAM COMPUSEC/1-87, 1/16/87

Computer Viruses: Prevention, Detection, and Treatment C1—Technical Report—001, 3/12/90

INFOSEC Catalogue

The *Information Systems Security Products and Services Catalogue* is a quarterly publication by NSA. It's published in complete form in January and July, with updates in April and October. It lists security products currently under evaluation by the National Computer Security Center and other parts of NSA. Individual copies are available from the GPO or from DOCKMASTER (described below). For further information about this catalogue. Contact:

> National Security Agency
> Attention: INFOSEC Office of Customer Relations
> 9800 Savage Road
> Fort George G. Meade, MD 20755-6000

Final Evaluation Reports

Final Evaluation Reports (FERs), written by the NCSC for successfully evaluated systems, are available from NTIS or from the following office:

> Director, National Security Agency
> INFOSEC Awareness
> Attention: S322
> 9800 Savage Road
> Fort George G. Meade, MD 20755-6000
> (301) 766-8729 or (301) 688-8742

FIPS PUBs

Federal Information Processing Standards Publications (FIPS PUBs) are prepared by NIST's Computer Systems Laboratory (CSL). The FIPS PUBs listed in the table below are relevant to computer security.

Order by FIPS PUBs number from:

> National Technical Information Service (NTIS)
> U.S. Department of Commerce
> 5285 Port Royal Road
> Springfield, VA 22161
> (703) 487-4650

If you are on the Internet, you can obtain many FIPS PUBs by anonymous FTP from **cert.sei.cmu.edu**. Ask your system administrator if you need help obtaining these documents.

Table E-2. FIPS PUBs

FIPS PUB	Title	Date
31	*Guidelines for ADP Physical Security and Risk Management* Contains guidance for organizations that are developing physical security and risk management programs to protect against natural disasters, system failures, and other problems.	6/74
39	*Glossary for Computer Systems Security* Contains definitions for computer security and privacy terms.	2/15/76
41	*Computer Security Guidelines for Implementing the Privacy Act of 1974* Provides guidance for organizations that are selecting methods for protecting personal data in computer systems.	5/30/75
46-1	*Data Encryption Standard* Contains the specification for the Data Encryption Standard (DES) DES algorithm, which can be implemented in hardware to protect sensitive unclassified information.	1/22/88
48	*Guidelines on Evaluation of Techniques for Automated Personal Identification* Contains information about the evaluation and use of personal identification devices.	4/1/77
65	*Guideline for Automated Data Processing Risk Analysis* Contains information to be used in conducting a risk analysis of a system facility and related assets.	8/1/79
73	*Guidelines for Security of Computer Applications* Contains a discussion of security objectives for computer systems and describes such controls as data validation, user identity verification, authorization, journaling, variance detection, and encryption.	6/30/80

Table E-2. FIPS PUBs (continued)

FIPS PUB	Title	Date
74	*Guidelines for Implementing and Using the NBS Data Encryption Standard* Companion to FIPS PUB 46-1. Contains guidance for the use of cryptographic techniques.	4/1/81
81	*DES Modes of Operation* Companion to FIPS PUB 46-1. Contains descriptions of the four modes of operation for the Data Encryption Standard: Electronic Codebook (ECB), Cipher Block Chaining (CBC), Cipher Feedback (CFB), and Output Feedback (OFB).	12/2/80
83	*Guideline on User Authentication Techniques for Computer Network Access Control* Contains guidance for the selection and implementation of authentication techniques for remote terminal users. Describes such techniques as passwords, identification tokens, verification by personal attributes, identification of remote devices, encryption, and computerized authorization techniques.	9/29/80
87	*Guidelines for ADP Contingency Planning* Contains considerations for developing a contingency plan for a computer facility.	3/27/81
88	*Guideline on Integrity Assurance and Control in Database Administration* Contains advice for achieving database integrity and security control.	8/14/81
94	*Guideline on Electrical Power for ADP Installations* Contains information about electrical factors that affect computer system operation. Describes power, grounding, static electricity, and lightning protection.	9/82
102	*Guidelines for Computer Security Certification and Accreditation*	9/27/83

Table E-2. FIPS PUBs (continued)

FIPS PUB	Title	Date
102 (cont.)	Contains information about establishing a program for certification (technical evaluation of a system to determine how well it meets its security requirements) and accreditation (official management authorization for system operation).	
112	*Standard on Password Usage* Contains a discussion of factors to consider in designing, implementing, and using access control systems based on passwords. Specifies a range of recommendations for systems at different levels of security.	5/30/85
113	*Standard on Computer Data Authentication* Contains the specification for the Data Authentication Algorithm (DAA), which automatically and accurately detects intentional and accidental unauthorized modification. The DAA is based on the Data Encryption Standard.	5/30/85
139	*Interoperability and Security Requirements for Use of the Data Encryption Standard in the Physical Layer of Data Communications* Contains the specification for the interoperability and security standard using encryption at the physical layer of the Open Systems Interconnection (OSI) model.	8/3/83
140	*General Security Requirements for Equipment Using the Data Encryption Standard* Contains security requirements for implementing the DES in telecommunications equipment.	4/14/82
141	*Interoperability and Security Requirements for Use of the Data Encryption Standard with CCITT Group 3 Facsimile Equipment*	4/4/85

Table E-2. FIPS PUBs (continued)

FIPS PUB	Title	Date
141 (cont.)	Contains the specification for interoperability and security standard for encryption with International Telegraph and Telephone Consultative Committee (CCITT) facsimile equipment conveying data and/or text.	
146-1	*Government Open Systems Interconnect Profile (GOSIP)* Contains the specification for GOSIP, a set of data communications protocols based on the OSI model.	4/91
161	*Electronic Data Interchange* Contains the specification for Electronic Data Interchange (EDI), the computer-to-computer interchange of messages representing business documents.	3/91

NIST Special Publications

NIST publishes documents describing the results of studies, investigations, and research conducted by the NCSL. The special publications (SPEC PUBs) listed in Table E-3 are relevant to computer security and risk management.

Order SPEC PUBs from the GPO or NIST, using the order numbers shown in the table. For a complete list, with prices, ask NIST for *Computer Security Publications* (NIST Publication List 91, March 1990). Contact:

National Technical Information Service (NTIS)
U.S. Department of Commerce
5285 Port Royal Road
Springfield, VA 22161
(703) 487-4650

Table E-3. SPEC PUBs

SPEC PUB	Title	Number/Date
500-20	*Validating the Correctness of Hardware Implementations of the NBS Data Encryption Standard* By Jason Gait. Describes the testbed used to validate hardware implementations of the DES.	NTIS: PB 81113524 9/80
500-27	*Computer Security and the Data Encryption Standard* By Dennis Branstad. Contains the proceedings of the Conference on Computer Security and the Data Encryption Standard held at NBS.	NTIS: PB 277695 2/78
500-54	*A Key Notarization System for Computer Networks* By Miles E. Smid. Contains a description of a system for key notarization, which can be used with an encryption device to improve network security.	NTIS: PB 80104698 10/79
500-57	*Audit and Evaluation of Computer Security II: System Vulnerabilities and Controls* By Zella G. Ruthberg. Contains proceedings of the second NBS/GAO workshop to develop improved computer security audit procedures.	GPO: SN 003-003-02178-4 4/80
500-61	*Maintenance Testing for the Data Encryption Standard* By Jason Gait. Contains descriptions of four tests that vendors and users can use to check the operation of data encryption devices.	NTIS: PB 80221211 8/80

Table E-3. SPEC PUBs (continued)

SPEC PUB	Title	Number/Date
500-67	*The SRI Hierarchical Development Methodology (HDM) and Its Application to the Development of Secure Software*	NTIS: PB 81115537 10/80
	By Karl N. Levitt, Peter Neumann, and Lawrence Robinson. Contains a description of a tool that can be used to design large software systems such as operating systems and data management systems that must meet stringent security requirements.	
500-85	*Executive Guide to ADP Contingency Planning*	NTIS: PB 82165226 7/81
	By James K. Shaw and Stuart W. Katzke. Contains questions and answers about the development of computer system contingency plans.	
500-109	*Overview of Computer Security Certification and Accreditation*	GPO: SN 003-003-02567-4 4/84
	By Zella G. Ruthberg and William Neugent. Contains a summary of FIPS PUB 102 (*Guideline to Computer Security Certification and Accreditation*) for computer system managers.	
500-120	*Security of Personal Computer Systems—A Management Guide*	GPO: SN 003-003-02627-1 1/85
	By Dennis D. Steinauer. Contains practical advice about PC security in the following areas: physical and environmental protection, system and data access control, integrity of software and data, backup and contingency planning, auditability, and communications protections.	

Table E-3. SPEC PUBs (continued)

SPEC PUB	Title	Number/Date
500-121	*Guidance on Planning and Implementing Computer Systems Reliability* By Lynne S. Rosenthal. Contains guidance for managers and planners about system reliability and management programs to improve system reliability.	GPO: SN 003-003-02628-0 1/85
500-133	*Technology Assessment: Methods for Measuring the Level of Computer Security* By William Neugent, John Gilligan, Lance Hoffman, and Zella G. Ruthberg. Contains information on technical tools and processes that can be used to measure the level of computer security.	GPO: SN 003-003-02686-7 10/85
500-134	*Guide on Selecting ADP Backup Process Alternatives* By Irene Isaac. Contains information on selecting backup processing methods and guidelines for management support.	GPO: SN 003-003-02701-4 11/85
500-137	*Security for Dial-Up Lines* By Eugene F. Troy. Contains techniques for protecting computers from intruders via telephone lines. Describes hardware devices that can be attached to computers or terminals to provide communications protection for unclassified computer systems.	NTIS: PB 862113097 5/86
500-153	*Guide to Auditing for Controls and Security: A System Development Life Cycle Approach*	GPO: 003-003-02856-8 4/88

Table E-3. SPEC PUBs continued

SPEC PUB	Title	Number/Date
500-153 (cont.)	By Zella G. Ruthberg, Bonnie Fisher, William E. Perry, John W. Lainhart IV, James G. Cox, Mark Gillen, and Douglas B. Hunt (authors and editors). Contains information about a process for auditing the system development life cycle (SDLC) of a computer system to ensure that controls and security are designed and built into the system.	
500-156	*Message Authentication Code (MAC) Validation System: Requirements and Procedures* By Miles Smid, Elaine Barker, David Balenson, and Martha Haykin. Contains information about the design of, and administrative procedures for, the Message Authentication Code Validation System (MVS) developed by NIST to test message authentication devices for conformance to standards.	GPO: 003-003-02860-6 5/88
500-157	*Smart Card Technology: New Methods for Computer Access Control* By Martha E. Haykin and Robert B.J. Warner. Contains information about smart card design, capabilities, and applications.	GPO: 003-003-02887-8 9/88
500-158	*Accuracy, Integrity, and Security in Computerized Vote-Tallying* By Roy G. Saltman. Contains information about problems in computerized vote-tallying and suggests	GPO: 003-003-02883-5 8/88

Table E-3. SPEC PUBs (continued)

SPEC PUB	Title	Number/Date
500-158 (cont.)	approaches to applying internal controls to this process. Suggestions include software for integrity and logical correctness, dedicated operation, improved design for systems that do not use ballots, and improved pre-election testing and partial manual recounting of ballots.	
500-160	*Report of the Invitational Workshop on Integrity Policy in Computer Information Systems (WIPCIS)* By Stuart W. Katzke and Zella G. Ruthberg (editors). Contains proceedings of the first invitational workshop on integrity policy. The workshop was held in response to the paper by David Clark and David Wilson entitled "A Comparison of Military and Commercial Data Security Policy."	GPO: 003-003-02904-1 1/89
500-166	*Computer Viruses and Related Threats: A Management Guide* By John P. Wack and Lisa J. Carnahan. Contains guidance for managers in controlling the threats of computer viruses and related software and unauthorized use.	GPO: 003-003-02955-6 8/89
500-168	*Report of the Invitational Workshop on Data Integrity* By Zella G. Ruthberg and William T. Polk. Companion to SPEC PUB 500-160. Contains the proceedings of the second invitational workshop on computer integrity (NIST, January	GPO: 003-003-02966-1 9/89

Table E-3. SPEC PUBs (continued)

SPEC PUB	Title	Number/Date
500-168 (cont.)	1989). The workshop focused on data integrity models, data quality, integrity controls, and certification.	
500-169	*Executive Guide to the Protection of Information Resources* By Cheryl Helsing, Marianne Swanson, and Mary Anne Todd. Contains a summary for executives of answers to questions regarding the protection of computer systems and data.	GPO: 003-003-02969-6 10/89
500-170	*Management Guide to the Protection of Information Resources* By Cheryl Helsing, Marianne Swanson, and Mary Anne Todd. Contains a summary of agency manager responsibilities for the protection of computer systems and data.	GPO: 003-003-02968-8 10/89
500-171	*Computer User's Guide to the Protection of Information Resources* By Cheryl Helsing, Marianne Swanson, and Mary Anne Todd. Contains a summary of user responsibilities for the protection of computer systems and data.	GPO: 003-003-02970-0 12/89
500-172	*Computer Security Training Guidelines* By Mary Anne Todd and Constance Guitian. Contains guidelines for determining the security training needs of employees who use computer systems.	GPO: 003-003-02975-1 11/89
500-174	*Guide for Selecting Automated Risk Analysis Tools*	GPO: 003-003-02971-8 10/89

Table E-3. SPEC PUBs (continued)

SPEC PUB	Title	Number/Date
500-174 (cont.)	By Irene E. Gilbert. Contains recommendations for selecting automated risk analysis tools. Describes the three elements that should be present in a suitable risk analysis tool: data collection, analysis, and output results.	
500-183	*Stable Implementation Agreements for Open Systems Interconnection Protocols, Version 5* By Tim Boland. Contains the text of the final agreements for implementing the OSI protocol.	GPO: SN 903-015-00000-4 12/91
800-1	*Computer Security in the 1980s: Selected Bibliography* By Rein Turn and Lawrence E. Bassham. Cites selected books and articles on computer security published during the 1980s.	GPO: SN 003-003-03060-1 12/90
NBSIR 86-3386	*Work Priority Scheme for EDP Audit and Computer Security Review* By Zella G. Ruthberg and Bonnie Fisher. Contains a methodology for prioritizing the work performed by computer system auditors and security reviewers. Developed at an invitational workshop attended by government and private sector experts.	NTIS: PB 86247897 8/86
NISTIR 90-4228	*Prototyping SP4: A Secure Data Network System Transport Protocol Interoperability Demonstration Project* By Charles Dinkel, Noel Nazario, and Robert Rosenthal. Describes a project, conducted in partnership with NSA	NTIS: PB 90-159609 1/90

Table E-3. SPEC PUBs (continued)

SPEC PUB	Title	Number/Date
NISTIR 90-4228 (cont.)	and industry, to demonstrate security at the Transport layer (layer 4) of the OSI model.	
NISTIR 90-4250	*Secure Data Network System (SDNS) Network, Transport, and Message Security Protocols* By Charles Dinkel. Contains four security protocol documents developed by NSA as a result of the SDNS project: security at layer 3 of the OSI model, cryptographic techniques, specifications for message security service protocol, and directory systems specifications for message security protocol.	NTIS: PB 90-198946 2/90
NISTIR 90-4259	*Secure Data Network System (SDNS) Access Control Documents* By Charles Dinkel. Contains three documents developed by NSA as a result of the SDNS project: principles and functions of the SDNS access control and authentication security services, a functional description of the access control system, and the capabilities of the Access Control Information Specification (ACIS).	NTIS: PB 90-188061 2/90
NISTIR 90-4262	*Secure Data Network System (SDNS) Key Management Documents* By Charles Dinkel. Contains four documents developed by NSA as a result of the SDNS project: implementation of SDNS Key Management services, services provided by the Key Management Application Service Element (KMASE), the protocol for the	NTIS: PB 90-188079 2/90

Table E-3. SPEC PUBs (continued)

SPEC PUB	Title	Number/Date
NISTIR 90-4262 (cont.)	KMASE protocol, and the framework of the SDNS security attribute negotiation service.	
NISTIR 4325	*U.S. Department of Energy Risk Assessment Methodology*	NTIS: PB 90-244484 5/90
	By Edward Roback. Describes a U.S. Department of Energy methodology in two volumes. Volume I includes risk assessment guideline instructions, a resource table, and a completed sample. Volume II contains risk assessment worksheets.	
NISTIR 4359	*Domestic Disaster Recover Plan for PCs, OIS, and Small VS Systems*	NTIS: PB 90-265240 8/90
	By Edward Roback. Describes a disaster recovery methodology developed by Advanced Information Management, Inc., under contract to the U.S. Department of State.	
NISTIR 4362	*Security Labels for Open Systems: An Invitational Workshop*	NTIS: PB 90-247446 6/90
	By Noel Nazario. Describes the results of a workshop on security labels covering labeling issues in end systems and in secure OSI networks.	
NISTIR 4378	*Automated Information System Security Accreditation Guidelines* By Edward Roback. Presents guidelines developed by the Federal Aviation Adminstration for documentation describing the security accreditation of automated information systems.	NTIS: PB 90-264102 8/90
NISTIR 4387	*U.S. Department of Justice Simplified Risk Analysis Guidelines (SRAAG)*	NTIS: PB 90-265257 8/90

Table E-3. SPEC PUBs (continued)

SPEC PUB	Title	Number/Date
NISTIR 4387 (cont.)	By Edward Roback. Contains a risk analysis methodology developed by the U.S. Department of Justice.	
NISTIR 4409	*1989 Computer Security and Privacy Plans (CSPP) Review Project: A First-Year Federal Response to the Computer Security Act of 1987 (Final Report)* By Dennis Gilbert. Describes a review effort conducted in response to the Computer Security Act of 1987 by a joint team from NSA and NIST.	NTIS: PB 91-107504 9/90
NISTIR 4451	*U.S. Department of Commerce Methodology for Certifying Sensitive Computer Applications* By Edward Roback. Describes a standard certification methodology employed by the Department of Commerce.	NTIS: PB 91-120162 11/90
NISTIR 4453	*SRI International Improving the Security of Your UNIX System* By Edward Roback. Provides a variety of suggestions for improving the security of systems running under the UNIX operating system.	NTIS: PB 91-120121 8/90

Other NIST Publications

The CSL also publishes the *Journal of Research of the National Institute of Standards and Technology*, as well as computer systems bulletins and research reports in the area of computer security. You can get a list of these bulletins by calling the CSL at (301) 975-2821.

Compartmented Mode Workstation (CMW) Publications

Note: These publications are available only to authorized organizations through their contracting officers.

Woodward, J.P.L., *Security Requirements for System High and Compartmented Mode Workstations*, MTR 9992, Defense Intelligence Agency, DDS 2600-5502-87.

Woodward, J.P.L., *Compartmented Mode Workstation Labeling: Source Code and User Interface Guidelines*, MTR 10648, Defense Intelligence Agency, DDS 2600-6215-89.

Compartmented Mode Workstation Standard User Interface Style Guide, Defense Intelligence Agency, U-15, 284/DSE-3.

COMSEC Program Publications

Note: These publications are available only to authorized organizations through their contracting officers.

Summary of the Commercial COMSEC Endorsement Program (CCEP), 1986.

Handling and Control of Controlled Cryptographic Items During Development and Manufacture/Assembly, NSA 86-44, 3/12/87.

Industrial Security Manual for Safeguarding Classified Information (DoD 5220.22-M), 1983.

COMSEC Supplement to DoD Industrial Security Manual (DoD 5220.22-S-1), 1983.

Industrial COMSEC Material Control Manual (NSA CSCM-1).

U.S. Government Contractors Controlled Cryptographic Item (CCI) Manual, 2/2/86.

TEMPEST Program Publications

Note: These publications are available only to authorized organizations through their TEMPEST project officers.

Memorandum for all Current and Prospective ITP Companies, "Decision to Restructure the Industrial TEMPEST Program," S-0068-88, 3/8/88.

NSA Objective Standards for Product Assurance, 11/12/85.

Endorsed TEMPEST Products Program, 1988.

Endorsed TEMPEST Test Services Program, 1988.

Endorsed TEMPEST Test Instrumentation Program, 1988.

PPL Product Transition Guidelines and Procedures

PPL Accreditation Standard Operating Procedures and Requirements

ITP Quality Assurance Procedures

ITP Standard Operating Procedures (ITPSOP-R), 8/3/89.

Other Security-relevant Government Publications

The following additional computer security publications are available from the GPO:

U.S. Congress, Office of Technology Assessment, *Defending Secrets, Sharing Data: New Locks and Keys for Electronic Information*, OTA-CIT-310 (Washington, DC: U.S. Government Printing Office, October 1987).

U.S. Congress, Office of Technology Assessment, *Federal Government Information Technology: Electronic Surveillance and Civil Liberties*, OTA-CIT-293 (Washington, DC: U.S. Government Printing Office, October 1985).

U.S. Congress, Office of Technology Assessment, *Federal Government Information Technology: Management, Security, and Congressional Oversight*, OTA-CIT-297 (Washington, DC: U.S. Government Printing Office, February 1986).

U.S. Congress, Office of Technology Assessment, *Federal Government Information Technology: Electronic Record Systems and Individual Privacy*, OTA-CIT-296 (Washington, DC: U.S. Government Printing Office, March 1987).

Government Program Contact Points

This section contains addresses and telephone numbers of government organizations that research, evaluate, and provide information about computer security. Note that although these names and addresses were accurate at the time we went to press, they are subject to change at any time.

Computer Security (COMPUSEC) Programs

Trusted Product Evaluation Program (TPEP)

Director, National Security Agency
Acquisition Policy and Business Development
Attention: X511
9800 Savage Road
Fort George G. Meade, MD 20755-6000
(301) 688-6581

Technical Guidelines

National Computer Security Center
Standards, Criteria, and Guidelines
Attention: C81
9800 Savage Road
Fort George G. Meade, MD 20755-6000
(301) 859-4452

Computer Security Technical Vulnerability Reporting Program

Director, National Security Agency
Computer Security Vulnerability Reporting Program
Attention: DDI/CSTVRP
9800 Savage Road
Fort George G. Meade, MD 20755-6000
(301) 688-6079

DOCKMASTER

National Computer Security Center
Attention: C81 Accounts Administrator
9800 Savage Road
Fort George G. Meade, MD 20755-6000
(301) 859-4360

Formal Verification Systems

National Computer Security Center
Office of Research and Development
Attention: 232, TAR Request
9800 Savage Road
Fort George G. Meade, MD 20755-6000
(301) 859-4360

Independent Research and Development Projects Program

National Computer Security Center
Information Systems Security Research and Technology
Attention: R206
9800 Savage Road
Fort George G. Meade, MD 20755-6000
(301) 859-6515

Degausser Evaluation Program

National Security Agency
Attn: L14 Degausser Evaluation Program
9800 Savage Road
Fort George G. Meade, MD 20755-6000
(301) 688-6581

Computer Security Standards and Research

Computer Security Division
National Computer Systems Laboratory
National Institute of Standards and Technology
Gaithersburg, MD 20899
(301) 975-2821

Communications Security (COMSEC) Programs

Commercial Communications Security Endorsement Program (CCEP)

Director, National Security Agency
Acquisition Policy and Business Development
Attention: X511
9800 Savage Road
Fort George G. Meade, MD 20755-6000
(301) 688-6581

Endorsed Cryptographic Products List (ECPL)

Director, National Security Agency
Attention: X51
9800 Savage Road
Fort George G. Meade, MD 20755-6000

Secure Data Network System (SDNS) Program

Director, National Security Agency
Multilevel Security Workstations
Attention: V531
9800 Savage Road
Fort George G. Meade, MD 20755-6000
(301) 859-4387

Electronic Funds Transfer Certification Program

Assistant Director, Security Programs
Department of Treasury
15th and Pennsylvania Avenue, NW
Washington, DC 20220
(202) 566-5152

TEMPEST Programs

TEMPEST Endorsement Programs

Director, National Security Agency
Attention: X512/TEMPEST
9800 Savage Road
Fort George G. Meade, MD 20755-6000
(301) 688-8728

Other Government Contacts

Restrictions on purchase and use of security products:

Director, National Security Agency
Attention: X51
9800 Savage Road
Fort George G. Meade, MD 20755-6000

Help with determining computer security needs of government agency or contractor:

Director, National Security Agency
Attention: INFOSEC Office of Customer Relations
9800 Savage Road
Fort George G. Meade, MD 20755-6000

Emergency Organizations

For help with an emergency over the Internet, contact:

Computer Emergency Response Team (CERT)
Software Engineering Institute
Carnegie Mellon University
Pittsburgh, PA 15213

Hotline: (412) 268-7090
By electronic mail: **cert@cert.sei.cmu.edu**

For emergency help with any Department of Energy system, contact:

Department of Energy's Computer Incident Advisory Capability (CIAC)
Lawrence Livermore National Laboratory
University of California
P.O. Box 808, L-303
Livermore, CA 94550

During business hours: (415) 422-8193
Emergency page: (415) 423-7705, enter pager number 2882, 5172, or 5173
By electronic mail: **ciac@cheetah.llnl.gov**

Standards Organizations

American Bankers Association (ABA)

To order ABA standards, contact:

American Bankers Association
1120 Connecticut Avenue, N.W.
Washington DC 20036
(202) 663-5000

American National Standards Institute (ANSI)

To order ANSI and ISO standards, contact:

American National Standards Institute
Attention: Sales Department
1430 Broadway
New York, NY 10018
(212) 642-4900

Computer and Business Equipment Manufacturers Association (CBEMA)

To order X3/SD-4, a document that lists all active X3 and related ISO projects and standards, contact:

Computer and Business Equipment Manufacturers Association
Attention: X3 Secretariat
311 First Street, Suite 500, N.W.
Washington, DC 20001-2178
(202) 737-8888

International Standards Organization (ISO)

For general information about ISO standards, contact:

International Standards Organization
1, Rue de Varembe
Gase Postale 58
CH-1211
Geneva 20, Switzerland

Institute of Electrical and Electronic Engineers (IEEE))

For information about the computer society, contact:

IEEE
345 East 47th Street
New York, NY 10017
(212) 705-7900

For general information about IEEE standards, contact:

IEEE
Attention: Standards
1730 Massachusetts Avenue, N.W.
Washington, DC 20036
(202) 785-2180

To order standards (e.g., POSIX), catalogs, and other publications, contact:

IEEE Computer Society
Attention: Customer Service
445 Hoes Lane
Piscataway, NY 08855
(201) 981-0060

X/Open

For general information about X/Open, contact:

X/Open Company Limited
Apex Plaza, Forbury Road,
Reading, England, RG1 1AX
+(44) (0)734 508311

To order the *X/Open Security Guide* and other volumes from the *X/Open Portability Guide*, contact:

Prentice-Hall
200 Old Tappan Road
Tappan, NY 07675

Security User Groups

The following organizations focus on computer security or have strong special interest groups in the security area. Many of them also sponsor computer security conferences on a regular or occasional basis.

Association for Computing Machinery (ACM)

The ACM supports computer security through its special interest groups (SIGs)—in particular, the SIG on Security, Audit, and Control (see the listing in "Security Periodicals") and the SIG on Computers and Society—as well as through sessions at conferences and various publications.

Association for Computing Machinery
11 West 42nd Street
New York, NY 10036
(212) 869-7440

American Society for Industrial Security (ASIS)

ASIS is oriented to overall security (not simply computer security). It publishes a bimonthly newsletter and a monthly magazine, *Security Management*, and sponsors an annual conference and exhibition.

> American Society for Industrial Security
> 1655 North Fort Meyer Drive, Suite 1200
> Arlington, VA 22209
> (703) 522-5800

Business Systems and Security Marketing Association (BSSMA)

BSSMA conducts sales and management training programs and administers competency tests for security equipment dealers and servicers. It publishes a monthly *BSSMA Newsletter* and sponsors an annual conference.

> Business Systems and Security Marketing Association
> 1411 Peterson
> Park Ridge, IL 60068
> (708) 825-8419

Computer Security Institute (CSI)

CSI, founded in 1974, publishes a *Computer Security Handbook*, an *Annual Buyer's Guide*, the semi-annual *Computer Security Journal*, and a bi-monthly newsletter. CSI also sponsors an Annual Computer Security Conference and Exhibition, and other conferences, seminars, and training courses. Members receive reduced rates on training and publications and access to a hot-line telephone referral service and a bulletin board system.

> Computer Security Institute
> 600 Harrison Street
> San Francisco, CA 94107
> (415) 905-2626

Computer Virus Industry Association (CVIA)

CVIA provides information on how to identify and eliminate computer viruses and sponsors conferences and seminars.

> Computer Virus Industry Association
> P.O. Box 391703
> Mountain View, CA 95039
> (408) 727-4559

Communications Security Association (COMSEC)

COMSEC's members are in communications security, information security, and investigations technology. It publishes a quarterly magazine, *COMSEC Journal*, and sponsors an annual conference and exhibition.

> Communications Security Association
> P.O. Box 7069
> Gaithersburg, MD 20898
> (301) 309-3731

Information Systems Security Association (ISSA)

ISSA consists of computer security practitioners representing banking, retail, insurance, aerospace, and other fields. It publishes a quarterly magazine, *Access*, and sponsors an annual conference and exhibition.

> Information Systems Security Association
> P.O. Box 9457
> Newport Beach, CA 92658
> (714) 250-4772

International Association for Computer Systems Security (IACSS)

IACSS offers testing programs for certification of computer systems security professionals, workshops, speakers' bureaus, and codes of ethics. It publishes a quarterly *Computer Systems Security Newsletter*, an annual directory of security products, a security guide, and other publications, and it sponsors an annual conference and periodic regional conferences.

> International Association for Computer Systems Security
> 6 Swarthmore Lane
> Dix Hills, NY 11746
> (516) 499-1616

International Information Systems Security Certification Consortium ((ISC)^2)

(ISC)^2 is a nonprofit organization working on development of a certification program for information systems security professionals.

> (ISC)^2
> P.O. Box 98
> Spencer, MA 01562
> (508) 797-3096

National Center for Computer Crime Data (NCCCD)

NCCCD distributes publications and sponsors seminars in the area of computer crime. It publishes a variety of magazines, statistical reports, and other documents, including *Computer Crime Chronicles*, *Computer Crime, Computer Security, Computer Ethics*, and the *National Center for Computer Crime Data—Statistical Report*.

> National Center for Computer Crime Data
> 1222 17th Avenue, Suite B
> Santa Cruz, CA 95062
> (408) 475-4457

National Computer Security Association (NCSA)

NCSA distributes a newsletter and sends all new members a Virus Self-Defense Kit. It makes available a variety of computer security books and research reports, including a *Computer Security Product Buyer's Guide*. It also sponsors seminars and supports an electronic bulletin board.

> National Computer Security Association
> 227 West Main Street
> Mechanicsburg, PA 17055
> (717) 258-1816

Smart Card Industry Association (SCIA)

SCIA promotes smart card technologies by providing speakers, compiling statistics, and raising public awareness. It publishes a monthly *SCAT News*, an annual directory, and proceedings of its annual conference.

> Smart Card Industry Association
> 2026C Opitz Boulevard
> Woodbridge, VA 22191
> (703) 490-3300

Other Groups

In addition, a number of system user groups have security subcommittees and provide security-related activities—for example, USENIX for UNIX users, DECUS for Digital Equipment Corporation users, IBM Share for IBM users, and Sun Expo for Sun Microsystems users. Groups for specific industries, such as the EDP Auditors Association, also provide extensive security activities and publications for members.

Electronic Groups

If your system is connected to a network, chances are there's an electronic bulletin board system on which you can exchange information about security issues. Ask your system administrator for information about resources available to you. The following sections describe the more popular electronic groups.

USENET

If you use a system that's connected to the USENET (a global news network that uses the UNIX UUCP facility to allow users to communicate with each other), you can participate in one of the many nationwide electronic forums for information about computer security and related issues. For example, the **comp.risks** news group (The Forum on Risks to the Public in Computers and Related Systems) moderated by Peter G. Neumann provides a digest of information about security events and vulnerabilities. The **comp.virus** (VIRUS-L) news group moderated by Ken van Wyk of CERT provides information about viruses and available anti-viral software.

A variety of other security-related news groups are active on USENET, including **comp.security.announce**, **sci.crypt**, **misc.security**, **alt.security**, and **alt.society.cu-digest** (Computer Underground Digest). For other information, see the various CERT groups; check with **cert-advisory**. In addition, be sure to read whatever groups apply to your own system, because postings on security issues of particular concern to you are likely to appear there first.

For information about using News, see your system administrator.

Commercial Bulletin Boards

CompuServe, The Source, and other commercial bulletin board systems also are a source of security information and anti-viral public domain and shareware software. Remember to be cautious about using any software obtained from such sources.

NCSC DOCKMASTER

DOCKMASTER is an unclassified electronic mail and bulletin board system used primarily by the NCSC and trusted system vendors and users. The system supports electronic mail connections to the ARPANET via direct mail, the MILNET, and the McDonnell Douglas Tymnet. DOCKMASTER allows its users to retrieve listings of trusted products (the Evaluated Products List is online) and provides an electronic bulletin board for the exchange of information about computer security products, conferences, and other security issues. See the INFOSEC catalogue (described under the section "Government Publications") for detailed information about using DOCKMASTER, or contact:

> National Computer Security Center
> Attention: C81 Accounts Administrator
> 9800 Savage Road
> Fort George G. Meade, MD 20755-6000
> (301) 859-4360

NIST Computer Security Bulletin Board

The National Institute of Standards and Technology provides an electronic bulletin board for the exchange of information about computer security publications, conferences, and other information. NIST also uses this bulletin board to disseminate information about security incidents. For information, contact NIST's Computer Sciences Laboratory at (301) 975-3362.

Computer Security Periodicals

> *Computer Crime Chronicles*
> *Computer Crime, Computer Security, Computer Ethics*
> National Center for Computer Crime Data (NCCCD)
> 1222 17th Avenue, Suite B
> Santa Cruz, CA 95062
> (408) 475-4457

> *Computers & Security: The International Source of Innovation for the Information Security and EDP Audit Professional*
> Elsevier Advanced Technology
> Mayfield House
> 256 Banbury Road
> Oxford OX2 7DH U.K.
> +44–(0) 865-512242

Computer Security Journal
Computer Security Institute
Miller Freeman Publications
600 Harrison Street
San Francisco, CA 94107
(415) 905-2626

Computer Security Products Report
Assets Protection Publishing
P.O. Box 5323
Madison, WI 53705
(608) 271-6768

Computer Systems Security Newsletter
International Association for Computer Systems Security (IACSS)
6 Swarthmore Lane
Dix Hills, NY 11746
(516) 499-1616

COMSEC Journal
Communications Security Association (COMSEC)
P.O. Box 7069
Gaithersburg, MD 20898
(301) 309-3731

Datapro Reports on Computer Security (subscription series)
Datapro Research Group
McGraw-Hill
600 Delran Parkway
Delran, NJ 08075
(609) 764-0100 or (800) 328-2776

Data Processing & Communications Security
Assets Protection Publishing
P.O. Box 5323
Madison, WI 53705
(608) 271-6768

Information Systems Security
Auerbach Publications
One Penn Plaza
New York, NY 10119
(212) 971-5005

ISPNews (INFOSecurity Product News)
498 Concord St.
Framingham, MA 01701-2357
(508) 879-9792

Newsletter of the ACM Special Interest Group on Security, Audit,
and Control (SIG SAC)
ACM, Inc.
11 West 42nd Street
New York, NY 10036
(212) 869-7440

SCAT News
Smart Card Industry Association (SCIA)
2026C Opitz Boulevard
Woodbridge, VA 22191
(703) 490-3300

Security Management
American Society for Industrial Security (ASIS)
1655 North Fort Meyer Drive, Suite 1200
Arlington, VA 22209
(703) 522-5800

Virus Bulletin
Virus Bulletin, Inc.
The Quadrant
Abingdon Science Park
Oxon OX14 3YS
United Kingdom
(+44) 235 555139
In the U.S., contact (203) 431-8720.

In addition, general computer periodicals devote occasional issues or major sections to security. For example, see the following:

Communications of the Association for Computing Machinery, Volume 32,
Number 6, June, 1989.

Communications of the Association for Computing Machinery, Volume 34,
Number 3, March, 1991.

UNIX Review, Volume 8, Number 2, February, 1988.

Computer Security Books

Conference Proceedings

Proceedings from the various computer and computer security conferences are an excellent source of current information. Consult the ACM, the IEEE, and other professional organizations for information about obtaining past proceedings. The National Computer Security Center also sponsors an annual conference at which proceedings are available.

Computer Security Textbooks

Davies, D.W. and Price, W.L., *Security for Computer Networks: An Introduction to Data Security in Teleprocessing and Electronic Funds Transfer*, John Wiley & Sons, New York (NY), 1984.

Denning, Dorothy E.R. *Cryptography and Data Security*, Addison Wesley, Reading (MA), 1983.

Fites, Philip E., Kratz, Martin P.J., and Brebner, Alan F., *Control and Security of Computer Information Systems*, Computer Science Press, Rockville (MD), 1989.

Garfinkel, Simson and Spafford, Gene, *Practical UNIX Security*, O'Reilly & Associates Sebastopol (CA), 1991.

Gasser, Morrie, *Building a Secure Computer System*, Van Nostrand Reinhold, New York (NY), 1988.

Pfleeger, Charles P., *Security in Computing*, Prentice Hall Englewood Cliffs (NJ), 1989.

Wood, Charles Cresson et al, (Garcia, Abel A., ed.), *Computer Security: A Comprehensive Controls Checklist*, John Wiley & Sons, New York (NY), 1987.

Viruses and Other Programmed Threats

Denning, Peter J., ed., *Computers Under Attack: Intruders, Worms and Viruses*, ACM Press/Addison-Wesley, Reading (MA), 1990.

Fites, Philip E., Johnston, Peter, and Kratz, Martin, *The Computer Virus Crisis*, Van Nostrand Reinhold, New York (NY), 1989.

Hoffman, Lance J., ed., *Rogue Programs: Viruses, Worms and Trojan Horses*, Van Nostrand Reinhold, New York (NY), 1990.

Hruska, Jan, *Computer Viruses and Anti-Virus Warfare*, Ellis Horwood, division of Simon & Schuster, New York (NY), 1990.

Spafford, Eugene H., Heaphy, Kathleen A., and Ferbrache, David J., *Computer Viruses: Dealing with Electronic Vandalism and Programmed Threats*, ADAPSO, Arlington (VA), 1989. (Order from ADAPSO: (703) 522-5055.)

Stang, David J., *Computer Viruses*, National Computer Security Association, Washington, DC, 1990. (Order from NCSA: (202) 244-7875.)

The Computer Worm: A Report to the Provost, (Order from Cornell University: (607) 255-3324.)

Computer Crime and Ethics

Best, Reba A., *Computer Crime, Abuse, Liability, and Security: A Comprehensive Bibliography*, 1970-1984 McFarland, Jefferson (NC), 1985.

BloomBecker, J.J. Buck, *Introduction to Computer Crime* National Center for Computer Crime Data, 1988. (Order from NCCCD: (408) 475-4457.)

BloomBecker, J.J. Buck, *Spectacular Computer Crimes*, Dow Jones Irwin, Homewood (IL), 1990.

Forester, Tom and Morrison, Perry, *Computer Ethics: Cautionary Tales and Ethical Dilemmas in Computing*, MIT Press, Cambridge (MA), 1990.

Johnson, Deborah G., *Computer Ethics*, Prentice-Hall, Englewood Cliffs (NJ), 1985.

Johnson, Deborah G. and Snapper, John W., *Ethical Issues in the Use of Computers*, Wadsworth Publishing Co., Belmont (CA), 1985

Parker, Donn B., *Computer Crime: Criminal Justice Resource Manual*, U.S. Department of Justice, National Institute of Justice, Washington, (DC), 1989.

Parker, Donn B., Swope, Susan, and Baker, Bruce N., *Ethical Conflicts in Information and Computer Science, Technology, and Business*, QED Information Sciences, Wellesley (MA), 1990.

Of General Interest

Kahn, David, *Seizing the Enigma: The Race to Break the German U-Boat Codes, 1939-1943*, Houghton Mifflin, Boston (MA), 1991.

Kahn, David, *The Codebreakers*, Macmillan Company, New York (NY), 1972.

Levy, Steven, *Hackers: Heroes of the Computer Revolution*, Anchor Press/Doubleday, Garden City (NY), 1984.

National Research Council, System Security Study Committee, et al., *Computers at Risk: Safe Computing in the Information Age*, National Academy Press, Washington (DC), 1991. (Order from (800) 624-6242.)

Stoll, Cliff, *The Cuckoo's Egg: Tracing a Spy Through the Maze of Computer Espionage*, Doubleday, New York (NY), 1989.

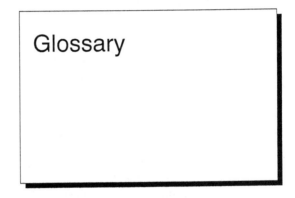

Glossary

access

The ability of a subject to view, change, or communicate with an object in a computer system. Typically, access involves a flow of information between the subject and the object (for example, a user reads a file, a program creates a directory).

access controls

Restrictions on the ability of a subject (e.g., a user) to use a system or an object (e.g., a file) in that system. Such controls limit access to authorized users only. Access control mechanisms may include hardware or software features, operating procedures, management procedures, or any combination.

access control list (ACL)

For a particular object, a list of the subjects authorized to access that object. The list usually indicates what type of access is allowed for each user. Typical types of access may include read, write, execute, append, modify, delete, and create.

accountability

> A security principle stating that individuals must be able to be identified. With accountability, violations or attempted violations of system security can be traced to individuals who can then be held responsible for their actions.

accreditation

> Official authorization and approval, granted to a computer system or network, to process sensitive data in a particular operational environment. Accreditation is performed by specific technical personnel after a security evaluation of the system's hardware, software, configuration, and security controls.

accuracy

> A security principle that keeps information from being modified or otherwise corrupted either maliciously or accidentally. Accuracy protects against forgery or tampering. Synonymous with *integrity*.

active threat

> A type of threat that involves the alteration, not simply the interception, of information. For example, an active tap is a type of wiretapping that accesses and compromises data, usually by generating false messages or control signals, or by altering communications between legitimate users. The danger of an active threat is primarily the authenticity of the information being transmitted. Contrast with *passive threat*.

add-on security

> The addition of security products and layers to an existing computer system.

administrative security

> Management rules and procedures that result in protection of a computer system and its data. Sometimes called *procedural security*.

assurance

> A measure of confidence that a system's security features have been implemented and work properly. Assurance is one of the primary issues addressed by the Orange Book.

attack

> An attempt to bypass security controls on a system. An active attack alters data. A passive attack releases data. Whether or not an attack will succeed depends on the vulnerability of the system and the effectiveness of existing countermeasures.

audit

> To record independently and later examine system activity (e.g., logins and logouts, file accesses, security violations).

audit trail

> The chronological set of records that provides evidence of system activity. These records can be used to reconstruct, review, and examine transactions from inception to output of final results. The records can also be used to track system usage and detect and identify intruders.

authentication

> The process of proving that a subject (e.g., a user or a system) is what the subject claims to be. Authentication is a measure used to verify the eligibility of a subject and the ability of that subject to access certain information. It protects against the fraudulent use of a system or the fraudulent transmission of information. There are three classic ways to authenticate oneself: something you know, something you have, and something you are. See also *identification*.

authenticity

> A security principle that ensures that a message is received in exactly the form in which it was sent. See also *message authentication* and *message authentication code*.

authorization

> The granting of rights to a user, a program, or a process. For example, certain users may be authorized to access certain files in a system, whereas only the system administrator may be authorized to export data from a trusted system.

availability

> A security principle that ensures the ability of a system to keep working efficiently and to keep information accessible. Contrast with *denial of service*.

back door

> See *trap door*.

backup

> Copying of data to a medium from which the data can be restored if the original data is destroyed or compromised. Full backups copy all data in the system. Incremental backups copy only data that's been changed since the last full backup. A sound backup plan involves keeping backup media off-site and developing procedures for replacing system components, if necessary, after a system failure.

bandwidth

A characteristic of a communications channel. The amount of information that can pass through the channel in a given amount of time. See *covert channel*.

Bell-LaPadula model

The computer security policy model on which the Orange Book requirements are based. From the Orange Book definition: "A formal state transition model of computer security policy that describes a set of access control rules. In this formal model, the entities in a computer system are divided into abstract sets of subjects and objects. The notion of a secure state is defined and it is proven that each state transition preserves security by moving from secure state to secure state; thus, inductively proving that the system is secure. A system state is defined to be "secure" if the only permitted access modes of subjects to objects are in accordance with a specific security policy. In order to determine whether or not a specific access mode is allowed, the clearance of a subject is compared to the classification of the object and a determination is made as to whether the subject is authorized for the specific access mode."

Biba model

An integrity model of computer security policy that describes a set of rules. In this model, a subject may not depend on any object or other subject that is less trusted than itself.

biometrics

The statistical study of biological data. In computer security, the use of unique, quantifiable physiological, behavioral, and morphological characteristics to provide positive personal identification. Examples of such characteristics are fingerprints, retina patterns, and signatures.

callback

A security procedure used with modems connected to terminals dialing into computer systems. When the computer system answers a call, it doesn't allow a direct login at that time. First, it calls back the telephone number associated with the authorized user's account.

capability

In capability-based systems, an identifier that identifies an object (e.g., a file) and specifies the access rights for the subject (e.g., the user) who possesses the capability (sometimes called a *ticket*).

category

An item in the nonhierarchical portion (the category set) of a sensitivity label. (The hierarchical portion is called the *classification*.) A category represents a distinct area of information in a system. When included in a sensitivity label in a system supporting mandatory access controls, it is used to limit access to those who need to know information in this particular category. Synonymous with *compartment*.

certification

The technical evaluation performed as part of, and in support of, the accreditation process that establishes the extent to which a particular computer system or network design and implementation meet a prespecified set of security requirements.

challenge-response

A type of authentication in which a user responds correctly (usually by performing some calculation) to a challenge (usually a numeric, unpredictable one).

channel

A path used for information transfer within a system.

checksum

Numbers summed according to a particular set of rules and used to verify that transmitted data has not been modified during transmission.

cipher

See *ciphertext*.

ciphertext

In cryptography, the unintelligible text that results from encrypting original text. Sometimes called "codetext," "cryptotext," or "cipher."

Clark-Wilson model

An integrity model for computer security policy designed for a commercial environment. It addresses such concepts as nondiscretionary access control, privilege separation, and least privilege.

classification

The hierarchical portion of a sensitivity label. (The nonhierarchical portion is called the "category set" or the "compartments.") A classification is a single level in a stratified set of levels. For example, in a military environment, each of the levels UNCLASSIFIED, CONFIDENTIAL, SECRET, and TOP SECRET is more trusted than the level beneath it. When included in a sensitivity label in a system supporting mandatory access controls, a classification is used to limit access to those cleared at that level.

clearance

A representation of the sensitivity level (the classification and the categories) associated with a user in a system supporting mandatory access controls. A user with a particular clearance can typically access only information with a sensitivity label equal to or lower than the user's clearance.

cleartext

See *plaintext*.

closed security environment

An environment in which both of the following conditions are true:

1. Application developers have sufficient clearances and authorizations to provide an acceptable presumption that they have not introduced malicious logic.

2. Configuration control provides sufficient assurance that applications and equipment are protected against the introduction of malicious logic prior to and during the operation of system applications.

communications security

Protection of information while it's being transmitted, particularly via telecommunications. A particular focus of communications security is message authenticity.

COMSEC

Short for communications security. The government program whose focus is the techniques (e.g., encryption) that prevent information from modification and unauthorized access while it's being transmitted.

compartment

See *category*.

compartmentalization

1. The isolation of the operating system, user programs, and data files from one another in a computer system to provide protection against unauthorized access by other users or programs.

2. The breaking down of sensitive data into small, isolated blocks to reduce the risk of unauthorized access.

compartmented mode workstation (CMW)

A trusted workstation that contains enough built-in security to be able to function as a trusted computer. A CMW is trusted to keep data of different security levels and categories in separate compartments.

compromise
Unauthorized disclosure or loss of sensitive information.

COMPUSEC
Short for computer security. The government program whose focus is the techniques (e.g., trusted systems) that prevent unauthorized access to information while it's being processed or stored.

computer security
Protection of information while it's being processed or stored.

confidentiality
A security principle that keeps information from being disclosed to anyone not authorized to access it. Synonymous with *secrecy*.

configuration management
The identification, control, accounting for, and auditing of all changes to system hardware, software, firmware, documentation, test plans, and test results throughout the development and operation of the system.

confinement
Prevention of leaking of sensitive data from a program.

confinement property
See *star property (*-property)*.

contingency plan
A plan for responding to a system emergency. The plan includes performing backups, preparing critical facilities that can be used to facilitate continuity of operations in the event of an emergency, and recovering from a disaster. Synonymous with *disaster recovery plan*.

countermeasure
An action, device, procedure, technique, or other measure that reduces the vulnerability of a system or a threat to that system.

covert channel
A communications channel that allows a process to transfer information in a way that violates a system's security policy.

covert channel analysis
Analysis of the potential for covert channels in a trusted computer system.

covert storage channel
A covert channel that allows a storage location (e.g., a location on disk) to be written by one process and read by another process. The two processes are typically at different security levels.

covert timing channel
A covert channel that allows one process to signal information to another process by modulating the use of system resources (e.g., CPU time) in a way that affects the response time observed by the second process.

cryptography
The study of encryption and decryption. From the Greek "kryptos" meaning "hidden" and "graphia" meaning "writing."

Data Encryption Standard (DES)
A private key encryption algorithm adopted as the federal standard for the protection of sensitive unclassified information and used extensively for the protection of commercial data as well.

decryption
The transformation of encrypted text (called *ciphertext*) into original text (called *plaintext*). Sometimes called "deciphering."

degauss
To demagnetize magnetic media (typically tapes) in a way that leaves a very low residue of magnetic induction on the media. This process effectively erases the tape.

denial of service
An action or series of actions that prevents a system or any of its resources from functioning efficiently and reliably.

digital signature
An authentication tool that verifies the origin of a message and the identity of the sender and receiver. Can be used to resolve any authentication issues between the sender and the receiver. A digital signature is unique for every transaction.

disaster recovery plan
See *contingency plan*.

discretionary access control (DAC)
An access policy that restricts access to system objects (e.g., files, directories, devices) based on the identity of the users and/or groups to which they belong. "Discretionary" means that a user with certain access permissions is capable of passing those permissions to another user (e.g., letting another user modify a file). Contrast with *mandatory access control*.

domain
The set of objects that a subject is allowed to access.

dominate

A relationship between security levels in a system supporting mandatory access controls. One subject dominates another if the first subject's classification is greater than the second subject's classification, and if the first subject's categories include at least all of the second subject's categories.

eavesdropping

Unauthorized interception of information. Usually refers to passive interception (receiving information), rather than active interception (changing information).

emanations

Electrical and electromagnetic signals emitted from electrical equipment (e.g., computers, terminals, printers, cabling) and transmitted through the air or through conductors. If the information carried by these emanations is intercepted and deciphered, sensitive information may be compromised. Also called "emissions."

encryption

The transformation of original text (called *plaintext*) into unintelligible text (called *ciphertext*). Sometimes called "enciphering."

end-to-end encryption

A type of encryption in which a message is encrypted when it is transmitted and is decrypted and then encrypted again each time it passes through a network communications node. Sometimes called "online encryption." Contrast with *link encryption*.

erasure

Removal of signals recorded on magnetic media. Simply reinitializing a disk or tape doesn't erase data; it simply makes the data harder to access. Someone who knows how to bypass ordinary volume checking mechanisms may still be able to access sensitive data on reinitialized disks or tapes.

export

Transfer of information from one system to another. Often used to refer to the transfer of information from a trusted system to an untrusted system.

file protection class

A code associated with a file that indicates the file type and associated file access. Typical classes are public (anyone can read or change the file), read-only (anyone can read, but only the owner and the system administrator can write the file), and private (only the owner and the system administrator can read or change the file).

file security

Protection of files stored on a computer system through discretionary access control and/or mandatory access control.

fingerprint system

A biometric system that compares a fingerprint pattern with a stored pattern to determine whether there's a match.

flaw

An error, omission, or loophole in a system that allows security mechanisms to be bypassed.

formal proof

From the Orange Book definition: "A complete and convincing mathematical argument, presenting the full logical justification for each proof step, for the truth of a theorem or set of theorems. The formal verification process uses formal proofs to show the truth of certain properties of formal specification and for showing that computer programs satisfy their specifications."

formal security policy model

From the Orange Book definition: "A mathematically precise statement of a security policy. To be adequately precise, such a model must represent the initial state of a system, the way in which the system progresses from one state to another, and a definition of a "secure" state of the system. To be acceptable as a basis for a TCB, the model must be supported by a formal proof that if the initial state of the system satisfies the definition of a "secure" state and if all assumptions required by the model hold, then all future states of the system will be secure. Some formal modeling techniques include: state transition models, temporal logic models, denotional semantics models, algebraic specification models."

formal verification

An automated tool used in designing and testing highly trusted systems. The process of using formal proofs to demonstrate two types of consistency:

1. Design verification: consistency between a formal specification of a system and a formal security policy model.

2. Implementation verification: consistency between a formal specification of a system and its high-level program implementation.

gateway

Typically, a system that is attached to two systems, devices, or networks that otherwise do not communicate with each other. Communications from one system or network to another are routed through the gateway. A gateway system may be used as a guardian or "firewall" between trusted and untrusted systems or networks. The gateway filters out any information that's not allowed to pass from the trusted system to the untrusted system or network, or vice versa.

granularity

The relative fineness or coarseness by which a mechanism can be adjusted. In the Orange Book, the phrase "to the granularity of a single user" means that an access control mechanism can be adjusted to include or exclude any single user.

group

A set of users in a system. A system security policy may give certain access rights to every member of a group.

handprint system

A biometric system that compares a handprint pattern with a stored pattern to determine whether there's a match.

identification

The process of telling a system the identity of a subject (e.g., a user or another system). Usually, this is done by entering a name or presenting a token to the system. See also *authentication*.

impersonation

Posing as an authorized user, usually in an attempt to gain access to a system. Synonymous with *masquerade*.

information label

A label associated with a particular subject or object in a system (e.g., file, process, window). Information labels are used in compartmented mode workstations and are similar to sensitivity labels. However, they differ from sensitivity labels in several ways:

1. In addition to a classification and a set of categories, information labels also contain dissemination markings and handling caveats (e.g., EYES ONLY).

2. They simply represent the sensitivity of the information in the subject or object; in contrast, sensitivity labels are used to make access decisions.

3. They are automatically adjusted as the information content of a subject or object changes (for example, the contents of a window); in contrast, sensitivity labels remain static.

information level

The security level implied by an information label's classification and categories.

information security

Protection of information.

INFOSEC

Short for information security. The government program whose focus is the techniques that increase the security of computer systems, communications systems, and the information they process or transmit.

import

Transfer of information into a system. Often used to refer to the transfer of information from an untrusted system to a trusted system.

integrity

A security principle that keeps information from being modified or otherwise corrupted either maliciously or accidentally. Integrity protects against forgery or tampering. Synonymous with *accuracy*.

kernel

See *security kernel*.

key

In cryptography, a secret value that's used to encrypt and decrypt messages. A sequence of symbols (often a large number) that's usually known only to the sender and the receiver of the message. See also *private key encryption* and *public key encryption*.

keystroke system

A system that compares a pattern of keystrokes with a stored pattern to determine whether there's a match.

labeling

In a system supporting mandatory access controls, the assignment of sensitivity labels to every subject or object in the system.

least privilege

A security principle stating that a user or a process should be granted the most restrictive set of privileges needed to perform a particular task and to keep those privileges only for the duration of the task. Least privilege limits the damage that can occur because of accident or system attack.

level

See *security level*.

life-cycle assurance

Confidence that a trusted system is designed, developed, and maintained with formal and rigidly controlled standards. In the Orange Book, the set of life-cycle assurances includes security testing, design specification and verification, configuration management, and trusted distribution.

link encryption

A type of encryption in which a message is encrypted when it is transmitted and is decrypted when it is received. Contrast with *end-to-end encryption*.

logic bomb

A type of programmed threat. A mechanism for releasing a system attack of some kind. It is triggered when a particular condition (e.g., a certain date or system operation) occurs.

login

The process of identifying oneself to, and having one's identity authenticated by, a computer system.

magnetic remanence

A measure of the density of the magnetic flux remaining after a magnetic force has been removed. Data remaining on a magnetic medium such as tape.

malicious logic

Code that is included in a system for an unauthorized purpose.

mandatory access control (MAC)

An access policy that restricts access to system objects (e.g., files, directories, devices) based on the sensitivity of the information in the object (represented by the object's label) and the authorization of the subject (usually represented by the user's clearance) to access information at that sensitivity level. "Mandatory" means that the system enforces the policy; users do not have the discretion to share their files. Contrast with *discretionary access control*.

masquerade

Posing as an authorized user, usually in an attempt to gain access to a system. Synonymous with *impersonation*.

message authentication

Ensuring, typically with a message authentication code, that a message received (usually via a network) matches the message sent.

message authentication code

A code calculated during encryption and appended to a message. If the message authentication code calculated during decryption matches the appended code, the message was not altered during transmission.

model

See *security model*.

modem

A device that connects a computer and a terminal via a telephone line. Short for modulator/demodulator.

multi-level

Used to describe data or devices. Multi-level security allows users at different sensitivity levels to access a system concurrently. The system permits each user to access only the data that he or she is authorized to access. A multi-level device is one on which a number of different levels of data can be processed. Contrast with *single-level*.

need to know

A security principle stating that a user should have access only to the data he or she needs to perform a particular function.

network

A data communications system that allows a number of systems and devices to communicate with each other.

node

A system connected to a network.

object

From the Orange Book definition: "A passive entity that contains or receives information. Access to an object potentially implies access to the information it contains. Examples of objects are: records, blocks, pages, segments, files, directories, directory trees, and programs, as well as bits, bytes, words, fields, processors, video displays, keyboards, clocks, printers, network nodes, etc."

object reuse

The reassignment to a subject (e.g., a user) of a medium that previously contained an object (e.g., a file). The danger of object reuse is that the object may still contain information that the subject may not be authorized to access. Examples are magnetic tapes that haven't been erased, workstations that hold information in local storage, and X Window System objects that haven't been cleared before they're reassigned.

one-time cipher
> A type of encryption in which a cipher is used only once. Two copies of a pad are created; one copy goes to the sender, and the other to the recipient. The pad contains a random number for each character in the original message. The pad is destroyed after use. Sometimes called a "one-time pad."

open security environment
> An environment in which at least one of the following conditions is true:

> 1. Application developers do not have sufficient clearance or authorization to provide an acceptable presumption that they have not introduced malicious logic.

> 2. Configuration control does not provide sufficient assurance that applications are protected against the introduction of malicious logic prior to and during the operation of system applications.

operational assurance
> Confidence that a trusted system's architecture and implementation enforce the system's security policy. In the Orange Book, the set of operational assurances includes system architecture, system integrity, covert channel analysis, and trusted recovery.

passive threat
> A type of threat that involves the interception, but not the alteration, of information. For example, a passive tap is a type of wiretapping that involves eavesdropping, monitoring, and/or recording of information, but not the generation of false messages or control signals. The danger of a passive threat is primarily the secrecy of the information being transmitted. Contrast with *active threat*.

password
> A secret sequence of characters that's used to authenticate a user's identity, usually during a login process.

penetration
> A successful, unauthorized access to a computer system.

penetration testing
> A type of testing in which testers attempt to circumvent the security features of a system in an effort to identify security weaknesses.

perimeter
> See *security perimeter*.

permission

A type of interaction a subject can have with an object. For example, file permissions specify the actions particular users or classes of users can perform on the file. Examples are read, write, and execute.

personal identification number (PIN)

A number or code of some kind that's unique to an individual and can be used to provide identity. Often used with automatic teller machines and access devices.

physical security

Protection of physical computer systems and related buildings and equipment from fire and other natural and environmental hazards, as well as from intrusion. Also covers the use of locks, keys, and administrative measures used to control access to computer systems and facilities.

plaintext

In cryptography, the original text that is being encrypted. Synonymous with *cleartext*.

playback

The recording of a legitimate message and the later, unauthorized resending of the message. Synonymous with *replay*.

policy

See *security policy*.

privacy

A security principle that protects individuals from the collection, storage, and dissemination of information about themselves and the possible compromises resulting from unauthorized release of that information.

private key encryption

A type of encryption that uses a single key to both encrypt and decrypt information. Also called symmetric, or single-key, encryption. Contrast with *public key encryption*.

privilege

A right granted to a user, a program, or a process. For example, certain users may have the privileges that allow them to access certain files in a system. Only the system administrator may have the privileges necessary to export data from a trusted system.

procedural security

See *administrative security*.

protocol
> A set of rules and formats for the exchange of information, particularly over a communications network.

protocol layer
> A component process within an overall communications process. Typically, each layer provides specific functions and communicates with the layers above and beneath it.

protocol model
> The conceptual basis for describing how to communicate within a network.

public key encryption
> A type of encryption that uses two mathematically related keys. The public key is known within a group of users. The private key is known only to its owner. Contrast with *private key encryption*.

read
> An operation involving the flow of information from an object to a subject. It does not involve the alteration of that information.

recovery
> The actions necessary to restore a system and its data files after a system failure or intrusion.

reference monitor
> From the Orange Book definition: "An access control concept that refers to an abstract machine that mediates all accesses to objects by subjects."

remanence
> See *magnetic remanence*.

replay
> The recording of a legitimate message and the later, unauthorized resending of the message. Synonymous with *playback*.

repudiation
> The denial by a message sender that the message was sent, or by a message recipient that the message was received.

residue
> Data left in storage or on a medium before the data has been rewritten or eliminated in some other way.

retina system
> A biometric system that compares a retina blood vessel pattern with a stored pattern to determine whether there's a match.

risk

The probability that a particular security threat will exploit a particular system vulnerability.

risk assessment

An analysis of a system's information needs and vulnerabilities to determine how likely they are to be exploited in different ways and the costs of losing and/or recovering the system or its information.

sanitizing

The overwriting of sensitive information. On magnetic media, degaussing. Sometimes called "scrubbing."

secrecy

A security principle that keeps information from being disclosed to anyone not authorized to access it. Synonymous with *confidentiality*.

secure state

A condition in which none of the subjects in a system can access objects in an unauthorized manner.

security

Freedom from risk or danger. Safety and the assurance of safety.

security kernel

From the Orange Book definition: "The hardware, firmware, and software elements of a Trusted Computing Base that implement the reference monitor concept. It must mediate *all* accesses, be protected from modification, and be verifiable as correct."

security level

A representation of the sensitivity of information, derived from a sensitivity label (consisting of classification and categories).

security model

A precise statement of the security rules of a system.

security perimeter

An imaginary boundary between the Trusted Computing Base (inside the perimeter) and other system functions (outside the perimeter). In a networking environment, sometimes used to refer to the boundary between trusted and untrusted systems and networks.

security policy

From the Orange Book definition: "The set of laws, rules, and practices that regulate how an organization manages, protects, and distributes sensitive information."

security testing

A type of testing in which testers determine whether the security features of a system are implemented as designed. Security testing may include hands-on functional testing, penetration testing, and formal verification.

self/group/public controls

A form of discretionary access control in which file access is determined by category. File permissions or some other scheme allow the owner of the file to specify what permissions he or she (self) will have, what permissions a group of users will have, and what permissions the rest of the world (public) will have. Typical permissions include read, write, and execute.

sensitive information

Information that, if lost or compromised, would negatively affect the owner of the information, would jeopardize the ability of the system to continue processing, and/or would require substantial resources to recreate. According to the U.S. government (NTISSP 2), "information the disclosure, alteration, loss, or destruction of which could adversely affect national security or other federal government interests."

sensitivity label

A label representing the security level of an object and describing the sensitivity of the data in the object. The label consists of two parts: a hierarchical classification and a set of nonhierarchical categories or compartments. In systems supporting mandatory access controls, sensitivity labels determine whether a particular subject will be allowed to access a particular object.

separation of duty

A security principle that assigns security-related tasks to several distinct individuals. Usually, each of them has the least number of privileges needed to perform those tasks.

shield

In TEMPEST technology, a container built around a piece of electronic equipment so the signals emanating from the equipment can't be intercepted and deciphered.

signature system

A biometric system that compares a signature with a stored pattern to determine whether there's a match.

simple security condition

> From the Orange Book definition: "A Bell-LaPadula security model rule allowing a subject read access to an object only if the security level of the subject dominates the security level of the object." See also *dominate*.

single-level

> Used to describe data or devices. Single-level security allows a system to be accessed at any one time only by users at the same sensitivity level. A single-level device is one used to process only data of a single security level at any one time. Contrast with *multi-level*.

smart card

> An access card containing encoded information and sometimes a microprocessor and a user interface. The information on the code, or the information generated by the processor, is used to gain access to a facility or a computer system.

spoof

> A trick that causes an authorized user to perform an action that violates system security or that gives away information to an intruder.

star property (*-property)

> From the Orange Book definition: "A Bell-LaPadula security model rule allowing a subject write access to an object only if the security level of the subject is dominated by the security level of the object. Also known as the confinement property." See also *dominate*.

subject

> From the Orange Book definition: "An active entity, generally in the form of a person, process, or device that causes information to flow among objects or changes the system state."

substitution cipher

> A type of cipher that replaces the characters being encrypted with substitute characters.

suppression

> In TEMPEST technology, an approach taken to build equipment in such a way that signals don't emanate from the equipment and thus can't be intercepted and deciphered.

system low

> The lowest security level supported by a system at a particular time or in a particular environment.

system high

The highest security level supported by a system at a particular time or in a particular environment.

system high workstation (SHW)

A type of compartmented mode workstation. Like a compartmented mode workstation, a system high workstation handles multiple compartments. Unlike a compartmented mode workstation, users must be cleared for all compartments on a system high workstation.

TEMPEST

A government program that prevents the compromising electrical and electromagnetic signals that emanate from computers and related equipment from being intercepted and deciphered.

threat

A possible danger to a computer system. See also *active threat* and *passive threat*.

ticket

See *capability*.

token

A physical item that's used to provide identity. Typically an electronic device that can be inserted in a door or a computer system to gain access.

top-level specification

A nonprocedural description of system behavior at an abstract level; for example, a functional specification that omits all implementation details.

topology

A network configuration; the way the nodes of a network are connected together. Examples include bus, ring, and star topologies.

traffic

The message flow across a network. Analysis of message characteristics (e.g., length, frequency, destination) can sometimes provide information to an eavesdropper.

transposition cipher

A type of cipher that rearranges the order of the characters being encrypted, but does not change the actual characters.

trap door

A hidden mechanism that allows normal system protection to be circumvented. Trap doors are often planted by system developers to allow them to test programs without having to follow security procedures or other user interfaces. They are typically activated in some unobvious way (e.g., by typing a particular sequence of keys). Synonymous with *back door*.

Trojan horse

A type of programmed threat. An independent program that appears to perform a useful function but that hides another unauthorized program inside it. When an authorized user performs the apparent function, the Trojan horse performs the unauthorized function as well (often usurping the privileges of the user).

trust

Reliance on the ability of a system to meet its specifications.

Trusted Computing Base (TCB)

From the Orange Book definition: "The totality of protection mechanisms within a computer system—including hardware, firmware, and software— the combination of which is responsible for enforcing a security policy. A TCB consists of one or more components that together enforce a unified security policy over a product or system. The ability of a TCB to correctly enforce a security policy depends solely on the mechanisms within the TCB and on the correct input by system administrative personnel of parameters (e.g., a user's clearance) related to the security policy."

trusted distribution

The process of distributing a trusted system in a way that assures that the system that arrives at the customer site is the exact, evaluated system shipped by the vendor.

trusted facility management

The management of a trusted system in a way that assures separation of duties (e.g., separate operator, system administrator, and security administrator roles), with duties clearly delineated for each role.

trusted path

A mechanism that allows a terminal user to communicate directly with the Trusted Computing Base. The mechanism can be activated only by the person or the TCB and cannot be initiated by untrusted software. With a trusted path, there is no way an intermediary program can mimic trusted software.

trusted recovery

The set of procedures involved in restoring a system and its data in trusted fashion after a system crash or some other type of system failure.

trusted system

A system designed and developed in accordance with Orange Book criteria and evaluated according to those criteria.

user

A person or a process who accesses a computer system.

user ID

A unique code or string of characters with which the system identifies a specific user.

validation

The performance of tests and evaluations to determine whether a system complies with security specifications and requirements.

verification

The process of comparing two levels of system specification to ensure a correspondence between them; for example, security policy model with top-level specification, top-level specification with source code, or source code with object code. The process may be automated. See also *formal verification*.

virus

A type of programmed threat. A code fragment (not an independent program) that reproduces by attaching to another program. It may damage data directly, or it may degrade system performance by taking over system resources which are then not available to authorized users.

voice system

A biometric system that compares a vocal pattern with a stored pattern to determine whether there's a match.

vulnerability

A weakness in a computer system, or a point where the system is susceptible to attack. The weakness could be exploited to violate system security.

wiretapping

The attaching of an unauthorized device to a communications circuit to obtain access to data. Taps may be active or passive; see *active threat* and *passive threat*.

worm

A type of programmed threat. An independent program that reproduces by copying itself from one system to another, usually over a network. Like a virus, a worm may damage data directly, or it may degrade system performance by tying up system resources and even shutting down a network.

write

An operation involving the flow of information from a subject to an object (e.g., the alteration of that information).

Index

O

Books That Help People Get More Out of Computers

Please send me the following:

❏ A free catalog of titles.

❏ A list of Bookstores in my area that carry your books (U.S. and Canada only).

❏ A list of book distributors outside the U.S. and Canada.

❏ Information about consulting services for documentation or programming.

❏ Information about bundling books with my product.

❏ On-line descriptions of your books.

Name _____

Address _____

_____

City _____

State, ZIP _____

Country _____

Phone _____

Email Address _____
(Internet or Uunet)

Books That Help People Get More Out of Computers

Please send me the following:

❏ A free catalog of titles.

❏ A list of Bookstores in my area that carry your books (U.S. and Canada only).

❏ A list of book distributors outside the U.S. and Canada.

❏ Information about consulting services for documentation or programming.

❏ Information about bundling books with my product.

❏ On-line descriptions of your books.

Name _____

Address _____

_____

City _____

State, ZIP _____

Country _____

Phone _____

Email Address _____
(Internet or Uunet)

NAME _____

COMPANY _____

ADDRESS _____

CITY _____ STATE _____ ZIP _____

BUSINESS REPLY MAIL

FIRST CLASS MAIL PERMIT NO. 80 SEBASTOPOL, CA

POSTAGE WILL BE PAID BY ADDRESSEE

O'REILLY & ASSOCIATES, INC.

103 Morris Street Suite A
Sebastopol CA 95472-9902

NAME _____

COMPANY _____

ADDRESS _____

CITY _____ STATE _____ ZIP _____

BUSINESS REPLY MAIL

FIRST CLASS MAIL PERMIT NO. 80 SEBASTOPOL, CA

POSTAGE WILL BE PAID BY ADDRESSEE

O'REILLY & ASSOCIATES, INC.

103 Morris Street Suite A
Sebastopol CA 95472-9902

About the Authors

Deborah Russell is an acquisitions editor for O'Reilly & Associates and also manages documentation consulting services for a joint venture of O'Reilly & Associates and Cambridge Computer Associates. In recent years, the focus of her consulting work has been computer security. Her consulting projects include work on the development of a secure UNIX kernel, several trusted operating systems, and a secure compartmented mode workstation. Ms. Russell has worked closely with a number of vendors during the "Orange Book" trusted system evaluation process. She has a degree from Harvard University and is currently developing additional books for O'Reilly & Associates on security and database topics.

G.T. Gangemi Sr. is Director of Wang Laboratories' Secure Systems Program. The Wang organization mirrors the structure of the U.S. government's Information Security (INFOSEC) program, encompassing computer security (COMPUSEC), communications security (COMSEC), TEMPEST, and physical access. Mr. Gangemi is responsible for all Wang security-related products designed for government and commercial use. He has previously held management positions at Wang in a variety of areas, including research and development, product management and marketing, account management, and business planning. He attended La Salle College and the Program for Senior Executives at Harvard University's Kennedy School of Government. He served in the U.S. Army and is a private pilot.

Colophon

Our look is the result of reader comments, our own experimentation, and distribution channels. Distinctive covers complement our distinctive approach to technical topics, breathing personality and life into potentially dry subjects. Computers can be unruly beasts. Nutshell Handbooks help you tame them.

The image featured on the cover of *Computer Security Basics* is a key. Locks and keys were first developed by the Egyptians for use on doors. The Egyptian wooden door lock was opened using a long wooden implement with thin wooden pegs of varying lengths set in one end. When inserted and lifted, the pegs on this key would raise similar pegs within the lock. When all the pegs were raised past a certain point, the door would open.

Metal locks and keys were developed by the Romans using a design similar to that of the Egyptian door lock. Over time the Romans refined this lock technique and embellished both locks and keys; locks were camouflaged as animals, flowers, or birds, keys were highly decorated and frequently worn as pendants.

Portable locks, otherwise known as padlocks, were invented by the early Chinese, Turkish, Indians, and Russians. In the late 16th century this was taken a step further with the invention of keyless locks, otherwise known as combination locks. Further refinement continued through the 20th century as greater precision in metal work allowed for closer parts tolerance and therefore greater security.

Edie Freedman designed this cover and the entire bestiary that appears on other Nutshell Handbooks. The images are adapted from 19th-century engravings from the Dover Pictorial Archive.

The text of this book is set in Times Roman; headings are Helvetica; examples are Courier. Text was prepared using SortQuad's sqtroff text formatter. Figures are produced with a Macintosh. Printing is done on a Tegra Varityper 5000.

System Performance Tuning

By Mike Loukides

System Performance Tuning answers one of the most fundamental questions you can ask about your computer: "How can I get it to do more work without buying more hardware?" Anyone who has ever used a computer has wished that the system was faster, particularly at times when it was under heavy load.

If your system gets sluggish when you start a big job, if it feels as if you spend hours waiting for remote file access to complete, if your system stops dead when several users are active at the same time, you need to read this book. Some performance problems do require you to buy a bigger or faster computer, but many can be solved simply by making better use of the resources you already have.

336 pages, ISBN 0-937175-60-9

Essential System Administration

By Æleen Frisch

Like any other multi-user system, UNIX requires some care and feeding. *Essential System Administration* tells you how. This book strips away the myth and confusion surrounding this important topic and provides a compact, manageable introduction to the tasks faced by anyone responsible for a UNIX system.

If you use a stand-alone UNIX system, whether it's a PC or a workstation, you know how much you need this book: on these systems the fine line between a user and an administrator has vanished. Either you're both or you're in trouble. If you routinely provide administrative support for a larger shared system or a network of workstations, you will find this book indispensable. Even if you aren't directly responsible for system administration, you will find that understanding basic administrative functions greatly increases your ability to use UNIX effectively.

466 pages
ISBN 0-937175-80-3

Practical UNIX Security

By Simson Garfinkel & Gene Spafford

If you are a UNIX system administrator or user who needs to deal with security, you need this book.

Practical UNIX Security describes the issues, approaches, and methods for implementing security measures—spelling out what the varying approaches cost and require in the way of equipment. After presenting UNIX security basics and network security, this guide goes on to suggest how to keep intruders out, how to tell if they've gotten in, how to clean up after them, and even how to prosecute them. Filled with practical scripts, tricks and warnings, *Practical UNIX Security* tells you what you need to know to make your UNIX system as secure as it can be.

"Worried about who's in your Unix system? Losing sleep because someone might be messing with your computer? Having headaches from obscure computer manuals? Then *Practical Unix Security* is for you. This handy book tells you where the holes are and how to cork'em up.

"Moreover, you'll learn about how Unix security really works. Spafford and Garfinkel show you how to tighten up your Unix system without pain. No secrets here—just solid computing advice.

"Buy this book and save on aspirin."—Cliff Stoll

512 pages, ISBN 0-937175-72-2

Computer Security Basics

By Deborah Russell & G.T. Gangemi Sr.

There's a lot more consciousness of security today, but not a lot of understanding of what it means and how far it should go. This handbook describes complicated concepts like trusted systems, encryption and mandatory access control in simple terms.

For example, most U.S. government equipment acquisitions now require "Orange Book" (Trusted Computer System Evaluation Criteria) certification. A lot of people have a vague feeling that they ought to know about the Orange Book, but few make the effort to track it down and read it. *Computer Security Basics* contains a more readable introduction to the Orange Book—why it exists, what it contains, and what the different security levels are all about—than any other book or government publication.

464 pages, ISBN 0-937175-71-4

COMPUTER
SECURITY
BASICS

Computer Security

Deborah Russell and G.T. Gangemi Sr.
O'Reilly & Associates, Inc.

Managing UUCP and Usenet

10th Edition
By Tim O'Reilly & Grace Todino

For all its widespread use, UUCP is one of the most difficult UNIX utilities to master. Poor documentation, cryptic messages, and differences between various implementations make setting up UUCP links a nightmare for many a system administrator.

This handbook is meant for system administrators who want to install and manage the UUCP and Usenet software. It covers HoneyDanBer UUCP as well as standard Version 2 UUCP, with special notes on Xenix. As one reader noted over the Net, "Don't even TRY to install UUCP without it!"

368 pages, ISBN 0-937175-93-5

Using UUCP and Usenet

By Grace Todino & Dale Dougherty

Using UUCP shows how to communicate with both UNIX and non-UNIX systems using UUCP and *cu* or *tip*. It also shows how to read news and post your own articles and mail to other Usenet members. This handbook assumes that UUCP and Usenet links to other computer systems have already been established by your system administrator.

While clear enough for a novice, this book is packed with information that even experienced users will find indispensable. Take the mystery out of questions such as why files sent via UUCP don't always end up where you want them, how to find out the status of your file transfer requests, and how to execute programs remotely with *uux*.

210 pages, ISBN 0-937175-10-2

Understanding DCE

By Ward Rosenberry, David Kenney, and Gerry Fisher

Understanding DCE is a technical and conceptual overview of OSF's Distributed Computing Environment for programmers and technical managers, marketing and sales people. Unlike many O'Reilly & Associates books, *Understanding DCE* has no hands-on programming elements. Instead, the book focuses on how DCE can be used to accomplish typical programming tasks and provides explanations to help the reader understand all the parts of DCE.

266 pages (estimated), ISBN 1-56592-005-8

Guide to Writing DCE Applications

By John Shirley

A hands-on programming guide to OSF's Distributed Computing Environment (DCE) for first-time DCE application programmers. This book is designed to help new DCE users make the transition from conventional, nondistributed applications programming to distributed DCE programming. Covers the IDL and ACF files, essential RPC calls, binding methods and the name service, server initialization, memory management, and selected advanced topics. Includes practical programming examples.

282 pages, ISBN 1-56592-004-X

Learning GNU Emacs

By Deb Cameron & Bill Rosenblatt

GNU Emacs is the most popular and widespread of the Emacs family of editors. It is also the most powerful and flexible. (Unlike all other text editors, GNU Emacs is a complete working environment—you can stay within Emacs all day without leaving.) This book tells you how to get started with the GNU Emacs editor. It will also "grow" with you: as you become more proficient, this book will help you learn how to use Emacs more effectively. It will take you from basic Emacs usage (simple text editing) to moderately complicated customization and programming.

The book is aimed at new Emacs users, whether or not they are programmers. Also useful for readers switching from other Emacs implementations to GNU Emacs.

442 pages, ISBN 0-937175-84-6

Learning the vi Editor

5th Edition
By Linda Lamb

For many users, working in the UNIX environment means using *vi*, a full-screen text editor available on most UNIX systems. Even those who know *vi* often make use of only a small number of its features. This is the complete guide to text editing with *vi*. Early chapters cover the basics; later chapters explain more advanced editing tools, such as *ex* commands and global search and replacement.

192 pages, ISBN 0-937175-67-6

Learning the UNIX Operating System

2nd Edition
By Grace Todino & John Strang

If you are new to UNIX, this concise introduction will tell you just what you need to get started, and no more. Why wade through a 600-page book when you can begin working productively in a matter of minutes?

Topics covered include:

- Logging in and logging out
- Managing UNIX files and directories
- Sending and receiving mail
- Redirecting input/output
- Pipes and filters
- Background processing
- Customizing your account

"If you have someone on your site who has never worked on a UNIX system and who needs a quick how-to, Nutshell has the right booklet. *Learning the UNIX Operating System* can get a newcomer rolling in a single session."—;login

84 pages, ISBN 0-937175-16-1

MH & xmh:
E-mail for Users and Programmers

2nd Edition
By Jerry Peek

Customizing your e-mail environment can save you time and make communicating more enjoyable. *MH & xmh: E-mail for Users and Programmers* explains how to use, customize, and program with the MH electronic mail commands, available on virtually any UNIX system. The handbook also covers *xmh*, an X Window System client that runs MH programs.

The basics are easy. But MH lets you do much more than what most people expect an e-mail system to be able to do. This handbook is packed with explanations and useful examples of MH features, some of which the standard MH documentation only hints at.

728 pages, ISBN 1-56592-027-9

UNIX Text Processing

Learning
GNU Emacs

Debra Cameron and Bill Rosenblatt
O'Reilly & Associates, Inc.

Guide to OSF/1: A Technical Synopsis

By O'Reilly & Associates Staff

OSF/1, Mach, POSIX, SVID, SVR4, X/Open, 4.4BSD, XPG, B-1 security, parallelization, threads, virtual file systems, shared libraries, streams, extensible loader, internationalization.... Need help sorting it all out? If so, then this technically competent introduction to the mysteries of the OSF/1 operating system is a book for you. In addition to its exposition of OSF/1, it offers a list of differences between OSF/1 and System V, Release 4 and a look ahead at what is coming in DCE.

This is not the usual O'Reilly how-to book. It will not lead you through detailed programming examples under OSF/1. Instead, it asks the prior question, What is the nature of the beast? It helps you figure out how to approach the programming task by giving you a comprehensive technical overview of the operating system's features and services, and by showing how they work together.

304 pages, ISBN 0-937175-78-1

POSIX Programmer's Guide

By Donald Lewine

Most UNIX systems today are POSIX-compliant because the Federal government requires it. Even OSF and UI agree on support for POSIX. However, given the manufacturer's documentation, it can be difficult to distinguish system-specific features from those features defined by POSIX.

The *POSIX Programmer's Guide*, intended as an explanation of the POSIX standard and as a reference for the POSIX.1 programming library, will help you write more portable programs. This guide is especially helpful if you are writing programs that must run on multiple UNIX platforms. This guide will also help you convert existing UNIX programs for POSIX-compliance.

640 pages
ISBN 0-937175-73-0

Managing NFS and NIS

By Hal Stern

A modern computer system that is not part of a network is an anomaly. But managing a network and getting it to perform well can be a problem. This book describes two tools that are absolutely essential to distributed computing environments: the Network Filesystem (NFS) and the Network Information System (formerly called the "yellow pages" or YP).

As popular as NFS is, it is a black box for most users and administrators. This book provides a comprehensive discussion of how to plan, set up, and debug an NFS network. It is the only book we're aware of that discusses NFS and network performance tuning. This book also covers the NFS automounter, network security issues, diskless workstations, and PC/NFS. It also tells you how to use NIS to manage your own database applications, ranging from a simple telephone list to controlling access to network services. If you are managing a network of UNIX systems, or are thinking of setting up a UNIX network, you can't afford to overlook this book.

436 pages, ISBN 0-937175-75-7

Power Programming with RPC

By John Bloomer

A distributed application is designed to access resources across a network. In a broad sense, these resources could be user input, a central database, configuration files, etc., that are distributed on various computers across the network rather than found on a single computer. RPC, or remote procedure calling, is the ability to distribute the execution of functions on remote computers outside of the application's current address space. This allows you to break large or complex programming problems into routines that can be executed independently of one another to take advantage of multiple computers. Thus, RPC makes it possible to attack a problem using a form of parallel or multi-processing.

Written from a programmer's perspective, this book shows what you can do with RPC and presents a framework for learning it.

494 pages, ISBN 0-937175-77-3

UNIX Network Programming

Power Programming with

RPC

John Bloomer

O'Reilly & Associates, Inc.

Practical C Programming

By Steve Oualline

There are lots of introductory C books, but this is the first one that has the no-nonsense, practical approach that has made Nutshell Handbooks famous. C programming is more than just getting the syntax right. Style and debugging also play a tremendous part in creating well-running programs.

Practical C Programming teaches you how to create programs that are easy to read, maintain and debug. Practical rules are stressed. For example, there are 15 precedence rules in C (&& comes before || comes before ?:). The practical programmer simplifies these down to two: 1) Multiply and divide come before addition and subtraction and 2) Put parentheses around everything else. Electronic Archaeology, the art of going through someone else's code, is also described.

Topics covered include:

- Good programming style
- C syntax: what to use and what not to use
- The programming environment, including *make*
- The total programming process
- Floating point limitations
- Tricks and surprises

Covers Turbo C (DOS) as well as the UNIX C compiler.

420 pages, ISBN 0-937175-65-X

Using C on the UNIX System

By Dave Curry

Using C on the UNIX System provides a thorough introduction to the UNIX system call libraries. It is aimed at programmers who already know C but who want to take full advantage of the UNIX programming environment. If you want to learn how to work with the operating system and if you want to write programs that can interact with directories, terminals and networks at the lowest level, you will find this book essential. It is impossible to write UNIX utilities of any sophistication without understanding the material in this book.

250 pages, ISBN 0-937175-23-4

Managing Projects with make

2nd Edition
By Steve Talbott and Andrew Oram

Make is one of UNIX's greatest contributions to software development, and this book is the clearest description of *make* ever written. Even the smallest software project typically involves a number of files that depend upon each other in various ways. If you modify one or more source files, you must relink the program after recompiling some, but not necessarily all, of the sources.

Make greatly simplifies this process. By recording the relationships between sets of files, *make* can automatically perform all the necessary updating. The 2nd Edition of this book describes all the basic features of *make* and provides guidelines on meeting the needs of large, modern projects.

152 pages, ISBN 0-937175-90-0

Checking C Programs with lint

By Ian F. Darwin

The *lint* program checker has proven itself time and again to be one of the best tools for finding portability problems and certain types of coding errors in C programs. *lint* verifies a program or program segments against standard libraries, checks the code for common portability errors, and tests the programming against some tried and true guidelines. *lint*ing your code is a necessary (though not sufficient) step in writing clean, portable, effective programs. This book introduces you to *lint*, guides you through running it on your programs and helps you to interpret *lint*'s output.

"Short, useful, and to the point. I recommend it for self-study to all involved with C in a UNIX environment."—Computing Reviews

84 pages, ISBN 0-937175-30-7

DNS and BIND

By Cricket Liu and Paul Albitz

DNS and BIND is a complete guide to the Internet's Domain Name System (DNS) and the Berkeley Internet Name Domain (BIND) software, which is the UNIX implementation of DNS. DNS is the system that translates hostnames (like "rock.ora.com") into Internet addresses (like 192.54.67.23) Until BIND was developed, name translation was based on a "host table"; if you were on the Internet, you got a table that listed all the systems connected to the network, and their address. As the Internet grew from hundreds to thousands and hundreds of thousands of systems, host tables became unworkable. DNS is a distributed database that solves the same problem effectively, allowing the network to grow without constraints. Rather than having a central table that gets distributed to every system on the net, it allows local administrators to assign their own hostnames and addresses, and install these names in a local database.

418 pages, ISBN 1-56592-010-4

sed & awk

By Dale Dougherty

For people who create and modify text files, *sed* and *awk* are power tools for editing. Most of the things that you can do with these programs can be done interactively with a text editor. However, using *sed* and *awk* can save many hours of repetitive work in achieving the same result.

This book contains a comprehensive treatment of *sed* and *awk* syntax. Plus, it emphasizes the kinds of practical problems that *sed* and *awk* can help users to solve, with many useful example scripts and programs.

"*sed & awk* is a must for UNIX system programmers and administrators, and even general UNIX readers will benefit. I have over a hundred UNIX and C books in my personal library at home, but only a dozen are duplicated on the shelf where I work. This one just became number twelve."—Root Journal

414 pages, ISBN 0-937175-59-5

Programming Perl

By Larry Wall & Randal Schwartz

This is the authoritative guide to the hottest new UNIX utility in years, co-authored by the creator of that utility.

Perl is a language for easily manipulating text, files and processes. Perl provides a more concise and readable way to do many jobs that were formerly accomplished (with difficulty) by programming in the C language or one of the shells. Even though Perl is not yet a standard part of UNIX, it is likely to be available wherever you choose to work. And if it isn't, you can get it and install it easily and free of charge.

482 pages, ISBN 0-937175-64-1

UNIX for FORTRAN Programmers

By Mike Loukides

UNIX for FORTRAN Programmers provides the serious scientific programmer with an introduction to the UNIX operating system and its tools. The intent of the book is to minimize the UNIX entry barrier: to familiarize readers with the most important tools so they can be productive as quickly as possible. *UNIX for FORTRAN Programmers* shows readers how to do things that they're interested in: not just how to use a tool like *make* or *rcs*, but how it is used in program development and fits into the toolset as a whole.

"An excellent book describing the features of the UNIX FORTRAN compiler f77 and related software. This book is extremely well written." —American Mathematical Monthly

264 pages, ISBN 0-937175-51-X